THE CONTEST FOR THE DELAWARE VALLEY

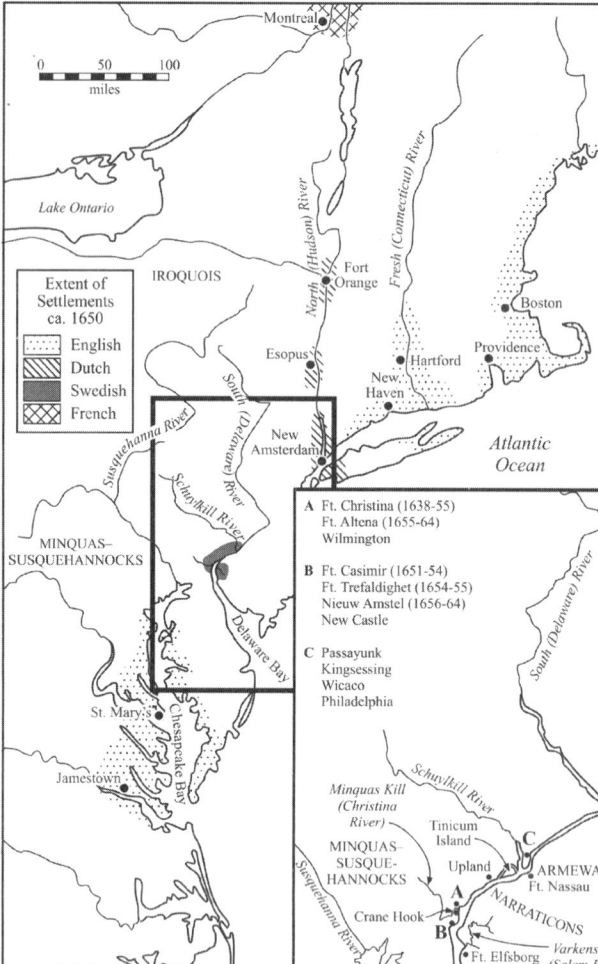
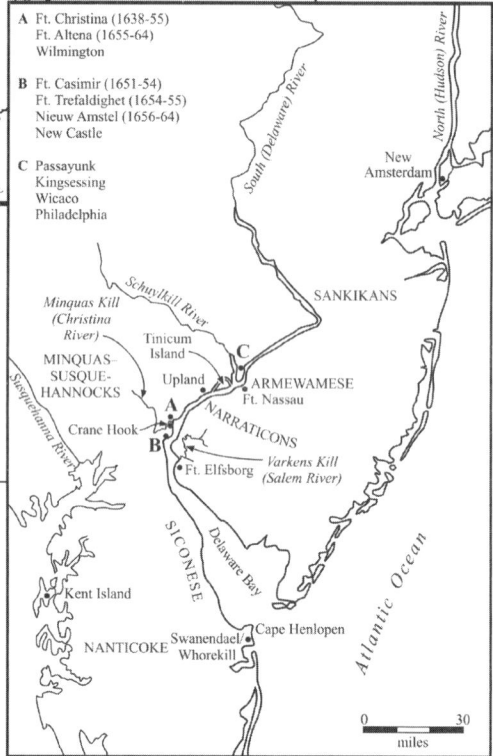

0   50   100
miles

Montreal

Lake Ontario

IROQUOIS

Fort
Orange

Fresh (Connecticut) River

North (Hudson) River

Boston

Extent of
Settlements
ca. 1650
.... English
///// Dutch
▓▓▓ Swedish
⊠⊠ French

Esopus

Hartford

Providence

New
Haven

Susquehanna River

South (Delaware) River

New
Amsterdam

Atlantic
Ocean

Schuylkill River

MINQUAS–
SUSQUEHANNOCKS

Delaware Bay

St. Mary's

Chesapeake Bay

Jamestown

A Ft. Christina (1638-55)
   Ft. Altena (1655-64)
   Wilmington

B Ft. Casimir (1651-54)
   Ft. Trefaldighet (1654-55)
   Nieuw Amstel (1656-64)
   New Castle

C Passayunk
   Kingsessing
   Wicaco
   Philadelphia

South (Delaware) River

North (Hudson) River

New
Amsterdam

Schuylkill River

SANKIKANS

Minquas Kill
(Christina
River)

Tinicum
Island

C

MINQUAS–
SUSQUE-
HANNOCKS

Upland

ARMEWAMESE
Ft. Nassau

A

Susquehanna River

NARRATICONS

Crane Hook

B

Ft. Elfsborg

Varkens Kill
(Salem River)

SICONESE

Delaware Bay

Atlantic
Ocean

Kent Island

NANTICOKE

Swanendael/
Whorekill

Cape Henlopen

0   30
miles

THE CONTEST FOR THE DELAWARE VALLEY

ALLEGIANCE, IDENTITY, AND EMPIRE IN THE SEVENTEENTH CENTURY

MARK L. THOMPSON

LOUISIANA STATE UNIVERSITY PRESS ✼ BATON ROUGE

Published by Louisiana State University Press
Copyright © 2013 by Louisiana State University Press
All rights reserved
Manufactured in the United States of America
First printing

Designer: Barbara Neely Bourgoyne
Typefaces: Garage Gothic, display; Ingeborg, text
Printer: McNaughton & Gunn, Inc.
Binder: Dekker Bookbinding

Library of Congress Cataloging-in-Publication Data
Thompson, Mark L., 1973–
  The contest for the Delaware Valley : allegiance, identity, and empire in the seventeenth
century / Mark L. Thompson.
      pages cm.
  Includes Bibliographical references and index.
  ISBN 978-0-8071-5058-0 (cloth : alk. paper) — ISBN 978-0-8071-5059-7 (pdf) —
ISBN 978-0-8071-5060-3 (epub) — ISBN 978-0-8071-5061-0 (mobi) 1. Delaware River
Valley (N.Y.-Del. and N.J.)—History—17th century. 2. Delaware River Valley (N.Y.-Del.
and N.J.)—Ethnic relations—History—17th century. 3. Delaware River Valley (N.Y.-Del.
and N.J.)—Social conditions—17th century. I. Title.
  F157.D4T45 2013
  974.9—dc23
                                                          2012039897

To my family

CONTENTS

ACKNOWLEDGMENTS

Oh, Time, Strength, Cash, and Patience!
—Herman Melville, "Cetology," *Moby-Dick*

The idea for this book was born in the late-twentieth-century Delaware Valley at a short distance from the Schuylkill River. Since then the pursuit of that idea has taken me to many places and left me with many debts. Time and again others have aided me so that I might be able to undertake and complete this book. Perhaps, then, we should add "Gratitude" to Ishmael's plea.

The project began when I was a doctoral student in the Department of History at The Johns Hopkins University, which provided me with a Lovejoy Fellowship in my first year. Subsequent support for my studies came from the United States Department of Education's generous Jacob K. Javits Fellowship. I presented early versions of parts of this book at the Research Seminar in Early Modern Colonial British America, led by Jack Greene, my mentor then and now. His support has always meant a lot to me. The participants in those seminars offered sharp advice and critique that shaped the arguments I have developed in this book. They were, and are, good friends. At Johns Hopkins I learned a great deal as well from my seminars with Michael Johnson, who continues to suggest fresh ways to think about my work. I later found a home in Philadelphia at the McNeil Center for Early American Studies. Led by Richard Dunn and then Daniel Richter, the McNeil Center provided me with office space, library privileges, and even travel support. Its associated faculty and many fellows made it a very stimulating place to work. It was there that I met Evan Haefeli, who introduced me to the Dutch and Swedes in the seventeenth-century Delaware Valley and continues to offer help and guidance. At the University of Pennsylvania Robert Naborn graciously gave me my first formal lessons in reading Dutch. Daniel Richter later offered useful advice for revising the manuscript.

I wrote, and rewrote, most of this book when I was a member of the Department of History at Louisiana State University (LSU). The university provided support in the form of research and travel grants from the Office of Research and Graduate Studies and a release from teaching. Those grants allowed me to conduct extended research into the Dutch and Swedish materials housed at the Historical Society of Pennsylvania and the New York State Archives, where I was later a Larry J. Hackman Research Fellow. Upstairs from the archive, Charles Gehring, the director of the New Netherland Project, gave me advice on my project, answered obscure questions, and freely shared his and Janny Venema's invaluable transcriptions and translations.

With the support of the LSU College of Arts and Sciences and an Andrew W. Mellon Long-Term Postdoctoral Fellowship from the John Carter Brown (JCB) Library, I was able to spend a year deepening and reshaping my manuscript. The JCB's director, Ted Widmer; staff members Valerie Andrews and Maureen O'Donnell; and librarians Susan Danforth, Dennis Landis, and Ken Ward were universally helpful. I especially enjoyed working alongside fellows Paul Cohen, Anoush Terjanian, and Sam Truett and attending the library's weekly luncheons and fellows' presentations with Amy Bushnell and Jack Greene.

Back at LSU I benefited from the help and camaraderie of many people (and their spouses) while I put together the manuscript. In particular I must thank Tiwanna Simpson, Chuck Shindo, Michael Fontenot, Maribel Dietz, Jordan Kellman, Christine Kooi, Steve and Yolanda Ross, John and Sylvia Rodrigue, Reza Pirbhai, Reem Meshal, Carolyn Lewis, Margherita Zanasi, Meredith Veldman, Nancy Isenstein, Alecia Long, Victor Stater, Paul Hoffman, John Henderson, Court Carney, Colin Woodward, Rand Dotson, Katie Henninger, Bill Boelhower, Andrew Sluyter, Kent Mathewson, Mark Martin, and Darlene Albritton. Special thanks go to Andrew Burstein, who helped me turn the manuscript into a book. Across campus at LSU Press, Alisa Plant offered early and strong support for my work and patiently shepherded the book to press. Mary Lee Eggart worked hard to translate the long list of features I gave her into a clear, elegant map. As the book's copyeditor, Elizabeth Gratch showed me what craftsmanship truly means.

Since coming to the University of Groningen in 2010, where final revisions of the manuscript were completed, I have had the chance to travel through the homelands of Peter Minuit and Pieter Stuyvesant, to stroll along the canals of Amsterdam, and to give my students a tour of the West India Company shipyard that was once down the street from our classroom. My new friends, neighbors, and colleagues have helped make Groningen our new home.

A number of libraries, archives, and institutions assisted me during my research. They include the Johns Hopkins University Libraries, the University of Pennsylvania Libraries, the Louisiana State University Libraries, the Tulane University Libraries, the John Carter Brown Library, the Brown University Libraries, the Providence Public Library, the Historical Society of Pennsylvania, the Library Company of Philadelphia, the Delaware Historical Society, the New York State Archives, the New York State Library, the New York Public Library, the Library of Congress, the British National Archives at Kew (formerly the PRO), the National Archives of Sweden (Riksarkivet), the National Library of Sweden (Kungliga Biblioteket), the National Archives of the Netherlands (Het Nationaal Archief, formerly Het Rijksarchief), the National Library of the Netherlands (De Koninklijke Bibliotheek), and finally the University of Groningen Libraries.

I am grateful to have had opportunities to present my research at talks and conferences sponsored by the McNeil Center for Early American Studies, the Society for Early Americanists, the Society for Netherlandic History, the Omohundro Institute of Early American History and Culture, the John Carter Brown Library, the American Antiquarian Society, and LSU History's Works in Progress Series. I especially appreciate the comments and suggestions made by the speakers, panelists, and audience members who attended those talks.

Friends, near and far, were a source of support whether they knew it or not. Among them were our neighbors in Baton Rouge, and John and Betty Chenier, who treated our family as part of their own. Patrick and Andrea Morris provided help in so many ways. The Nortons met us once in Breaux Bridge and another time in southern Arkansas—I hope we can caravan again soon. I was happy to see their fellow Texan Jimmy McWilliams again during our mutual sojourns in New England. The Boston apartment of Beran Rose and Marcela Escobari was like a second home, while Dante Ramos, a fellow New Orleanian and old friend, lived down the street. Across the river were other friendly faces: Vincent Brown and Ajantha Subramanian and their growing family as well as my sister, Julliette, her husband, Rob Ehlert, and now their new son, Zachary. Back in Providence, the McNeil Center's benevolent influence persisted, home to former fellows and fellow travelers Paul Erickson, Seth Rockman, and Marty Rojas. Old friends Garrett Anderson and Matt Klemm offered long-distance advice. More recently, I was glad to share a panel at the Omohundro Institute annual conference with Elizabeth Mancke, who provided a close, incisive reading of my manuscript. At the New Netherland Institute's annual conference Frans Blom and Henk Looijesteijn shared their research on New Amstel, and Christian Koot offered ideas and a view into his recent work on Augustine Herrman.

Ultimately, I am most grateful to my family. My parents have been a great source of support. I wrote this book, but they provided me with the means, in every way, to write it. I continue to turn to my brother, Neil, and my sister, Julliette, for important advice, and I look forward to reunions with them and their families in the years to come. My wife, Cortlyn, and my son, Phineas, have had to make many sacrifices so that I could finish this book. Judy Edwards made many of those sacrifices easier to bear by making her home our home. Cortlyn and Phineas have weathered our long journeys with strong resolve and good cheer. I look forward to discovering this strange country and continent with them and building a new life out of the old. Their love, and the assurance of that love, makes everything possible.

THE CONTEST FOR THE
DELAWARE VALLEY

INTRODUCTION

From Hudson to Penn

We begin with two voyagers to the Delaware Bay, one at the start of the seventeenth century, the other at its finish.

The first was Henry Hudson, "an Englishman late of London," who cruised into the bay on a warm, clear day late in August 1609.[1] Over the two previous summers he had sailed in "the company of our troublesome neighbours, Ice with fogge," searching for a way through the Arctic to China. First the coasts of Greenland and Spitsbergen and then the frozen archipelago of Novaya Zemlya had thwarted him. The ice, once troublesome, turned murderous. At Novaya Zemlya, a day after observing such a "great plenty of Ice, [that] the hope of passage . . . was taken away," he and his men had spent twelve hours "fending off with Beames and Sparres" a wall of ice "driving upon us, very fearfull to looke on."[2] During that voyage his employer had been the English Muscovy Company, a chartered trading company whose founders included one "Henry Herdson," probably the navigator's grandfather.[3] Since then, Hudson had left behind England, the Muscovy Company, and his relations—or they had left him. When he entered the Delaware Bay, he was in the service of the Heren XVII der Vereenigde Oostindische Compagnie, the Seventeen Lords of the Dutch East India Company.

Before sailing the *Halve Maen* into the balmy waters of the mid-Atlantic, Hudson had attempted one final time to push through the ice floes north of Norway. "After much trouble with fogges, sometimes, and more dangerous of Ice," his restive crew, better suited to the South Seas than to the Barents Sea, had forced him to turn back. Hudson duly pointed the yacht toward "faire cleere Sun-shining weather" and North America.[4] Inspiration for the detour came in part from Hudson's correspondence with Captain John Smith, commander of the newborn settlement at Jamestown, whose Indian informants had plied him with tales of an open sea to the north of Virginia. Although the Powhatans' passage evaded Hudson, he did find a "great Bay,"[5] the Delaware Bay, as well as a "goodly river, into the which he sailed with his ship fifty leagues up." Along this river, later known as "Hudson's River," he received a friendly welcome from native inhabitants who possessed a "great plenty of their country corn" and furs they were eager to trade.[6]

Short of supplies and willing sailors, the *Halve Maen* returned to Europe. Instead of proceeding directly to Amsterdam, however, the vessel stopped first at Dartmouth, a deepwater port along England's southwestern coast. News of the voyage spread far beyond the walls of the ship—as, no doubt, Hudson had intended. By the time he had received orders to return with the ship and its crew to Holland, Crown officials had confiscated his papers and maps and demanded that he and the other Englishmen reenter English service. Although a copy of Hudson's journal eventually reached the Netherlands, the Dutch East India Company lost the talents of the navigator himself.[7] Hudson would undertake his next voyage in the name of his native country and its king.

This expedition, Hudson's last, ended in June 1611, when mutineers abandoned him, his seventeen-year-old son John, and seven other men in a shallop in "Hudson's Bay" and then sailed for England.[8] "What is otherwise become of them [he] knoweth not," mariner Robert Byleth later testified. The bill for Byleth's indictment suggested otherwise—it stated that Hudson and the others "came thereby to their death and miserably perished."[9] Soon afterward Dutch and English settlers, officials, and historians began asserting and disputing linkages between the departed captain's national origin and the areas he had explored in 1609. For advocates of English claims to North America, Hudson was first and foremost a native Englishman, and the rights to his discoveries belonged to his natural sovereign, the King of England. For defenders of Dutch colonial claims, more important than Hudson's place of birth was the fact that he had been in the service of a company chartered by the Lords of the States General in the Netherlands. The navigator's Dutch sponsors owned the rights to whatever he found while under their protection.

Hudson, the focus of all these debates, may not have cared which sovereign, nation, or company claimed his discoveries—his actions suggest that he was willing to entertain all offers, whatever their origin. His ultimate loyalties seem to have been to God and to a geographic imagination that drove him and his men into that "blacke blue Sea" at the boundary between life and death.[10] In order to reach that limit, however, he needed the support of Heren and gentlemen, of companies and kings, and in their world allegiances mattered a great deal. So even if Hudson's own attachment to his *"Prince and Countrie"* was conditional, when he returned from North America in November 1609, he found that the bond between national origin and allegiance, once flexible, had become fixed.[11] As Sir Edward Coke had asserted in his report on Calvin's Case a year earlier, "Ligeance and obedience is an incident inseparable to every subject; for as soon as he is born he oweth by birth right ligeance and obedience to his Soveraign."[12] Born an English subject, Hudson would die an English subject. His charts, his discoveries, and his loyalties became the English Crown's inheritance.

By entering the Delaware Bay in 1609, Hudson and his polyglot crew unwittingly began a colonial contest that only came to an end seven decades later. The arrival in 1682 of our second English voyager, William Penn, signaled the conclusion to this era of conflict. The Quaker proprietor had come to take possession of Pennsylvania, a territory that Hudson had helped to create and that English soldiers and sailors had ultimately secured. Penn's colony was only the latest of many European efforts to settle the Delaware Valley. Inhabitants who had lived under previous Swedish, Dutch, and English regimes already had established farms, churches, and courts within the generous bounds of Penn's grant. Indeed, part of the proprietor's mission was to assure the "ancient settlers" that he and his government would protect their rights and their possessions.

The ritual incorporation of these settlers took place in a series of assemblies along the Delaware River, where Penn's vessel, aptly named the *Welcome,* landed in October 1682. Later accounts of his arrival, nearly all celebratory, claimed that the old settlers happily accepted the proprietor as their new lord. At the little river town of New Castle, once the site of the Dutch Fort Casimir, the Swedish Fort Trefaldighet, and the town of New Amstel, *"Dutch, Swedes* and *English* . . . received and entertained him with great expressions of Joy." Seventeen miles upriver, at Upland, the town's Swedish and Finnish inhabitants were said to be "very Joyful." The Swedes, in particular, dispatched a representative to tell Penn that *they would Serve, Love, and Obey him with all they had, and that it was the best Day they ever saw.*"[13] According to minister and historian Israel Acrelius, who led the Swedish Lutheran congregation in Philadelphia from 1749 to 1756, the *Swenske* welcomed their "new fellow-citizens with great friendliness, carried up their goods and belongings from the ships, and lodged them in their houses without charge—as many old Quakers still relate with pleasure."[14]

Whether the river's non-English settlers were really so joyful or were merely being pragmatic, they quickly sought to ensure that the new English regime would honor Penn's promises of "Spiritual and Temporal Rights, Liberty of Conscience and Civil Freedoms."[15] In early December 1682 they came forward at the first Pennsylvania assembly convened at Upland, which had been newly renamed "Chester." There "the Swedes, Finns, Dutch & others who were not English Men" petitioned Penn and the general assembly to grant them "the same Power, Libertyes and Priviledges as English Men who are Inhabitants of the Province of Pennsylvania . . . and territories thereof." The assembly acceded to their request by passing a generous naturalization law. Soon afterward a group of influential Swedish men appeared before Philadelphia's first county court. They promised "faith and Allegiance" to the King of England and "fidelity and Lawfull obedience" to William Penn. They only did so, however, with the assurance of receiving English liberties in return.[16]

This was not the first time these settlers had made such promises. Once many of them had been colonists in New Sweden. Since the fall of the colony in 1655, they had also been subjects of the governments of New Netherland, New Amstel, New York, New Netherland again, New York again, and now Pennsylvania.[17] At some, if not all, of those points of transition—three invasions and three peaceful handovers—officials had required that settlers swear oaths of allegiance to their new (or old) political masters in order to demonstrate their loyalty. They usually did so willingly, knowing that allegiance was their avenue to liberty. For the older Swedes and Finns their promises to Penn and the King of England in 1683 may have represented the seventh or even the eighth time that they had promised their fealty to a colonial regime and its sovereign. Penn's arrival marked a change. Although officials and settlers in Pennsylvania, Maryland, and the Delaware counties continued to struggle over their respective boundaries until the 1760s, the

Delaware Valley's European inhabitants remained bound by allegiance to the Crown of England until American Independence. The contest to decide which nation would rule the Delaware was over.

During the years between Hudson's and Penn's voyages, no less than ten different colonial regimes sought to assert their authority in the Delaware Valley.[18] The land was never free for the taking. Native peoples had their own claims to the territory and its trade, and they asserted those claims vigorously. The resulting struggle for power had effects on both sides of the Atlantic Ocean. In Europe the controversies produced a torrent of commissions, deeds, charters, affidavits, and protests extending to the highest levels of government. In North America officials engaged in their own epistolary battles, accompanied by a series of choreographed encounters, angry standoffs, and armed assaults. In and around the Delaware Valley native peoples forged alliances and enmities with one another and with the newcomers. They witnessed, provoked, and intervened in intercolonial conflicts. Because of these complex rivalries, the Delaware Valley's status as colonial territory remained unsettled for most of the seventeenth century.

These different disputes were united by a basic theme: that settlers, officials, and even Indians belonged to "nations." The defining characteristics of a nation varied considerably in the early modern era, to be sure. In colonial settings such as the Delaware Valley, Europeans used the term primarily to identify a people bound together by a common allegiance. They conceived of subjecthood and peoplehood as related statuses and identified individuals, communities, and sovereigns as coparticipants, however unequal, in cultural and political collectivities called "nations." The term applied to Europeans as well as peoples outside of Europe. Although early modern Europeans were not and could not be programmatic nationalists in a modern sense, they were quite comfortable imagining social and political relationships in national terms.[19] Drawing on medieval conceptions of kingdoms as both territories and peoples, they believed that individual peoples had distinctive natures and customs shaped by their region; persisted over long stretches of time; exercised agency in a world divided among other peoples; and commonly possessed their own languages, laws, territories, and governments.[20] The multiple and overlapping meanings attached to the word *nation* are evident in John Minsheu's multilingual dictionary *Ductor in Linguas, The Guide into Tongues,* first published in London in 1617. Minsheu listed synonyms for *Nation* in seven modern languages (in Dutch it was *Natie*) while cross-referencing it with "Countrie," which he defined as a "region" but also as "natiue soile," "Pátria," and "Vaderlandt." "People, *or Nation*" was the headword for an entry that included *populus, Volk,* and *Lieden.*[21] Nations evoked peoples, places, and powerful attachments to those places. The early modern sense of what constituted a nation differed from the modern, but it was not so different as many have supposed.[22]

Colonizers conventionally emphasized the political dimension of nationhood—the ties of authority and allegiance that bound together a people. They blended references to sovereigns and nations in order to assert territorial claims; to articulate linkages between settlers, officials, and their sovereigns; and to differentiate themselves and their fellow subjects from their neighbors and competitors. Discourses about nations, empires, and allegiances that once had framed relationships and rivalries within Europe now extended into the Atlantic World and beyond.[23] Yet nations were not invoked only to justify empire. As early modern states, colonizers, and commercial enterprises extended their global reach, a view of the world as divided into nations helped to make sense of European colonial competition as much as it helped to make it possible. Nations became relatively stable, familiar, and recognizable categories of distinction, even as forms of authority multiplied and divided in the extra-European world.[24] In the Delaware Valley, as in other contested colonial zones, indigenous peoples, too, were keenly aware of colonizers' national affiliations and employed this knowledge in their negotiations with traders and officials.[25] Drawing from their own existing and developing understandings of peoplehood, the representatives of native communities also identified themselves and other indigenous peoples as nations in their dealings with Europeans.[26] Nation-ness proliferated in the colonial encounter.[27]

National affiliations could be sticky, persistent forms of identification. In large part this was because nations were understood first and foremost as peoples, even if they were treated generically in political and diplomatic contexts as communities of subjects loyal to a sovereign. Commonalities of language, religion, history, and place also characterized nations as peoples. Unlike allegiance, which could formally be dissolved under certain conditions (and in practice was taken up and dropped by many mobile Europeans), national affiliation often adhered to the very character and body of a person as a form of ethnicity.[28] Even during peaceful periods in the colonies, foreign-born settlers were identified by their national origin. Outside their own communities colonists routinely identified friends and foes according to their nation.

These national differences were articulated most clearly at sites of conflict, but they also mattered once hostilities had ceased. In the Delaware Valley national affiliations powerfully affected how settlers, officials, and Indians related to one another in the aftermath of handovers and invasions. Although colonial authorities commonly treated subjecthood as a political status based on allegiance, not national or ethnic origin, they often doubted the loyalties of nonnative subjects, especially those who had recently belonged to a rival regime. Writing at the beginning of the seventeenth century, English jurist and philosopher Francis Bacon noted that the most effective method "to assure and retain obedience in countries conquered" was *not* "by colonies, and intermixture of people, and transplantation of families, . . . [in] the Roman manner," which he claimed was "an old relick, much reverenced and almost never used." Rather, he recommended "the modern manner, . . . almost wholly in practice and use," which was "by garrisons and citadels, and lists or companies of men of war, and other like matters of terror and bridle."[29] Bacon's brutal skepticism often seemed warranted in contested colonial settings where settlers maintained collective identities that tied them to one another and to their former sovereigns even after their conquest. The colonists' indigenous neighbors also recognized that the old settlers and the new regimes belonged to different nations. Several years after the English invasion of New Netherland, a large group of "wel Loded" Lenape men told Finnish and Dutch settlers along the Delaware River that they "would do us no hurt but for the English and all new Castll thay would kill man woman and Child and burne the howll plase."[30]

Actors high and low worked within, around, and sometimes against national affiliations as circumstances required. Officials were most wedded to discourses linking colony, people, and sovereign, but settlers also participated in and appropriated these discourses for themselves. As Frederick Cooper has argued in another context, imperial subjects' "claims for resources, rights, or access . . . on the basis of *belonging*" were important instruments of power that "rulers of empire in certain circumstances needed to take seriously."[31] These claims could be made in relation to subjects' own authorities, as Cooper notes, but they were arguably more useful in making claims against outsiders. Settlers acted as transgressors against other colonies and defenders of their own, and they justified their actions by asserting their allegiances and identifying themselves with national communities that shared in the rights of their sovereigns. National identities, then, were hardly limited to a small, literate elite who sought to impose them on the ignorant rabble below, as scholars of modern nationalism often seem to suggest. Nor were these identities necessarily metropolitan in origin—discourses of national identification were often born within the colonies and elaborated in response to local conditions. Common settlers latched firmly onto the idea of a nation as a community formed of sovereign and subjects. They drew on national allegiances to make demands of higher authorities and to legitimate their own actions in contested situations. "At once opposing and using the state for its own ends, local society brought the nation into the village," Peter Sahlins has written of the communities that occupied the eighteenth-century border between France and Spain. In the seventeenth-century Delaware Valley settlers brought the nation into the colony.[32]

Natural subjects were more likely to assert their national allegiances than naturalized aliens, although one can find neo-patriots among the latter group as well. Instead, foreign subject populations—colonial "immigrants" as well as the more numerous settlers who stayed behind after the conquest of their colony—typically adopted a posture of legal privilege and ethnic difference. When large enough to wield collective power, they offered their obedience in exchange for generous conditions regarding land, trade, and the ability to preserve a separate corporate status. In the case of postconquest settlements officers of new regimes often agreed to grant conquered populations distinctive statuses as "English," "Dutch," or "Swedish" in order to obtain their willing consent. Here they were following practices common in Europe, where conquered subjects sometimes received similar concessions. Dutch jurist Hugo Grotius, for example, recommended in *De Jure Belli et Pacis* (1625) that even "when the Conquered are altogether deprived of their Empire," they should be allowed to retain "power over their private Estates, and some smaller things that are publick; as their own Laws, Customs and Magistrates." The conquered should also be permitted to retain "free exercise of their Religion."[33] And indeed, the remnants of defunct colonies in the Delaware Valley commonly retained implicit or explicit rights to choose their own local officials, to make collective demands of higher officials, to organize and regulate their own churches, to run their own local courts, and sometimes even to continue trading with their native countries. National identities once oriented toward empires became ethnic identities associated with customary rights and liberties attached to specific communities.[34]

Over time nonnative settler communities crafted national identities that were more communal and less state oriented than they were in previous incarnations. Examples included the "Swedish nation" and the "English nation" in New Netherland and "the Swedes, Finns, Dutch & others who were not English Men" in early Pennsylvania. These reinvented "nations" preserved their autonomy by acting as loyal, obedient subjects, as most of their members chose to do. Demonstrating fidelity to their new masters enabled "aliens" to gain access to the rights, privileges, and *power* that accrued to individuals with the official status of subjects. Sometimes, in fact, they retained rights that were withheld from other colonists or gained privileges that they had not had before. In the parallel contest for seventeenth-century Acadia, historian John Reid writes, "invasion inevitably brought threats and disruptions. It also brought opportunities."[35] Avowals of allegiance permitted preexisting structures of communal authority to survive, and even to strengthen, under new regimes. Loyalty had benefits not only for privileged male intermediaries but also for the communities of men, women, and children they claimed to represent.

The bond between "People, *or Nation*" and "Countrie" did not break easily. Allegiances and identities remained hard to keep separate even (or especially) when colonial competition seemed to force them apart.[36] Some settlers openly or secretly sought to restore the natural allegiances of their naturalized communities, and the anxious officials of new regimes made concerted efforts exactly to prevent such "revolutions." Only when a state acquired stable authority did such fears subside. Yet achieving this stability in the seventeenth-century Atlantic World was a feat few states were able to accomplish for long. In the Delaware Valley it required a large and loyal population to secure that territory, something no Dutch, Swedish, or English colony could boast before William Penn's arrival.

Only with the assurance offered by the presence of thousands of new British settlers could Penn confidently grant the so-called aliens in his province the rights of Englishmen. He denied them, however, the corporate privileges and autonomy that they once had possessed or might have expected to gain. Pennsylvania developed into a pluralistic colonial society in part because Penn made sure that its institutions incorporated every nation within that society on the same terms. Unlike in earlier regimes, in which different populations of settlers within a colony were often separate and *unequal,* in Pennsylvania the diverse subjects in the colony would be as "one people" and one nation. By the end of the next century, if not sooner, many European settlers in the colony had come to see themselves as members of one *race* too.[37]

The category of the nation operated at many levels in the early modern Atlantic World. It shaped relations between states in Europe, between rival colonies, between Indians and Europeans, and between settlers and officials within individual settlements. Yet as ubiquitous as it could be, the nation had very real limits as a category for organizing social relations in imperial settings. In the Delaware Valley, where no colonial regime was capable of establishing uncontested authority until the last quarter of the century, the same conditions that promoted identification with nations and empires also encouraged subjects to forge relationships that bridged or undermined those national and imperial boundaries.

One way that European traders, settlers, merchants, and officials and their Indian counterparts responded to the colonial contest for the Delaware Valley was by constructing transnational, or "cosmopolitan," forms of affiliation. Their cosmopolitanism was not the kind formulated by Immanuel Kant or the philosophes. Rather, it was the actual practice of forming intercultural or transnational relationships among actors of various social strata.[38] In recent decades this view of cosmopolitanism as practice has attracted researchers in a wide range of different fields, including history. Margaret C. Jacob, for example, has written in her study of early modern European cosmopolitanism that "we need a history of cultural practices, of de facto mores, not simply high ideals."[39] This sort of lived, everyday cosmopolitanism has become a major theme in many recent works on the seventeenth-century Atlantic World, which have challenged the notion that imperial divisions functioned effectively as cultural boundaries. The authors of these works point to the diverse origins and experiences of settlers, the activities of merchants who traded across colonial and imperial boundaries, and the ways in which members of different cultural groups cooperated in everyday life. *Communication* and *connection* are their watchwords.[40]

While newer research on the Atlantic World has emphasized collaboration and mixture among various colonial populations, an older and influential historiographic tradition has stressed the weakness of national loyalties and identities during this period. Historian Hans Kohn asserted nearly seventy years ago that "national feeling was yet unknown" in early modern Europe. The work of Eric Hobsbawm, which has acknowledged the existence of early modern "proto-nations," is typical in other respects in stating that the "basic characteristic of the modern nation and everything connected with it is its modernity."[41] Recent scholarship on colonial identities in the Atlantic World continues to argue that early modern Europeans identified themselves primarily by their locality or region, not by their nation.[42]

The seventeenth-century Delaware Valley offers many examples to support the cosmopolitan interpretation of intercultural relations as well as the older "localist" model of early modern identity that still wields great influence today. The initial efforts to colonize the Delaware Valley were born from the wide-ranging imagination of Willem Usselincx, a displaced Antwerper who envisioned Europeans from various nations working together under the protection of a sovereign state. The first settlements diverged from Usselincx's cosmopolitan vision but nonetheless relied heavily upon commerce with outsiders. Likewise, despite their frequent disputes over territory, authorities often tried to work together when they had interests in common. Over the course of the seventeenth century Dutch, English, and Swedish officials attempted to coordinate Indian diplomacy; to corral runaway servants, debtors, and criminals; and to prevent European wars from spreading to North America. In their letters to one another they appealed frequently to Christian friendship and neighborliness.

Although appeals to principle and a common faith often met with little success, prospects of mutual profit sometimes led to more productive outcomes. "Special colonial interests" could override "national prejudices and animosities" through commerce and communication, Claudia Schnurmann has argued. It was also true that national loyalties themselves were sometimes up for negotiation.[43] In keeping with the localist model, allegiances often seemed quite weak, and not only among the settlers. Officials frequently pursued their own interests alongside (or instead of) those of their masters. Consider Dutch official Alexander d'Hinoyossa, who announced in 1662 that if his superiors in Amsterdam did not treat him better, he would "go and bring the Englishman or the Portuguese, the Swede or the Dane. What the devil do I care whom I serve?"[44] D'Hinoyossa was simply following in the footsteps of the "founding fathers" of colonial settlement in the Delaware Valley, Henry Hudson and Peter Minuit, notorious national shape-shifters in their own right. Yet there were significant risks attached to such strategic disloyalty. After giving up Minuit's hometown of Wesel to French forces during the *rampjaar* of 1672, d'Hinoyossa was beheaded. He had "abandoned his post, demonstrated great faintheartedness, [caused] riotous quarrels and mutiny, and further provoked others."[45]

In comparison to their officers, settlers were usually less bold in word but more daring in deed—as occupants of a contested territory, they had to be. During the 1640s and 1650s, for example, many of New Sweden's inhabitants fled to Maryland in order to escape the obligations, punishments, and privations of their own colony. Lord Baltimore's long-standing desire to claim the Delaware's western shore made these Swedish and Finnish runaways welcome additions, particularly as they helped to populate his province's thinly occupied northern frontier. The old inhabitants of a territory could be very accommodating to newcomers too. After the English took over the Delaware Valley in 1664, some Dutch residents and English soldiers married into Finnish and Swedish families. Local officials, later drawn from their ranks, had origins that were just as diverse. Once order became established, a pragmatic pluralism took root.

There were, however, significant limits to this amalgamation of peoples. A few settlers became fluent in indigenous languages and cultures, and some Indians became well versed in European ways, but European and indigenous societies generally remained separate. Yet it was a familiar distance, often bridged, that was the product of decades of close contact. The Lenape and the Minquas-Susquehannock actively fostered this interaction in the early seventeenth century by encouraging rival European traders and colonizers to come to the river. Indeed, Indian peoples' relationships with other indigenous and European communities, near and far, created political and commercial networks that shore-bound Europeans barely understood.[46]

Taking into account the critical perspectives offered by the cosmopolitan and localist approaches to early modern identity, this study seeks to define the extent and limits of national identities and their alternatives in the Delaware Valley. The argument here ultimately breaks from those models, however, by charting the ways that sources of authority and power— and settlers' identification with those sources—reinforced national forms of identification while undermining broader transnational and narrower local forms of attachment. Indeed, just as a "growing consensus" among scholars of cosmopolitanism suggests that "cosmopolitanism sometimes works together with nationalism rather than in opposition to it," this study argues that cosmopolitan forms of interaction and communication coexisted with, and indeed reinforced, national identities.[47] Likewise, it argues that empire fostered an interpenetration of the local and the national in the colonial setting. Pursuing their own interests—or the interests of their families, friends, neighbors, and compatriots—colonizers and colonists embedded themselves within national contexts.

This interplay between the local, the national, and the transnational is what makes the seventeenth-century competition for the Delaware Valley more than another old story about imperial rivalries. Even as settlers trumpeted their national affiliations and struggled over colonial territory, they created unique creole communities in North America in which interactions across national boundaries became routine. At the end of the century, however, the conditions for interaction changed dramatically. As the English empire in America expanded and consolidated, the rivals in its midst were swallowed up. New Netherland became New York (twice), and the Swedish monarchy's hopes of regaining New Sweden died their final death. The indigenous nations in the Delaware Valley and its hinterlands became weaker and less able to shape the terms of their relationships with Europeans. This large-scale change, the product of English imperial success, is essential to understanding the significance of nations and ethnicity in colonial North America. Imperial nations struggled over territories in the seventeenth century that belonged to a single multinational empire in the eighteenth. The descendants of those conquered subjects became naturalized subjects of the British Empire. The character of group identity changed from national to ethnic. Under these new conditions subjects from various nations forged a new British nationality in America. Following a pattern set by their seventeenth-century predecessors, the inhabitants of the eighteenth-century Delaware Valley turned loyalty into liberty.

1

Claiming Hudson and His Discoveries

In his 1612 account of Henry Hudson's two voyages to North America, Hessel Gerritsz remarked that the English navigator's first voyage in 1609 had achieved "nothing memorable."[1] Not all of Gerritsz's own contemporaries were so dismissive, but the Dutch chronicler had a point. Giovanni Verrazzano and doubtless several other European explorers had already visited "Hudson's River" in the previous century, if not more recently. Hudson had neither discovered a passage to Asia via Novaya Zemlya, where his employers had contracted with him to go, nor found a route that passed through the North American continent. Perhaps worst of all, he had revealed nothing especially valuable in the areas he had explored.

Of course, Hudson had achieved something memorable in 1609. Although he was not the first European to navigate the North American coastline between 39 and 41 degrees of latitude, he and the sailors aboard his ship were the first to produce detailed navigational and cartographic knowledge of this region. More important, because his explorations became known in England and the Netherlands soon after his return to Europe, his voyage allowed other navigators to reproduce the journey and to seek out commodities that might make the territory profitable after all. In 1612 Hudson's voyage might not have seemed memorable, but in subsequent years it would be remembered, and re-remembered. Hudson's accomplishments became noteworthy most of all because others found profit in the areas he visited and because Dutch and English authorities alike sought to legitimate their own ambitions by avowing his discoveries as their own. In time the struggle to claim Hudson became a struggle to claim the mid-Atlantic coast of North America.

When Hudson left London for Amsterdam in early 1609, he quickly became entangled in the rival commercial and imperial ambitions of Dutch merchants, the French monarchy, and his own native kingdom.[2] He went seeking the patronage of the Dutch East India Company (Vereenigde Oostindische Compagnie, or VOC), which the States General had chartered in 1602 with the aim of monopolizing commerce between the United Provinces and east and southeast Asia. The company minimized competition and maximized profits for its members at the same time that it coordinated efforts to chip away at the Iberians' eastern trading empire. The trade with Asia was lucrative, but it remained costly, time-consuming, and dangerous, not least because the Spanish and Portuguese monarchies claimed sovereignty over the sea-lanes around Africa's Cape of Good Hope and South America's Straits of Magellan, the only navigable routes to Asia. Of course, the Asian trade appealed to many Dutch merchants exactly because it undermined the Iberian empire, whose sovereign, Philip III, continued to seek the Dutch Republic's subjugation. Across the Channel like-minded English proponents of commerce and colonization also encouraged an expanded overseas presence in order to challenge the Spanish and Portuguese empire at its vulnerable periphery.[3]

Direct confrontation appealed to some Dutch and English militants, but the burgeoning science of geography suggested that patriotic (Protestant) merchants might be able to achieve their goals without sailing the southern routes dominated by the Spanish and the Portuguese. If they could find a viable (and much shorter) northern route via the Arctic or through the unexplored regions of North America, then they would be able to avoid the military and diplomatic hazards inherent in flouting the Iberians' claims. The French ambassador at The Hague, Pierre Jeannin, reported that such a northern voyage could be finished in six months "without approaching any of the harbours and fortresses of the King of Spain," while the most common route around the Cape of Good Hope "generally requires three years, and one is besides exposed to meet and to fight the Portuguese."[4] The discovery would benefit merchants and states alike. A northern passage held out the potential of undermining Iberian political and commercial hegemony, spreading Christianity, gaining glory for sovereigns and nations, and making all involved ever richer. Inserted into this nexus of politics, religion, and commerce, Henry Hudson appeared to be a very valuable man.

Because Hudson's ideas were unproven, however, he was a risky investment. He had already failed twice in the service of the English Muscovy Company, and the VOC initially proved unwilling to gamble further on his speculations. Company officials listened to Hudson's proposal but declined to sponsor him. Another patron soon expressed interest. Isaac Le Maire, a prominent merchant in Amsterdam who had attracted the attention of Jeannin, presented Hudson with an offer of French royal backing. Eager to imitate the successes of the VOC, the French king Henry IV had instructed Jeannin to seek out potential Dutch investors in a French East India Company, and the maverick Le Maire seemed a good place to start.[5]

Jeannin strongly urged his sovereign to give Hudson his support. Although the enterprise might fail, Jeannin insisted "the risk would not be very great." He testified to the experience and ability of Le Maire and encouraged the French king to imagine the great rewards such a "glorious enterprise" might offer. Jeannin prompted Henry to consider his own resemblance to another monarch who had sponsored a discoverer with bold and unproven ideas: "When Ferdinand of Spain received the offer of Columbus, and caused three ships to be fitted out for him, to sail to the West Indies, the proposal seemed still more hazardous, and all the other potentates, to whom he had applied, had laughed at him, considering his success as impossible, yet he has obtained such great results." Henry Hudson, Jeannin hinted, might make Henry IV the founder of a new eastern empire.[6]

The French ambassador had even taken the added step of speaking with the VOC's famed geographer, Domine Petrus Plancius, who had met previously with Hudson and shared his theories regarding northern routes to Asia. Plancius's consultations with Hudson and other pilots had convinced him, Jeannin reported, that "there must be in the northern parts a passage corresponding to the one found near the south pole by Magellan." Plancius predicted this passage would be open to navigation because Hudson's previous voyages had shown that "the more northwards he went, the less cold it became." The geographer reasoned that "near the pole the sun shines for five months continually," rendering the climate "temperate" enough to accommodate men and animals. Just as the tropics had proven to be "habitable, temperate, fertile, and favourable to the existence of man," so would the lands in the far north prove more hospitable than the ancients had thought. In fact, Plancius and other geographers believed that "in the

northern parts there are many countries which have not yet been discovered, and which God may be keeping for the glory and the profit of other
princes, unwilling to give everything to Spain alone."[7] Geography and the
Almighty seemed to be on the side of the Iberians' challengers. Here, however, Jeannin's efforts to harness discovery to empire proved to be in vain
because once VOC officials learned Hudson was considering other offers,
they immediately recalled him. Company officials soon negotiated a contract with Hudson and began making preparations for his voyage.[8]

Hudson's service as an Englishman to a Dutch trading company may
seem unremarkable when we consider the context. London and Amsterdam are just over two hundred miles apart—a little more than the distance
between Boston and New York. That proximity facilitated a long history
of interaction and exchange between England and the United Provinces,
Holland in particular.[9] Dutch armies fielded English soldiers, among them
Hudson's correspondent Captain John Smith as well as numerous other
men who would later serve as officials in England's colonies.[10] English Protestants settled in Holland's cities, among them the Separatists from Leiden
who founded the New Plymouth colony in 1620. The flow of migrants went
the other way as well. Many Dutch and Walloon Protestants migrated to
England in the sixteenth and seventeenth centuries as skilled tradesmen.[11]
Jodocus Hondius, one of the VOC geographers who consulted with Hudson
before the 1609 voyage, was a mapmaker in England for ten years before
returning to the Netherlands in 1593 and later becoming an advisor to the
VOC.[12] Emanuel van Meteren, whose history of the Netherlands is one of the
best contemporary sources regarding Hudson's voyage, lived in England for
most of his life.[13]

Yet cosmopolitanism had its limits. During Hudson's four months in Amsterdam news of his discussions with VOC officials, the geographer Plancius,
and the merchant Le Maire did not remain within the borders of the United
Provinces. Contemporary Spanish diplomatic correspondence suggests
strongly that members of the English government knew of Hudson's activities.
Writing from Brussels a month after Hudson had departed, the Marqués de
Guadeleste informed his monarch, Philip III, that the VOC had equipped two
ships to seek a northern passage to China. The voyage, led by "un ingles,"
had proceeded despite the fact that "his master (*amo*) had not allowed it."[14]
The term *master* is somewhat ambiguous, but it suggests that either the
English Crown or Hudson's former employers in the Muscovy Company had
sought to block Hudson from entering the service of a foreign employer.

This express prohibition may help to explain Hudson's fate when he returned to England at the end of his voyage. As a prodigal or a truant, Hudson reentered the service of his "master" once he returned to his king's domain.

Henry Hudson, Englishman

In the early months of 1609 Hudson had been at the center of a remarkable competition for his talents. Representatives of the French king had courted him, English officials had attempted to obstruct him, and the directors of the Dutch East India Company had hired him, all while Spanish agents were spying on him. A wily entrepreneur who recognized his own value in the imperial marketplace, Hudson had immersed himself in the competitive commercial politics of exploration and emerged with the sponsorship he desired. His Englishness had played a part in the process—the English government had sought to block his voyage, and virtually all those who commented on the voyage referred to him as an "Englishman"—but his national origin had not prevented him from obtaining the VOC's support.

The national identities of Hudson and his crew seem to have directly affected the voyage once it was under way. According to historian Emanuel van Meteren, the United Provinces' longtime consul in London, the crew aboard the *Halve Maen* consisted of "eighteen or twenty men, *Engelsche ende Nederlanders.*"[15] Hudson probably could not speak Dutch, but he would have had officers who could communicate his orders to the sailors.[16] That communication often seemed to break down during critical moments in the voyage. According to van Meteren, when Hudson first directed the vessel into the Arctic Sea, the members of the crew who had been to the East Indies could not endure the cold, and the "Englishmen and Netherlanders" turned against one another. Hudson's way of settling the dispute and continuing the voyage was to give them the option to seek a passage in the west, where they ultimately decided to go.[17] The crew split along national lines on other occasions too. When the *Halve Maen* reached the coast of New France in mid-July, the explorers discovered that the region was good for fishing and for trading for skins and furs. Yet the promising trade quickly came to an end when the *Schipvolck* (the sailors) abused the *Landtvolck* (the Indians), violently seizing their goods. The quarrel with the native inhabitants again led to divisions among themselves. Fearing reprisals from the Indians, the "English" refused to explore any further.[18]

After leaving the coast of New France, Hudson and his disorderly crew traveled south to the mouth of the Chesapeake Bay. Despite approaching "the entrance into the *Kings* River in *Virginia,* where our *English*-men" were settled, Hudson chose not to make contact with the English colonists there.[19] Hudson's decision to avoid Virginia seems all the more curious given that Captain John Smith, who had provided him with maps of the region, was commander there. Hudson may have wished to avoid delaying his mission, but it seems just as likely that he sought to avoid precipitating a dispute with Virginia's officials. Whatever his motivation, Hudson turned the vessel to the north and soon reached Delaware Bay. Although the bay appeared too shoaly to navigate safely, the strength of the current suggested that a "large river" discharged into it. Continuing north, Hudson and his men entered the harbor at Manhattan. They explored the great river there as far north as contemporary Albany, encountering numerous Indian communities along the way. They finally turned around once they had given up their hopes of finding a passage to Asia at the river's headwaters.[20]

Hudson had failed on this third effort to find a passage to Asia, but he still expected to find a route in the northern reaches of North America. The decision to return to Europe, rather than staying to explore further, is therefore somewhat puzzling. Again, we find evidence that disputes among the crew and officers may have led Hudson to change his plans. Van Meteren reported, for example, that one of the officers, a "Netherlander," thought that they ought to stay in Newfoundland for the winter and search for the northwestern passage in the spring. Hudson opposed this plan, van Meteren wrote, in part because of the danger posed by the oncoming winter. Hudson also "feared his crew would mutiny, because at times they had boldly menaced him." Van Meteren's account also suggests that Hudson's own officers may have forced him to stop the ship in England instead of returning to their port of origin. Van Meteren noted that Hudson became suspicious that "no one . . . spoke of returning to Holland" when the officers were trying to decide whether to return to Europe. Perhaps because he feared mutiny, Hudson cut short the return voyage by stopping in England in early November 1609.[21]

Despite the difficulties of the previous voyage, Hudson seemed determined to continue searching for the passage. According to van Meteren, when Hudson and his men arrived at the port of Dartmouth, they sent a report of their voyage to "their masters, the Directors in Holland," and proposed to set out on another voyage to explore the northwest.[22] Indeed, Hudson told Thomas Holland, the mayor of Dartmouth, that he intended to stay only ten days before returning to America.[23] "A long time elapsed," however, before the report reached the directors in Amsterdam. When they finally received it, they commanded Hudson and the crew to return immediately to the Netherlands. By then it was too late. Thanks to Hudson's candid conversation with Mayor Holland, English royal officials had also learned of Hudson's activities in North America. When the ship was about to leave—in January 1610, two months after it had arrived—officials ordered Hudson and the other Englishmen to stay and "serve their own country."[24]

Van Meteren, no doubt reflecting the viewpoint of interested Dutch observers, considered the seizure of Hudson, his English crewmembers, and the records of the voyage to be illegitimate. He wrote that many found it "strange" that officials in England would prevent the leaders of a voyage intended "for the common benefit of all kinds of navigation" from making a report of their service to their masters.[25] Van Meteren supposed that officials had intervened because the English intended to send Hudson and the English crewmembers "to Virginia to explore further the before mentioned river."[26] Instead of seeking the "common benefit" of all, English officials had sought selfishly to appropriate the service and the records of Hudson and his men, who were still in the service of the VOC's directors when English officials seized them.

Embedded in van Meteren's account was a hierarchical language of masters and servants that helps to explain the responses of English and Dutch officials to Hudson's voyage. From the Dutch officials' perspective Hudson had agreed to serve the directors of the VOC and was obliged to fulfill the terms of his contract. The contract defined the relationship between Hudson and the VOC in specific terms. The company would provide a fully equipped vessel and pay Hudson eight hundred guilders to undertake the voyage. The directors promised further to provide a small sum (two hundred guilders) to his wife should Hudson fail to return safely. If Hudson succeeded in his quest—if he "found the passage so good and convenient that the company should again make use of it"—then the company promised to reward him "for his hazards, troubles, and skill." Hudson was poised to profit handsomely if his theories proved correct.[27]

Such success, however, would have come at a cost. If the company desired to retain Hudson for future missions, Hudson would have had to take up residence in Holland with his wife and children and to "let no-one other than the company use him."[28] Although the terms of the contract did not imply a permanent relationship of subservience or any kind of feudalistic form of allegiance, the contract did speak of "service" (*dienst*) and made clear that the directors of the VOC had the greater authority to interpret the terms of the contract. In this sense the contract was a typical example of how early modern Europeans understood agency within hierarchical relationships: those in the subordinate position expressed their moral freedom by choosing to serve their superiors, and those in the superior position offered aid and protection in exchange for that faithful service. In the terms of van Meteren's account the officers and crew of the *Halve Maen* were in the service of "their masters, the [VOC's] Directors in Holland." By disrupting that relationship, the English government was interfering with one of the most basic and important ways of organizing social and economic life.

Just as Hudson's contract and van Meteren's account reflected a "master-servant" discourse, so did the English interpretation of Hudson's voyage. We have seen already that the Spanish agent at Brussels had reported that Hudson's master denied him permission to make the voyage with the VOC. Hudson's master in this case was James I or possibly his former employers at the Muscovy Company. From the perspective of English officials (and English historical memory) James I was Hudson's natural liege lord and his *true* master as the King of England. Natural allegiance bound Hudson as a subject to his king, who ultimately had the legal prerogative to command Hudson's service and to forbid him to serve another. Such a command probably did not apply directly to the other Englishmen aboard Hudson's vessel, but they too were natural subjects of the English Crown and thus were obliged to "serve their own country" (and the monarch who ruled that country) once they arrived at Dartmouth.

The claim that Hudson and the *Halve Maen*'s English sailors were actually in the service of the King of England during the 1609 voyage soon became ingrained in English historical memory. For generations to come, English settlers, officials, polemicists, and historians insisted that Hudson had been in the service of his sovereign, not the VOC, when he explored the North American coastline between the Chesapeake Bay and the New York harbor. In April 1633, when navigator and colonizer David de Vries and officials at New Amsterdam came into conflict with the master of a merchant vessel from New England, the Englishman claimed that the land there belonged to the English. According to de Vries, the English captain argued that "David Hutson [i.e., Henry Hudson], had found this river first, and wasn't he an *Engelsman?*"—implying that Hudson's Englishness gave the English first rights to his discoveries. Dutch officials responded by agreeing that

Hudson had "found the river in the year nine [1609]" but countered that "he was outfitted by the East India Company at Amsterdam at their expense, and it was now named Mauritius River, after our Prince of Orange."[29] Although New Netherland's officers acknowledged Hudson's English origin, they emphasized that Hudson had been in the service of a Dutch company and that "Hudson's River" was never truly Hudson's. His Englishness did not matter because he was acting in the name of a chartered Dutch company. Insisting upon the river's official name also highlighted the United Provinces' historical claim to the river and demonstrated that the monarch-like authority of the Prince of Orange extended over this colonial territory. If the dispute was between equal sovereigns, then the Dutch had as legitimate a claim to the region as the English.

Several published English accounts of Hudson's discoveries also asserted that Hudson was serving his native sovereign in 1609. In *Cosmographie* (1652) Peter Heylyn wrote that "the *Netherlanders*" traced their title to New Netherland in part from "having bought *Hudsons* Cards and Maps, and otherwise contented him for the charge and pains of his *Discovery, An.* 1609."[30] According to Heylyn's account, however, "the *Hollanders* . . . were hardly warm in their new habitations, when Sir *Samuel Argal*[l], Governour of *Virginia,* specially so called (having dispossessed the *French* of that part of *Canada,* now called *Nova Scotia, An.* 1613) disputed the possession with them." Argall denied their right to the territory, "alledging that *Hudson,* under whose sale they claimed that Country, being an *Englishman,* and licensed to discover those Northern parts by the King of *England,* could not alienate or dismember it (being but a part or Province of *Virginia*) from the Crown thereof." Supposedly after being confronted with this argument based on Hudson's national origin and his natural allegiance, "the *Dutch* Governour submit[ted] himself and his Plantation to his Majesty of *England,* and the Governour of *Virginia* for, and under him." The King of England's restored right would have remained intact if only "a new Governour being sent from *Amsterdam*" had not spoiled the bargain by refusing to pay "the conditioned Tributes," fortifying the colony, and "entitl[ing] those of *Amsterdam* to a just propriety" without English consent. Heylyn thus accepted that Hudson had established a commercial relationship with the Dutch. But such a relationship was immaterial because the King of England had already licensed Hudson to explore those regions and Hudson, as an Englishman, could not sell or transfer a right to territories that already belonged to his natural sovereign.[31]

The nationalized account of Hudson's explorations in 1609 remained a part of English legal and historical tradition long after the governments of England and the Netherlands had settled their disputes over the territory. For example, in his 1757 history of New York William Smith reported that "Henry Hudson, an Englishman, according to our authors, in the year 1608, under a Commission from the King his master, discovered Long Island, New-York, and the river which still bears his name; and afterwards sold the country, or rather his right, to the Dutch." Yet Smith noted that Dutch writers offered a substantially different account. Their writers contended that Hudson had been "sent out by the East-India Company in 1609, to discover a North-west passage to China," during which voyage he had discovered Delaware Bay and the Hudson River. "It is said, however," Smith wrote, "that there was a sale, and that the English objected to it, though they for some time neglected to oppose the Dutch settlement of the country." Aware that the English and Dutch accounts did not mesh, Smith nonetheless affirmed the basic outline of the English account of Hudson's voyage, including the submission of New Netherland's governor to Sir Samuel Argall (and King James) in the first years of the settlement. The territory was English either way.[32]

Dutch writers also fashioned links between nationality and sovereignty in their narratives of the discovery of New Netherland. Hudson's Dutch chroniclers tended to offer less fanciful accounts than their English counterparts, although they too sought to use history to justify claims to colonial territory in North America. Before discussing Hudson's 1609 voyage to North America in *De Nieuwe Wereldt* (1625), for example, geographer and West India Company (WIC) director Johannes de Laet wrote that "our *Nieuw-Nederlandt*" received its name because "our *Nederlanders*" had discovered it at their own expense, sailed there in subsequent years, and built a fort and settlements in the territory. These *Nederlanders* did so under the authority of "the High and Mighty Lords of the States General of these United Provinces," which had issued them their own "special charter." Only after certifying the Dutchness of New Netherland did the WIC historian relate how the "first discovery" came in 1609 when "the Directors of the chartered East India company sent the yacht the *Halve Maen,* which *Hendrick Hudson* led as skipper and merchant, to search in the northeast for a passage to *China.*" Henry had become "Hendrick," and his English origin remained unmentioned. Afterward Dutch merchants began trading in the region, obtained a charter from the States General, and built a fort and a "small occupation." There, de Laet wrote, "our people" remained year-round in order to trade with "de Wilden." For these reasons, he concluded, "this quarter has rightly acquired the name of New Netherland." Hudson's voyage was merely the first in a series of efforts by Netherlanders to exploit and occupy this territory.[33]

Later Dutch accounts of New Netherland's origins were just as partisan but ever more inventive. Adriaen van der Donck, a former official in New Netherland, acknowledged in *Beschryvinge van Nieuvv-Nederlant* (1655) that "*Hendrick Hudson* [was] born an Englishman" but insisted that he "had long trafficked among the Netherlanders and . . . [at that time was] in the service and monthly pay of the East India Company." Van der Donck offered historical evidence as well as the testimony of the territory's indigenous peoples to prove that the Dutch "were the first Christians and discoverers there." Their discoveries, and the resulting claims to territory, stretched from "the South Bay at *Cape Hinlopen*" up to "the great North River, . . . that some English still want to name *Hutsons Rivier,* but which [the Netherlanders] called *Mauritius Rivier,* after *Prince Maurits,* who was then stadhouder in Netherland," and then on to "*Cape Codt,* where they also took possession, and named *Nieuw Hollant.*" In subsequent years "our Netherlanders" continued to visit "these possessed places," where they traded, built forts and plantations, settled families, and purchased land from the Indians. Van der Donck argued that it was "very strange, indecent, and beyond reason that some other nations"—namely the English and the Swedes—were claiming a right to territories that had been discovered, settled, and purchased by his fellow countrymen.[34]

Other Dutch authors added different twists to the Hudson story. Writing in 1612, after incorrect reports had reached Europe that Hudson had discovered a northwestern passage during his final voyage, Hessel Gerritsz suggested that Hudson had intentionally avoided the most promising route in 1609. He reported that Hudson "did not go the correct way (so people here say) in order to do these lands [the Netherlands] no service."[35] Later writers minimized Hudson's importance and gave the honor of discovery to Dutch merchants. Nicolaes Wassenaer, chronicler of the WIC's early efforts in New Netherland, noted as an aside that Hudson, "the famous English pilot," had once visited the area of Manhattan, but the Dutch writer averred that "this country, or the River Montagne [the Hudson River], called by ours Mauritius, was first sailed to by the worthy Hendrick Christiaesz of Cleves."[36] Like the eighteenth-century Anglo-American historian William Smith, latter-day Dutch historian N. C. Lambrechtsen sought to redeem Hudson's memory for a national history. Lambrechtsen wrote that Hudson, "though born in England," felt such a strong connection to the Dutch East India Company that he gave the territory he discovered the name of his "adopted Fatherland," calling it "New Holland." The mistaken renaming of Cape Cod in de Laet's account had become evidence for Hudson's new allegiance to the Dutch Republic.[37]

For Lambrechtsen and van der Donck, Hudson was a virtual Netherlander whose relationship to his employers' fatherland was as affectionate as it was pragmatic. For other Dutch commentators Hudson's Englishness may have been worth remarking upon, but it was nonetheless irrelevant to the matter of right. The English captain was merely a proxy for a greater body formed of, and by, Netherlanders with greater authority. These writers acknowledged that Hudson's voyage was a remarkable achievement but argued that he had achieved his discovery only by virtue of Dutch sponsorship. In English history and memory, by contrast, Hudson was an Englishman in the service of the English king, and his discoveries rightfully belonged to his sovereign, even if he did sell his charts or claims to the Dutch. Ultimately, neither Dutch nor English histories seemed to offer much room for the other except by altering the facts. Hudson may have been a cosmopolitan free agent in 1609, but his discoveries could only be English or Dutch.

Patriots and Pilgrims

Hudson's explorations became part of Dutch and English colonial narratives of possession, although the navigator had not set out to plant colonists or flags. The Dutch merchants and traders who began to frequent Hudson's discovered lands during the next decade also expressed little interest in costly, risky permanent settlements. Instead, they sought the most valuable item Hudson's voyage had revealed: an untapped supply of furs readily collected and traded by the region's indigenous inhabitants. Better yet, Hudson's journey had shown that the territory had no other European competitors.

The rush to profit from this trade inevitably led to conflict among the handful of trading operations now active in the region. Unable to police themselves or to outmaneuver their Indian counterparts, in early 1614 the leading participants and the States General agreed to establish a system of registering discoveries through charters.[38] Later that year a group of these merchants established the Nieuw-Nederland Compagnie and sought to register their discoveries with a charter. They asserted that they had "discovered and found New Netherland," a territory they described as being "situate[d] in America between New France and Virginia." Although the merchants were mainly interested in trade, they nonetheless dressed up their claim with patriotic, national language. They gave the name "New Netherland" to the territory and represented it as the third major colonial province in the northern part of North America. In the map that they submitted with their claim, they promoted the idea that the northeastern coast of North America was divided, without overlap or gaps, between colonies belonging to France, the Netherlands, and England.[39]

None of these early trading efforts attempted to put settlers in North America. Besides the obvious expenses associated with colonization, founding a settlement had political risks. Just five days after Hudson began his voyage on the *Halve Maen*, the United Provinces officially began a twelve-year truce with the King of Spain. A new colonizing effort might have endangered the new peace. By 1620, however, the truce was nearing its end, and Dutch zealots were preparing for war. Greater Dutch involvement in the Americas held out the promise of preying upon the Spanish monarch's wealthy colonial dominions. With plans for a West India Company starting to circulate, the idea of setting up a permanent outpost in New Netherland began to appear more attractive.

In 1620, once the New Netherland Company's charter privileges had expired, a group of the company's former directors addressed the States General and the Prince of Orange with a proposal to send settlers to New Netherland.[40] They offered to dispatch more than four hundred families from the Netherlands and England. The prospective colonists had been recruited by an English preacher residing in Leiden and "versed in the Dutch language." Appealing to God and country, the petitioners attested that the settlers would propagate "the true, pure Christian religion" (i.e., Reformed Protestantism), instruct the Indians and convert them to Christianity, and "plant there a new Commonwealth" under the command of the Prince of Orange and the States General. In more practical terms the petitioners claimed that the settlers would be able to contribute to the proposed new West India Company by turning the territory's "large abundance of timber" to ship building. In return for their services the petitioners asked the Prince of Orange and the States General to protect them from "all violence on the part of other potentates."[41]

The United Provinces' traditional enemy, the King of Spain, was not the only violent potentate who threatened the venture. The King of England, the petitioners warned, was "disposed to people the aforesaid lands with the English nation, and by force to render fruitless their possession and discovery, and thus deprive the State of its right." The English were already behaving aggressively toward Dutch vessels and sought to "surprize the ships of this country which are there." Emphasizing the patriotic goals of the project, the petitioners argued that placing settlers in New Netherland "under the protection of this country" would contribute to the "preservation of this country's rights" in North America. In recognition of Spanish and English threats to these rights, the petitioners asked the States General and the Prince of Orange to provide them with two warships to secure this valuable territory and its settlers.[42]

These merchants had identified the crucial difficulty New Netherland's officials would face for the next five decades: English encroachment on their colonial claims. In order to solve that problem, they suggested that large-scale settlement should be supported by military force. Yet the Lords of the States General hesitated to back the venture. They considered the proposal for two more months but eventually rejected it when the United Provinces' Admiralty declined to provide the requested ships. The Admiralty feared offending the English and French governments, whose colonies adjoined (or claimed to include) the territory of New Netherland. As the Twelve Years' Truce drew to a close, Dutch authorities may have been eager to fight the Spanish, but they had to maintain alliances with the English and the French in order to do so. Colonization would have to wait.

By the time the States General came to this decision, the would-be colonists from Leiden had already found sponsors for their venture in England. Their narratives of this period suggest that the decision to settle in "New England" and not "New Netherland" was more choice than accident. They also suggest that the Separatists' Englishness profoundly shaped that choice, notwithstanding their earlier self-imposed exile from England.[43] New Plymouth's founders may have seen themselves as pilgrims on a journey to heaven, but they seemed confident that the road signs to the end of time were posted in English.[44]

One form of this Englishness was an antipathy toward those who were not English. The longtime governor of New Plymouth, William Bradford, seemed to harbor little affection for the Netherlands or the Dutch. In his famous account *Of Plymouth Plantation* Bradford not only made the Netherlands appear to be morally suspect; he also depicted their inhabitants in a way that suggested a resemblance to the "heathens" in America. On the Separatists' arrival at Amsterdam in 1609, Bradford wrote, they had "heard a strange and uncouth language, and beheld the different manners and customs of the people, with their strange fashions and attires; also so far differing from that of [the Separatists'] plain country villages (wherein they were bred and had so long lived) as it seemed they were come into a new world." Although awed by the wealth of Amsterdam, the Separatists soon had to confront their own poverty. They found life nearly as difficult in Leiden, where they resettled a year later. Yet what was "more lamentable, and of all sorrows most heavy to be borne," was not their poverty but that many of the Separatists' children were subject to "the great licentiousness of youth in that country, and the manifold temptations of the place." Their children "were drawn away by evil examples into extravagant and dangerous courses" and were disregarding their parents' moral authority. "Some became soldiers, others took upon them far voyages by sea, and others some worse courses tending to dissoluteness and the danger of their souls, to the great grief of their parents and dishonour of God," Bradford wrote. Rather than see "their posterity . . . in danger to degenerate and be corrupted" in the Netherlands, the Separatists at Leiden chose to leave Europe altogether.[45]

Other accounts suggest English national feeling motivated New England's founders, at least when they were trying to justify their project to audiences back home in England. In the preface to "Mourt's Relation," published in London in 1622, "G. Movrt." (George Morton) prayed that the settlement at Plymouth might further "the kingdome of Christ . . . [and enlarge] the bounds of our Soueraigne Lord King *Iames*."[46] Even the "Mayflower Compact" described its signatories as "loyall Subiects of our dread soveraigne Lord King IAMES" and proclaimed their purpose as "the glory of God, and advancement of the Christian Faith, and honour of our King and Countrey."[47] Edward Winslow also emphasized the patriotic motivations of the congregation at Leiden. In *Hypocrisie Unmasked,* printed in London in 1646 to counter criticisms of New England's leadership, he recounted how the Separatists' leaders found it "grievous to live from under the protection of the State of *England*" and feared losing "our language, and our name of English." By contrast, settling in America would gain them "so much favour with the King and State of *England,* as to have their protection there, where wee might enjoy the like liberty," he wrote. Under such protection, and with God's blessing, they would show their "tender Country-men" where they could "live, and comfortably subsist and enjoy the like liberties" while keeping "their names and Nation" and enlarging the dominions of England and the Christian church. Winslow concluded by noting that the founders of New England thought that they "might more glorifie God, doe more good to our Countrey, better provide for our posterity, and live to be more refreshed by our labours, than ever wee could doe in *Holland* where we were."[48]

A generation later, writers in New England continued to elaborate the patriotic theme. In 1669—five years after the invasion of New Netherland and two years after England's war with the United Provinces had ended—Nathaniel Morton published *New-Englands Memoriall* in Massachusetts. Expanding upon Bradford's complaints about life in the Netherlands, Morton described the founders' fear that "their Posterity would in few generations become *Dutch,* and so lose their interest in the *English* Nation; they being desirous to enlarge His Majesties Dominions, and to live under their Naturall PRINCE."[49] The Separatists' chroniclers redeemed their original flight to the Netherlands by framing the founding of the Plymouth colony as an expression of patriotic feeling. They obviously had not lost "their interest in the *English* Nation."

Natural Animosities and Interests of State

The subsequent history of the Plymouth colony's founding is a familiar one, or once was. After the winter of 1620–21 only half of the original migrants were alive, but over time the small community persevered and made history as the first permanent English settlement in New England. The international consequences of the Plymouth settlement are less recognized although no less important. Not only had Dutch officials lost to their English rivals a ready group of zealous, voluntary colonists, but these colonists had established a settlement that undercut Dutch claims to the northeastern half of "New Netherland," which by earlier reckonings extended to the 45th parallel. Moreover, the settlement of the Plymouth colony in 1620 preceded by several years the WIC's first attempts to settle New Netherland. English polemicists thus had a good basis for their claims that their countrymen had established first possession of eastern North America from the 34th to the 45th parallel. The Plymouth settlement was only the latest proof of the claim's validity. The Virginia Company's charter of 1606 had already asserted as much before Hudson ever set foot in North America.

James I's Privy Council used similar arguments late in 1621, when it drafted instructions for the English ambassador to the United Provinces, Sir Dudley Carleton, to make a formal complaint to the States General about "Hollanders" who were settling in New England. The council wrote to Carleton with news that in "the yeare past the Hollanders have entered upon some parte [of New England], and have left a Colonie and given new names to the severall ports appertaining to that part of the Countrie, and are now in readinesse to send for their supply six or eight shipps." It ordered Carleton to demand that the States General put a stop to this "plantation" and prevent any additional Dutch ships from visiting the territory. The letter outlined the English claim to the territory by recounting how subjects of the King of England had "many years since taken possession of the whole precinct, and inhabited some parts of the North of Virginia (by us called New England), . . . [and] some yeares since by Patent granted the quiet and full possession unto particular persons."[50]

Before presenting the protest, Carleton privately inquired about the extent of Dutch involvement in North America. He seemed to have made a thorough investigation. He spoke with merchants in Amsterdam, the Prince of Orange, and various other officials. His contacts in commerce and government revealed that two companies of merchants in Amsterdam had begun to trade in "those parts betwixt 40 and 45 degrees, to [which] after their manner they gave their own names of New Netherlands a south & a north sea, a Texel, a Vlieland, & the like." The trade was merely in furs, however, and only a handful of men were posted there in order to trade with the "savages." He found no evidence of a colony or of one in the planning. In fact, during the previous months "divers inhabitants of this country to a considerable number of familyes have been suters unto me, to procure them a place of habitation among his [Majesty's] subjects in those parts," he wrote. If Dutch merchants had been planning a colony, he reasoned, these suitors would not have sought places in an English settlement, as "there is small apparence they would desire to mingle w[i]th strangers & be subject to their government." From Carleton's nation-centered perspective the idea that Dutch settlers would freely choose to live among Englishmen and submit themselves to English rulers only made sense if no Dutch alternative existed.[51]

Whether the States General ever replied directly to Carleton's protest is unclear, but according to a note in the Book of Resolutions of the Council of New England from 1622, "upon complaint of Sir Dudley Carleton . . . it was answered that there was no plantation or settlement to impeach the English right."[52] In 1632, at a more critical moment in Anglo-Dutch relations, Captain John Mason (a later member of that council) explained what he understood had happened ten years earlier. He said that "ye Lords ye States by answer (as I take it) of their ambassador Sir Nowell Carronne did disclayme, disavowing any such act that was done by their people w[i]th their authority."[53] Soon afterward, however, "the sayd Dutch under a pretended authority from ye West India Company of Holland, maintayned as they sayd by commission from ye said Prince of Aurange did return to ye foresayd river of Manahata and made plantation there, fortifying themselves in two several places." The Dutch established the settlement despite the fact that the New Plymouth colony had warned them that they were encroaching on the King of England's territories, Mason said. Moreover, the Dutch interlopers responded with "proude and contumacious answers (saying they had commission to fight against such as should disturbe their settlement)," they continued to plant and trade, and they persisted in "vilefying o[u]r Nation to the Indians and extolling their owne people and countrye of Holland."[54] Dutch traders were trying to sabotage English claims by spreading their own national prejudices among North America's native peoples.

The Lords of the States General were being truthful, although not wholly so, when they claimed that no Dutch plantation existed in 1622. Until the early 1620s Dutch merchants had come to North America to trade. Populous English-style colonies did not fit their model of low-cost, high-profit commerce. But just as the formation of the English East India Company had spurred the founding of its Dutch counterpart, the vocal English opposition to the Dutch presence in North America may have encouraged a more direct commitment to New Netherland.[55] If the newly chartered Dutch West India Company wanted to protect the fur trade, it would have to secure the territory with settlers.

The decision to colonize New Netherland came at a low point in relations between English and Dutch officials. In 1624, the same year that the WIC dispatched its first group of settlers, news of the "Amboina Massacre" reached Europe. Although accounts of the incident vary even in modern historical literature, it appears that in early 1623 the Dutch governor of the East Indian island of Amboina ordered the torture and execution of ten English traders, ten Japanese traders, and one Portuguese trader for plotting to assassinate him.[56] News of the executions riled the English political class and reawakened fears of the commercial and colonial ambitions of the Dutch, whose VOC had been engaged in a quasi-war with English merchants in the East Indies for two decades. (One twentieth-century historian described the "massacre" as "merely a dramatic epilogue" to the history of violent conflict between English and Dutch traders in the East Indies.)[57] In later years "Amboina . . . became a byword for Dutch treachery [and] a shibboleth among devoted Hollandophobes," historian Benjamin Schmidt writes. Although "both the Dutch and English agreed that it had been an 'unjust' mistake," English polemicists strove to keep its memory alive. They published several accounts of the event after the episode and again during various Anglo-Dutch conflicts later in the century.[58]

The Amboina incident is a good example of the way that the colonial-commercial projects of European states, state-authorized companies, and individual merchants could make different national affiliations the focus of discussion, dispute, and violence. Despite their likenesses as Europeans and as Christians, the organizers and participants in these ventures expected bloodshed and prepared themselves accordingly. As English geographer and super-patriot Peter Heylyn noted, "naturall Animosities, . . . seconded by their severall interesses and Reasons of State, hath left almost no people without some such enemy, as doth particularly and perversly cross them in all their Counsels." He wrote that in "the state of humane affairs, . . . there is almost no Nation without a more particular Enemy. The English are enemies to the French, the Scots to the English; the Portuguese have the like inveterate hatred against the Spaniards." Heylyn, a royalist writing in the aftermath of the English Civil War, wished that instead of fighting among themselves, the English had turned their martial prowess against such past or present enemies as the French, Spanish, Dutch, Scots, or Irish because of "the dishonor," "the barbarous butchery," "the insolencies," and "the rebellions" these other nations had inflicted upon the English. "How happy had it been if we had found some other field to have tried our valour in?" he wondered.[59]

In the early seventeenth century Europe's imperial nations found fertile fields in the Indies, east and west, to try their valor and to vent their "naturall," and national, animosities. Dutch chronicler Nicolaes Wassenaer, describing the West India Company's first settlement of a colony along the Delaware River in 1624, wrote that "to go forward safely, it is first of all necessary that [the settlers] be placed in a good defensive position and well provided with forts and arms, since the Spaniard, who claims all the country, will never allow any one to gain a possession there."[60] The earliest regulations and instructions for the WIC's initial settlement along the South River directly addressed the possibility of conflict, mainly with Indians but also with other Europeans. According to these regulations, all settlers and officers could be required to "take the field" if ordered to do so.[61]

The depredations of Spaniards were foremost in Dutch planners' minds when they established the first settlements in New Netherland, but cannon could repulse New Englanders and French Canadians just as well as conquistadores. The WIC's officials hoped to avoid conflicts with these occasional allies, if possible. The orders for the first director of New Netherland, Willem van der Hulst (or "Verhulst"), instructed him to "avoid getting into any dispute with the French or English, and especially [to] avoid all acts of violence, unless he be obliged to defend himself and those who are committed to his charge against open aggression."[62] Verhulst's directions turned out to be very timely. By 1625 agents from France and England had already disputed the WIC's right to settle in what it called "New Netherland." When the first settlers reached the "River Mauritius," the Hudson River, they found "a Frenchman lying in the mouth of the river, who would erect the arms of the King of France there." An armed escort ushered the French vessel out of the river, but it simply headed south to the Delaware River, where Dutch traders again turned it away.[63] In the decade that followed, New Netherland's defenders would face more formidable challenges from English and Swedish colonizers, who would not be deterred so easily.

In the aftermath of Hudson's voyage of 1609, Dutch and English explorers, merchants, officials, and writers and their indigenous counterparts transformed a little-known part of the North American coastline into a contested colonial territory. In Europe the motivating force behind this transformation was the increasingly close relationship between commercial actors and political regimes. As merchants and governments came to rely upon each other for financial support and moral legitimacy, their mutual dependence fostered commercial expansion and competition. Commercial interests intertwined with imperial ambitions, and the possession of a distant region for purposes of trade became a matter of national honor.

Patriotic in principle, many of these projects proved cosmopolitan in practice. The dynamics of commercial competition encouraged merchants and officials to seek out talent and capital wherever they could find them, often with little regard for national affiliations. Yet while trade rivalries sometimes fostered transnational attachments and allegiances, the national dimensions of these competitive ventures made international or transnational cooperation difficult to sustain.[64]

This imperial and commercial competition encouraged European subjects to imagine themselves as belonging to larger social and political groupings that extended across space from an origin in the home country, or *patria*. Such early modern imperial "nations" were rife with contradictions and ambiguities, yet they had persistent effects on discourse and social life. Just as "empire building . . . influenced state formation through the networks of economic and political power that overseas expansion engendered," so did it shape nation formation in the larger Atlantic world.[65] In this contested realm nations were integral bodies composed of sovereigns and subjects, each sharing in the rights of the other and each relying upon the other to defend their interests. As Peter Heylyn explained, "The Rights of the *English* Nation . . . [are] inherent personally in their Kings, by way of publick interess in the Subject also; as the whole body doth partake of that sense and motion, which is originally in the Head."[66] This linkage of sovereign and subject through nation, allegiance, and rights—the very root of the struggle over Hudson's discoveries—would produce many more conflicts in the decades to follow.

2

Cosmopolitan Patriotism and the Founding of New Sweden

Since the 1590s Willem Usselincx had tried, and failed, to win a charter for a trading company that would turn the wealth of the Atlantic basin to patriotic purposes. In pamphlets and memorials he wrote by the dozen, he claimed his company would produce profits for its investors, promote industry and employment, bring Protestant Christianity to the Americas, and deprive the King of Spain of the fortune he spent each year to subdue the Dutch Republic.[1] The Antwerper's drive had nearly succeeded, but just as it was gaining momentum, the governments of Spain and the United Provinces declared a truce in 1609, and everything came to a halt. Usselincx remained undaunted. When the treaty came to its scheduled end twelve years later, the architect of the peace had been beheaded, the partisans of war were in the ascendant, and the time seemed right for his company to rise again. Yet now Usselincx's voice was just one of many, and men more practical and politic than he became the leaders of the new West India Company. After three decades of advocacy, his arguments and advice went ignored just as his triumph seemed secure.

Usselincx had not given up on his fellow Netherlanders, even though he had lost faith in their governors. Instead, he decided to test his luck among his itinerant countrymen in the port cities of northern Europe: at Glückstadt, Friedrichstadt, Copenhagen, Göteborg, and ultimately, Danzig. The influence of Dutch shippers and merchants had transformed not only these towns but the entire Baltic into "the backyard of the Netherlands," as historian Milja van Tielhof has written. "Dutch ships dominated traffic on the seas, Dutch capital and entrepreneurs prevailed in trade, Dutch coins were a common and popular means of payment, and Dutch language and culture spread in the Baltic cities," many of which were designed, built, and occupied by Netherlanders.[2] The most important of them all was Danzig, or Gdańsk, a German-Polish city that was the "main Dutch centre" in the region.[3] In addition to being the biggest city in the Baltic, it was also the most important port in the kingdom of Poland, whose monarch, Sigismund III Vasa, had once ruled as king of Sweden (1592–99) and through a series of wars with Sweden continued to seek restoration. Usselincx would wend his way through these Netherlandish enclaves in search of his next success.[4]

Usselincx never made it to Danzig. After pitching his proposals for a trading company to Scandinavia's two modernizing monarchs, first to Christiaan IV of Denmark and then to Gustav II Adolf of Sweden, Usselincx cut off his journey at Göteborg. There he received his long-awaited charter and set to work building his visionary enterprise. Linking the cosmopolitan and the patriotic, the proud Antwerper promised to transform the Swedish kingdom into a trading power through a transnational commercial alliance open to all, including subjects, princes, and even cities belonging to other states. Everyone who participated would prosper, individually and collectively, and all shareholders would have their say, whether they were Dutch merchants, Swedish aristocrats, German burghers, or Finnish clergymen. The King of Sweden would protect the investors and their gains, and those investors would turn the Swedish *rike*, rich in natural resources but poor in capital, into a new commercial power.

As with so many of his quixotic projects, Usselincx's plans for the Söderkompaniet, or the Swedish South Company, did not turn out as he had hoped. Tethered to a small and ill-funded administration composed of landed aristocrats whose interests did not match his own, the restless merchant found that he could control the workings of Swedish administrators no better than he could manage the wranglings of the diverse provincial assemblies of the United Provinces. And while Usselincx may have been familiar with disappointment, he was not one to waste time; after several years of struggling to find financing for the company, he abandoned it to the feckless Swedes and returned to the Netherlands. Yet he was careful to keep up his correspondence with the *rikskansler,* Axel Oxenstierna, the most powerful figure in the Swedish government after the king himself, and he was able to revive support for the company in the early 1630s just as the "Lion of the North," Gustav Adolf, extended his influence into Protestant Germany. The resurrected project was all too short-lived. The king was killed in battle in 1632, and his army's losses in 1634 caused the kingdom's German allies to abandon it, and the company, shortly thereafter.

Despite this latest failure, Usselincx's efforts to promote state-sponsored commerce in Sweden did produce a basic, if fractured and incomplete, foundation upon which others soon began to build. His successors, also Netherlanders, were more modest, more pragmatic, and more successful, at least in the short run. They retained Usselincx's plan for a multinational company under a national flag, only on a much smaller scale. Yet they also discovered that transnational alliances were easier to propose than to maintain, and in time their project, like Usselincx's, came to rely on the thinly stretched resources of the Swedish state. The colony they founded, Nya Sverige, or New Sweden, soon became dependent upon officials absorbed in the power politics of the Baltic and only fitfully attentive to their ill-equipped outpost across the Atlantic. The Netherlanders ultimately abandoned the project, and the colony's Swedish directors divested it of its cosmopolitan origins. New Sweden was to be Swedish after all.

Cosmopolitan Patriotism and the Swedish South Company

Usselincx's biography offers a virtual template for the "cosmopolitan patriot" of the early modern era.[5] Born into a mercantile family in Antwerp in 1567, he spent much of his early life in the Azores, where he served as a factor. There, positioned on an island trading post, he was able to observe the importance of Atlantic commerce not only to the Low Countries but also to Portugal and Spain. In 1591 Usselincx took this Atlantic knowledge with him back to the Netherlands. His relocation was shaped twice by expressions of Spanish power: the capture of the Azores from the Portuguese in 1583, two years after Philip II had seized the Crown of Portugal; and the occupation of Antwerp, which had fallen to Spanish forces in 1585, after a yearlong siege. Apparently quite wealthy by this time, Usselincx resettled in Middelburg in Holland while continuing his activities as a merchant. Soon afterward he began to advocate for the founding of a West India Company. By 1600 he had begun to seek a wider audience for his ideas and started publishing his appeals within the United Provinces. The company that he

imagined would serve a variety of commercial, religious, and patriotic purposes. Among them was the redemption of the southern Netherlands, and
Antwerp in particular, from Spanish rule. But the coming of the peace with
Spain in 1609—and the rush to establish the WIC as the peace neared its
end—had left him with a bountiful supply of ideas and a Dutch reading
public that was no longer interested in them.[6]

In Sweden Usselincx found the opportunity to repackage his proposals
and to present them anew. His proposals continued to blend patriotic and
cosmopolitan themes but the relationship between those themes changed
as his circumstances changed. The project had started firmly in the realm
of the patriotic—Gustav Adolf had given his support to Usselincx because
the Netherlander promised to make Sweden into a great commercial power.
But Usselincx's own goals for the company extended far beyond Sweden
and cosmopolitanism was essential to its structure. Soon Usselincx sought
a wider circle of investors, especially as it became clear that support for the
company was not so great as promised or expected. Where the balance of
elements once favored the patriotic and the national, over time the cosmopolitan and the transnational came to predominate.

Usselincx intended the company to serve the purposes of the Swedish
monarchy, but he also wanted to draw participants from all over Europe.
Appeals went out to investors in the Netherlands, France, Sweden's Baltic
provinces, and the Holy Roman Empire. He anticipated that such "strangers"
might have their own motives for joining, so he sought to show that the company could sustain their local patriotisms as well as their pecuniary interests. After all, he was no Swede, and he wanted his readers to know that the
company was open to all who wished to participate. The company would not
merely offer a return on an investment, although Usselincx promised it would
do that as a matter of course. Rather, the company would do many things
at once: develop economies, build navies, enrich merchants, and employ
workers. It would provide for a whole portfolio of interests, high and low,
that participants could employ as they saw fit, where they saw fit. A variety
of patriotisms would flourish under the aegis of the cosmopolitan company.
Yet as Usselincx's audiences grew larger and more diverse, the company's
connection to reality became increasingly tenuous. It risked, finally, floating
off to that ethereal plane where only Usselincx's imagination ranged.

After making his initial decision to support the company, Gustav Adolf
had no need to trouble himself with the details of its founding. Usselincx
quickly offered drafts of a prospectus, a charter, and his own commission.[7]

The prospectus, printed on November 10, 1624, was drawn directly from the proposals Usselincx had written for the Dutch West India Company just a few years earlier.[8] The commission appeared in print six weeks later. But because Gustav Adolf renewed his war with Poland in the spring of 1625, Usselincx had to wait another eighteen months before the king signed the company's charter. In the meantime Usselincx worked to promote the project and to obtain subscriptions for the company, issuing a steady stream of publications that explained and justified what it was going to do.[9]

The earliest appeal for support in Sweden appeared in the "Contract" of 1625, in which Usselincx listed the personal and the patriotic rewards available to the kingdom's investors. He noted that Sweden was just as well suited to transoceanic trade as Spain and the Netherlands, whose power and wealth had grown so great through navigation and commerce.[10] International trade offered opportunities for individual profit, but it also had more general benefits for Sweden, including conversions that would add to "God's glory"; added revenues for the king and the Crown; and stronger defenses against the state's enemies. Best of all, these advantages would accrue without requiring any additional taxation. There were benefits particular to each order in Swedish society as well. Members of the nobility would see their own incomes and status grow, while their children and relatives found opportunities to serve as officers in the company. The clergy could turn its gains into new schools. Merchants would profit from the growth in trade and could find employment for their sons. Farmers and common folk would see their fortunes rise with the increase in demand for their products. The company's revenues would reduce the pressure of conscription too; Gustav Adolf would be able to hire foreign troops to fight his battles, and farmers could pay other men to serve in place of themselves or their sons. Usselincx concluded that participation in the company would benefit "every sincere and pious man, be he of high or low degree, who cherishes the glory of God, loves his Lord and King and desires to promote the general welfare as well as his own." Even a poor patriot could afford to subscribe a small sum that would eventually achieve a substantial return.[11]

Usselincx aimed this first appeal at a Swedish audience then turned his attention abroad. The first texts printed in support of the project appeared in Swedish but also in German, which had a semiofficial status in Sweden's empire and was widely used in commerce throughout northern Europe. Usselincx was looking beyond the Baltic littoral too; by the summer of 1625 he had begun to seek subscriptions among Calvinist merchants in France.[12]

More important, he had designed the very structure of the company to encourage foreign investors to participate and to give them special privileges
within it. The charter of 1626, for example, noted that "all countries, cities, companies or private persons, foreign as well as native," who invested
100,000 daler would have the power to appoint their own director in the
company.[13] Moreover, "each Nation" was entitled to its own special contract
that allowed it to decide who would handle its money, and participants
could select "which Nation" would receive their subscription. Foreigners
who invested 25,000 daler and wanted to live within the kingdom would
enjoy full *Bürgerrecht* in those places where they settled and would be free
from all taxes. They would be free to travel in and out of the country as they
pleased, and at their deaths their heirs could collect their property and remove it from the country without penalty. Even the subjects of a "King, Prince,
Republic or Community" engaged in conflict with the King of Sweden would
be allowed to withdraw their capital just as the king's own "subjects and
inhabitants" could.[14]

In addition to these more general references to foreign communities and
sovereigns and their subjects, Usselincx also made direct appeals to certain foreigners, namely his own fellow Netherlanders. In the preface to the
Außführlicher Bericht he issued a call to "all pious Netherlanders, who on
the confession of their faith and the freedom of the fatherland of Brabant,
Flanders, Wallonia and other conquered Netherlands are scattered over Europe." He complimented "de goede Patriotten in Hollandt" for their actions
against Spain, and called for his *Landtslieden,* or "countrymen," to join the
project. He boasted that "no king in Europe" was better loved by foreigners
in his kingdom than Gustav Adolf and in no other country were foreign subjects treated as well as native subjects. Usselincx even urged his countrymen
to move to Sweden, where opportunities were so much more abundant than
elsewhere in wartorn Europe. Under Swedish rule Netherlanders would be
able to preserve their "language, good manners, ways, morals, and domes-
tic arrangements" better than they could in other places where they had
to "mix with other nations." Their children and their children's children
would retain their privileged status in a place where many foreigners had
been promoted to positions of authority. Indeed, those who had settled in
Göteborg had their own government and freedom of religion, just as in the
Vaterlandt, Usselincx asserted.[15]

The body of the *Außführlicher Bericht* also included a broader appeal
to foreigners, in which Usselincx sought to convince his readers that the

kingdom of Sweden and its inhabitants would be good hosts to the company and its investors. Usselincx had a long list of "false notions and slanders" to counter: "that this is a bad, poor, and barren country"; that it was "very and exceedingly cold"; that it had "intemperate and unhealthy air"; that its constitutions, laws, and rules of justice were bad; and that the inhabitants "hated foreigners," drank and ate immoderately, and even managed their households badly. The Sweden that critics imagined, reflected here in Usselincx's prose, was a bleak place filled with rude, conniving people.[16]

Usselincx, of course, had an answer to every one of these complaints. Most interesting were his attempts to burnish the reputation of the Swedes, in particular their relations with foreigners, as it was here that the complications of Usselincx's cosmopolitan patriotism became more apparent— namely, that it was a challenge to convince foreign merchants to invest in a country as provincial as Sweden, in part because of the national reputation of the Swedes themselves. Usselincx was intent, for example, to counter the Swedes' reputation as *unhöfflich und unfreundlich,* "impolite and unfriendly." He emphasized that foreigners were treated very well in Sweden. Indeed, he said it was little known how much "friendliness, politeness, and modesty" Swedes possessed. He found that the nobles were possessed of "quality" and were friendly, whether they were from the country or the city. The people in the cities, he noted, were genial hosts who happily shared their entertainments. Sweden's farmers possessed "humanity, affability, and civility" and offered their guests a hearty welcome and a good word. Even if a stranger were to arrive in the dark of night, a farmer would rise to let him in and set down food and drink for him. According to Usselincx, a man could travel the whole kingdom bearing gold and silver and suffer no harm because robbers were unknown there. The subtitle of one section of this litany could stand in for the whole: "That nowhere are foreigners so loved and honored."[17]

Usselincx spent the mid-1620s trying to build support for the company in Sweden, only to find that the king's extended absences and distracted attention made it virtually impossible to get anything started or to get paid. Eager to acquire investors wherever he could, Usselincx toured Sweden's Baltic domains for nearly a year in search of subscriptions. Even as he complained about the impoverished state of Estonia, Finland, and Livonia, he claimed that he had found eager audiences at the edge of the Swedish empire. But his remark that the only opposition came from "drunken fellows that sat on alehouse benches railing without ground or reason" suggests that his more sober critics may simply have been holding their tongues—Usselincx, after all, was an authorized agent of the king. Whatever his reception in the provinces, Usselincx's time abroad proved mortal to his reputation in the metropolis. He returned to Stockholm in April 1628 only to discover that he was rumored to be dead.[18]

In the fall of 1628, amid complaints about his salary and the condition of the company (and curious claims that the Dutch East India Company wanted him to serve as a general in the East Indies), Usselincx decided to return to the Netherlands. Arriving in early 1629, he remained there a short while before attempting to return to Sweden. His luck turned ever worse when he was captured at sea by a Spanish ship, imprisoned, and ordered to be tortured. He managed to escape this punishment, however, when the commander of the imperial forces, Albrecht von Wallenstein, ordered Usselincx and the other agents of the King of Sweden to be set free. Soon the tireless Netherlander was trolling for subscriptions in Germany, following Gustav Adolf and his army as it moved south. Finally, at Nuremberg in October 1632 the king gave his assent (but not his signature) to an amplified charter that expanded the company's powers and its ambit. Usselincx's latest hope was that German investors would provide the company the support it needed to get off the ground. Under different circumstances they might have. A month later Gustav Adolf was killed in battle.[19]

Even at this dark time, Usselincx still saw bright prospects ahead. In 1633 he and Sweden's highest official, chancellor Axel Oxenstierna, arranged for the publication of *Argonautica Gustaviana,* a compilation of the various commissions, charters, and promotional writings issued in the 1620s as well as some newer pieces designed to advertise the company's latest incarnation. Printed in Frankfurt and addressed to the "German Evangelical Nation," the *Argonautica Gustaviana* referred to the late king's affection for "die Teutschen Lande" (the German countries) and noted that the company had been organized especially to allow participation by the "German and especially Evangelical Nations."[20] The *Mercurius Germaniae,* one of the texts published in *Argonautica Gustaviana,* aimed its appeal directly at German readers. Usselincx wrote that Germany had suffered from the predations of "tyrants and robbers" and that it had been almost "completely ruined" by the armies of Spain and the Holy Roman emperor, but, he insisted, the company could help. It would expand commerce in the German states, improve their ability to sustain themselves, and benefit the whole community.

The company would help Sweden in its struggle against Spain, although the greater gain would actually go to the Germans themselves. The Germans' privileged place in the company was a sign of the *herzliche Affection* (sincere affection), *inbrünstiger Affection* (ardent affection), and *Väterliche Affection* (fatherly affection) that Gustav Adolf felt for Germany and the Germans, Usselincx claimed. But it was also because the German states were better situated to trade with the rest of Europe. They had more workers, produced more, and had better access to waterways and the sea, he explained. They could establish their own local chambers within the company, which would be run by merchants, not the Crown. In order to take advantage of this opportunity, Usselincx urged "all who are good Christians and true Patriots who loved their Fatherland" to contribute to the cause. Everyone who had "a German heart or a drop of German blood remaining in him" ought to support the company and its efforts to improve the condition of Germany and the German nation.[21]

Usselincx's attempts to rally patriotic investors in Germany had as much success as his efforts to win over sponsors in Sweden, the Netherlands, France, Finland, Estonia, Livonia, and Pomerania. He presented his proposals at the meeting of the Heilbronn League in the summer of 1633 and a year later at the league's conference in Frankfurt. Just a day after the latter proposal was read, news arrived that the Swedish army and its allies had been defeated at Nördlingen. Soon the League was in disarray, and Usselincx was on his way to peddle his next plan: a joint French-Swedish trading company. When that scheme failed to attract interest, he returned to the Netherlands with a proposal to merge the Swedish South Company with the Dutch West India Company. After the WIC rejected the proposal in the fall of 1637, Usselincx took the next logical step and proposed to form a company that would join together all the governments in Europe (and their subjects) that were opposed to the King of Spain and the emperor. Usselincx's biographer J. Franklin Jameson, unimpressed by the heights of cosmopolitan patriotism that the Antwerper had reached, called it a "wild project."[22]

In the midst of these ever grander visions, Usselincx offered his thoughts about a voyage to North America that was being organized by certain members of the Swedish government and some Dutch investors. Responding to a query from Vice Admiral Klas Fleming, one of the officials who was planning the venture, Usselincx wrote that the Dutch West India Company had already established populous settlements in the region and that there was "noth-

ing to get there except furs or skins and tobacco."[23] Usselincx was wrong
about many things, but he was right about New Sweden. For the Rhinelander
who planned it, furs, skins, and tobacco were exactly what he wanted.

Homo Versipellis

Peter Minuit was just the sort of man that Usselincx had sought for his
Swedish project. Although born in the German town of Wesel, Minuit was
descended from a merchant family that had fled the southern Netherlands
in the late sixteenth century, as had the "pious Netherlanders . . . scattered
over Europe" to whom Usselincx had addressed the *Außführlicher Bericht*.
Peter's father, Johan Minuit, seems to have come originally from the Calvinist stronghold of Tournai in Wallonia, near the border with France. After
leaving Tournai, perhaps to avoid religious persecution, Minuit's father appears to have reestablished himself as a merchant in Antwerp then to have
moved to Wesel before 1584, when he purchased citizen's privileges there.
His first son, the founder of New Sweden, was probably born in Wesel a few
years later.[24]

    Located near the contested border between the United Provinces and the
Spanish-held Low Countries, Wesel had welcomed Lutheran and Reformed
congregations since the beginning of the Reformation. It received the title
"Vesalia Hospitalis" from a group of grateful Dutch and Walloon exiles in
1578, but the city's more common nickname was "klein Antwerpen," or "little
Antwerp," because so many of its inhabitants had settled there.[25] Wesel had
an especially strong tie to Tournai, whose exiles first arrived in the German
city in the 1540s, and the connection only grew stronger as time passed.[26]
Both towns participated in the iconoclastic *wonderjaar* of 1566, and in the
crackdown that followed, some of the most prominent men of Tournai left
for Wesel.[27] The nominally German city soon boasted a strong Reformed
presence, one that over time grew more influential than the Lutheran. It
became "the centre of Calvinism on the Lower Rhine" during the sixteenth
century,[28] hosted the Synod of Wesel in 1568, and its congregations formally belonged to the Dutch Reformed Church until 1610.[29] (An anonymous
sixteenth-century Jesuit saw Wesel's relationship to Calvinism in a different light. He rhymed that "Genff, Wesell und Rochelle, seindt des Teuffels
andre Hell" [Geneva, Wesel, and La Rochelle are the Devil's other Hell].)[30]
According to one historian, at the beginning of the 1600s "Wesel was in all

but name another Dutch city."[31] Usselincx would likely have found a friendly audience there.

Peter Minuit might also have recognized himself in Usselincx's appeals to the Germans. Wesel, like many other parts of Germany during the Thirty Years' War, had become entangled in the rivalries of great powers and suffered greatly because of it. It belonged to the Duchy of Kleve, a contested territory that fit like a wedge into the Netherlands, between the rebellious provinces of the north and the Spanish-dominated provinces of the south. It happened also to be placed where it was "easiest for the Spaniards to . . . penetrate into the Dutch interior."[32] Its history in this era was consequently one of sieges and occupations. Spanish troops besieged the fortified city "almost continuously" from 1586 to 1590. A plague followed that may have killed as many as thirteen thousand.[33] An account from 1589 offered a long list of offenses committed by the occupying soldiers: "rebellions, theft, murder, burning, seizure, fighting, ransoming, tormenting[,] . . . the destruction of the countryside, the closure of river ways and roads, shooting at merchants and traders, and other inhumane and unchristian deeds."[34] In 1598, twenty-four thousand Spanish troops arrived outside the city's gates and held it for several months, meanwhile demanding a large tribute and the placement of Catholic priests in the city's Protestant churches.[35] The stadholder Maurits of Orange subsequently used Wesel as a base for his army in the first decade of the 1600s, but in September 1614 the Italian general Ambrogio Spinola captured the town and placed a garrison of nearly three thousand men there to hold it.[36] Consequently, Minuit not only knew what it was like to be an exiled Netherlander but also understood, as Usselincx wrote, "how Germany was almost completely *ruined* by tyrants and robbers, [and] . . . the wild and disorderly conduct of Imperial and Spanish soldiers who robbed it of its trade and wealth."[37]

Minuit may have left Wesel, however, before the Spanish captured it in the fall of 1614. He had married the daughter of the burgomaster of Kleve in August 1613, and by 1615 he and his wife were living in Utrecht, where he appeared in local records as "Pierre Minuit," a diamond cutter and citizen of Wesel. He reappeared in Wesel's records in 1619, 1620, and again in May 1624, when he was recorded as having departed the city, no doubt as part of his engagement with the WIC, which began in early 1625.[38] Whether he was motivated by Usselincx's desire to strike out at Spain through its colonies is unclear. He certainly would have known intimately the effects of the Spanish occupation of Wesel. A contemporary source also suggests that he was either a deacon or an elder in a "church under the cross" that was defined as much by resistance to Roman Catholicism and Spanish power as by its doctrines.[39] Perhaps Minuit was too prudent to be a fire-breather while his city was under occupation, but did the WIC's promise to disembowel the Iberian empire appeal even to a respectable burgher nearing forty years of age? Or was he simply seeking better opportunities than beleaguered Wesel had to offer?

Whatever Minuit's motivations may have been, during his first voyage under the command of director Willem Verhulst, he was assigned several important tasks: investigating the "minerals and crystals" of the North and South Rivers (the Hudson and the Delaware, respectively); exploring the upper reaches of those rivers; and trading with the Indians he encountered during his travels.[40] The former diamond merchant must have impressed the directors of the WIC's Amsterdam chamber, for when he returned to the Netherlands in 1625, he was sent back to manage the company's fur trade. Verhulst, by contrast, was a disaster as director, and within three months of Minuit's return to New Netherland, the colony's council asked him to take Verhulst's place. With the support of the company's leading men in Amsterdam, Minuit held the title of director for six years before he, too, was accused of mismanagement and corruption and was forced to return to Europe. In the meantime as director he had acquired an extensive understanding of the region, its trade, and its native neighbors. Yet the company stripped him of his position and may have banned him from returning to the colony, as it had done to several other disgraced officials. Embarrassed and abused by the WIC, Minuit shared yet another attribute with Usselincx. Deprived of his place within the Dutch company, Minuit offered his knowledge and his services to the Swedish kingdom.

Minuit's experience as director of New Netherland had centered on Manhattan and the Hudson Valley, but he knew the Delaware Valley nearly as well. He may have explored the river in 1625 under Verhulst's command, and one of his first decisions as director was to relocate a group of Walloon settlers living on "High Island" on the Delaware River to Manhattan. More important, Minuit became acquainted with the various native groups who were active along the river. Shortly after he began serving as director, thirty or forty "Minquaes" (or Susquehannock) came to Manhattan "from the south" seeking the friendship of the colony's officials. The colony's secretary and commercial agent, Isaack de Rasière, appears to have handled negotiations with them (perhaps because Minuit was away), but as director Minuit would have participated in subsequent discussions about establishing trade and friendship and negotiating peace with their native rivals along the Delaware.[41] Minuit was also involved in the purchase of lands along the Delaware Bay for the "patroonships" founded by several of the WIC's directors. On June 1, 1629, for example, Minuit met with Queskakons and Eesanques, deputies of the "Sakmah or King" of the Siconese, to certify that they had sold the land for Swanendael along the southern shore of the Delaware Bay.[42] A year later the two Siconese representatives again visited Minuit at Manhattan, where they confirmed the previous year's purchase, this time in the form of patents issued to the patroons Samuel Godyn and Samuel Blommaert.[43] Minuit also would have learned of the terrible consequences of bad diplomacy, as he was director when the Siconese later destroyed the patroons' settlement at Swanendael in 1631.

Minuit's skills as a merchant suited him well in the American woods. Over the late spring and summer of 1626 he acquired a small fortune in animal skins for the company: 6,360 beavers, 614 otters, 48 minks, and 10 lynxes. Over his entire term as director the colony exported over 52,000 pelts, worth over 400,000 guilders.[44] Although most of these skins were acquired through trade with Indians in the Hudson Valley, a significant portion came from the Delaware.[45] Even when Minuit was forced to return to the Netherlands, he continued to offer advice about opportunities along the South River. On his arrival at Amsterdam in 1632, for example, he reported to WIC director and patroon Kiliaen van Rensselaer about the possibilities for whaling along the Delaware, noting that its native inhabitants "wear on their heads mostly small feathers made of whalebone."[46] He also told van Rensselaer about a new method for growing tobacco in New Netherland that he had learned from "Rutger Moris," an English runaway from Virginia whom he had brought into his own service.[47]

Minuit may have become a proficient planter and fur trader during his time as director of New Netherland, but he also appears to have learned something about how allegiances came into play in the colonial setting. The circumstances of his appointment as director are revealing in this regard. The colony's council had accused Minuit's predecessor, Willem Verhulst, of many misdeeds, among them sloppy recordkeeping, harsh and capricious rule, and "bad government." Ultimately the council decided to remove Verhulst from power and to banish him "now and forever" from New Netherland because he had stated publicly that "if he were not serving the Honorable Lords [of the West India Company] here, he knew other Lords who would help him, and he would know well how to avenge himself." Verhulst's remarks were interpreted as a threat that he might return "in the service of the French or English," whose colonies, after all, were located just a short distance away. The council barred him from the colony so that if he did come back they would have the power to prosecute and to sentence him. They hoped that evidence of this order would appease the "Prince or Lord" who might take the faithless Verhulst into his service—and who might protest if the colony's officers punished him.[48] Minuit, then, was chosen to lead New Netherland because his predecessor had announced that he would offer his allegiance to a rival if the WIC removed him from office. Later, of course, Minuit did exactly what his disgraced predecessor had threatened to do. Verhulst's words must have echoed in Minuit's ears as he set sail for Amsterdam in 1632 to answer the charges against him.

The accusations leveled at Minuit during his term as director suggest that his enemies sensed an inconstancy in him. In 1630 Jonas Michaëlius, the colony's minister, identified Minuit as "homo versipellis"—literally, "man who changes his skin" (i.e., a shape-shifter; a sly, cunning, crafty man). Michaëlius said that "under the treacherous mark of honesty [Minuit] is a compound of all iniquity and wickedness." He was "accustomed to lies, of which he is full," and to "oaths and most awful curses." He was "not free from fornication," and he was "the most cruel oppressor of the innocent." Along with his allies on the council—a "mixture of the most pestilent kind of people"— the director was cheating the company. Above all, Minuit favored only those who were "of his ilk."[49]

At the time Michaëlius wrote this letter, he was engaged in a factional dispute with Minuit that eventually led the WIC to recall both of them and several of their peers. Michaëlius's grievances certainly colored his comments. But the minister may have had reason to criticize the director. One wonders, for example, whether Minuit's "ilk" included his brother-in-law Jan Huygen, who initially served as the colony's *ziekentrooster,* a kind of lay leader of religious services, until Michaëlius arrived.[50] Together the three men (along with a fourth, Bastiaen Jansz Krol, who was commander at Fort Orange) formed the consistory, or governing council, of the congregation at New Amsterdam. Shortly after his arrival at the colony, Michaëlius had given notice that political and religious matters "must not be mixed but kept separate in order to prevent all confusion and disorder," despite the inherently mixed character of the consistory itself.[51] The minister may have found that the in-laws from Wesel had their own notions about how authority should be shared.

The presence of a distinct population of Walloons, men such as Minuit's father, may also have had something to do with Michaëlius's troubles. He admitted, for example, that he could not preach extemporaneously in French and had to read from a written script when ministering to the colony's *Walen ende Francoisen*.[52] Testimony made against Minuit after his return to Amsterdam suggests that as director he may have favored some Walloons in the colony while waging a vendetta against another. Michaëlius and the colony's former miller, Abraham Pietersz, testified that Minuit had boycotted Francois Versaert's mill, abused his servant, and refused Versaert's family its allotment of grain and livestock.[53]

Minuit's order, defined by local and familial connections that superseded established hierarchies, may have appeared to Michaëlius as the very opposite of order. Yet as Usselincx would have understood, these attachments were what motivated men such as Minuit to leave behind their families and to risk their lives and fortunes. Minuit's fatherland, after all, was not the WIC or the United Provinces, however much he identified himself as a Netherlander. His homelands were plural: Tournai, Wesel, Kleve, and now New Amsterdam. Putting aside his attachments would have meant disregarding the very reasons he had gone to New Netherland. Those attachments led him back to New Netherland six years after he had left it in disgrace.

Diamonds, Copper, Gold, and Furs

Usselincx's proposals might have appealed to Peter Minuit, but it was another Netherlander who brought him into Swedish service. Minuit's new patron, Samuel Blommaert, had much in common with Usselincx. Both were natives of Antwerp, both had extensive knowledge of trade with the "Indies," and both were leading figures in the founding of the Dutch West India Company. Blommaert also mirrored Usselincx in his energy and his ambition, and he, too, had known failure. But unlike Usselincx's abortive enterprises, Blommaert's failures produced captains, cargoes, and crews, and in New Sweden his failure was Sweden's success.

Born in Antwerp in 1583, Blommaert spent his youth in England, where his father was a merchant. After schooling in Germany and the Netherlands, he began his career in commerce, trading in Hamburg, Amsterdam, and Vienna. Then in 1603 he received the opportunity, in his own words, "to go around the world and to seek . . . adventure" as an officer in the service of the

Vereenigde Oostindische Compagnie. He returned to Amsterdam after eight years abroad, mostly in western Borneo, with "a good quantity of diamonds," an avowed aversion to cold weather, and a global perspective on commerce and colonization.[54] Soon afterward he married into a well-connected family with its own impressive overseas portfolio—his father-in-law Gerrit (or Gerard) Reynst was a founding director of the VOC and was sent to Jakarta as its second governor-general in 1613.[55] A decade after leaving the service of the VOC, Blommaert was selected by Amsterdam's *burgemeesters* to serve as a director in the newly chartered WIC. His interest in the Atlantic trade probably drew from his experience trading in Angola in the 1610s. As a director of the WIC, he soon found himself planning ventures in America too.[56]

Blommaert never seemed satisfied, however, with his supervisory role. Instead, he eagerly pursued opportunities inside and outside of the company. He was one of the activists in the WIC's Amsterdam chamber who sought to promote settlement and later the establishment of privately sponsored patroonships in New Netherland. For his own patroonship, chartered in November 1629, Blommaert chose a location along the "Fresh River," or the Connecticut River, which he intended to rename after himself. In April 1630 he also received a patent to establish a colony on "*St. Martin* or on *Barbadas,* among the Caribbean Islands." Two colonies apparently were not enough for the new patroon. Deciding to pool their capital and share their risks, he and several other WIC directors in 1630 established a partnership in which each invested in the projects of the others, so Blommaert also became a minority investor in patroonships in the upper Hudson Valley and along the eastern and western shores of Delaware Bay. Kiliaen van Rensselaer's closely supervised *colonie* on the upper Hudson managed to survive, but all the others failed. In fact, Blommaert's patroonships in the Connecticut Valley and the Caribbean were "not begun at all," according to van Rensselaer. Likewise, the patroonship on the east side of the Delaware Bay was never started, and Swanendael, on the west side of the bay near Cape Henlopen, was destroyed in 1631 by its Siconese neighbors. In 1635 the WIC purchased the patroons' claims to both sides of the bay. All that Blommaert got for his trouble was the name of a creek near the mouth of the bay ("Blomaerts kil"), and even that would disappear from later maps. Like so many other colonial companies before and after, the patroons' promising partnership turned into an engine for destroying capital.[57]

The Delaware was far from Blommaert's mind when he first met Axel Oxenstierna, the chancellor of Sweden, during a visit to Amsterdam in

1635. Like map-drunk Usselincx, Blommaert had fantasies of linking the tropical and the polar. In particular, his experience trading in Angola in the 1610s and serving as a director of the WIC during the 1620s had impressed upon him the strong demand for copper in western Africa. Based in Amsterdam, the leading marketplace for copper in Europe, he also knew that its value there was depressed because of oversupply.[58] The fall in its price had a particularly strong impact on the economy of Sweden, Europe's leading producer of the metal. Copper was not only one of Sweden's most important exports; it was the regime's primary link to sources of capital in the Netherlands. Blommaert also knew that Sweden's leaders were eager to promote commerce at home and abroad and that Oxenstierna in particular intended to reorganize Sweden's copper industry, which was already subject to extensive control by the government.[59] Finally, Blommaert was probably most aware that great fortunes could be made in copper by cultivating the patronage of Sweden's government. Netherlanders Elias Trip and Louis de Geer had proven as much when they obtained a monopoly on Sweden's copper production during the 1620s.[60] Blommaert must have impressed the Swedish chancellor with his understanding of the copper market. Soon afterward Blommaert began sending regular reports to Oxenstierna, who seems to have welcomed having a director of the Dutch West India Company in his employ.[61]

In the months that followed, Blommaert continued to advise Sweden's officials about the copper trade, but he had begun to look to the future. By the end of 1635, even before his own service had officially started, Blommaert began recommending other men for employment by the Swedish government. One was a captain with extensive experience along the coast of Guinea. The other was "very experienced in another place"—a place that Blommaert was reluctant to mention. This second prospect "lived in the land of Cleve," but his homeland was "so full of war" that he had sought out Blommaert to tender his service. He had also offered to visit the chancellor in Sweden to discuss what service he could provide. The unnamed resident of Kleve was none other than Peter Minuit.[62]

Nova Sweediae

Sickness and war had dogged Minuit for much of his life. Northern Germany suffered heavily from both during the 1630s, with waves of disease striking communities that already had experienced the miseries of life under siege. Although Spain had lost its hold on the Lower Rhine by the time that Minuit had returned from New Netherland, it began a new counteroffensive against its Dutch and French enemies during the summer of 1635.[63] Minuit and his fatherland were caught in the middle once again. He had resettled in the city of Kleve, his wife's hometown, intending to take up the business he had left in her hands while he was away. A sign of his commitment to this new life appeared in the city's records in May 1635, when he officially became a burgher.[64] Just two months later, however, Spanish forces captured Schenckenschans, "one of the most vital Dutch fortresses on the Lower Rhine," located less than four miles away from Kleve. Twenty thousand soldiers now occupied the territory; at the end of the year two thousand were based in the city itself.[65] Worse yet, typhus and the plague swept across the Netherlands and northern Germany in the mid-1630s.[66] No wonder, then, that Minuit went to Amsterdam in late 1635 seeking Blommaert's patronage. He soon turned Blommaert's gaze from the south to the west.

Since 1632 Blommaert had promoted the idea of establishing a Swedish-sponsored company for trading copper in Guinea. Minuit offered a new direction to his plans. By June 1636 he was writing directly to Axel Oxenstierna about the prospects for "a voyage to the Virginias, New Netherland, and other places thereabouts, [and] certain places well known to me, of a very good climate, which would be named *Nova Sweediae*." Minuit explicitly framed the project in national and dynastic terms. Employing language that Usselincx would have recognized, he asserted that "many kingdoms and countries flourish" through navigation and that the West Indies "gradually have been occupied by the English and French and Netherlanders." The Crown of Sweden should not be left out, he argued. It should "spread its name in foreign lands" just as the other colonizing nations had done.[67]

In his letter Minuit described all that would be necessary for the voyage. He would need a ship of one to two hundred tons, supplied with a dozen cannon and ammunition; twenty to twenty-five men, with provisions for a year; and ten to twelve thousand guilders' worth of adzes, axes, kettles, duffels, and other merchandise. If the Crown were to provide a yacht, ammunition, and twelve soldiers, the cost of the whole endeavor might reach only sixteen thousand guilders. The bulk of the cost would be the merchandise the ship would be carrying. Those goods were to be sold to the *wilden*, the Indians whom the voyagers would seek to befriend in hopes of obtaining four to six thousand beaver pelts in return. Although the trade for furs was the primary motivation for the voyage, there were other opportunities for profit too. The land they would occupy was good for planting tobacco and grains. At sea Spanish and Portuguese ships could be captured and brought as prizes to Sweden. From "this small beginning," Minuit predicted, the enterprise would acquire "a large capital" that would allow them "to undertake something greater." He asked for an exclusive twenty-year charter from the Crown of Sweden, extending in jurisdiction from Newfoundland to Florida, along with ten years' freedom from import and export duties. Ultimately, if they acted quickly so that no others could occupy the territory, the voyage would produce a "great benefit" to the Crown of Sweden.[68]

The work of Blommaert and Minuit soon began to bear fruit. In September 1636 Oxenstierna offered to the Swedish *Riksrådet* (Council of State) a proposal for a "Guinean company, which probably could be established with some in Holland."[69] By November Blommaert had received a commission from Pieter Spierinck Silfvercrona (known in Sweden as Peter Spiring), a recently ennobled Netherlander who served as Sweden's agent at The Hague and who presented the plans to Oxenstierna.[70] By the end of the year preparations had already begun to move forward in the Netherlands. Blommaert could now write openly about "the person of Pieter Minuit, living at Emmerick," coming to discuss a "certain voyage."[71]

In January 1637 Blommaert, Minuit, and Spiring met to decide what course the company should take. Ultimately, they chose to put aside Blommaert's original plan to exchange copper for gold along the African coast because the capital for such a venture was out of reach. Instead, they resolved to go ahead with Minuit's proposal to create a company that would establish outposts and trade along the North American coast. By the first of February they had produced a sheaf of documents outlining the form of the company and the plans for the first voyage. Minuit personally carried this valuable cargo of papers to Sweden, traveling via Hamburg and Helsingör before he finally reached Stockholm in early March—a monthlong winter trek of about a thousand miles. Not surprisingly, he became very ill upon reaching Sweden. He was only able to begin preparations for the voyage two months later.[72]

While Minuit languished in Stockholm during the spring of 1637, Blommaert was working to supply the voyage with its cargo and its men. He ordered great quantities of cloth for the trade in North America, at one point shipping more than a mile and a half of material to Stockholm. He also recruited the officers and crew for the voyage, although he had to obtain the permission of the United Provinces' States General before he could send them to Sweden. At the end of July the remaining cargo and the sailors departed for Göteborg, where the two ships were supposed to have been ready for departure since June. Instead, the ships remained at Stockholm until late August. Despite the delays, Minuit returned to Amsterdam that month to report to Blommaert and to hire additional officers. By early September he was back in Göteborg, still trying to get the ships ready. Eventually, in late October, the *Kalmar Nyckel* and the *Fogel Grip* were set to depart, several months later than originally planned.[73]

The problems only worsened once the ships entered the North Sea. "The start of the voyage . . . stumbled badly," Blommaert wrote. "First the long delay of the ship and yacht at Göteborg required that all the crew who were sent from here had to be maintained at great cost, [and] the nice summer season was lost." Then, after leaving Göteborg, the ships became separated and for a month wandered at sea in bad weather. The *Kalmar Nyckel* suffered damage to its bow and was leaking badly, so it sailed into the Dutch harbor town of Medemblik, where it was joined by the battered yacht more than a week later. Along with the high cost of repairing the ship, their supplies of food dwindled even further, so more had to be purchased. Blommaert estimated that the total capital required for the voyage was now thirty-six thousand guilders, more than twice what Minuit had projected in his letter to Oxenstierna in June 1636. Eventually, on the last day of 1637, some two months after they had left Göteborg, the vessels set out to sea with "a beautiful fleet of 150 ships, . . . some destined for the East Indies, the West Indies, Brazil, the Strait [of Gibraltar], France, and other places."[74]

"Nations or Peoples"

According to testimony later provided by four officers who had served on the voyage, Minuit and his officers followed their instructions closely upon their arrival at the Delaware in March 1638. Their affidavit stated that they sailed into the Minquas Kill (Christina River) then sought to determine whether any other "Christians" inhabited the territory. After finding the territory empty of other European colonizers, Minuit and his officers met with its native owners and requested that they sell the river and all the land around it. According to the officers' testimony, the inhabitants assented to Minuit's proposal "with the common consent of the Nations." Then, or soon thereafter, five "sachems or chiefs" acting in the names of their "nations or peoples" granted them all of the territory they had requested. With the aid of one of the officers who knew their language (another New Netherlander whom Minuit must have recruited), the sachems unanimously declared that they had "transported, ceded, and transferred the said land with all its jurisdiction, sovereignty, and rights to the Swedish Florida Company [i.e., the New Sweden Company] under the protection of the most illustrious and high mighty Princess and Virgin Christina, elected Queen of the Swedes, Goths, and Wends." In the sachems' presence Minuit and his men erected the arms of Sweden and performed "other solemn ceremonies" to signify the Crown's possession of "the land named *New Sweden*." Soon afterward Minuit's men raised a fort at the site, which they named "Christina" in honor of the Swedish monarch. Most of the officers were Netherlanders of one sort or another, but through these symbolic "ceremonies of possession," staged with the cooperation of the territory's sachems, they had become spokesmen and agents of Swedish royal authority.[75]

Despite having orders to the contrary, Minuit seems to have sought out a confrontation with the West India Company's agents on the Delaware. The director of New Netherland, Willem Kieft, reported in April 1638 that Minuit and his men had recently attempted to sail past Fort Nassau. When the fort's commander demanded that Minuit display his commission and explain himself, Minuit refused, replying that "his Queen had as much right there as the Company."[76] A week later Kieft drafted a protest for the commander to present to Minuit. The document stated that "the entire South river of New Netherland has been for many years in our possession and secured above and below by forts and sealed with our blood, which took place during your honor's administration of New Netherland and is well known to your honor" (a reference to the massacre at Swanendael in 1631). Kieft protested against Minuit's intrusion and said that the occupiers' presence would "never be suffered by us." The director added that "we are also well assured that her Royal Majesty of Sweden has not given you any orders to build fortifications on our rivers or along our coasts." Kieft's letter explained further that he and his superiors would protest any additional damages to their colony, including "all accidents, shedding of blood and trouble," that might arise in the future. Minuit apparently ignored the protest, but Kieft's official warning set a precedent for future action against the Swedish colony.[77]

In his wranglings with New Netherland's officials, expressed in fluent Dutch, Minuit had given bold notice of New Sweden's territorial claims. He also sought to establish contact with his English neighbors to the south by sending the *Fogel Grip* to Virginia to trade for tobacco. Jerome Hawley, Virginia's treasurer, recounted the ship's visit in a letter to Secretary Francis Windebanke in England. Hawley explained that "a Dutch shipp wth comission from the yong Queene of Sweaden and signed by eight of the Cheife Lordes of Sweden" had arrived at Jamestown and requested permission to trade for tobacco there. Governor William Berkeley had informed the *Grip*'s captain that he could not permit the trade without instructions authorizing him to do so. The ship nonetheless remained at Jamestown about ten days in order to resupply.[78]

During the vessel's stay the Virginians learned that the Swedish vessel was "bound for the Delaware Baye." Hawley noted that the bay was located within "the confines of Virginea and New England, and there they p[re]tend to make a plantation and to plant tobacco, w[ch] the Dutch do allso already in Hudsons River, w[ch] is the very next river Northard from Delaware Baye." Like so many other Englishmen in North America, Hawley believed that all the lands between Virginia and New England were "His Ma[jesty's] terretorys." If the king wished to take action against these intruders, Hawley suggested, then his "subjects of these parts making use only of some English ships that resort heather for trade yearly" could remove them and prevent others from settling in the king's territory. Best of all, English subjects in the colonies would undertake the action "at no charge at all" to the king.[79] In short order Minuit and his officers had alerted English and Dutch authorities of the existence of the new Swedish colony and initiated a new stage in the contest for the Delaware Valley.

Homo Bulla

Minuit never made it back to the "lant van Cleeff."[80] In keeping with his instructions, after leaving New Sweden he had sailed to the island of Saint Christopher, or St. Kitts, in order to sell some wine for tobacco. He may also have hoped to capture a "rich Spanish ship" to recoup the great expense of a voyage that he knew by now had cost far more than it had earned.[81] In his eagerness to secure its success, however, he failed to take fully into account the hazards of these isles, "where this *Hurri Cano* is frequent." The native inhabitants of St. Kitts, on the other hand, knew a storm was on its way some three or four days before it struck, on August 5, 1638. Indeed, according to eyewitness John Taylor, "the *Dutch* and *English* had warning of the comming of it, by the knowledge that the *Indians* had by observation of the Moone." But instead of seeking protection from the storm in "holes[,] Caves, pits, Dens and hollow places of the earth," as did the burrowing Caribs, Minuit and his skipper, Jan Hendricksz van de Water, sought shelter behind the caulked and tarred walls of the *Vliegende Hert*, a vessel from Rotterdam anchored at St. Kitts. No doubt the gentlemen initially felt secure while they enjoyed the *gezelligheid* offered by their host. Yet ill fortune, which Minuit had evaded so well in Christian lands, finally caught him here, where there remained "many Heathens, *Indians,* and barbarous Nations unconverted." The hurricane struck just a half-hour after Minuit and van de Water boarded the other vessel.[82]

Taylor's account reveals that the best of intentions were washed away with the storm: "All possible meanes was used for the safeguard of men, ships, and goods, yet when it came, the force of it was so great, and continued so vehemently the space of foure days and nights without intermission, that maugre all the industry that could be, it sunke five Shipps, whereof two were *English,* and three were *Dutch,* and of *Englishmen, Dutchmen,* and *Indians,* it did drowne and kill to the number of Seventy and five persons, besides the harme it did to many Houses and goods."[83] Among the more than twenty ships blown out to sea was the *Kalmar Nyckel,* whose sailors managed to steer it back a few days later. The *Vliegende Hert* and its guests, however, never returned, and eventually the *Kalmar Nyckel* and the *Fogel Grip* departed for Europe without their two highest-ranking officers, now presumed to be dead.[84]

Afterward Blommaert blamed Minuit for many of the mistakes in the planning, preparation, and execution of the voyage, even finding fault with the way he kept his records. Yet on this last count Blommaert admitted that his leading officer had not realized that his life was about to be cut short. Writing to Oxenstierna in November 1638, Blommaert observed that with Minuit "the pen was spared all too much, not thinking he was to come to such a pitiful end."[85]

By the end of 1638 Minuit was dead, the Dutch investors in the venture wanted to pull out, and Blommaert's own commitment to the company was in question. Klas Fleming reported to Oxenstierna in June 1639 that he had learned that "Blommaert does not want to continue it, whether [because] he does not dare [do so] on account of the West India Company, of which he is a director, or because he also [may have] been persuaded by them to change his mind."[86] A month later Peter Spiring complained from Holland that Blommaert's continuing participation in the WIC had endangered the success of the project. After Blommaert advertised his status as a Swedish commissioner in Amsterdam, the directors of the WIC had "reproached him rather severely and remonstrated with him that though he should be a Royal Swedish servant and should hold a seat on their Board, he would do them no service but rather harm, and therefore [he was] not only useless but also harmful on their Board." Moreover, by seeking investments from other members of the WIC, Blommaert had only further complicated matters. When Spiring chastised him for the "evil he had done, in that he had introduced the Company here, or some members of it, into our [company]," Blommaert "made excuses, wanting to blame everything on Minuit, but he could not quite pull himself out of it." Blommaert's partners in the Netherlands made their own intentions clear when they declined to contribute any additional funds for a return voyage to New Sweden.[87]

The difficulty of coordinating the Dutch and Swedish halves of the New Sweden company had become apparent even before Minuit's voyage began. Preparing the voyage in Sweden while most of the goods, crew, and planners were in the Netherlands caused a variety of problems. Most were attributable to Sweden's primitive commercial economy. Minuit, for example, wrote Blommaert from Sweden to report that he could not obtain adequate cooperage, a basic necessity for an Atlantic voyage. Cargoes that had been produced and purchased at great expense in the Netherlands had to be shipped to Sweden to be loaded on the ships there. The sailors and officers also came from Holland and had to be transported to Sweden. Problems communicating across such a great distance added to their troubles, as was evident when Blommaert hired a crew and sent it to Göteborg. Blommaert had expected that the ships would be prepared to depart by the time the men arrived, but because of the delays in Sweden, the men had to be paid and maintained in port for several months before the ships were finally ready. Minuit, who was overseeing the preparations, had to sail back to Amsterdam during the summer of 1638 not only to confer with Blommaert and the other Dutch investors but also to acquire additional supplies.[88]

Unlike the company's Swedish sponsors, its Dutch investors were mainly skilled and experienced merchants. Based mostly in Amsterdam, several were already actively trading in New Netherland, while nearly all appear to have been relatives of either Blommaert or Minuit.[89] Joris Hoefnagel, who held a one-sixteenth share in the company, was probably a cousin on

Blommaert's mother's side of the family, the Hoefnagels, originally of Antwerp.[90] "Hüygens von Arnheim," who also owned a one-sixteenth share, may have been another relative—Blommaert's uncle through marriage was Christiaan Huygens, secretary to William of Orange and the Council of State in the United Provinces.[91] Or he may have had some connection to Minuit, whose nephew Hendrick Huygen (the son of Jan Huygen, New Netherland's first *ziekentrooster*) was the commercial officer on the first voyage and retained a leading role in the colony's affairs until its surrender. Adam Bessels, who held a one-sixteenth share, was a merchant with a diverse portfolio of interests that ranged from the Mediterranean to Russia to New Netherland. He was Blommaert's brother-in-law and one of the investors in Rensselaerswyck.[92] Gillis Verbrugge, a native of Haarlem, held a sixty-fourth share. During the 1640s, when the WIC opened up the fur trade to outsiders, Verbrugge's "trading house was by the far the most important in New Netherland," according to historian Jaap Jacobs.[93] Verbrugge was probably related through marriage to Isaac van de Water, perhaps also from Haarlem, who had purchased a three-sixty-fourth share; the odd proportions of Verbrugge's and van de Water's shares might be attributable to their close relationship to one another.[94] Isaac, in turn, was probably related to Jan Hendricksz van de Water, the skipper of the *Kalmar Nyckel* who was lost at sea with Minuit. Isaac also appears to have been Minuit's relative, as a notarial record from 1662 suggests that he was married to Maria Hasenkamp, the daughter of Minuit's sister.[95] A web of capital and kin tied the Dutch investors together.

The different motivations and attitudes held by the Swedish and Dutch investors created problems that were difficult to resolve. For the Swedish sponsors, all high officials in the government, the overriding goal of the project was to improve Sweden's commercial economy so that it could support such ventures on its own, without needing secretive and self-interested Dutch partners to prop them up. The Dutch investors, by contrast, wanted a return on their investment in the early modern equivalent of an offshore company. Both sets of investors were slow to contribute their share of the capital. Swedish officials were absorbed in more important affairs of state—namely, the Thirty Years' War—and their wealth was derived from rents, taxes, and revenues that could be expropriated as needed. For the Dutch merchants who supplied the rest of the company's funds, the capital invested was very real indeed and was meant to produce real outcomes. Otherwise, they could have and would have invested their money elsewhere.

Recognizing that their partners might not in fact contribute their portion, they withheld their capital until the Swedish government put in its part. During the previous decade Usselincx had argued that the Swedish government was a reliable commercial partner, but the participants in this venture were not so sure. They knew that it would be nearly impossible to recover their investment if these high-ranking officials decided that they wanted it for other purposes.

The Dutch sponsors were wise to be wary. Because of the project's patriotic goals, the interests of the Dutch investors frequently fell to the wayside (or in this case the quayside). When the *Kalmar Nyckel* returned to Amsterdam with only a fraction of the number of furs that Minuit had promised, the Dutch investors protested that the costs of founding a colony were none of their concern. They groused that "the whole capital would be consumed by the expenses and that it was not possible to support such great expenses upon such little trade." They thought the plans to attack Spain's shipping in the Caribbean were foolish and argued that their aim was only to trade. They reiterated their commitment to a self-sustaining enterprise when they asserted that the costs of new cargoes should be paid from the returns of the fur trade: "They said their intention has been nothing other than to go for the trade; the fact that the Crown wanted to bring its population had nothing to do with them."[96]

For Clan and Country

New Sweden was born of hybrid stock, an unlikely, fragile graft of the cosmopolitan and the patriotic. Its founders imagined that they could join the knowledge and the capital of the Netherlands with the patronage and the protection of the Swedish Crown. Willem Usselincx hoped to turn Sweden into a refuge for a Dutch diaspora and to forge a Protestant alliance that would overthrow the Iberians' Atlantic empire. Samuel Blommaert's motivations were less lofty, although he, too, saw opportunities for improving Sweden and helping Netherlanders and Germans beset by war. While these projectors looked abroad in order to escape the WIC's monopoly, their counterparts in Sweden had reasons of their own for bringing foreigners into the service of the Crown. Sweden's high officials wanted to transform their poor, primitive kingdom into a modern empire whose power and influence at sea would match that of its armies on the Continent. Northern Europe offered numerous examples of the prosperity Dutch merchants could create under foreign patronage and protection. If Netherlanders happened to profit as a consequence, then so be it—Swedish subjects would benefit too.

Usselincx and Blommaert believed that they, the expert merchants, would lead the companies they founded, but they soon discovered that even Antwerp's and Amsterdam's cleverest *kooplieden* could not outmaneuver Sweden's aristocratic bureaucracy. Usselincx worked for years to establish a Swedish trading company that would span the Atlantic only to see its meager capital turned into an ill-managed rope manufactory in Norrköping.[97] Blommaert later spent great sums on the first voyages to New Sweden but received little in return. To add insult to injury, once the WIC's directors discovered that he was organizing a colony at the edge of New Netherland, they discharged him as a director.[98] When he and his complicit countrymen finally quit their partnership with the Swedish Crown in 1641, they managed to get half of their principal back but no more.[99] They were fortunate to get even that for their trouble. Minuit lost his life.

The early voyages to New Sweden revealed the difficulty of managing a "multinational" commercial venture in the early modern era. Communication was slow, leadership was diffuse, and the personnel and the supplies required for the voyage were hard to find outside of the Netherlands. But the failure of the partnership at the heart of the company was not simply a matter of poor logistics. It was the failure of a concept. Usselincx had articulated the concept in his early writings, and Blommaert had revived the idea in his proposals from the mid-1630s—to establish an Atlantic colonial company organized by Dutch merchants under the patronage of the Swedish Crown. The plan promised the satisfactions of profit and patriotism. In Usselincx's strong formulation Netherlanders and Swedes could seek both with a good conscience; cosmopolitan patriotism would reward all involved. In Blommaert's more pragmatic imagining the project would benefit Sweden's government and improve its commerce, and the Dutch investors would have to be content with the profits reaped in trade and in piracy against the Spanish enemy.

Several related problems prevented the concept from becoming a reality. The sponsors' differing motivations never meshed as easily as Usselincx promised they would. New Sweden's Dutch investors wanted to focus on the fur trade, while its Swedish sponsors were more concerned with the prospects of permanent occupation and settlement. Nor did there appear to be much interest in sponsoring a large-scale Swedish trading company outside of Sweden itself, despite Usselincx's claims to the contrary. Where the itinerant promoter was able to attract support, it was in places that were under direct or indirect Swedish rule. And when Gustav Adolf and his chancellor, Axel Oxenstierna, turned their attention to other matters, Usselincx's company reverted to its most real form—a thick stack of pamphlets and prospectuses and little else.

The investors' divergent allegiances also created conflicts that could not be resolved easily. Blommaert and his partners who had ties to the WIC, for example, tried to retain their positions in the Dutch company even as they sponsored a rival venture under the Swedish flag. When their duplicity became public knowledge, a controversy erupted, Blommaert lost his directorship, and the other Dutch investors quickly sought an exit from the Swedish venture. Sweden's officials soon lost their taste for the arrangement too. They welcomed the departure of their Dutch partners as an opportunity to make the company more Swedish in every respect. The cosmopolitan core of New Sweden quickly collapsed.

The only leading figure in the project who had real experience in America was Peter Minuit. New Sweden had been his inspiration, and his plans for it reflected his own cosmopolitan and patriotic commitments. He had proposed in 1636 that the Crown of Sweden establish a colony, *Nova Sweediae,* for purposes of trade and settlement, and he had provided precise details regarding what it would require. His prospectus left out his own personal motivation for leading the voyage. According to Blommaert, Minuit aimed to become a patroon and to place settlers from Kleve, his *patria,* in the new colony he was to govern. Minuit's death disrupted this plan, but echoes of his intentions survived him. The chief commercial officer in the colony was his nephew Hendrick Huygen. After his uncle's death, Huygen remained in a position of influence as an officer, merchant, and investor in the colony. Also accompanying Minuit on the first voyage was another nephew, Gotfried Harmer, Huygen's young cousin. Harmer later became New Sweden's (and Huygen's) leading trader with the Minquas-Susquehannock. In 1653, following his elder cousin's advice, Harmer left New Sweden for northern Maryland, where he eventually became a prosperous landholder.

In the final accounting those who gained the most from the founding of New Sweden were not officials or investors in Europe but men such as Huygen and Harmer, cosmopolitan patriots of a lesser sort. Their connections to one another and to friends and relatives in New Netherland and Europe helped make distant foreign provinces into a new homeland for themselves and their progeny. Minuit knew that by leading this venture, he was risking his life—his instructions described what should happen if he were to die during the voyage. But he also recognized that death was no stranger to his homeland and that his relations and his countrymen might find a better life in America than in the wrecked, plaguey world they had left behind.

3

Good Friends and Doubtful Neighbors

At the end of April 1623 the tulips were blooming, and Willem Usselincx was at The Hague trying to take credit, and receive payment, for his contributions to the Dutch West India Company. Holland's *bloemisten* had reason to be excited—a bulb called "Semper Augustus" had just sold for one thousand guilders. "No tulip was ever more esteemed," Nicolaes van Wassenaer wrote of the flower, whose scalloped white petals, emerging from a deep blue base, were streaked red as though they were aflame.[1] Usselincx's esteem for himself led to expectations of an even greater reward. Rejecting the offer by the States General of a salary of four thousand guilders per year, he demanded "two per cent of all the subscriptions he got beyond five millions, one fifteenth of all the profits the state should derive from the company, and one fourth of the brokerage."[2] The West India Company was his prized bloom, bearing the marks of his cultivation, and he wanted the recognition that was his due. Six months later he was on his way to Sweden.

As Usselincx petitioned for his pay, a fleet of eleven ships was preparing to depart from the Goeree Gat, an outlet of the Maas River about thirty miles south of The Hague. A great parade of worthies from the capital came to inspect the vessels. Among them were the stadholder Prince Maurits of Nassau; his brother Prince Frederik Hendrik; the deposed king and queen of Bohemia; the Duke of Saxe-Weimar; along with "many other Barons, Captains, Officers, and Nobles, as well as noble ladies," borne by thirty carriages and eight coaches.[3] The maritime might on display mirrored the quality of the spectators on shore. The flagship *Het Wapen van Amsterdam* carried forty-two cannon and 237 men, and its partner, *Het Wapen van Delft,* matched it with forty cannon and 242 men. Each of these "leviathans" weighed eight hundred tons, ranking them among the largest ships in Dutch service.[4] The other ships—the *Arend,* the *Eendracht,* the *Griffioen,* the *Hollandia,* the *Hoop,* the *Koning David,* the *Mauritius,* the *Oranje,* and the *Windhond*—were comparably armed and manned. The fleet went to sea on April 29 with nearly three hundred cannon and over 1,600 men in all, including 600 soldiers.[5] It was the "greatest force ever sent to the South Seas," a contemporary declared.[6]

The "Nassau Fleet," named for Prince Maurits's role in sponsoring the expedition, was inspired in part by the voyage of Joris van Spilbergen, who had led a series of naval attacks along the Pacific coast of South America in 1615. The Nassau Fleet was twice as large as van Spilbergen's expedition, and its goals were grander: to capture Spain's treasure fleet and to foster an uprising among Spain's indigenous and enslaved African subjects.[7] Van Spilbergen's voyage offered an example for the Nassau Fleet to follow, but Usselincx's ideas, and those of men like him, brought these fantasies of liberation to life. Since the beginning of the Dutch Revolt in the late sixteenth century, Netherlanders had identified their own struggle against Spain with the plight of the natives of the Americas. In his efforts to promote the Dutch West India Company and then its Swedish counterpart, Usselincx had taken this older patriotic tradition and translated it into the commercial language of the seventeenth century.[8] Commerce with America's indigenous peoples, he argued, would forge alliances, promote conversions, and earn profits. Indians would offer their own goods in a free and fair exchange, resulting in a "very big trade." Eventually, the natives would acquire "civility" and Christianity as well. Through "patronage and friendship with so many different peoples" Christian traders would bring "peoples and nations who up to now lived in blindness, idolatry, and godlessness . . . to the light of truth and eternal bliss." Various Protestant nations would participate in these efforts. In time, Usselincx predicted, these partners in commerce and faith would challenge Spanish power on both sides of the ocean.[9]

Samuel Blommaert and Peter Minuit, alumni of the actual West India Company, showed little interest in a transatlantic anti-Iberian alliance. Yet their own conception of New Sweden, modeled after the WIC's New Netherland, retained several core precepts from Usselincx's original vision: the natives of America were free to trade with whomever they wished; they could make alliances and contracts with outsiders; and their aid, cooperation, and ultimately their conversion would follow from this friendly trade. This "contract theory" of colonial commerce—elaborated more fully by Hugo Grotius in *Mare Liberum* (1609)—formed the ideological basis for the contest for the Delaware Valley.[10] It defined colonizer and native as equals according to the law of nations, recognized natives' capacity and desire to facilitate trade and consensual settlement, and encouraged competition among colonizers who sought to legitimize possession not through a priori claims but through actual negotiations and exclusive agreements with native landowners. This model was especially suited to the Delaware Valley because Europeans and Indians alike were incapable of controlling the space through force. Instead, friendly trade offered the means to establish, maintain, and renew peace. So, while Blommaert and Minuit probably did not expect the founding of New Sweden to lead to widespread Christian conversions or to the overthrow of Spain's empire in the Americas, they did recognize the importance of making agreements with the native peoples of the region. New Sweden would not become the proving ground for Usselincx's Euro-American cosmopolitanism, but it would become a colony intimately dependent upon "good friendship" with its Indian allies.

The colony would also come to rely on friendly commerce with its Dutch and English neighbors. Blommaert and Minuit knew that planting a trading post in the Delaware Valley would not be received well by officials in the Netherlands, old or new, but they did expect to gain their neighbors' eventual cooperation, if not their formal consent. In keeping with Usselincx's proposals, mutually beneficial commerce among fellow Protestants would smooth the way. As in Usselincx's and Minuit's imaginations, New Sweden would be first peopled by a mix of Protestant subjects, including Netherlanders. But these nations did not mix well for long. Although Swedish officials initially supported the participation of Dutch investors in the colony, they ultimately chose to restrict the Netherlanders' influence. At the same time, metropolitan officials in the United Provinces and in England, along with their spokesmen on the Hudson and the Chesapeake, decided that the Delaware Valley and its trade were too valuable to give up to Swedish interlopers. Enterprising colonizers from England and New England soon joined the contretemps, seeking to plant their own settlements along the river. The result was a multisided international and intercolonial competition to possess the Delaware Valley and its trade.

In the chorus of claims that followed, disputants frequently invoked their sovereigns and nations to justify their assertions and actions. Colonizers and colonists defined themselves and others by their national allegiances, even (perhaps especially) when their actual backgrounds and origins were more complicated. The heightened attention to national differences need not have led to conflict, of course. During the first half of the seventeenth century the states of England, the Netherlands, and Sweden were allies, not enemies. In an age of confessional wars all were formally associated with Protestant churches. Yet officials failed to forge lasting cooperative relationships from these affinities. Commercial relationships could thrive—trade was these little colonies' lifeblood—but only when individual traders formally acknowledged the authorities and nations that laid claim to this space. Good friendship, then, might depend on merchants subordinating their national allegiances, on the one hand, while officials asserted them, on the other. Cosmopolitan commerce could flourish when national loyalties were acknowledged and then set aside. "Bloody threats" were the usual alternative.

The main audience for these performances of allegiance was made up of other colonizers, but the indigenous inhabitants of the region entered the conversation about national differences too. In fact, it was their fickle patronage—their decisions about who their "good friends" would be—that had fostered the colonial rivalry in the first place. And while they were not so well attuned as Europeans to the fine distinctions within and between nations, the native occupants of the Delaware Valley and its hinterlands were keen learners. They quickly identified those nations that were cultivating their favor or their displeasure, and they acted accordingly. They proved to be just as free as Usselincx imagined them to be.

Civil Disputes

Minuit's purchases from Lenape landowners and their Minquas-Susquehannock allies in the spring of 1638 supposedly gave the Swedish Crown rights to land from the Delaware Bay to the falls of the Delaware River. In reality, for the first two years of its existence "New Sweden" was little more than an armed trading post occupied by twenty-five men.[11] Fort Christina was in many ways a mirror image of New Netherland's Fort Nassau, which held about twenty men of its own at a site thirty miles upriver.[12] The occupants of the Swedish fort, a mix of Swedes and Netherlanders, even may have resembled those who lived across the river, as the WIC commonly re-cruited soldiers from all over northern Europe, including Scandinavia.[13] Fort Christina's officers had diverse national origins too. Its commander was Måns Nilsson Kling, a Finnish soldier who seems to have served in a regiment in southern Sweden before becoming the chief military officer in the colony.[14] William Laury was the provost marshal, the officer in charge of discipline at the fortress. His name suggests he was of British origin, perhaps Scots.[15] The leading commercial officer, or *commis,* was Minuit's nephew, Hendrick Huygen, a Dutch-speaking native of Kleve.[16] The collec-tion of nations in the colony's officer corps reflected the mixed origins of its sponsors, although it may also have indicated a desire to work with the colony's Dutch and English neighbors.

The prospects for such peaceful coexistence were poor from the start. Since the founding of the Swedish trading post, New Netherland's officers had seen their gains on the river dwindle nearly to nothing. The colony's director, Willem Kieft, wrote in July 1638 that Minuit had "attracted all the peltries to himself by means of liberal gifts." A year later he wrote that trade on the Delaware had been reduced to a "small amount, because the Swede, by underselling, had depressed, and continues to keep down the market." The director's frustration was apparent. "To behold this contentedly, to be thus hectored, deprived of the trade and robbed of our land, is a vast an-noyance," Kieft wrote. "Since their arrival there, we have fallen short full 30,000 [skins] in the trade, and still daily suffer through their means."[17] By offering Indian suppliers better terms, the newcomers had drawn away most of the furs and skins that once had gone to the WIC's men upriver.

The Swedish colony's new commander, Peter Hollander Ridder, was nonetheless keen to maintain peaceful relations with his counterparts at Fort Nassau. Ridder was a good candidate for the post—he was of Dutch and perhaps Finnish descent, and he had served as a lieutenant in the Swed-ish admiralty under powerful Finnish aristocrat Klas Fleming.[18] It did not take long before Ridder learned that good intentions and Dutch ancestry did not count for much. Just a day after his arrival at Fort Christina, three of his officers, all of Dutch origin or background, decided on their own authority to sail their sloop past Fort Nassau.[19] Their goal was to purchase land for the colony and to conduct trade with the Indians who lived across the river from the Dutch fort. Threats from the WIC's soldiers quickly turned them back. Afterward Ridder criticized his fellow officers, noting that they had no orders to wage "great naval war by force." Moreover, they were supposed to behave "amicably" toward their neighbors. Their superiors had specifically directed them to "build without a quarrel" and then to see how their rivals responded.[20]

Ridder blamed his colleagues for their rash provocation, but when he attempted to sail past Fort Nassau a few days later, the WIC's soldiers fired four warning shots at his vessel. Ridder was philosophical about the show of opposition: "The balls drown; [let us] build for those to come." Proceeding upriver, he and his men arranged to buy lands from the Lenape inhabitants and then set up border posts on the riverbank across from Fort Nassau to signify Sweden's possession. Afterward Ridder returned to the Dutch fort to deliver a message written by Samuel Blommaert himself, but it seemed to have little effect. When Ridder's assistant, Gregorius van Dyck, attempted to sail past the fort a week later, the soldiers fired on their vessel again. Following Ridder's orders, van Dyck asked the fort's commander why he had shot at them. The head officer replied: "So that you shall not sail up. The whole river belongs to the West India Company, you have no business here, and if you come again we shall shoot again."[21] Although both sets of officers were Dutch in origin, cooperation at this moment proved to be impossible.

Disputes with the Dutch at Fort Nassau created uncertainty, but conflicts between the Dutch and Swedish personnel *within* New Sweden also posed problems. At the beginning of July 1639, as preparations for Ridder's voyage were under way, Admiral Klas Fleming wrote to Axel Oxenstierna that the government should recruit new soldiers for the fort. He also suggested trying to find "especially some artisans, such as blacksmiths, shoemakers, carpenters, master masons, and what else is needed daily, among them three or four who are married and would be willing to take their wives along, who should be able to brew, bake, and wash for the people." Men and women (and eventually children) from the Swedish kingdom would help to build and populate the colony. Fleming's ultimate goal was to "garrison the fort with Swedish people only, . . . as I learn that the Swedes and the Dutch who have been there before cannot get along well, and consequently good discipline [can]not be kept there."[22]

Even the Dutch skippers hired for Ridder's voyage caused trouble. Fleming's choice as captain, Cornelis van Vliet, connived to profit from the huge expenses associated with preparing the *Kalmar Nyckel*'s second voyage to New Sweden. Blommaert later attributed the voyage's delays and extraordinary costs to van Vliet, whom he described as "most disloyal" in his service to the Crown. The passengers aboard the ship accused the captain of mismanagement, while van Vliet's own officers asserted that he "acted only according to his own personal view." "Wasting the summer time most shamefully," van Vliet had neglected the ship during its long stay at Göteborg and instead had spent his time "continuously" in the more comfortable surroundings of an inn. He was an embezzler too—large quantities of supplies never reached the ship. Missing were two tons of butter, two tons of herring, seven barrels of beer, and a hundred loaves of rye bread. Blommaert even hinted that the captain might have hired carpenters who knowingly damaged the ship's leaky hull so that more extensive repairs were required. "Who knows how many thefts he committed," Blommaert wrote.[23]

Van Vliet was eventually dismissed by Pieter Spierinck Silfvercrona (Peter Spiring), a Netherlander who served as Sweden's resident in The Hague and a stockholder in the New Sweden Company. Van Vliet's replacement, Pouwel Jansen, another Dutchman, created problems of his own. Although Blommaert said that he had a reputation as an "able person," during the voyage Jansen abused the Swedes aboard the ship, belittled the Lutheran religion, cursed at the Swedish minister, and prevented fellow officer Gregorius van Dyck, a native of The Hague, from participating in the Swedes' religious services.[24] According to van Dyck, Jansen declared that while it was acceptable for the Swedes to practice Lutheranism in their own kingdom, van Dyck could not, as he was from Holland, where Lutherans were not permitted to practice openly. Meanwhile, Jansen spent every evening during the voyage drinking brandy and smoking tobacco with the factor Joost van Langdonk, another Dutchman.[25] "God knows, I cannot get along with this clerk," Ridder later wrote of van Langdonk.[26]

Eventually, Blommaert, too, came to the conclusion that New Sweden should employ fewer Netherlanders. Drawing from the example of van Vliet's perfidy, Blommaert noted that the Dutch captain had been in the Swedish service for ten years before his "untrustworthy" character was revealed. "The government has to watch most closely that it gets faithful people in its service—people who can be relied upon in time of distress," Blommaert advised. "Therefore the government must try to raise in her own nation people who will be trained for the navigation to faraway regions."[27] Foreigners could not be trusted in endeavors that required a strong patriotic commitment. Blommaert, of course, did not mention that others might have said (and almost certainly did say) the same thing about him.

The danger of weak loyalties was certainly evident at Fort Christina, whose occupants had watched two years pass without any support arriving from Sweden. Described as "halfe starved and tottered" in one English source, they decided in early 1640 that they had waited long enough for relief to come.[28] Just as they were about to abandon their fortress and seek the protection of Dutch authorities at New Amsterdam, however, a ship came from Sweden bearing "fresh settlers and goods." It was the *Kalmar Nyckel,* piloted by Captain Jansen and carrying the contentious officer corps of Ridder, van Langdonk, and van Dyck. The ship's arrival headed off the mass desertion and renewed the competition along the river. "They have greatly injured, and still do harm to the Company—the trade is wholly ruined," Willem Kieft, the director of New Netherland, reported shortly afterward. Several months later he noted that "they are beginning to exhibit much hostility, such as forcibly sailing up past our fort, trading, threatening to run off with our sloop, and so forth." Despite Ridder's desire for friendly relations and Kieft's promise "to treat the Swedes with all civility," the contest for the Delaware Valley had taken a new, more aggressive turn.[29]

Dutch Settlers in a Swedish Colony

By 1640 the problems inherent in the New Sweden Company's Dutch-Swedish partnership were more evident than ever. Blommaert's and Minuit's associates in the Netherlands were negotiating to sell their stakes back to the Swedish government, and officials in Sweden, led by Klas Fleming, had begun to reorganize the company so that it would be truly a Swedish venture. Yet the Netherlanders who first proposed and organized the project were the ones who actually possessed the knowledge and experience necessary to manage a colony. Minuit, in particular, knew better than anyone how to organize a settlement and to conduct trade with the Indians in the region. His death at sea was not simply the loss of a seasoned colonial administrator. The hurricane that took Minuit's life also swept away the plans to populate New Sweden with his beleaguered countrymen from Kleve.

Yet Blommaert thought that he could attract new settlers. All he needed was another figure like Minuit, a "capable person" who could recruit colonists. Blommaert found such a person in Netherlander Joost van den Bogaert. Like Minuit, van den Bogaert had served the WIC in a commercial capacity during New Netherland's early years. By the late 1630s he was in Brazil, where he witnessed the birth of the son of Isaack de Rasière, who had served with Minuit as an officer in New Netherland in the 1620s.[30]

Van den Bogaert now represented two prominent participants in the WIC: the nobleman Godard van Reede, Heer van der Nederhorst; and Hendrik Hooghkamer, an officer in the Admiralty of Amsterdam and the son of Jacob Pietersz Hooghkamer, a founding director of the WIC.[31] Like Minuit and his compatriots in Kleve, these supporters of colonization were motivated by the difficulties of life at home. "The people of Utrecht, seeing that the burdens on the country became heavier and heavier, [and] that the farmer could hardly make a living," had sought to come to an agreement with the WIC to establish a settlement in New Netherland, Blommaert explained to Oxenstierna. Yet they had been frustrated by the company's unwillingness to cooperate with their demands. So they had turned to the organizers of New Sweden, "seeing that the Crown of Sweden had chosen a good place situated between New Netherland and Virginia." Recruiting these settlers would allow the Crown to "gain a populated land without cost," Blommaert claimed. In time the colony would bring benefits to the Crown and to Sweden's navigation.[32]

Officials in Sweden were wary, however, when they first discussed the proposal in the spring of 1639. Chancellor Axel Oxenstierna noted that privileges were easy enough to grant, especially when they were to places the Crown did not already possess, but he worried about planting Dutch settlers in a Swedish colony. He wrote to Klas Fleming that "if we make the resolution to allow the Hollanders, who besides us claim it, to populate the country with their own people, and to appoint a Governor of their nation over it, we confirm them in it, who today or tomorrow will not be very considerate of us; and the trade will not, in the long run, come to our country, but to others, and thus we shall have the name [only] and no benefit."[33] Fleming responded that in the past he had supported sending Dutch settlers to the colony "but not more than we always could manage." He agreed that Oxenstierna's concerns were legitimate and that the colony should be peopled by Swedes, not Netherlanders. "In my humble opinion, the foundation of our activity seems to rest on the country being populated as soon as possible with Swedish people," Fleming wrote. If the Dutch investors wished to withdraw, then let them go. The project was necessary "for the reputation of the Crown as well as for the profit and advantage" that would follow from it.[34]

Eventually, the parties were able to agree, and in January 1640 the Swedish government issued a charter for the "Patronen" in the name of Hendrik Hooghkamer. The *octroy* granted the participants a wide range of rights and privileges, including rights to own property, to trade, and to practice

Reformed Protestantism.[35] There were important limits, though: exports had to go directly to Sweden; laws had to be submitted for approval to the local Swedish governor; and Lutheran and Reformed congregants alike were instructed to "live peacefully with one another." In return the Swedish government promised to protect the "Patronen" and their colonists from outside aggression and to promote their best interests just as it did for "our other faithful subjects." Recognizing that these Dutch settlers possessed multiple allegiances, the regulations declared that they would be exempt from military service in the colony. In other words, if the WIC chose to attack the Swedish colony, the settlers from Utrecht would not be pressed to fight. Nonetheless, even during wartime they would be expected to remain loyal to their new Swedish masters.[36]

Shortly after the charter was issued, van den Bogaert left Sweden for the Netherlands in order to prepare for the voyage. These preparations soon stalled when a dispute with Denmark led the States General to restrict voyages to the Baltic and to prohibit Dutch sailors from entering the service of foreigners. The result was that many Netherlanders were hesitant to contribute to the new project for fear of suffering public punishment.[37] Although Spiring finally obtained an official release for the ship, allowing it to proceed, great power politics had left their imprint on the voyage. Worse yet, the WIC's officials were now trying to block the effort. Rumors had spread that the soldiers at Fort Christina had abandoned the colony and had fled to New Amsterdam (as indeed they almost had done); that the director of New Netherland was planning to transport Fort Christina's soldiers back to the Netherlands if support did not arrive soon; and even that the *Kalmar Nyckel* had been captured by Turkish pirates on its return to Europe. WIC officials in Amsterdam also warned that if the settlers from Utrecht were placed anywhere besides along the Minquas Kill (Christina River), then its agents would treat them as trespassers against the WIC's charter, confiscate their property, and prosecute them. For the moment the WIC was willing to tolerate Fort Christina's presence in order to prevent a public dispute with the Swedish Crown. The company would permit nothing more than what little ground the Swedish settlement already occupied.[38]

Uncertainty and politics delayed the voyage, but it finally began in late July or early August 1640. The *Freedenburgh* reached Fort Christina in early November, carrying perhaps fifty colonists, a large number, considering that the entire population of the settlement may have numbered only about one hundred at this time.[39] They settled at a site about eighteen miles north of the fort on land that Ridder had selected for them.[40] How long their colony retained its semiautonomous character is unknown, as neither Dutch nor Swedish sources refer to them after 1642. John Winthrop wrote in his journal in August 1642 that "sickness and mortality" had struck the inhabitants of the Delaware River that summer, so perhaps their community had dissolved then. Some of the survivors may have joined the population at Fort Christina, while others probably departed for New Amsterdam or returned to Europe.[41] By choice, necessity, or mortality, van den Bogaert and his fellow Netherlanders left New Sweden to the Swedes.

The Empire of New Haven

As the Utrecht colony collapsed, a new English effort to settle the Delaware Valley was emerging from New Haven. The two leaders of the "Dellaware Company" were important and wealthy men. According to a tax record of 1643, merchant George Lamberton's estate was worth one thousand pounds, ranking him among the ten richest men in New Haven.[42] He was truly an Atlantic entrepreneur—during the 1630s, among other trading ventures he "had dabbled, with limited success, in the West African trade in gold and 'elephant's teeth,'" historian L. H. Roper has revealed.[43] Lamberton's partner, Captain Nathaniel Turner, was nearly as rich—his estate was worth eight hundred pounds.[44] Since 1640 he had officially possessed "the comaund and ordering of all martiall affayres" of New Haven.[45] Turner's plot in the town was just around the corner from those belonging to two of the settlement's founders, Theophilus Eaton and John Davenport, "the *Moses* and *Aaron* of the Christian Colony," as Cotton Mather later described them.[46] They had invested in the Delaware Company too.[47] Several other investors were also leading figures in New Haven's government and its church.[48]

The goal of the Delaware Company, like that of New Haven itself, was to pursue trade. Ipswich minister William Hubbard noted in his history of New England (written ca. 1680) that the "main founders of New Haven were men of great estates, notably well versed in trading and merchandising, strongly bent for trade." Two decades later Mather wrote, "Being *Londoners,* or Merchants, and Men of Traffick and Business, their Design was in a manner wholly to apply themselves unto *Trade.*"[49] They had placed their original settlement at Quinnipiac, far beyond existing English settlements, exactly because "there was then no settled place of trade, at least of any great moment, in the country," Hubbard wrote. Soon after their arrival, they had begun to pursue opportunities beyond New England: "they built some shipping, and sent abroad their provisions into foreign parts, and purchased lands at Delaware, and other places, to set up trading houses for beaver."[50] By Hubbard's accounting the Delaware Valley actually belonged to the English. He wrote that New England extended from "about Delaware Bay to the south of Nova Francia."[51]

The Delaware Company's first voyage set off in the spring of 1641 and almost immediately created an intercolonial controversy.[52] Before heading south, the New Haveners sailed into the harbor at Manhattan, where word spread that the visitors aimed to place settlers along the Delaware, New Netherland's "South River." On April 8 Director General Kieft warned the captain of the vessel, Robert Cogswell, "not to build nor plant on the South River, lying within the limits of New Netherland, nor on the lands extending along it, as they lawfully belong to us." Kieft was ready to allow the travelers to proceed, however, if they promised to "settle under the Lords the States [General], and the Hon[orable] West India Company, and swear allegiance and become subject to them, as other inhabitants do." That is, if these English colonists were willing to become *Dutch* subjects, Kieft would permit their settlement along the Delaware.

Other New Englanders had accepted the colony's conditions for settling within New Netherland. Such migrants, however, sometimes aroused the ire of New England's officials, "not for going from us, but for strengthening the Dutch, our doubtful neighbors," as John Winthrop wrote of some families from Lynn and Ipswich, Massachusetts, who had moved to Long Island and sworn an "oath of fealty" to the Dutch. By accepting the authority of Dutch officials, the settlers had forsworn their natural allegiances and strengthened a rival nation. When it came to defining New England's borders—and settlers' loyalties—Winthrop and his fellow Puritans could employ the language of nation and subjection as well as any.[53]

Captain Cogswell would have known of the Dutch regime's openness to English settlers, and he led Kieft to believe that his passengers might accept the offer to become sworn subjects. He said that his goal was to land the settlers where the States General had no jurisdiction, but if he could not find such a place, the passengers would either settle within New Netherland under Kieft's terms or return to New Haven. Kieft took him at his word. He allowed the vessel to proceed and ordered New Netherland's commissary at Fort Nassau to treat the English in a friendly manner.[54] But Cogswell seemed to hold a very constricted notion of the States General's jurisdiction. When the voyagers reached the Delaware, they quickly arranged to purchase lands from Indian sachems on both sides of the river.[55] New Sweden's commander, Peter Ridder, tried to disrupt the sale at Varkens Kill (present-day Salem River, New Jersey), but the visitors from New Haven were undeterred. Meanwhile, the New Englanders disrupted the unstable Dutch and Swedish duopoly over the fur trade. New Sweden's head trader, Hendrick Huygen, later wrote that "it may be feared and it is already evident that the trading will be spoiled."[56]

The following spring the merchant George Lamberton led another, perhaps much larger, expedition from New Haven to the Delaware.[57] This time Lamberton purchased lands near the mouth of the Schuylkill River, almost directly across the Delaware from New Netherland's Fort Nassau. The influential sachem "Matthorne," or Mattahorn, and "severall other Indian Sayamoes" sold the land to him; Mattahorn had also participated in the sale of the land for New Sweden's Fort Christina in 1638.[58] Lamberton then sent notice of the purchase to New Sweden's officials, warning them not to place settlers within the Englishmen's limits.[59] New Netherland's officials ultimately had more at stake. After a series of similar disputes, some violent, with New Englanders along the Connecticut River, Dutch authorities may have realized that only a show of force could halt their spread.[60]

When they learned of New Haven's occupation of the Schuylkill during the peak season of the fur trade, Kieft and his council quickly resolved to expel the Englishmen. Within a week they had dispatched two yachts to the Delaware bearing orders for commissary Jan Jansen to confront the English colonists and to remove them from their new settlement but doing so "in a friendly way in order that no blood be shed." If the English refused to leave, Jansen had permission to seize them and ship them to New Amsterdam. Kieft and the council pointedly reminded their subordinate that he must "remain master of the situation" while he "maintain[ed] the reputation of their High Mightinesses [the Lords States General] and the honorable West India Company." Although Jansen was directed to preserve and inventory the trespassers' property, he was also commanded to "raze the said settlements to the ground."[61]

According to a subsequent English account, Jansen did just that. He and his "armed men . . . by force in a hostile way burnt theire trading house[,] seized and for som time detained the goods in it[,] not suffering their servants soe much as to take a just Inventory of them." The witness claimed that

the soldiers also "seized theire boate and for a while kept theire men Prisoners." Adding to the affront, Kieft "compeled Mr Lamberton theire Agent
by force or threatenings to give in at the Manhattoes an account of what
beavers he had traded within Newhaven limits at Delaware and to pay recognition for the same."[62] Not only had the WIC's soldiers destroyed the trading post at Schuylkill and transported the New Englanders as prisoners to
Manhattan, but they also had demanded that Lamberton pay customs duties
or damages for trading without the permission of New Netherland's authorities.[63] One man apparently suffered burns from the incident, and later protests charged that Kieft's men had caused one thousand pounds in damages.[64]

New Netherland's officials took the lead in displanting Lamberton's trading post at the Schuylkill, near Fort Nassau. Authorities in New Sweden
were left to confront the new English settlement at Varkens Kill, downriver from Fort Christina. Its greater size may have deterred direct action by agents of the Dutch and Swedish colonies—English and Swedish
sources suggested its inhabitants numbered twenty families, or about sixty
persons.[65] Ridder's unwillingness to confront them also suggests that he
lacked the resources to displace them. Perhaps he expected that the isolated
colonists would willingly submit themselves to Swedish authority, much as
Kieft had hoped that Cogswell's passengers from New Haven would accept
the government of New Netherland as their own. Ridder's successor, Johan
Björnsson Printz, would be left with the task of transforming these "New
English" into "New Swedes" or forcing them from the river.

Making New Sweden Swedish

Printz would serve over ten years as governor of New Sweden. At the peak
of his power the colony's territory extended to both sides of the Delaware
River, and its fortresses controlled trade along every major artery employed by Indian fur suppliers. But when the flow of ships from Sweden
came to a sudden stop in the late 1640s, Printz's aggressive methods no
longer worked. New Sweden's Indian allies turned to their old Dutch trading partners, and a reinvigorated administration in New Netherland forced
the governor to scale back his ambitions. The colony's settlers reacted to the
change as well. Although New Sweden's population grew to as many as two
hundred people during Printz's tenure, by the time his replacement arrived
in 1654, only about seventy inhabitants remained. When the future seemed

secure, officials such as Printz could demand obedience and rely on their subjects' national loyalties as a base for support. When collapse seemed imminent, allegiances frayed, and the cohesive power of national attachments soon reached its limit.

Shaping the national character of the colony was one of Printz's first priorities as the new governor. Printz was the first native Swede to occupy the post, whose powers had expanded with his appointment. With the departure of the investors from the Netherlands, the company was now entirely under the control of Swedish officials and investors who sought to replace the Dutch servants, soldiers, and officers with Swedes. As a former officer in the Swedish army and now a servant of the Crown, Printz directly embodied and represented a distinctively Swedish imperial authority. He suited the colony well in another respect too—having been court-martialed in 1641 for surrendering the German city of Chemnitz to Imperial forces during the Thirty Years' War, Printz knew the consequences of failure and the weight of disgrace. Like many of his own colonists, Printz found in New Sweden the opportunity to seek redemption from past misdeeds. In trying to save themselves, Printz and his colonists also promoted Swedish officials' ambitions to transform their kingdom into a colonial power.[66]

Drafted in Sweden in 1642, Printz's instructions represented the practical expression of official Swedish national identity. They emphasized the importance of using Swedish law, customs, and practices in the colony. In government and the administration of justice Printz's superiors commanded him to act in the name of the Queen and the Crown of Sweden. Similarly, Printz was ordered to govern "according to Swedish law and justice, custom and usage . . . [and to] adapt and fit the laudable customs, habits and usages of this most praiseworthy kingdom" to conditions in the colony.[67] Per Brahe, a member of the Swedish Council of State, later instructed Printz that the "Swedish language should be kept, spoken, and written, purely without any mixture of other languages." Even the "rivers and streams as well as herbs and woods" should have "old Swedish names," Brahe wrote. Above all, Printz was to "abolish all expressions from the Dutch which now seem to be somewhat ingrained." In sum "both in manners and customs, as far as possibly can be managed, everything should be conformed to old Swedish."[68] The kingdom, its laws, its language, and its customs were to be united in the colony, and the Dutch influence was to be rooted out.

The governor's instructions also demonstrated the importance of Swedish Lutheranism. Printz was well suited to the colony in this respect too.

He came from two generations of Lutheran ministers, had trained for the priesthood himself, and once had been licensed to preach in his home congregation at Bottnaryd in Småland.[69] Now, as governor of New Sweden, he had responsibilities in the church once again. He was ordered to "take all good care that divine service be zealously performed according to the true Augsburg Confession, the Council of Uppsala, and the ceremonies of the Swedish Church" and that "all good church discipline be [duly] held and exercised."[70] The church and its liturgy should even *look* distinctively Swedish. Brahe directed Printz to "decorate your little church and your priests in a Swedish manner with chasuble in order that you may be different from the English and the Hollanders, fleeing from all Calvinistic leaven."[71] Printz duly followed his orders and in July 1644 reported that "the divine service with its ceremony are here held just as in Old Sweden, in the good old Swedish language." Their pastor was wearing his chasuble, and their church differed "in all manners from the other sects hovering around us here."[72]

Even as Printz sought to make New Sweden more Lutheran and more Swedish, the Delaware Valley remained a space penetrated by other religious persuasions and other peoples. At the time that Printz's instructions were written, officials in Sweden expected that the Dutch settlers from Utrecht—"those of the Holland nation"—would still be part of the colony. They were also aware of the English settlers at Varkens Kill and the Dutch traders and soldiers at Fort Nassau. Meanwhile, outside the Delaware Valley were more Netherlanders and Englishmen who claimed it. Native peoples surrounded the colony. Printz's instructions with regard to these other "nations" reflected the cautious, ambivalent attitudes of nearly all the European colonizers of this space. On the one hand, he was supposed to treat his neighbors and rivals with "grace and propriety," but on the other, he was supposed to be ready to use deadly force against them if necessary. Ultimately, it was Printz's duty to negotiate these dangerous, fraught relationships to the greatest advantage of his patrons.

Regarding the Utrecht settlers, for example, Printz was ordered to respect their privileges to the "exercise of the Reformed religion" but also to keep them at a safe distance from Fort Christina.[73] Although Printz's superiors wanted the added population and labor the colonists provided, they still feared that the Netherlanders might assist their countrymen if the West India Company were to attack.[74] Of greater concern were the English settlers who occupied the mouth of Varkens Kill a dozen miles downriver. Printz was commanded to "bring these English families under the jurisdiction, devotion and dominion" of Queen Christina and the Swedish Crown. The English colonists might welcome the offer of protection from the Swedish colony, "as it is rumored that they, as a free people [*fritt folck*], would submit themselves to that government, which can maintain and protect them." If their numbers were to expand, as was feared, then the need to incorporate them was all the more pressing.[75] The preferred solution, however, was to remove them in a "peaceable manner." Wary of any English claims to the Delaware River, officials in Sweden worried that allowing the settlers to remain might encourage further sorties from New England and the Chesapeake. At the same time, Printz had to exercise great caution, for he risked alienating English authorities in the colonies and at the metropolis if he mishandled the situation.[76]

Printz also had to keep his neighbors from New Netherland at bay—his superiors warned that if the English were displaced, the Dutch would try to seize the entire eastern shore of the Delaware River. Printz was directed to meet with the officials at Fort Nassau and to treat them with "mildness and propriety" as he argued for the right of Swedish subjects to "a free exercise of commerce" along the river. If New Netherland's officials reacted in a hostile manner, then he was permitted to repel force with force. Otherwise, Printz was to uphold "good friendship and neighborhood" with the Dutch at Fort Nassau and New Amsterdam. At the same time, Printz was supposed to maintain friendly relations with the English in Virginia without infringing upon any of the lands they "actually possess[ed]." That qualification was significant—even as Swedish royal officials commanded Printz to establish friendly relations with his Dutch and English neighbors, they also empowered him to dispute claims of possession that were not based on actual settlement.[77]

Finally, the *Wilde Nationer* (wild nations) who surrounded the colony required careful consideration. While treating them with all "humanity and respect," Printz was to see that the Indians were instructed in Christian religion and "brought to civility and good public manner, as though led by the hand." He was to assure the Indians that the Swedish colony intended them no harm and wanted only to trade with them. Printz was also instructed to offer them higher prices for their furs than "the Hollanders from Fort Nassau, or the adjacent English." Lured by better terms of trade, the "legitimate masters of the lands" would withdraw from their relationships with these competing nations and turn to "our own [people]."[78] Unlike the members of the English or Dutch nations settled along the river, the members of these "wild nations" were not imagined to be potential subjects of the Swedish Crown or inhabitants of the colony. They *were* expected to welcome the Swedish colony, to accede to its program of expansion, and to trade freely with its inhabitants. Yet as Printz's instructions hinted, the Indians of the Delaware Valley ultimately had the power to choose which nation they would favor.

English and Indian Challengers

As soon as Printz arrived at the colony in February 1643, he set out to expand its influence and power. Within a year the men under his command had constructed several new forts and blockhouses along the Delaware and Schuylkill Rivers. The most significant was Fort Elfsborg, which was placed a short distance downriver from the English settlement at Varkens Kill.[79] Named after the imposing fortress Älvsborg near Göteborg, Fort Elfsborg was important for several reasons. For the first time New Sweden had an armed post on the eastern side of the Delaware River, which had previously been considered the de facto (if not de jure) domain of New Netherland. Unlike Fort Christina, which was set at a distance from the Delaware River, Fort Elfsborg gave the Swedish colony the ability to exercise direct control of navigation along the river. It was fitted with eight heavy guns and a mortar and manned by thirteen soldiers, the largest contingent at any of the Swedish forts.[80] Its proximity to the English settlers at Varkens Kill gave them little choice but to leave their lands or to become subjects of the Swedish Crown. (Some of them appeared to have accepted the offer to join the colony, as Printz later shipped out tobacco that he said had been grown by "our English at Varken's Kill.")[81] Several other new forts—at Tinicum Island, at Upland (contemporary Chester, Pennsylvania), and along the Schuylkill River—extended the regime's reach even further. New Sweden's authorities were now in position to control nearly all access to the fur trade in the Delaware River's western hinterlands.[82] All of this was possible, apparently, with fewer than fifty officers and soldiers.[83] Despite the growth in military strength, a shortage of goods and the pressure from outside traders, especially the English, had led to disappointing results in the fur trade. Making up for these losses was a booming trade in tobacco, some grown by New Sweden's own farmers but most coming from English planters in the Chesapeake.[84]

The rise of the tobacco trade reveals that not all outsiders were excluded from the river. Instead, Printz used Fort Elfsborg's strategic location to channel commerce to his colony at the same time as he restricted colonization and trade farther upriver. English and Dutch merchants who wished to trade with New Sweden were allowed through, provided that they stopped and were given permission to proceed. One of those visitors was New Haven captain Robert Cogswell, who had clashed with Kieft and Ridder in 1641; two years later his name appeared in Hendrick Huygen's account book, indicating that he had traded with the colony.[85] WIC vessels that tried to pass without recognizing the fort, on the other hand, might be fired upon, and visitors who hoped to plant settlements or trade directly with the Indians were blocked altogether.[86] Printz wrote that his goal was to "oppose the pretensions of the Hollanders and the Puritans and the other Englishmen in this place" and to force them to "correspond and trade with us and do our will and bring to us what we ask for."[87] The strategy seemed to work, especially with regard to New Netherland. Although Governor Kieft protested the construction of the new Swedish forts, he and Printz soon established a cooperative relationship. Indeed, Printz wrote that while the Hollanders "do not gladly see us here . . . yet they have nevertheless since I came here kept and still keep with us unity and good friendship, especially their commander in Manathans, called Willem Kiefft." The two men passed news to each other, permitted trade between their colonies, and worked to keep their mutual rival, the English, from gaining a foothold in the Delaware Valley.[88]

The first English attempt to colonize the Delaware Valley during Printz's tenure came from Virginia, one of the main sources of Printz's tobacco. The expedition landed, raggedly, in May 1643, a few months after Printz's arrival. Stopped at Fort Elfsborg, the ship's passengers were brought to Fort Christina, where a maid-servant confessed that the captain and the passengers had mutinied against their leader, Sir Edmund Plowden, an English gentleman and Roman Catholic who was attempting to plant a new colony along the river. Before reaching the Delaware, the mutineers had abandoned Plowden on an uninhabited island near the entrance to the Chesapeake Bay, where English rescuers later found him "half dead and black as earth." In the meantime Printz sent the mutineers as prisoners back to Virginia.[89] Printz also dispatched to Kieft a friendly if cryptic letter warning him of "certain events" that affected not only his colony but also their respective sovereigns.[90] Plowden's efforts did not stop after this setback, as he continued to dole out commissions in Virginia to those who wished to trade with the Indians of the river. He also announced that he was "expecting ships and people out of Ireland and England" to occupy the territory he called the "Province of New Albion."[91] Plowden eventually appeared in Massachusetts five years later. He had spent the intervening years at Kecoughtan in Virginia, renting a store and engaging in a series of lawsuits. Now, according to John Winthrop, he was on his way to England to get supplies in order to "returne, & plante de la ware, if he could gett sufficient strengthe to dispossesse the Swedes."[92]

While Plowden continued to seek metropolitan support for his colonial claims, Printz worried more about the "Puritans" of New England. In the report he drafted in 1644, Printz described the assaults that New Englanders had committed against New Netherland's servants at the Connecticut River and predicted that further attempts to colonize the Delaware would soon follow.[93] The Swedish governor was right to worry—during the previous summer he had arrested and tried merchant George Lamberton, one of the leaders of New Haven's Delaware Company. At the end of June 1643 Lamberton and his partner, Nathaniel Turner, had purchased lands near Varkens Kill from several sachems, including Usquata, sachem of the Narraticons, and Wewhewsett, sachem of Wattsesinge.[94] Printz arrested Lamberton and subjected him to a humiliating trial. Before a court consisting of Dutch officers from Fort Nassau, New Sweden's own officials, and several of New Sweden's freemen, Printz accused the English merchant of a variety of offenses against the colony. The Dutch and Swedish officers along the river may have disagreed about their respective boundaries, but they could agree to thwart English intruders and Lamberton, in particular.

In addition to charging Lamberton for illegal trading and for purchasing lands already claimed by New Sweden (and New Netherland), the court accused the merchant of inciting Indians to murder the Dutch and Swedish settlers along the river. Two of New Sweden's officers, Timon Stiddem and Gotfried Harmer, testified that "Mr. Lamberton had bribed all the Savages in order to murder us, frightening the Governor and the people here, the women and children crying." The freemen Peter Kock and Lasse Bonde claimed that the other English settlers on the river had "intimated that as soon as Mr. Lamberton arrived the English and the Savages should unite and strike us Swedes dead and chase [us] out of the River." As proof of these claims, the court described how the Minquas and their allies had come to Fort Christina bearing their weapons "in a very hostile manner," as though they intended to attack the fort.[95] The court found Lamberton guilty of this most severe charge—that Lamberton "had [bribed] the savages to miserably murder all the Swedes and Hollanders, together with women and innocent children, here in the South River"—but it commuted its decision when Printz declared that he "wished to treat Mr. Lamberton with mercy and . . . [to] let such a criminality pass for this time."[96] Lamberton's arrest and trial set off a flurry of correspondence between Dutch, English, and Swedish colonial authorities, each offering a different interpretation of the merchant's innocence or guilt.[97]

Despite Lamberton's difficulties with Dutch and Swedish authorities along the Delaware, New Englanders continued to stage visits to the river. In the summer of 1644 William Aspinwall and a company of investors from the Massachusetts Bay Colony organized an expedition to discover the source of "the great trade of beaver, which came to all the eastern and southern parts."[98] They, like so many others before them, speculated that the Delaware River led to a "great lake." Although authorities in the Bay Colony were at first unwilling to give their sanction to the effort, they eventually provided the company's members with a commission and issued them "letters from the governour to the Dutch and Swedish governours."[99]

The endorsement from Massachusetts Bay's officials appeared to have the desired impact on New Netherland's authorities. When Aspinwall and his cohorts landed at New Amsterdam, Governor Kieft merely issued a protest but did not stop them from proceeding. Unknown to the New Englanders, however, he had secretly sent orders to Fort Nassau to sink the ship if it attempted to go beyond the fort. There would be no need to do so. According to John Winthrop, when Aspinwall's ship "came to the Swedes [at Fort Elfsborg], the fort shot at them, ere they came up." Forced to anchor, the ship could go no farther. Later Aspinwall met with Printz, to whom he "complained of the lieutenant's ill dealing, both in shooting at them before he had hailed them, and in forcing them to weigh anchor on the Lord's day." According to Winthrop, although Printz supposedly admitted fault in both cases and "promised all favor," the "Dutch agent" from Fort Nassau soon came downriver, brandishing an order from Kieft that instructed him to block the vessel's progress. The final insult came when Printz's lieutenant permitted the voyagers to depart only after they had paid forty shillings for the shot that he had fired at them.[100] Printz's account differed somewhat from Winthrop's. He claimed that he had allowed Aspinwall's ship to proceed upriver but that New Netherland's men had stopped them at Fort Nassau.[101] If the Swedish governor had hoped to avoid English blame for this subtle maneuver, he had failed.

For the moment Printz had the power to stop these English incursions. But his use of this power profoundly disturbed New Sweden's native allies along the river, who were directly affected by his colony's actions. The depth of their alienation became clear in early March 1644, when, shortly after the Swedish ship *Fama* landed, Lenape fighters committed a series of murders against New Sweden's inhabitants. Printz had "told them the whole year that we shall receive [many] people with our ships, but . . . [when] they observed that there was only one ship and no people, they fell in between Tinnakungh and Uplandh [i.e., between Tinicum and Upland] and murdered a man and a wife in their bed, and a few days afterwards they killed two soldiers and a workman."[102] The attacks might have continued, but Printz's decision to gather the outlying settlers caused sachems on the river to come together "from all places" to deny responsibility for the killings. At the meeting the governor told them that if they "hereafter practised the smallest hostilities against our people then we would not let a soul of them live." Although the Lenape sachems signed the agreement and offered gifts of beaver and wampum, Printz concluded that "they do not trust us and we trust them still less."[103]

The Swedish governor linked the killings to recent attacks in neighboring colonies. "The Savages here in West India set themselves up against the Christians in one place after another," he wrote. He described the effects of "Kieft's War" against the Munsee around Manhattan, which Printz claimed had led to the deaths of over a thousand colonists. In Virginia "several thousand savages" had joined together and "attacked and fearfully murdered over six hundred Christians"—the coordinated assault on Jamestown and surrounding settlements by the Pamunkey leader Opechancanough in 1644.[104] Just beyond New Sweden's own perimeter, the Minquas-Susquehannock were at war with Maryland, even managing to capture two cannon in battle. All this violence, Printz claimed, had led the Indians to become "very proud here in the river" too.[105]

The recent killings inspired Printz to imagine how, with sufficient military support, he could wipe out the Indians on the river, notwithstanding the fact that their supplies of maize kept his settlers alive.[106] "Nothing would be better than to send over here a couple of hundred soldiers, and [keep here] until we broke the necks of all of them in this River, especially since we have no beaver trade whatsoever with them but only the maize trade." If these natives could be swept away, then "each one could be secure here at his work, and feed and nourish himself unmolested without their maize, and also we could take possession of the places (which are the most fruitful) that the savages now possess; and when we have thus not only bought this river, but also won it with the sword, then no one, whether he be Hollander or Englishman, could pretend in any manner to this place either now or in coming times." With no other competitors on the river, Indian or European, the Swedish colony could monopolize the beaver trade with the "Black and White Minquas" and win four times as much of the trade. "Not a single savage would be allowed to live in this River," and the route from the Delaware to Manhattan, "three small days' journeys across the country," would be free for travel and trade.[107] Killing and dispersing the river's indigenous inhabitants, Printz claimed, would bring security as well as the benefits of increased commerce with their Christian neighbors. As Printz dreamed of a cosmopolitan coastline cleansed of its original inhabitants, he expressed his hope that in the future his beleaguered Dutch and English colleagues would not "press so hard . . . [and] be contented with what has passed." He hoped in vain.[108]

Bloody Threats

In the early 1640s New Netherland's officials did not actively resist the expansion of Swedish authority, even as they refused to give up the West India Company's claims to the Delaware Valley. They only tolerated the Swedish colony's presence because their own colony was at war with its Munsee neighbors.[109] By 1645 the war had nearly come to an end, and officials on New Netherland's "North River," the Hudson, could afford to be less congenial to their newly fortified rivals along the Delaware. In that year surveyor Andries Hudde became the commander of Fort Nassau. His task was to keep track of the ways the Swedish colony hurt the WIC's interests and to prevent its expansion. Shortly thereafter, the WIC recalled his superior, Director General Kieft, to account for his role in the disastrous war with the Munsee. Kieft's successor, Pieter Stuyvesant, would push New Sweden to the point of collapse.

Stuyvesant arrived as the director general of New Netherland in May 1647. He, like Kieft, sought to maintain good relations with English officials at his colony's eastern frontier so he could rein in New Haven's aggressive expansion. He also wanted to strengthen New Netherland's authority at its southern edge. In both efforts he succeeded. He negotiated a treaty with New England's officials that gave away most of New Netherland's eastern territorial claims—by now rendered moot by expanding English settlement—but at last established a provisional border between the two colonial regions. The Hartford Treaty (1650) also served to delay the transfer of their sovereigns' mutual antagonisms, which soon erupted in the First Anglo-Dutch War (1652–54).[110] Meanwhile, Stuyvesant expanded upon Hudde's and Kieft's earlier attempts to reclaim the Delaware Valley's fur trade and to block the expansion of New Sweden. His most important allies in this effort would prove to be the region's native headmen, who turned to the leaders of New Netherland to counter the Swedish colony growing in their midst.

Hudde began compiling evidence of the misdeeds of New Sweden's officers soon after his arrival as commander of Fort Nassau in 1645. In the fall of 1648 he traveled to New Amsterdam in order to provide Stuyvesant with a lengthy report of his wranglings. His report depicted New Sweden's officials, especially Governor Printz, as intent on monopolizing the river's fur trade, seizing territory that belonged to New Netherland, and humiliating the Dutch colony's officers and servants. The account he presented to Stuyvesant in 1648 reveals just how vituperative these face-to-face meetings could be. His report also shows that Europeans and Indians alike saw their different communities as nations contending for control of this space.

The first clash that Hudde described took place in the summer of 1646. It began when a trading vessel from New Amsterdam sailed into the Schuylkill River to trade with the Minquas-Susquehannock, the main suppliers of furs in the Delaware Valley. New Sweden's men had built several blockhouses in the area to prevent outside access to this trade. "Consequently there are no places open to attract these Minquas," Hudde wrote, yet without this trade "this river is of little importance."[111] Posted nearby were Swedish officers who confronted the ship's supercargo, Jurriaen Blancke, and demanded that the vessel "leave the [Swedish] Crown's territory." Several heated exchanges between Dutch and Swedish officers followed. Placing their dispute in an imperial context, Hudde warned the Swedish colony's officers that "the alliance between Their High Mightinesses [the Lords of the States General] and Her Royal Majesty [the Queen of Sweden] should be kept in mind here." A miscalculated act of aggression could have wider repercussions in Europe. Printz eventually declared that the Dutch merchant could trade if he remained on the Schuylkill, but Blancke decided to depart for fear that New Sweden's officials would confiscate his vessel and cargo.[112]

Printz also undermined the Dutch in less obvious ways, as Hudde discovered on a journey upriver to look for mineral specimens. A sachem named Wirachkehon stopped the Dutch commander at the falls of the river

(Trenton Falls) and prevented him from proceeding further. When Hudde asked why the sachem would not permit him to go upstream, Wirachkehon replied that he had learned that New Netherland's men were planning to massacre all the Indians in the area. According to Wirachkehon, Printz had told Meer Kadt, a sachem who lived near Tinicum Island, that the Dutch were planning to build a fort upriver so that "with the expected ships 250 men were to be sent here from Manhattan, and they were to kill the Indians from the lower to the upper [Delaware] river, and that the men, who would be stationed in the house which we intend to build up there, would turn back the Indians above so that none could escape." The proof that the Dutch were going to do this, Wirachkehon said, was that "we [the Dutch] would come up with a small vessel to inspect the place there, and we would kill two Indians in order to obtain a pretext." According to Wirachkehon's story, Governor Printz had promised to protect the Indians and fight the Dutch; he had told Meer Kadt that he "would not allow it, rather he wants to drive us [the Dutch] out of the river." Printz's stories seemed to have worked. Describing his attempts to travel upriver, Hudde said he had "tried various means to proceed . . . [but] was repeatedly barred and as often met with the aforesaid reason." Hudde had to give up his plans. Kieft's brutal war against the Munsee around Manhattan had spoiled the Netherlanders' reputation as a nation. Meanwhile, by manipulating Indians' perceptions of the Dutch, Printz had successfully positioned himself as an ally to the Lenape nations along the river and framed the Dutch as their mutual enemies.[113]

Printz's officers continued to harass Hudde and other representatives of New Netherland. In September 1646, when Hudde arranged the purchase of a stretch of land (later known as "Wicaco") across the Delaware River from Fort Nassau, another series of disputes began. Although the land's indigenous owner—"Megkirehondom, sachem of Pemipagha"[114]—escorted Hudde to the place where "the arms of the honorable Company were attached to a pole and set in the ground," New Sweden's officials tried to block settlement at the location. Under orders from Governor Printz, commissary Hendrick Huygen dismantled the posted arms and exchanged angry words with Hudde. One source of contention was that Hudde had arrested and briefly imprisoned Gregorius van Dyck, New Sweden's Dutch quartermaster, after a previous confrontation regarding the purchase. Hudde threatened the two men with even more severe action if they continued, saying that he himself would "carry out punishment as one is accustomed to inflict on such troublemakers."[115]

The cycle of protests continued. Printz responded with a long letter of warning to Hudde, demanding that he "immediately abstain and desist from the offenses" that he had committed against the Queen of Sweden. Through a litany of references to the queen, Printz sought, like Hudde, to emphasize the imperial significance of these confrontations. He argued that Hudde's "nation or masters" had no interest in coming into conflict with the Queen of Sweden over "such a trifle," particularly because Hudde lacked "the slightest justification for these rude actions against Her Royal Majesty."[116]

Hudde did not respond immediately to the Swedish governor's protest. In the meantime Printz had ordered his colonists not to trade with the Dutch along the river. At the end of October 1646 Hudde finally sent a reply in which he denied Printz's charges that the purchase was illegal. He said that he had purchased the land in good faith from its legitimate owner and that the "places we occupy, we occupy in rightful ownership." In fact, the WIC's servants had "occupied them perhaps before the South River was heard of in Sweden." Hudde added that New Sweden's commissary, Hendrick Huygen, had not only torn down the WIC's arms on the purchased land but had directed "many bloody threats" at Hudde and his men. Indeed, Huygen had vowed to Hudde that "even had it been the flag of His Royal Highness, the illustrious Prince of Orange, standing there, he would have trampled it . . . under his feet"—an affront that was all the more remarkable considering Huygen's own Dutch ancestry. Hudde asserted that these abusive words and actions concerned "not only my nation or masters but also the supreme authority of their High Mightinesses, the Noble Lords the States General, as well as His Highness the illustrious Prince of Orange, and the honorable directors who have been thereby insulted." Finally, Hudde cautioned that "we, who are Christians, do not ourselves become subjects of mockery to the heathen Indians." In these disputes over their sovereigns' rights and reputations, the "Christians" of the Delaware River risked exposing themselves to the ridicule of their "heathen" neighbors. Appealing to Christian fellowship seemed to be just as ineffective, however, as appeals to right and precedent.[117]

Hudde's quartermaster, Alexander Boyer, delivered the message to the Swedish governor, who then "took it from his hand and threw it over to one of his men who was standing near him, saying, 'There, take care of it.'" The man "picked it up from the ground and put it away," Boyer later reported to Hudde. When Boyer asked the governor for an answer to the letter, Printz's men "pushed [him] out the door." Printz was so enraged by the request that he took "a gun from the wall in order to shoot [Boyer], but was restrained." Verbal disputes were moving closer to open violence.[118]

Hudde's report offered a long list of Printz's offenses as governor of New Sweden. Printz intended to make the representatives of New Netherland "suspect before everyone; among the Indians as well as among the Christians." His abusive words toward the officers of the WIC were matched by his actions against "the subjects of the honorable Company, freemen as well as servants," whom Printz treated so poorly that "they return[ed] home bloody and bruised." Hudde accused Printz of urging the river's natives to attack Fort Nassau, as he claimed had occurred on May 12, 1647, when the Armewamese Indians who lived in the hinterlands of the fort sought to overrun it. Printz's repeated claims that the West India Company had no rights to trade or land along the river were ever more offensive. In regards to the WIC's claims of precedence, Printz had told Hudde (in the presence of the officer's wife) that "the devil was the oldest owner of hell, but that he sometimes admitted a younger one." Netherlanders may have been the first to claim the river, but that fact would not stop the Swedes from seizing everything the Dutch could not hold.[119]

Governor Printz viewed his rivalry with the New Netherlanders from a perspective that was, of course, very different from that of Stuyvesant and Hudde. In his report of February 1647 he insisted that removing the Dutch from the Delaware was of the "utmost necessity." The Hollanders, he wrote, were "destroy[ing] our trade everywhere," providing guns, shot, and powder to the Indians, encouraging the Indians to attack New Sweden, buying land from the Indians within New Sweden's boundaries, placing the arms of the WIC in territory belonging to New Sweden, and referring to Swedish territory as though it were part of New Netherland. "In short, they appropriate to themselves alone every right here, hoist high their own flags, and will not pay the least attention to H[er] R[oyal] Maj[esty]'s flags and forts, unless they are reminded [of it] by a couple of cannon shots." Printz claimed that some of the Dutch had even settled among the Minquas-Susquehannock in order to ensure that their trade did not reach the Swedish colony. He had protested these offenses to New Netherland's governor, but his complaints had had no effect, "for they see very well that we are weak here, and do nothing serious in the matter, therefore their malice against us increases more and more as time goes on."[120]

Printz hoped that the colony's new forts would "prejudice the trade of the Hollanders" and stave off their attempts to weaken the colony. The posts along the Schuylkill River were situated along one of the major routes connecting the Delaware to the inland areas where the Minquas-Susquehannock lived. In order for the "great traders, the Minquas" to reach New Netherland's Fort Nassau, they first had to pass the Swedish forts. Provided with sufficient cargoes, New Sweden could have monopolized the fur trade. Yet because the colony's sponsors in Europe had not dispatched any merchandise between 1644 and 1646, New Sweden's agents had been unable to participate in the trade. Since then, the Dutch had "drawn the principal traders (who are the White and Black Minquas) from us, [and] we shall be able only with great difficulty to regain them." The arrival of the *Gyllenhaij* from Sweden in 1646 permitted a brief revival of the trade. When the ship landed, Printz immediately sent two officials and some soldiers to the Minquas-Susquehannock to alert them of the arrival of new goods and terms of exchange more generous than those offered by the Dutch.[121] If only the colony were provided with sufficient settlers, workers, soldiers, and weaponry, Printz pleaded, "the Hollanders, as well as other nations," would recognize the Swedish Crown's commitment to its colony and return to their cautious and deferential ways.[122] But those days were over, and the European and Indian nations of the Delaware Valley acted accordingly.

The Consent of the Indians

The Minquas-Susquehannock, among others, did not simply stand by as the Swedish colony's officers sought to take control of their trade. In July 1647 "two chiefs of the Minquaas named Aquarichque and Quadickho" visited Willem Kieft, New Netherland's former governor, to relate Printz's promises to them. They reported that Printz had said that he could "sell them powder, lead, and guns enough, but the Netherlanders, being poor tatterdemalions, could not do so." He had told them that "the Netherlanders were bad and the Swedes were good men." Although Printz had requested permission from the sachems to set up a trading post in their territory, they said that they had refused him. Clearly, these Minquas leaders, if not all of the Minquas-Susquehannock headmen, were keen to encourage competition between the two sets of colonizers.[123]

Yet the Netherlanders had their own problems with the Indians along the Delaware River. Sometime during the fall of 1647 a trader or agent belonging to New Netherland beat to death a Minquas chief. Under suspicion was

Govert Loockermans, one of the colony's most active traders on the Delaware—and well-known for selling guns, powder, and lead to his native trading partners.[124] When Stuyvesant questioned the merchant upon his return to New Amsterdam, Loockermans claimed that he had merely threatened the chief because "the sachem had wounded the skipper, Andries, [in the] face with a pistol." Yet Stuyvesant later instructed Hudde to make amends with the Minquas "before it is thoroughly examined and the truth is discovered, which Govert Loockermans shall have to [deny]." Ultimately, Loockermans continued to trade on the river, but there is no indication that anyone else was suspected or punished for the sachem's death.[125]

Stuyvesant was keen to turn the Minquas-Susquehannock and their trade to New Netherland's side. In the spring of 1648 he gave permission to Peter Ebel, Claes Jansen, and Simon Root (a German, a Dutchman, and an Englishman) to travel to the "Minquas country" in order to trade there, "since the Swedes do the [same] and try also to [alienate] the savages from us."[126] Yet Stuyvesant was hesitant to send traders into territory where they were not actually welcome. He warned Hudde to send the men only if "the Commissary Hendrick Huygen or some of the Swedes go to the Minquas country." Stuyvesant was wary of upsetting this important and powerful nation even as he wanted to counter New Sweden's men.[127]

Although sachems from the Lenape and the Minquas-Susquehannock offered to continue trading with the Netherlanders, they expected generous treatment in return. "They say we must have a constant supply of goods at our place," Adriaen van Tienhoven wrote in the fall of 1648, noting that "they also ask for guns, powder, and lead." The terms of the trade were steep—like his Swedish rival, van Tienhoven complained that the trade had been "badly spoiled." Taking advantage of the competition, his Indian counterparts were demanding two fathoms of white wampum and one fathom of black wampum for every beaver, or one fathom of cloth for two beavers. Moreover, the savvy native traders, who measured the Netherlanders' goods in arm-lengths, chose "their largest men to trade," driving costs even higher.[128] Loockermans, writing to his employer, merchant Gillis Verbrugge, blamed the proliferation of small traders. They "go inland with their goods, and so make themselves the slaves of the *wilden*, which is entirely contrary to nature."[129]

Dutch and Swedish traders may have thought the fur trade had been "spoiled," but it seems to have suited the native occupants of the Delaware just fine. They actively sought to encourage it. In April 1648 several Lenape sachems along the Schuylkill invited Hudde to establish a trading post in an area where the Swedes were already building. They, too, hoped to disrupt the Swedish colony's attempts to control trade on the river. The sachems then "summoned the Swedes" to the location for the new Dutch post, where they declared that the Swedes should remove themselves from the area. They denounced New Sweden's men for "surreptitiously" coming to the place and occupying it "against their will." They informed New Sweden's officers that they were giving the land to Hudde "for the time being" and were permitting him to build there. Two of the principal chiefs at the meeting, Mattahorn and Wissemmenetto, "themselves planted the prince's flag there and ordered me to fire three shots as a sign of possession," Hudde wrote afterward. Later that evening Hendrick Huygen and seven or eight men from New Sweden visited the Dutch officer and demanded his justification for building at the spot. Hudde responded that he had acted by "order of my superior and the consent of the Indians." The sachems' active role in the affair suggests that they had consciously sought to employ Hudde and the Dutch as a counterweight to the overweening influence of the Swedish colony. They did so in part by manipulating the Europeans' own symbolic rituals of possession.[130]

The sachems who were attending the meeting heaped criticism upon Huygen and his companions. New Sweden's expansion had obviously upset these Indian leaders. They pressed Huygen to explain by what right the Swedes had built there. Was it "not enough that they occupied Moetinnekonck, the Schuylkil, Kinsessingh, Kakarikonck, Upland, and other places settled by the Swedes, all of which they had stolen from their people"? The colony's first commander, Peter Minuit, they said, "had purchased no more than a small piece of land at Paghahackingh in order to plant some tobacco," half of which was supposed to go to the land's true owners. They expressed dismay at the way that "they (pointing to the Swedes), by coming to them and buying one piece of land, should be able to take further all that adjoins it, as they (the Swedes) had done here in the river and still were doing." Hudde reported that the sachems were amazed that the Swedes "wanted to prescribe the law to them, the native owners, so that they would not be able to do with their own possessions whatever they wanted," especially considering that "they (the Swedes) had only recently come into the river and had already seized and occupied so much of their land." By contrast, the WIC's servants had "never taken away any land from them . . . [despite] frequenting here for over 30 years."[131] The natives of the Delaware had their own narratives of possession—and dispossession—and sought Dutch support to check the aggressive Swedish regime.

Hudde and his men began building a fort at the disputed location soon thereafter. They surrounded their blockhouse with palisades to prevent the Swedes from demolishing it, as Printz's soldiers had done to the previous Dutch trading post along the Schuylkill River. Before the fort was complete, however, Måns Kling, the lieutenant at the Swedish fort on the Schuylkill, marched to the fort with twenty-four "fully-armed men with loaded weapons and burning matches." According to his own account of the incident, Hudde did not back down when presented with these threatening visitors. When Kling asked Hudde whether he intended to proceed with the building of the fort, Hudde replied, "What has been started must be completed." Kling then ordered his men to put aside their weapons and to cut down all the trees around the fort, presumably in order to delay its construction.[132]

Despite continued protests from New Netherland's officials, Printz continued to resist their attempts to send traders and freemen to the Schuylkill. When Dutch trader Hans Jacobsz began to build along the river—part of a larger effort to reach the "Minquas' country"[133]—Printz sent his son, Gustaf Printz, to command Jacobsz to dismantle what he had built. When the settler refused, the younger Printz "did it himself by burning it down, and threatened that if [Jacobsz] came there again to build he would be sent away with a beating." An Englishman who wanted to settle along the river under the authority of New Netherland received similar treatment from New Sweden's officials. Thomas Brown—"Tomes Broen" in Dutch sources—was at the same location for about three hours, Hudde wrote, when the "Swedes" under command of officer Gregorius van Dyck arrived, tore down what Brown had built, warned him to leave, and threatened to "drive him off with a beating" if he returned.[134]

Hudde was obliged to go to New Amsterdam in the autumn of 1648 to report to Stuyvesant and to answer certain charges made against him. While he was away, Printz ordered the construction of a fort directly in front of Fort Beversreede, the new Dutch fort. The Swedish fort was not especially large—Alexander Boyer, Hudde's quartermaster, said it was thirty to thirty-five feet in length and twenty feet wide—but it blocked access to the Schuylkill River in a provocative, even ludicrous fashion. It was placed so that when Dutch vessels "come to anchor there under the protection of the fort, . . . [the Dutch] fort can scarcely be seen." The Swedish fort was intended "to mock our lords," Boyer said, as demonstrated by the fact that the rear of the

Swedish stockade stood only twelve feet in front of Fort Beversreede's front gate.[135] The Swedes even planted corn around the Dutch fort so that there was not enough land to keep a "small garden."[136] The reason Printz could get away with such outrages was clear enough—at the time only "six able-bodied men capable of bearing arms" were posted at New Netherland's two forts along the Delaware River.[137] In the face of such weakness Printz had no reason to expect anything but continued success in his contest with the Dutch.

After Hudde returned to his post, New Sweden's men assaulted the short-handed Fort Beversreede under the cover of darkness. Hudde wrote that "one of the Swedish servants named Pieter Jochim contemptuously pulled the palisades of Fort Beversreede apart and broke through them, making use of great insolence by words as well as deeds." The Swedes also attacked a nearby house constructed by Dutch settlers, tearing it down "with great force, chopping the timbers to pieces."[138] Hudde later complained to Printz about the attack, which his subordinate had accomplished with "hacking and chopping until nothing was left . . . [while] directing shameful, scornful, and abusive language towards those who were seeking to carry out their master's orders." According to testimony taken after the event, the Swedish lieutenant in charge, Sven Skute, had told them that he had orders "not to allow even a stake to be planted in the name of Their High Mightinesses, but whatever had been set up *de facto* to trample under foot." When Hudde presented him with a protest against the action, Skute declared that Hudde was "a villain and a scoundrel, and had nothing to do with [the Swedes'] government." Alexander Boyer then replied to Skute, "You must be a villain yourself to abuse a man behind his back so that he cannot answer for himself." Upon hearing these words, Skute "grabbed the aforesaid Boyer by the hair, but they were prevented from coming to further blows."[139] As Adriaen van Tienhoven later wrote, "The Swedes do here whatever they please."[140]

By excluding and underselling New Netherland's traders, Governor Printz had managed to expand New Sweden's influence, but he had also alienated his native neighbors. According to a later account, in April 1649 Printz attempted to purchase lands upriver of Fort Nassau from their Indian owners. Describing his own efforts to block Printz, Hudde wrote that Printz had "labored greatly among the Indians" to purchase these lands but that "he could not persuade them."[141] The owners of the land were willing, however, to sell it to Hudde and New Netherland's freemen on the river. Stuyvesant approved of Hudde's decision to join with the freemen in buying the tract in question, and he encouraged his subordinate to purchase additional land on the east side of the river "from the Narraticonse Kil to the bay, while the Indians are offering it for sale, in order thereby to exclude others."[142] So, even as Printz was "pressuring the Indians heavily" to sell lands on the east side of the river, native communities there continued to cultivate the Dutch as a counterweight.[143] Without regular voyages from Sweden, Printz had little leverage to persuade native leaders to do otherwise.

No additional support reached the colony during the next several years, despite Printz's repeated pleas for assistance. When Printz wrote to Per Brahe in August 1650, more than two years had passed since the last vessel from Sweden had visited the colony. Stuyvesant had just informed him that a Swedish ship on its way to the colony had been "seized and confiscated by the Spaniards at Puerto Rico, and that the governor and his family were being held in detention."[144] Hans Amundsson, Printz's long-awaited replacement, would never arrive.[145] In the meantime no further communication from Sweden had come. Nonetheless, the colony seemed to have a stable, if limited, foundation. In 1647 the total population was over 180, and Dutch and English traders offered for sale "everything which one's heart may desire," even if it was at three times the normal price.[146] The freemen were producing good harvests of rye and barley, they had planted "orchards with splendid fruit trees," and their cattle "increase and multiply greatly," Printz wrote. All they lacked were servants and wives.[147]

Yet the West India Company now monopolized trade on the river, and without a ready supply of goods, New Sweden risked falling out further with its Indian neighbors, who had turned decisively to the Dutch. "All the trade has this year been in the hands of the Hollanders, for we have had no cargoes at all," Printz wrote, "and as long as we are without cargoes, we must fear the Savages."[148]

The Great Sachem of the Manhattans

Within a year of his arrival Stuyvesant had begun plotting against the Swedish colony. Secret plans to make a show of force in the spring of 1648 came to nothing, however, when contrary winds and rumors that "the Northern Indians were gathering against us and our nation" prevented him from making the voyage.[149] More important, his aggressive and populous neighbors in New England continued to threaten New Netherland. In June 1649 Stuyvesant wrote in a panic that he had heard several reports from the

"English as well as our own nation, that the English are preparing five or six ketches or vessels to seize control of the South River under English commission or on their own authority." An English incursion into the Delaware Valley was worrisome in its own right, but it also endangered New Netherland's core settlements in the Hudson Valley. "If the people of this nation were to go [settle] there," Stuyvesant wrote, "they would not only steal this river from us and the Swedes but would also attempt to occupy, from behind, this [North] River between the [Rensselaerswyck] Colony and this place, and thus divert the entire trade and separate the Colony of Rensselaerswyck from this place." The director-general was so worried that he even authorized Hudde to cooperate with Printz in blocking the effort.[150]

In the meantime New Netherland's officers had been busily engaged in diplomacy with New England's officials to address their contested boundary. The product of their successful efforts, the Hartford Treaty of 1650, settled existing disputes by ceding to the English virtually everything their settlers already occupied.[151] Now that his eastern border had been secured, Stuyvesant could turn his attention once more to the south. In his dealings with New England's officials Stuyvesant had relied on diplomacy. Facing off against New Sweden's officials during the 1650s, he employed threats of force.

Aiding him were members of the Lenape and Minquas-Susquehannock who wanted to restore the balance of power on the river. Throughout the 1640s they had played Dutch and Swedish agents against one another, and they continued to do so. In a letter from July 1650 Stuyvesant reported giving guns, powder, and lead to an unnamed person who appeared to have been a Minquas leader. This leader suggested that loyalties in Minquas country were "divided in half . . . half for the Swedes, while he and the others were for our nation." The representative of the Dutch-allied Minquas said that the Swedes had won the other side's affection through gifts of "powder, muskets, and lead" and that he had come to Stuyvesant to give him the opportunity to provide them with the same. Stuyvesant acknowledged that "by giving the muskets, blame will be earned by me and the Company, however, it could not be otherwise at this time."[152] The price for Indian alliances was now higher.

As Stuyvesant consulted with native leaders, he revisited his plans to confront the Swedish occupants of the river. Printz observed the first sign of Stuyvesant's intentions in May 1651, when "a vessel well manned and equipped with cannon, arrived from New Netherland and stationed itself . . . below our Fort Christina and thereby closed the River so that no vessel at all could go up and down unmolested." The Swedish governor responded by sending an armed yacht against the larger vessel. This action reopened the river, as the captain of the Dutch ship chose not to engage the Swedish yacht. The failure of this gambit seemed to convince Stuyvesant that a more vigorous show of force was necessary. Six weeks later he traveled overland with 120 soldiers from New Amsterdam to the Delaware. At the same time, eleven ships from New Netherland sailed into the river from the south and met the governor's men at Fort Nassau.[153] Together they formed a force as large or larger than New Sweden's entire population. Knowing that the Swedish colony was too weak to respond, Stuyvesant and his small fleet sailed up and down the river, "drumming and cannonading."[154]

Stuyvesant did not confront the Swedish colony directly. Instead, in early July 1651 he called for a meeting at Fort Nassau with three of the river's sachems, "Mattehoorn, Pemenatta, and Sinquesz." Their spokesman, Mattahorn, had extensive experience negotiating with European colonizers. He had participated in the original sale of land for New Sweden in 1638 along with four other sachems of the "Ermewormahi" (Armewamese) and the "Mante and Minqua nations." In 1648 he had granted land to Hudde at the Schuylkill River and had chastised the Swedish for making illegitimate claims to his territory. Now he was being asked to testify to the true history of the land that New Sweden's officers claimed. The history they told together was a history of nations.

With Alexander Boyer serving as the interpreter, Stuyvesant proposed a number of questions to the sachems. He first asked whether the sachems were the "Chiefs and Proprietors" of the lands where the Swedes had settled. Mattahorn answered that "they were great Chiefs and Proprietors of the lands, both by ownership and descent and appointment of Minquaas and River Indians; wherefore they had power to sell and to make over the lands; and what they did that should be done and remain." Stuyvesant then inquired how much land the Swedes had purchased from the sachems along the river. Mattahorn replied by asking Stuyvesant why he did not address these questions to the "Sachem of the Swedes." Stuyvesant responded that he had invited Printz, but the Swedish governor had chosen not to attend. Mattahorn then told Stuyvesant that "all Nations coming to the river were welcome to them, and that they sold their land indiscriminately to the first who asked it." Mattahorn added that the people of the "Dutch nation" were the earliest visitors and discoverers of the river as well as the first to settle along it. The Indians of the river had always maintained "good friendship and commerce with the Dutch," as was evident from the history of gifts they had exchanged with one another.[155]

Mattahorn's indirect response to Stuyvesant's questions about Swedish territorial claims caused the governor to rephrase and repeat his query. Stuyvesant explained that "it was neither his nor his nation's custom to buy or occupy any lands which were rightfully bought and occupied by any other nations; he, therefore, requested, before proceeding to purchase any more lands, first to know what lands the Swede had bought, and of whom, and what lands were now free, and who were the right owners." Mattahorn replied that when Peter Minuit first came to the river in 1638, Minuit had requested of him "as much land as Minuyt could set a house on, and a plantation between six trees," which Mattahorn had agreed to sell to him. Yet Minuit had not followed through with the terms of the sale. Mattahorn further declared "that neither the Swedes nor any other nation had bought lands of them as right owners, except the patch on which Fort Christina stood, and that all the other houses of the Swedes, built at Tinnecongh [Tinicum], Hingeesingh [Kingsessing] in the Schulkil and at other places were set up there against the will and consent of the Indians, and that neither they, nor any other natives had received anything therefor." Printz had purchased other lands farther north, but according to Mattahorn, those lands did not belong to the sachems who had sold them. "The land which the Swede at present occupies, was bought neither by him nor by any other nation," Mattahorn attested, "except where Fort Christina stands" and at the Schuylkill, where an agent from New Netherland had purchased a piece of land seventeen or eighteen years ago.[156]

Stuyvesant pressed the sachems to declare whether they were the rightful owners of the lands currently occupied by the Swedes along the western shore of the Delaware River and whether they were willing to sell those lands to the mouth of the river. The sachems replied with their own questions: "If we sell the Great Sachem of the Manhattans the land from the Schulkil down to the Bay, where then will the houses of the Swedes remain? Will the Sachem of the Swedes, then, not do us harm, on that account, or put us in prison or beat us; thus making, through fear, some [sachems] scruple to sell the intermediate lands occupied by the Swede[?]" The director-general told Mattahorn and his fellow sachems that they need not fear violence from Printz. Assuring them that "he was not disposed to make any trouble nor to buy any lands that were purchased by the Swede or any other nation, but what were free and unsold," Stuyvesant then asked a final time whether the lands along the western side of the Delaware from the Minquas Kill, or the Christina River, to the mouth of the river were "free and unsold" and whether the sachems were willing to sell them. The exasperated sachems responded, "Why, Sachem, do you ask that question so often? We told you the lands are not sold to any person."[157]

After consulting with one another, the sachems finally said, "The Swede builds and plants, indeed, on our lands, without buying them or asking us. Wherefore should we refuse you, Great Sachem, the land?" Rather than sell Stuyvesant the land that he desired, however, the sachems resolved to provide it as a gift, so that they would not incur his displeasure "should the Swedes again pull down the Dutch houses and drive away the people." Pemenatta, the proprietor of the territory in question, then formally presented the land to Stuyvesant, requiring in return that "whenever anything is the matter with his gun, it shall be repaired for nothing, and when he come empty among our people, they shall remember [to give] him some maize, and again a token of friendship."[158]

When Printz learned that "Peminacka and his friends" had given the land south of Fort Christina to Stuyvesant, he summoned the heirs of the sachem who had previously sold that territory to the Swedish colony. The heirs claimed that Peminacka/Pemenatta only had hunting rights on that land and therefore had no right to sell it. The original owner, Mitatsimint, had sold the land to the Swedes, and "nobody else, whatsoever nation it be, had any right or pretension to it, to dwell upon it or to incorporate it." Mitatsimint's widow, Notike, and three of his children testified to the Swedes' right in a document drafted days after the sale to Stuyvesant.[159]

Printz dispatched a copy of the document to Stuyvesant, but the Dutch governor ignored the counterclaim. Instead, he and two hundred of his soldiers left Fort Nassau and sailed to the new site. "Tamecongh," or Sandhook, was located just five miles south of Fort Christina and the Minquas Kill. There Stuyvesant confirmed the purchase once more in a meeting with Mattahorn, Pemenatta, Sinquees, and a fourth sachem named Ackehoorn. At this meeting the sachems specified the limits of the territory, which extended "to the bounds and limits of the Minquaes country," and they asserted that these "lands were never before sold or conveyed to any nation in the world." Four Minquas sachems and thirteen New Netherlanders acted as witnesses to the sale. The Lenape sachems ceded the lands entirely, except for hunting and fishing rights, in exchange for various European goods, including guns and powder.[160] Shortly thereafter the sachem Wappanghzewan joined them, offering to give Stuyvesant nearby lands on both sides of the river. Although Printz had tried to buy these tracts from him a week earlier, "the Sachem now was not inclined to sell nor to convey to the Swedish Governor because said Governor, without acknowledging him as proprietor, had taken the land and had, against his, the Sachem's will, and without asking permission, settled it in part without offering him any satisfaction." With a "solemn" handshake and an ornate signature, Wappanghzewan gave his support to "the much respected General, the great Sachem of the Manhattans."[161]

Once completed, the new fort, "Casimir," gave New Netherland's officials the power to regulate trade and navigation along the Delaware River, much as Fort Elfsborg once had done for New Sweden. Stuyvesant used this newfound strength to assert New Netherland's authority. Writing to Axel Oxenstierna in August 1651, Printz described the current state of affairs. He claimed that Stuyvesant had ordered his forces to cut down the arms of the Queen of Sweden within New Sweden's territory and was now blocking outside commerce with the colony. Along with demanding customs duties from foreign traders who visited the river, the Dutch governor had seized vessels from Virginia and compelled them to pay customs on the trade they had conducted with the Swedish colony. Stuyvesant even had attempted to convince New Sweden's freemen to break their oath to the Swedish queen and to place themselves "under the Holland flag." If the settlers did not switch their allegiances, then Stuyvesant "threatened to drive them from their houses and homes." Finally, New Netherland's governor continued to draw away the trade of the Minquas and the friendship of the river's Indians, who now acted in "fear of his great power and the large number of his people."[162]

Stuyvesant's maneuvers also endangered New Sweden by encouraging English plans to take the Delaware River. "I am . . . [no] longer safe from the English," Printz wrote. In fact, Stuyvesant may have acted when he did in order to block yet another English attempt to place a colony along the river. In April 1651, two months before he and his forces left for the Delaware, a ship bearing fifty men from New Haven had stopped at New Amsterdam on its way to the Delaware River. Stuyvesant arrested the men and only released them when they promised not to proceed any farther, but he knew that he could not keep the New Englanders at bay for long. Printz, by contrast, asserted that New Sweden needed only "two good men-of-war" to be stationed at the colony for a few years in order to stop further affronts from "the Hollanders and the English."[163]

Printz's reports regarding the sad state of New Sweden did not bring about their desired effect, at least in the near term—the colony had not received any direct communication from Sweden since 1647.[164] Officials in the metropolis either lacked the political leverage to provide the support the colony needed or were preoccupied with Sweden's own military demands.[165] As a result, New Sweden's autonomy and reputation continued to slip away. Visitors "tell us at present to our face, that we do not belong to any government at all," Printz reported. "The Puritans treat us with violence and encroachment upon our rights," he wrote, "and the Hollanders . . . wrong us wherever they can and intrude upon us on all sides." The Dutch were attempting to turn the Indians against the Swedish colony and "hasten them upon our neck." The lack of support from Sweden was also destroying the morale of the colony's inhabitants and employees. No longer trusting that relief would come, many of the colony's employees had run away, and "the rest are daily on the point of leaving," wrote Printz. The governor claimed that if aid did not arrive soon, he would be unable to "hold them any longer, officers as well as common soldiers." Finally, although New Sweden's forts were still securely garrisoned, they were unable to prevent the "Hollanders" from placing large numbers of settlers freely on both sides of the Delaware River.[166]

Printz stayed on as governor for a year longer, until October 1653, overseeing the colony and about two hundred settlers.[167] Among the colonists the free farmers continued to do well for themselves, but those dependent on provisions from the colony, namely its soldiers and employees, were in much worse shape. In the spring of 1653 Printz wrote that the colony's servants sought every opportunity to escape, with or without permission. The trade with the English that once had supplied the colony's needs had disappeared since war had begun between England and the Netherlands. Worse yet, backcountry warfare between the "Arrigahaga" and the "Susquahannoer" had disrupted the supply of furs.[168] Since 1638 the Swedish colony's officials had been able to maintain peace with the river's Lenape nations, but without goods to trade, "there is no friendship any longer," Printz wrote.

For Printz the Dutch were still an annoyance, although they were no longer an immediate threat once the First Anglo-Dutch War had intervened. It had begun unofficially with English efforts to enforce the Navigation Acts in its colonial territories during the fall of 1651 and officially with a series of sea battles in the summer of 1652. Faced with the prospect of war with New England—whose officials enthusiastically welcomed the opportunity to invade New Netherland—Stuyvesant had consolidated the settlements along the Delaware around Fort Casimir, where about twenty-six families had settled. Their reduced strength ultimately gave the Swedish colony a chance to rise again. For even as Printz was sailing back to Europe on a vessel from New Netherland, new officials, soldiers, and settlers were on their way from Sweden.[169]

Friendship, Peace, and Concord

Six years before Printz departed, Charles Ondaaiondiont, a Catholic Huron, visited New Sweden with a party of "Andastoeronnons," or Minquas-Susquehannock. "Charles did not fail to tell them that he was a Christian, and requested them to take him to their Church, that he might perform his devotions; for he thought that it was like those in our French settlements," Jesuit Father Paul Ragueneau later reported. "They replied that they had no place set apart for their prayers."[170] Nor did the inhabitants seem especially pious. The settlement's young men, for example, behaved inappropriately toward some of the women in the party. Struck by what he saw, Ondaaiondiont "took occasion to speak, with zeal, of their indifference to their salvation and to reproach them because they thought only of the fur trade, and not of instructing the Savages with whom they are allied."[171]

As Ondaaiondiont discovered, trade was the key to New Sweden's relationship with its native neighbors in the Delaware Valley. Both Europeans and Indians recognized this as a fact as plain as the sun. Of course, trade need not have precluded conversion. Usselincx, for one, had predicted that commerce between Christian and heathen would work to spread the Holy Word. Yet there is little evidence to suggest that Indians in the Delaware Valley received much spiritual instruction, direct or indirect, from their partners in trade.[172]

Ondaaiondiont's reproach applied just as well to the other Europeans seeking a place along the river. The Puritan leaders of New Haven's "Dellaware Company," George Lamberton and Captain Nathaniel Turner, planted settlers at Varkens Kill in order to get a foothold in the fur trade. William Aspinwall's voyage of 1644, licensed by the government of Massachusetts Bay, came up the river in a fruitless search for the source of the "great trade of beaver."[173] Sir Edmund Plowden's efforts to establish New Albion were more self-consciously imperial in nature—he and his partners claimed in 1635 that it was a "great matter of state to have it planted"—but the colony's planners imagined that trade with the Indians would be one of its major sources of wealth.[174] The priorities of New Netherland's agents were no different. For years their sole outpost on the river was Fort Nassau, which could manage the seasonal trade well enough but did little to exclude rivals or to promote settlement. New Netherland's only settlers during the 1640s were a handful of freemen from New Amsterdam who wanted the colony's protection so they could participate in the fur trade. Several were not Dutch. Only after Fort Casimir was established in 1651 did Dutch settlers come to the river in significant numbers.

The one person on the Delaware River who seems to have taken seriously the task of conversion was Johan Campanius Holm, who accompanied Printz to New Sweden in 1643 and served six years as the Lutheran minister for the colony. During his time there Campanius compiled a vocabulary in the "Americaners Språk," the language of the river's Lenape inhabitants. Later in life he translated Martin Luther's *Der kleine Cathechismus* (1529) into the "American-Virginian language," which was published posthumously in 1696 in Sweden and then distributed in Pennsylvania.[175] Yet even Campanius was acutely aware of the importance of trade for the colony, as is apparent in a chapter of *Kort Beskrifning om Provincien Nya Sverige* (1702) titled "Pijri Simaeckan" (Conversation), which was essentially a long dialogue representing an encounter between a Swede and a Lenape. The *nitáppi,* or "good friends," exchanged goods and food, struggled over a knife, then concluded with a discussion of the Lenape speaker's impoverished state. The Swede's wares were revealed at the start of their conversation: *Zææband* (money, or wampum), *Aquijvan* (cloth), *Paxickan* (knife), *Tamhichan* (ax), *Hyperænn* (hoe), *Massáppi* (*Coraller,* or beads), and *Etzkans* (needles). Elsewhere Campanius followed a list of animal names with a short dialogue in which a Lenape offered deerskins in return for cloth, a kettle, linen, and shirts.

The trade was more than a simple exchange of skins for manufactured goods. An earlier chapter on the household included terms for guns, bullets, and gunpowder.[176] An accompanying vocabulary for the language of the "Myncqueser or Mynckussar" (Minquas-Susquehannock) was also in the form of a dialogue about trade. As answers to the question "Will you sell or barter something?" Campanius offered the words for cloth, shirt, stockings, and shoes, along with those for gun and sword.[177] Campanius's vocabularies reveal that by the 1640s selling guns to Indians had become a relatively routine practice in the Delaware Valley.[178] Some of this trade may have been illicit, but at times it was conducted with the full knowledge and support of colonial officials. If we are to believe their protests, officials permitted gun sales to the Indians only because their indigenous allies forced them to do so. Some Mohawks stated the matter bluntly, informing their Dutch allies that they "allowed the Christians to live there, because they should convenience them with everything, and otherwise the Christians might just as well cross the great water again."[179] If the Dutch did "not do what they wished, they threatened to kill the [farm] animals, and even the Christians."[180]

All of these agents of empire, Dutch, English, and Swedish, came to the Delaware Valley seeking trade. From the beginning they recognized that they needed the cooperation of the area's native inhabitants. Colonizers trumpeted their sovereigns' and their own authority over this space, but they all had to negotiate with the "rightful owners of the country" in order to realize their claims.[181] And indeed, virtually all of the colonizers active in the Delaware Valley shared the belief that the native inhabitants owned their lands.[182] Because Europeans offered this recognition of their autonomy and status, the native owners of the Delaware Valley were generally willing to accept all comers, whether they were Dutch, English, or Swedish. The clearest exponent of this principle of hospitality was Mattahorn, the sachem who told Stuyvesant in 1651 that "all Nations coming to the river were welcome to them."[183] The sachem's deeds demonstrated the truth in his words. He had sold land to Minuit in 1638, to Lamberton in 1642, to Hudde in 1648, and to Stuyvesant in 1651. Mattahorn may have been the most enterprising sachem among the "River Indians," but his fellow headmen also welcomed the competition. The frequent complaints from Dutch and Swedish officials about rivals "spoiling the trade" merely indicate that their Indian counterparts were negotiating good terms for the skins they sold.

When indigenous communities became discontented with one European nation, they knew they could turn to another. Minquas sachems Aquarichque and Quadickho visited Manhattan in 1647 to inform officials there that Printz had promised to supply them with weaponry while the Dutch could not. These sachems were inclined to support the Dutch regime, but they needed New Netherland's officials to show their generosity in order to counteract Swedish-inclined sachems within their own community. Among the Lenape, Printz's efforts to control trade provoked other forms of opposition. In 1648 Mattahorn, Sinquees, and Alebackinne sold a piece of land along the Schuylkill River to Andries Hudde in order to undermine Printz's efforts to control this crucial trading route. Two of the "most principal chiefs" at the sale, Mattahorn and Wissemenetto, personally choreographed a show of Dutch opposition so they could voice their own protests against New Sweden's expansion. If the point of the performance was not obvious enough, they made it clear when they excoriated New Sweden's officials for stealing their land.[184]

When protests failed, violence could follow. Printz documented a variety of hostile actions directed at New Sweden that were connected to rivals' visits to the river or to the colony's failure to satisfy its native hosts. Minquas who were upset with Printz's treatment of George Lamberton, for example, approached Fort Christina "in a very hostile manner" in 1643, setting off rumors that the New Haven merchant had "bribed all the Savages in order to murder us."[185] In the spring of 1644 Lenape men killed five settlers and soldiers belonging to New Sweden after it became apparent that Printz's claims of additional support arriving from Sweden were not true. The rivalry with New Netherland only added to the Swedish colony's difficulties. According to Printz, the Dutch encouraged the natives on the river to assault New Sweden.[186] In earlier years, of course, Printz had played the same game. In 1646 he had spread rumors that the Dutch were planning to massacre all the Indians on the river, and a year later Hudde accused him of inciting the Armewamese to attack Fort Nassau. Europeans knew their Indian neighbors had the power to destroy them—since the 1630s natives along the river had killed Englishmen, Netherlanders, and Swedes. They knew of the destruction of Swanendael and its thirty-odd settlers in 1631; they had heard accounts from Virginia and New Netherland of attacks that had killed hundreds during the mid-1640s; and they knew firsthand that nine settlers, soldiers, and traders had been killed on their own river in 1644 and 1645.[187]

An imaginative expression of these interconnected themes of nation, trade, friendship, and murder appeared in another dialogue that the minister Campanius set in the fall of 1645. In it the Lenape sachem "Matta Horn" (Mattahorn) consults with his son "Agga Horn" and an assembly of his people to consider whether to "go out and kill the Swedes and completely exterminate them" or to allow them to stay. The Swedes, or *Achoores,* had built forts and buildings on their land yet had no goods to sell and nothing to barter. Matta Horn asks his people for their advice: "What should we do with the Swedes? They have no cloth (red, blue or brown frieze) nor do they have kettles, brass, guns, gunpowder, lead—they have nothing that they want to sell to us. But the English and Dutch have all kinds of good merchandise." Although one sachem answers that it would be "good if one killed the Swedes because they have nothing in their stores that we can get trading with them," all the other speakers defend the Swedes or discourage acting against them. Others mention that the Swedes would soon bring a large ship full of good products and that they live in "good friendship" with the "Renàppi" (Lenape). Agga Horn points out, too, that "the Swedes are shrewd at waging war." Ultimately, Matta Horn announces that the native people of the country would "love the Swedes," treat them as their good friends, and trade with them always: "We shall not war against them and exterminate them."[188]

The Lenape in Campanius's dialogue chose love, not war. The Europeans who struggled over this territory also claimed that they preferred cooperation and good relations to threats and bloodshed—they, too, wanted cosmopolitan friendship to prevail. All of the officers involved in these disputes were commanded to avoid violence, and their letters to one another brimmed with friendly wishes. The correspondence between Winthrop and Printz in the mid-1640s is instructive. After Winthrop wrote to Printz in 1643 to protest Lamberton's treatment as "not only unusual but . . . [unworthy] of the name of Christian," Printz wrote back with a vigorous defense of his actions alongside expressions of friendship.[189] He noted in his response (like Winthrop's, written in Latin) that his "most gentle Queen" had instructed him to "nourish friendship, peace, and concord with all provinces" in America.[190]

Printz went to great lengths to defend his good treatment of the English settlers and traders on the river and to demonstrate his own personal affection for the English nation in general. He presented his case to Winthrop in the form of a remarkable list, noting at the start the "friendship and the bonds of a very friendly joined harmony between England and Sweden." The Swedish governor went on to describe the strong connection between their two nations in Europe, personified in his own case by the "very honorable" Englishmen who had served with Printz during his twenty-two years of military service. English generosity to the Swedes extended to the New World too. In the West Indies, Virginia, and New England "the bestowal of kindnesses on me was not very little," he wrote. Printz concluded by saying that, "If I should only repay such and other services and kindnesses of this extraordinary nation with insult and contempt, I would be worse than a barbarian brute"—here offering an implicit reference to the native peoples of America, who served as cultural foils for both men. Drawing his plea to a close, Printz urged Winthrop to ignore the claims of "that ruiner [Lamberton], who is so shamelessly eager to stain my innocence." Rather, he hoped that Winthrop would continue to "embrace and cherish friendship, peace, harmony and correspondence with my country Sweden."[191]

Winthrop's response, written during the spring of 1644, offered a different tone. He thanked Printz for his "very kind letter" and for "the spirit of good will and greatest friendliness therein displayed towards us and the English people." Winthrop promised that this spirit of goodwill and the "ancient and closest bond of intimacy between the English and the Swedes" assured Printz and all his men of good treatment "by us and the Englishmen who live in these lands."[192] A second letter written a month later expressed the wish that Printz's treatment of William Aspinwall, who was on his way to the Delaware Valley, would "correspond with your most friendly words" and thereby "lay the foundation of a mutual correspondence and friendship of no small use between us."[193] After Aspinwall came to the river—and was turned away by Dutch and Swedish officers—Printz wrote back that he had given the New Englander all possible assistance and aid but that Dutch authorities had stopped him at Fort Nassau. Printz's innocent pose apparently did not convince Winthrop, whose journal reveals that he assigned much of the blame to the Swedish officers on the river.[194] Notwithstanding his friendlier tone, Winthrop probably still mistrusted "this Swedish governour," who "demeaned himself as if he had neither christian nor moral conscience" and who was "a man very furious and passionate, cursing and swearing, and also reviling the English of New Haven as runagates."[195]

Winthrop's own impassioned words reveal that despite all their avowals of amity, the Delaware Valley's colonizers could not help challenging one another's claims and employing force, or the threat of it, to secure those claims. Underneath their calls for friendship and cooperation was a more basic sense of their difference, not simply as spokesmen for their individual colonies but also as representatives of their sovereigns and their nations. These opposing identifications were actually related. It was their very status as Dutch, English, and Swedish subjects that allowed colonial officials to consider one another "good friends" and allies, even as those national affiliations formed the basis for the rivalries and disputes among these "doubtful neighbors." Although they often appealed to a shared status as Christians that was not enough to prevent them from selling guns, powder, and shot to "heathen" trading partners. Protestantism, too, was a weak glue. Dutch, English, and Swedish officials proudly advocated and enforced their own orthodoxies while pouring disdain on those of their neighbors. Cosmopolitanism of every sort struggled under these conditions. In a world in which "the Law of Nations, and the Law of Nature, is the same thing," as Thomas Hobbes wrote in *Leviathan* in 1651, loyalties to sovereign and nation were more lasting. Yet even those loyalties had their limits during a "time wherein men live without other security, than what their own strength, and their own invention shall furnish them withal."[196]

4

Rebels and Good Swedish Men

On March 11, 1644, the *Fama* reached New Sweden after ten weeks at sea. Rumbling in its hold was the colony's future, packed and crated: 6,000 bricks, a ton of lime, 3 saws, 2 millstones, 8 grindstones, 2 stones for a hand mill, 5 anchors, 6 pumps, 20 augers, 4 compasses, 250 copper kettles, 200 barrels of flour, 20 barrels of salt, 10 casks of wine, a cask of brandy, several hundred yards of cloth, 10 flagpole knobs, 300 pairs of shoes, 200 pairs of stockings, and 147 shirts.[1] Several soldiers were also aboard the *Fama*, among them Anders Jönsson from Jönköping.[2] He had been recruited by Johan Papegoja, a young, high-strung nobleman who was returning on the *Kalmar Nyckel*, Peter Minuit's old ship, to court the governor's seventeen-year-old daughter. Papegoja was posted at Fort Christina—fifteen miles downriver from young Armegot and her father—while Jönsson and the other soldiers were sent across the river to Fort Elfsborg. They would be guarding the colony's newest and most important fortress, the symbol and instrument of Governor Printz's ambition to control the Delaware River.[3]

Situated on the east side of the river near the mouth of modern-day Salem River in New Jersey, Fort Elfsborg was well suited to challenge vessels entering the mouth of the river. But its marshy site made it a miserable place to live—and to die. During the previous summer its miasmas had claimed the lives of nine men; Jönsson surely wondered whether he would be the next to die at the fort nicknamed *Myggenborgh,* or "Mosquito Castle." Per Lindeström later wrote that it had such "an immense number of [mosquitoes] that they almost ate the people up." During the day the insects swarmed so that the men "could not see with their eyes," and at night they "could neither rest nor sleep" for all the mosquito music. The "continued stinging and sucking" made the men so sick, weak, and swollen that they appeared to have "some horrible disease." Perhaps if the soldiers had smeared themselves with bear grease, as their Lenape neighbors did, they might have suffered less—and smelled no worse.[4]

By the time Lindeström saw Fort Elfsborg in 1654, it had been abandoned for several years and was "totally in ruins."[5] The imaginative engineer blamed the insects, but it was really Peter Stuyvesant's construction of Fort Casimir in 1651 and New Sweden's slow, steady decay that had led its officers to give up the fort.[6] Just as Fort Elfsborg had become "dilapidated and abandoned," so had New Sweden, which had not received any support from Sweden since 1648.[7] Morale in the settlement had collapsed, and the governor was deeply resented by free settlers, soldiers, and company employees alike. Already some colonists had left or attempted to leave. Some headed west to the upper Chesapeake, where Marylanders were planting tobacco and needed workers. Others escaped downriver to the Dutch post at Fort Casimir or fled north to New Amsterdam.

Finally, in the summer of 1653 a group of freemen and soldiers confronted their governor. The protestors could not fault Printz for the failures of their fatherland, but they did blame him for depriving them of their rights and for abusing their fellow settlers. On July 27 they presented him with a listing of their grievances and informed him that they were sending two men to the Crown and the company "in the fatherland, to find out whether we are entirely disowned." They wanted to know once and for all whether the Swedish Crown intended to protect them.[8]

The twenty-two signers were among the most senior residents of the colony. A majority had been in New Sweden longer than Printz, and only one or two appear to have lived there less than ten years.[9] Other colonists were involved in the protest who had not attached their names. The most prominent among them was the colony's minister, Lars Carlsson Lock, who may have drafted the petition. The most unfortunate participant was the soldier from Jönköping, Anders Jönsson, whom the governor blamed for instigating the rebellion. On August 1, four days after Printz received the petition, Jönsson was executed before a firing squad of his fellow soldiers.[10] Printz left for Sweden two months later. Like John Falstaff, his literary double, Printz knew the value of discretion—and when to exit the scene.

The "mutiny" of 1653 revealed the fractured character of loyalties in New Sweden. The people who had committed their lives to building the colony were neither of one body nor of one mind. They varied in origin, status, employment, and their ability to bear the privations of frontier life. Their ranks included Swedes, Finns, Netherlanders, Germans, and even a handful of Britons. Some came as officers, others as free people, and many more as contracted employees or soldiers. A sizable proportion had been sent over as punishment for a crime or some misdeed. Some lived and worked on their own farms, while others served as laborers in the company's tobacco fields or as soldiers at its forts. Yet their statuses often overlapped and changed over time. Some soldiers worked in the fields as part of their service to the colony, while they and other company employees often became free farmers once they had finished their contracts. Situation, as well as class, shaped relationships to authority and to the colony, but the most fundamental difference was between the officers and everybody else.

Each group relied on the colony in a different way. For the freemen and their families the colony's administration was useful so long as it preserved their lives, liberties, and properties. Their farms could usually feed them, but they needed guarantees of security in order to justify such difficult labor, especially given that the company actually owned the lands they worked. The soldiers and servants of the company, by contrast, were dependent upon officials for basic needs such as food and shelter. The governor's ability to purchase supplies from foreign merchants and their Indian neighbors was therefore essential to their survival—Printz had to cooperate with outsiders in order for the colony to sustain itself. By the early 1650s Printz could satisfy neither his freemen nor his subordinates—this they shared in common. Their allegiance was conditioned upon protection that their governor and their fatherland could not provide.

Printz resisted releasing the company's men from their service, and he denied indebted free settlers permission to travel. New Sweden's colonists freed themselves nonetheless. Settlers without their own lands knew that they could find refuge in neighboring colonies, where labor was in strong demand, their debts would be forgiven, and a hearty dinner was assured. Freemen who hoped to keep their farms had to consider whether cooperating with the English or the Dutch might serve them better than relying on their own distracted fatherland and its imperious but hamstrung governor. Outside rivals threatened more than the colony's territorial claims—they threatened to dissolve the ties that bound together the colony as a whole.

When reinforcements from Sweden finally arrived in the spring of 1654, those who still remained in the colony—some seventy in all—warily renewed their allegiances to the Crown and to their new commander, Johan Claesson Risingh. Joining them were the new arrivals, over two hundred sick and weary Finns and Swedes, as well as a group of settlers and soldiers from Fort Casimir, which Risingh's soldiers had captured. Risingh encouraged New Netherland's former subjects to place themselves under New Sweden's protection, and many had sworn oaths of loyalty to the new regime. Their fidelity was never guaranteed. As was the case with New Sweden's jaded old settlers, their allegiances would depend on officials' ability to defend the colony's expansive claims to the river.

Risingh tried to assure himself of the faithfulness of his people, but the colonists had their own judgments to make. They had seen support for the colony wax and wane as ships came and went, and they knew that they had to protect themselves against shifts of fortune. Their loyalties would stand at the center of the struggle to claim this contested space. Some chose patriotism, while others preferred accommodation. Many more suffered from the destructive effects of the rivalry.

Stranded in New Sweden

Johan Printz left Sweden in October 1642 expecting to be back in Sweden three or perhaps four years later. He realized that his new posting offered the opportunity to redeem his fallen military career, but he hoped that his term of penance would be short. He soon felt trapped. In July 1644, after just over a year in the colony, he asked his patron Per Brahe to consider his advanced age and the possibility of promotion when he returned to his "dear fatherland." Instead, he found that his superiors wanted him to stay longer. Then he heard nothing for years. By 1650 Printz had not had any word from Sweden in "two years and three months," and he wrote openly of his own imminent mortality: "I feel indeed myself and believe this strongly, that God will soon relieve me of all my distress, for I become weaker daily, and the longer [I live] the more inclined towards [the] earth." The governor began to see his service in New Sweden as a death sentence.[11]

Printz foretold his own doom, but the numerous freemen in the colony were managing well enough on their own. In 1650 they had produced enough of a surplus to sell a few hundred barrels of grain. The colonists who were still in the service of the company as workers, soldiers, and officers, on the other hand, "long[ed] and yearn[ed] with great desire to be released and to come again to the fatherland." Freeing them from their service was imperative, Printz warned, "so that they by chance in the future might not undertake something else"—that is, run away or revolt.[12]

Yet no word came. A letter to Axel Oxenstierna in August 1651 described Stuyvesant's construction of Fort Casimir and Printz's inability to resist with the men and resources he had. As though he were marking time on the wall of his cell, he wrote that "during three years and six months [I have] received no orders at all or assistance from the fatherland, but [I] am waiting daily for it with great anxiety." He, too, hoped to be set free from his bondage. "God knows how I here in these long years have suffered," he wrote. A year later Printz noted that despite sending frequent communications to Sweden over the past five years, "during the whole space of that long time and not to this day [have I] received a single letter, messenger or message from the fatherland." Worse yet, the condition of the colony was declining as each day passed without new support.[13]

New Sweden's isolation was as plain to outsiders as it was to the colonists themselves. The English and the Dutch "tell us . . . to our face, that we do not belong to any government at all," Printz wrote. Meanwhile, their Indian neighbors knew that the Swedish colony had possessed nothing to trade for a long time. The colony's weakness meant that "we day and night now have more to fear of them than they of us," a great reversal of fortune for the belligerent officer who once had dreamed of wiping out the river's native population. New Sweden's inhabitants had also given up hope in the face of pressure from English and Dutch rivals and the possibility of attack from the river's Lenape inhabitants. The colonists "now doubt altogether [the arrival] of vessels and of their relief (although I have assured them of it)," he explained. "Part of them have already run away and the rest are daily on the point of leaving, so that if aid does not soon arrive it is impossible for me to be able to hold them any longer, officers as well as common soldiers." A year passed, and the situation had deteriorated further. Although the freemen on their farms could provide for themselves, "the sustenance of the soldiers and others who still serve under the Company is very poor; [they] look every day for means and opportunities to get away from here," with or without his permission.[14]

In July 1653 Printz sent off another letter from New Sweden in which he noted, "I now in six years and a half have not had a letter or message from my fatherland." His outlook was still bleak, but the governor still held out hope for redemption. He had more at stake than his career, as he had been granted a substantial amount of land at Tinicum Island and was intent on reaping whatever reward he could from his long service. "God knows what difficult eleven years, and now soon twelve years, I have experienced among the heathens and a turbulent people, with so little assistance from the King-dom, yet done everything gladly, only I might have the grace and favor of H[er] R[oyal] Maj[esty] for it, wherefore I have always and in all my days strived and still hereafter shall strive, while I live."[15]

Printz eventually left the colony in October 1653—he was counting his twelve years of service from France, where he had arrived "with a leak-ing ship and half dead." Nonetheless, he offered to return to New Sweden if the Crown asked him to do so, though it is clear that he had no desire to go back. In a letter to Brahe he claimed that the colony was prosper-ing, notwithstanding the gloomy warnings that had filled his earlier cor-respondence. To the secretary of the company, Johan Beier, he was more frank about the state of the colony, which had had no contact with Sweden in five years. "No one of us Swedes, nor of the strangers, could any longer think that we were still dependent upon our dear fatherland or our gra-cious superiors," he wrote. The settlers had become "confused" and were "led astray by the Hollanders." By the time he had left, "they not only no longer wish[ed] to obey commands, but almost all of them [were] on their feet ready to commit as great an excess as they possibly [could] and then flee from there." Printz claimed that he had prevented the colony's collapse, however, and that he had convinced "the Christians as well as the Savages" that within a year either he or a ship from Sweden would return to inform them of the colony's status in Sweden.[16]

The Mutiny

The "rebels" who confronted Printz in 1653 represented a remarkable cross-section of New Sweden's population. One signer, Claes Johansson, came over with Peter Minuit on the *Kalmar Nyckel*, became a freeman on land across from Fort Christina, and seems to have resided in the colony until its very end. Most of the other petitioners had been there nearly as long. Sven Gunnarsson was sent to the colony as punishment in 1640 with his wife and two children. He was working in the company's tobacco fields near

Fort Christina in 1644, became a freeman in 1645, and later settled upriver at Kingsessing (along contemporary Cobb's Creek in West Philadelphia). On the same voyage was the signer Per Rambo. Born near Göteborg, Rambo started as a farmhand, became a freeman in 1644, then settled at Kingsessing, where after 1647 he lived with his Finnish wife, Brita Mattsdotter. Måns Andersson came on the same ship and served in the tobacco fields outside Fort Christina with Gunnarson, Rambo, and a third signer, Finnish glassmaker Mårten Mårtensson. All three were freemen by 1648.[17]

A number of the protest's signers came to New Sweden on a single ship, the *Charitas,* in 1641. Several had been sent to the colony as punishment for misdeeds in Sweden. The first name on the petition to Printz, Matts Hansson, belonged to a man who once had served as a soldier under Admiral Klas Fleming at Borgå/Porvoo in Finland but was sent to the colony because he had "committed some offense and must go along as punishment."[18] Another former soldier was Hans Månsson, who was arrested in 1640 for cutting down six apple trees and two cherry trees in the Royal Garden at Varnhem. Swedish officials allowed him to "choose whether he will go with his wife and children on our ship from Göteborg across to New Sweden or otherwise hang." He served for six years as a tobacco worker and later became a freeman.[19] Peter Kock had served as a soldier at Stockholm but was sent to the colony for some transgression. In 1644 he was a laborer on a tobacco plantation along the Schuylkill. Another of the signers, Henrik Mattson, joined him there. Mattson may have accompanied Kock on the *Charitas.*[20]

On the same voyage as the exiled soldiers were the Stille brothers, Olof and Axel. Olof, whom Printz accused of being one of the ringleaders of the rebellion, had a history of confrontations with his betters. A feud with his landlord's widow resulted in two jailings. The second came for breaking into the widow's castle, freeing a former servant from a dungeon, and waving a sword as he announced, "I defy you to come and take me!" This move earned him a death sentence, which was commuted for a large fine that he probably found impossible to pay. Three years later Stille came to the colony as a millwright with his wife and two children, seven-year-old Ella and one-and-a-half-year-old Anders. Olof's brother Axel, meanwhile, first served as a field worker but later became a freeman.[21]

Several other voyagers on the *Charitas* signed the petition. Matts Hansson was a gunner at Fort Christina until he became a freeman in 1646. His brother Anders was a regular soldier until he, too, became a freeman. "Lars Thommeson Bross" was a sailor aboard the *Charitas* who served on the colony's sloop during the 1640s and was a freeman by 1654. Others from the voyage included Evert Hendricksson and Oluf Ericksson, who were still serving as farmhands in 1648 but were probably freemen by 1653.[22] They may have been so-called forest Finns, who had been rounded up by Swedish authorities in the 1640s for pursuing slash-and-burn farming in Sweden's protected forests.[23] Later arrivals whose names were on the petition included Petter Jochim and Anders Andersson "the Finn," who came to the colony with Printz in 1643, and Valerius Loo, who sailed with Anders Jönsson in 1644.[24] In 1644 Jochim, Andersson, Loo, and Jönsson were serving together as soldiers at Fort Elfsborg. There was even an Englishman among the signers, "Johan Hwiler" (John Wheeler), who had married Catharine Lom, the daughter of a prominent Swedish settler. How Wheeler became attached to the colony is unknown, although the Loms, like so many of the protesters, had come across on the *Charitas* in 1641.[25] Wheeler and Olof Stille may have been the only men who signed the petition who had not been officially bound to serve the company.

The men began their petition to Printz by complimenting him and avowing their loyalty, calling him their "kind promoter" and promising "our obedient and faithful service . . . so long as we live." A long list of grievances followed. Most pressing was their safety. "We . . . are situated [so] that at no time or hour are we secure to our life and welfare," they wrote. Printz's policies had made life even harder. They claimed that the governor had "strictly forbidden us all trade with the heathen and the Christians." He threatened them with fines and capital punishment, even as he had engaged in his own private trade with outsiders.[26] He had denied them basic rights to "fishing waters, trees, the rye, the grass on the ground, and the land to plant on, from which we could have our sustenance." They had to pay to use the company's flour mill, which they had helped to build. Moreover, the governor had abused a number of Finnish settlers and their wives "without trial and judgment," so that some "have now lost their mind and soul . . . and must go with their small children and beg [for] bread."[27] Printz had dispossessed Anders Andersson of his land, and now his family was at risk of starving to death. Finally, the governor had denied them ownership of their property, saying that "all that we own belongs to him," even as some colonists had built up debts to the company that they could never repay. The petitioners had thus decided to send two men to Sweden to register their complaints against Printz and to discover whether officials there intended to support the colony.[28]

Six days after they presented the petition and two days after the soldier Anders Jönsson was executed, Printz responded to the petitioners in writing. Point by point he refuted their charges. Security against the Indians was never certain, though he hoped that the "tumult" that had led to the petition and the "treachery" (*förräderij*) by Jönsson would never occur again. He acknowledged that the fur trade with the Indians was not open to the settlers, although he said that he had never forbidden trading tobacco with foreigners. Nor did he deny them use of the colony's waters and lands except for two islands that had been set aside for his own residence. Printz claimed that the mill was open to their use, that they had not actually paid any toll for the past two years, and that their debts should have been paid long ago. As for the Finns he was said to have abused, Printz noted that Anders Andersson had suffered a legal judgment against him, whereas the Finnish couple Lasse and Karin had been condemned for witchcraft and separated from the rest of the settlers. Indeed, Printz thought he had been rather generous to the pair, as their debts were three times as great as what their farm was worth. Finally, in response to accusations that he had imposed forced labor on them, Printz proposed that after careful examination they might receive some compensation in the future. Regarding the petitioners' plan to send two men to Sweden, Printz was defiant, saying, "The sooner the better." After all, he intended to join them.[29]

The Aftermath

Two months later Printz was gone. New Sweden's settlers were not wistful. Almost immediately after the governor left the colony, New Netherland's director general, Pieter Stuyvesant, wrote to his superiors in Amsterdam to inform them that the "Swedes on the South River would be well inclined to repair among us, in case we will take them under our safeguard."[30] Stuyvesant ultimately declined the settlers' offer, as he did not have explicit permission to incorporate them as a group. Some settlers fled to Dutch jurisdiction anyway. Måns Andersson, Axel Stille, and John Wheeler, for example, joined a group of Swedish freemen who had settled around Fort Casimir.[31]

Anders Hansson and Valerius Loo took off for Maryland. They were following in the footsteps of settlers who had already left New Sweden for English protection. Hansson may have fled to Maryland once before—on April 5, 1652, he and three others at Kent Island had sworn an oath of loy-

alty "to the Commonwealth of England, without King or House of Lords."
The other two men's names appeared as "John Errickson" and "Andrew Anderson." The former was almost certainly Johan Ericksson, who had come
to New Sweden aboard the *Charitas* in 1641 and served as a laborer and a
soldier. He deserted in 1651, however, leaving behind him a huge debt of
1,017 guilders.[32] His name appeared frequently in the court records of Kent
County in subsequent years.[33] Anderson may have been the much-suffering
"Anders the Finn," dispossessed by Printz because of his extensive debts.[34]
Loo, whose name was usually recorded in Maryland's records as "Valerus
Leo," was a regular at Kent County's court during his brief time there. "Swan
Swanson" may have come with them; Maryland planters James Homer and
Henry Morgan sued him along with Hanson and Loo in October 1655.[35]
Swanson, or Sven Svensson, was the eldest son of Sven Gunnarsson, one of
the signers of the petition against Printz.[36]

According to the governor's replacement, Johan Risingh, fifteen men fled
the thinned ranks of New Sweden's settlers after Printz's departure.[37] Left
in charge was Vice Governor Johan Papegoja, who seemed to have learned
all the wrong lessons from his father-in-law and had hired some Indians
to track down the runaways. (Papegoja probably realized that his own soldiers would not accept the task—ten years earlier he had written that the
soldiers under his command carried "a secret hate towards me so that if
they would find a small fault in me they would possibly murder me.")[38]
The Indian trackers returned to Fort Christina with the heads of two of
the men.[39] The settlers understandably viewed Papegoja's actions as "too
severe," especially as they seemed to set a precedent whereby Indians might
"become accustomed to slaughtering our Christians"—something, Risingh
wrote, they were "only too willing to do." Risingh concluded that "if our ship
had not arrived, the majority of our people would have run away to Virginia
[i.e., Maryland] at the encouragement of evil folk."[40]

The new commander did not fault Papegoja or Printz. Instead, he attributed the unrest to the machinations of the English, who "claim the right
to this *Rivier* through the grant of King James." He also blamed former
settlers and employees who had left for Maryland and encouraged others
to join them.[41] Risingh would soon receive his own share of blame for the
colony's misfortunes. By taking Fort Casimir, he had given Stuyvesant and
the West India Company the casus belli they needed to justify an invasion
of New Sweden.

Reviving New Sweden

Risingh and about 350 colonists left Göteborg on February 2, 1654, in the middle of "a cracking cold winter" that had frozen their outlet to the sea. They were nearly trapped there but ultimately were able to hack through the ice and out to sea. The colonists had already suffered a great deal even before they had begun the voyage on the *Örn*. They had been forced to wait at Göteborg for eleven weeks before departing. Others had been turned away at the ship. Unlike on previous voyages, "persons of evil repute were mustered out"—there were to be no convicts and exiles among this group. In fact, there was so much demand that "about 100 families, good honest people, who had fine recommendations and a splendid reputation, had to remain [behind] in the [old] country with their wives and children, unable to get on the ship for want of room for such a great number." The consequences were tragic. "These people were very much to be pitied, because they had sold all their household articles, cattle and all their property and all that they possessed, turned it into money and necessary commodities [for the voyage]," engineer Per Lindeström recounted. Those who were fortunate enough to find space on board were mustered once more on January 27. On the deck of the *Örn*, as the Swedish colors flew overhead, they swore the oath of allegiance and promised to be "loyal and faithful" to their queen, to their fatherland, and to the company.[42]

These "faithful subjects and servants" soon discovered that they had left provincial Sweden and entered an arena of rival nations. During their passage through the English Channel three English warships confronted their vessel and demanded that the *Örn*'s captain come aboard. When the captain, Jan Jansson Bockhorn, a native of the Netherlands, voiced his refusal in Dutch and demanded the English captain visit his own vessel, the English ships fired several shots at them, one at the rudder and others that tore the tackling and the bowsprit from the ship. "Then they raised the red flag, presented their broadsides, and made themselves ready for action," Lindeström wrote. The English captain suspected that "we were concealing a Dutch ship under our Swedish flag," at a time when the war between the English and Dutch republics had not yet ended. Finally, Captain Bockhorn dispatched an officer bearing the ship's passport from Queen Christina to clear up the dispute. The English captain later apologized and "extended us his friendship, even permitting his people to bring water and other provisions" to their ship, which had to go to Dover to obtain a pass before it could proceed. Bockhorn, however, "was not kindly disposed towards the English" and refused the offer, ordering the ship to set sail. Ten days later the officers aboard the ship were able to enjoy the hospitality of their English counterparts during a stop at Falmouth Harbor. With their host, the vice governor at the port, they discussed the visit of the English ambassador Bulstrode Whitelocke to Sweden, and Risingh "expressed a wish for good friendship between our nations, which pleased both him and the others."[43] According to Lindeström, it was a noisy and boisterous affair—after each toast the English fired off a double salute, so there was "uninterrupted shooting from the time we began to drink the toasts during the meal and until we took leave in the night." The cannonade demonstrated the enduring friendship between the *svenske och engelske.*[44]

In the English Channel the *Örn* had taken fire, but the shots had merely grazed it. At Gran Canaria, in the Spanish Canary Islands, "three live shots were fired upon us and struck the ship."[45] Unaware that a little citadel near the capital was guarding the harbor, the Swedish ship had not given the proper salute. Again, Bockhorn went ashore to present his passport and to obtain supplies for the Atlantic crossing. The island's governor was a generous host, granting each officer the services of an African escort bearing a sunshade and treating them to a banquet of "100 dishes of sweetmeats" made from the island's fruit. The governor and the officers exchanged toasts to their respective monarchs and fired double salutes after each one.[46]

The city's inhabitants were less gracious. When the Swedish officers traveled through the streets, the locals threw stones at them, injuring many, until the island's governor interceded. The passengers on the ship were suffering much worse. "Our people, both the crew and passengers, were by now seriously ill and dying, and some also died there in the harbor," Risingh wrote. The contagion had been in full flower as they sailed past the coast of Portugal, where "many died and were cast overboard." New supplies poured into their hold, however: fish, oranges, lemons, potatoes, bananas, and fresh water, which were much more useful to the expiring passengers than the ballast stones they displaced.[47]

Despite gaining new provisions, within three weeks of their departure from the Canaries, over 130 people on the ship were sick, and the ship's council decided to sail to St. Christopher (St. Kitts) instead of New Sweden. The cramped conditions aboard the ship meant that disease spread rapidly and destructively. Passengers were struck with fevers and dysentery, especially women giving birth. "There was such lamentation and misery, yes, lamentation above lamentation, so that a person, even if he had a heart of stone would have felt sorrow and grief on account of the miserable condition," Lindeström wrote. At roll call in the morning, sometimes there would be "3, 6, 8, or 9 corpses" laid out on the deck of the ship. Their bodies were wrapped in sheets or skins, and weights were placed at their feet so that they might sink faster. After the minister performed a ceremony, their bodies were thrown overboard. Some among the living became so delirious that they tried to drown themselves. The men aboard the ship were able to save some who went overboard by day but "could rescue none of those who jumped through the portholes at night." Always eager to embroider his tale, Lindeström blamed the music of the "sirens," whose playing was so lovely that feverish passengers leaped into the sea.[48]

In mid-April the ships finally arrived at St. Christopher, where, once more, they were greeted with cannon fire until their national origin became apparent.[49] The English governor provided them with fresh supplies, and a rich planter hosted the officers on shore. Later Lindeström and Risingh rode eighteen miles under a burning tropical sun—on horses, according to Risingh, and on mules, according to Lindeström—to meet with the governor of French St. Christophe on the other side of the island. They wished to discuss the affair of the *Katt,* the ship that had wrecked off the coast of Puerto Rico in 1649. Some of the passengers had been taken to the French island of St. Croix, where they had been robbed and abused. The governor treated them "very politely" but denied that any of the people remained on the island. He promised, however, that "Swedes would be properly welcomed in all French settlements, would be free to trade there, and would be treated as brothers throughout French territory." Upon returning to the English part of the island, Risingh signed a contract with the governor there to exchange New Sweden's lumber and furs for the island's sugar and tobacco. Amid this conviviality those aboard the *Örn* remained so ill that Risingh purchased a large ox to be butchered and served to the distressed passengers.[50] Lindeström noted morbidly that even the sick Finns were able to hold down their food, eating "until they gave up the ghost, as horses and sheep do."[51]

More than a month passed before the *Örn* reached the entrance to the Chesapeake Bay, which the captain first mistook for the Delaware Bay. Meanwhile, passengers were dying each day. Finally, the *Örn* reached Fort Elfsborg on May 20, 1654 (Old Style), nearly four months after it had left Göteborg. Printz's prized fortress had decayed, but four freemen who came across the river from Fort Casimir gave the Swedish officers reason for hope. "The Dutch stayed on our ship overnight and were well satisfied with that," Risingh wrote. "They said that it did not matter who had the fort, as long as they could only remain free and secure in the territory."[52] The passengers aboard the *Örn* no doubt agreed, though they might have asked for security in their lives too. They had already seen a hundred of their number dumped into the sea.

Fort Casimir and the Freemen

When the *Örn* arrived at the mouth of the river, the soldiers and freemen at Fort Casimir could see the ship, but they could not tell "whether she was Dutch, English, or of some other Nation."[53] To investigate, Gerrit Bicker, the officer in charge, sent the four freemen to the *Örn* with Adriaen van Tienhoven, a local official in the settlement. Van Tienhoven had experience challenging Swedish claims to the Delaware River—six years before he had urged Stuyvesant to resist Printz's efforts to take control of the Schuylkill River.[54] As it was already evening when they set out, the men stayed overnight on the *Örn*. When they returned to shore at eight o'clock the next morning, they revealed that indeed it was "a Swedish ship, having on board a new Governor of the Swedes, and many other people . . . [and] that the Swedes intended to surprise and capture said Fort Casimir for the Crown of Sweden."[55]

The fort was poorly equipped to respond, possessing at most a dozen soldiers. The freemen were few—there were just twenty-one houses at the settlement—and unlikely to fight.[56] Stuyvesant had abandoned Fort Nassau a few years earlier, deciding to concentrate his men at Fort Casimir instead, so there were no reinforcements nearby. Moreover, officials at New Amsterdam had no men to spare because they were preparing to defend themselves against an imminent invasion from New England. The very day that the *Örn* arrived on the Delaware, Stuyvesant presented a list of propositions to the colony's council at New Amsterdam that revealed the depth of their desperation. "Nothing seems to be left," he wrote, "but to consider, how for the sake of our and the nation's honor, we ourselves may defend us against surprises and massacres." The colony needed to repair its fortifications, enlist troops, raise money for soldiers' salaries, and collect arms in order to resist the Puritans' attack. The director general even proposed bringing the soldiers at Fort Casimir to Manhattan and requiring the freemen at the fort to defend themselves. Stuyvesant had misgivings about this plan, noting that the inhabitants might not be able or willing to repulse an attack, especially as they were "in danger or at least fear to be massacred by the savages." The few settlers there had already requested additional soldiers to protect them, "or else they would leave the river altogether." Finally, he worried whether withdrawing the soldiers would be "equivalent to giving up absolutely the possession and . . . surrender[ing] that fine river to others." And if New Netherland's English neighbors did not attack New Amsterdam, "how shall we justify our abandoning it?"[57] He could not have imagined that Fort Casimir would face a heavily armed Swedish ship just a day later.

After returning from the *Örn,* the freemen and soldiers at the fort assembled to discover what their commander would do. Bicker, the fort's commander, seemed resigned to defeat. "What should I do? We have no [gun] powder," he replied. Three hours later Captain Sven Skute and Lieutenant Elias Gyllengren arrived with eighteen musketeers from the *Örn.* According to various witnesses, Bicker gave no orders to defend the fort. Indeed, by his own account he "welcomed [them] as friends." Accounts differ about what happened next, but soon Gyllengren's men rushed into the fort, where they disarmed the soldiers inside and took up positions along its walls. Risingh's account minimized the coercion involved, as his orders only permitted him to "force other nations from the territory . . . without hostilities."[58] Bicker, by contrast, claimed that Skute demanded the surrender of the fort "at the point of the sword" and that upon a signal from the Swedes' ship, the soldiers stripped his men of their arms and threatened "to fire at them, because they did not surrender their pieces."[59] By force or by consent Fort Casimir had fallen.

An inventory of the fort's armaments revealed that Bicker had been correct: inside the fort were "twelve iron cannon and one brass three-pounder, but no powder, nor ammunition whatever, except 1000 musket balls and 60 three-pound cannon balls."[60] Risingh later wrote that "the cannon which the Hollanders left are mostly useless."[61] Even if Bicker had wanted to resist, the fort would have been unable to fire its weapons. Testimony about the takeover revealed why. According to Jan Adamse, a twenty-eight-year-old corporal from the German city of Worms, the fort once had "plenty of ammunition." Yet he had overheard Bicker's wife, Aaltje, tell her husband it would be better to trade the gunpowder for beavers than to give it to the soldiers.[62] Consequently, each soldier only received three spoonfuls of powder, enough to fire his own weapon perhaps but little more.[63] The Indians' demand for gunpowder—and the Bickers' avarice—had emptied the fort of the most basic materiel for its defense.

New Netherland's last outpost on the Delaware had fallen, but the officers, soldiers, and colonists who had occupied this Dutch corner of the Delaware Valley still remained. Whether they would become loyal subjects of the Swedish regime was an open question. Even before Risingh's men seized Fort Casimir, the freemen who visited the *Örn* had given him reason to believe that Dutch settlers would accede to his rule so long as their rights were respected. Risingh, in turn, had extended an offer of "friendship to all the Dutch freemen." Later, during negotiations with Fort Casimir's commander, Risingh informed the freemen of "all the fine and fair conditions they would receive: freedom for their persons, property, work, religion, and the privilege of trading freely with Sweden." The WIC's men and their families would be free to stay or to go, with all their property, as they saw fit. If Bicker, his soldiers, or colonists decided to stay, they would have the same liberties as other Swedish subjects in the colony. According to Risingh, Bicker and the freemen accepted these conditions and accordingly promised to swear allegiance to the queen and the company.[64]

Bicker and the freemen came to Fort Christina two days later. According to Risingh, they all wanted to "be placed under Swedish protection in order to enjoy the freedom and rights" possessed by the Swedish population of the colony. The officers asked the assembled people "if they wished to be the loyal subjects of Her Royal Majesty and our honest neighbors and citizens," to which the settlers and officers "all assented with one voice, and there under the open sky swore an oath that they would be humble and loyal subjects of Her Royal Majesty in Sweden and in the territory behave as honest men with our patrons and colony." The scene of the oath swearing had the feeling of a celebration. The colony's new subjects were plied with food and drink and were in "high spirits." The former officers of Fort Casimir promised to act as loyal subjects to the Swedish regime too. Bicker "pledged an especial allegiance and well-willingness and offered to assist our people with the means that he had." Even Andries Hudde, New Sweden's longtime adversary at Fort Nassau, "promised that he would hereafter counteract the designs of Stuyvesant in the same way that he had previously served against us."[65]

Yet Risingh identified some troublemakers among the Netherlanders. Adriaen van Tienhoven was not considered trustworthy. Another, Cornelius de Boer, "had scornfully talked about Her Majesty and said that the Swedish kingdom had been put up on the stock exchange in Amsterdam, and he had otherwise caused difficulties among our people in the colony and much more harm." Risingh and his council decided to banish him from the colony but let him stay until further notice. Alexander Boyer, the former quartermaster and interpreter at Fort Nassau who had struggled with Governor Printz and Sven Skute in the 1640s, was found to be a "malicious and hateful man" and might have been banished too, but he had married a Swedish woman and was permitted to stay.[66] Likewise, Risingh and his council considered ordering two Englishmen, Simon Lane and Thomas Brown, to depart but allowed them to remain when they promised to be "loyal and honorable." Like Boyer, these two swore their allegiance to the Swedish Crown and the colony's officers then left for Manhattan shortly afterward. Of the Dutch soldiers at Fort Casimir, three decided to stay in the colony as freemen, while six others requested permission to return to New Amsterdam to be discharged of their duties. Although these six claimed that they wanted to become freemen, they soon slipped out of the colony too.[67]

After all was said and done, the Swedish colony gained twenty-two colonists from New Netherland. In return for their loyalty the freemen received their own separate court of law and generous freedoms regarding "their persons, goods, trade, economy, and their religion," with only a few stipulations, the most important being that none of the Hollanders should "provoke or agitate our Swedes."[68] Swedish officials spoke as if they were generously granting these "privileges," but in fact New Netherland's former colonists would have abandoned the river if they had disliked the terms of their incorporation. Restricting their liberties would have provoked resistance and flight, if not outright rebellion.

Faithful Subjects

New Sweden's officers may have entertained doubts about the loyalty of their new subjects, but they also had to be concerned about the fidelity of the colony's existing population. They had to offer generous terms to their own settlers to ensure their loyalty too. On June 4, 1654, Risingh and his officers traveled upriver to Tinicum Island, the site of Printz's manor house and the ruins of the fort Nya Göteborg. After a sermon at the settlement's church, they announced before the assembled freemen that Queen Christina intended to support the colony and "grant its residents all possible freedoms and continue hereafter with timely relief," so that in the future

New Sweden alone would possess the river. The news of additional support from the Crown greatly pleased the assembled freemen, Risingh claimed, although he admitted that "a great many of them had little hope in this matter." They had heard the same promises many times before. Yet prompted by their officers, who called them "good Swedish men," they promised they would "live and die Her Royal Majesty's faithful subjects."[69]

Risingh and his officers returned to Tinicum on June 9 to attend the day's church service. This time they assembled the area's freemen in order to confirm their loyalty and to investigate the causes of the "uprising and mutiny against Governor Printz." Risingh wanted public affirmation of their allegiance, especially in the wake of the mutiny against Printz, "when many had been of such evil disposition, that they had run away from their nation and colony to other places." The colonists' disaffection with the former governor seemed nearly total. One of the settlers, "Hans Nylänning" (probably Matts Hansson), went so far as to blame Printz entirely for the "rebellion" and the loss of so many settlers.[70] Incredulous, Risingh asked the assembled settlers whether they agreed. "They all cried with one voice, Aye." In light of this hostility to Printz, the officers wanted assurances from the settlers that they would continue to be honest, sincere subjects and "not accept any rebellious mutineers, but rather reveal them." In exchange for the privileges presented to them, the colonists once again promised their loyalty and swore an oath of fidelity to their sovereign and her officers.[71]

New Sweden's settlers had reason to mistrust their officials, but they also had reason to worry about the demands that officials would make of them. When Risingh and his officers visited Kingsessing, "where most of our freemen live," they informed the settlers that Queen Christina had granted to Captain Skute lands on both sides of the Schuylkill River, including Kingsessing. The freemen, who may have included new arrivals from the *Örn*, vigorously protested, saying that "they had all too recently come to the colony to now become *frälsebönder* [tenants to a noble] as they still had not yet enjoyed their freedom." Risingh calmed their fears when he informed them that Skute would have rights to the land but not to their labor, to their improvements to the land, or to their persons. He also promised that in time each settler would receive "pieces of land with perpetual ownership and freedom."[72] Quite apart from seeking to turn the freemen into feudal tenants subject to the corvée, Risingh promised the settlers that they would eventually have permanent ownership of their properties. They would finally have the right to own land the way their Dutch and English neighbors did. During an era in Swedish history that saw a "tremendous shift in favor of the nobility," New Sweden's freemen were gaining, not losing, rights to their lands.[73]

Having acknowledged their allegiances to the new regime, the settlers put their officers to work, wrangling a promise from them to hold a court date at Tinicum two weeks hence.[74] At that meeting Risingh and his officers considered some of the unresolved questions regarding the mutiny. Before he left, Printz had accused two established figures in the colony, clergyman Lars Lock and freeman Olof Stille, of collaborating in the rebellion.[75] Several witnesses testified, however, that before the mutiny's supposed leader, Anders Jönsson, was executed, he had exonerated Lock from any wrongdoing. The witnesses' testimony released Lock from further suspicion. Stille, on the other hand, was unapologetic. He posted bail and asked to be tried according to the law. In response to these questions regarding the mutiny, the colonists complained "much and long about Governor Printz" and presented Risingh with the list of grievances they had given to Printz. The freemen welcomed the new governor's suggestion that they compile their new complaints in writing so that he could report their concerns to his superiors in Sweden. No longer would they be "treated more against law than according to law."[76] With Risingh's help the colonists hoped to have the last word in their feud with Printz.[77]

"Wild Nations"

The settlers at Fort Casimir (now called Fort Trefaldighet) and the old inhabitants of New Sweden had promised their loyalty to Risingh in exchange for promises of liberty and security. The native communities of the Delaware Valley made their own demands of the new governor. Their burning of the Schuylkill's Fort Korsholm after Printz's departure suggests that they had their own ideas about ownership and possession in this contested territory.[78]

Risingh first met with some of the river's sachems at Tinicum Island, the same place where he had consulted with the discontented Finns and Swedes of his own colony. There twelve "sachems or chiefs" came to make "a pact of friendship and alliance" and to receive gifts from the new leader.[79] They then confirmed the colony's previous land purchases and promised to remain "good friends" in the future. Each of the major sachems received an arm's length of cloth, a kettle, an ax, a hoe, a knife, a pound of gunpowder, a bar of lead, and six awl points.[80] The sachems requested that the colony place a fort and some houses at Passayunk, the site of "the major village where most of them live." They promised that they would try to keep "their common Lenape" from causing any harm to the colony's settlers and pledged that they would treat the colony's enemies as their own. Speaking for the others, Naaman said that together they should keep a "very firm friendship," as they had during the days of *Meschatz,* or "Big Belly," their name for Printz. Just as they had been as "one body and one heart" during that time, now they would be "as one head with us," Naaman said.[81]

The Lenape leaders seemed to accept Risingh as the new "sachem" of the Swedes. Three weeks after the meeting at Tinicum, two important sachems, Ahopameck and Peminecka (or Pemenatta), came to Fort Christina to present the colony with grants of land. The gifts were not without controversy, as Pemenatta had given one of the areas in question to Stuyvesant in 1651. New Sweden's officers reproached the sachem for selling the land to the Dutch, but he said that he had merely accepted some presents from Stuyvesant and "in return allowed him to build houses there but had made or given no deeds on it."[82] Although the Swedish colony already claimed to own these lands, Ahopameck's and Pemenatta's gifts served to reinforce those claims and to undermine the counterclaims of their European rivals.[83]

On June 17 several leaders of the Lenape had confirmed their alliance with Risingh. A day after that meeting a Minquas sachem named Agaliquanes visited Fort Christina. The colony's officers gave the sachem presents and sought to confirm their peoples' continued friendship and trade. Agaliquanes informed the new commander that the Minquas wanted to "retain friendship with the Swedes and trade with them." This relationship was in stark contrast to the English of Maryland, who were "accustomed to shooting [the Minquas] to death wherever they find them." These Minquas "look upon themselves as our protectors," Risingh wrote, and "can supply us with the most beaver and goods for trade." About six weeks later Risingh dispatched the colony's vice factor, Jakob Svensson, to win their support. When Svensson returned in mid-August, he came bearing the good news that the Minquas had received him well. They promised to visit the colony in the fall to present gifts to the colony's leaders as well as to provide the colony with a piece of land. The Minquas also promised to be "reliable friends and protect us against attack by all the other Indians." As had the Dutch freemen and the Swedish and Finnish settlers, the Minquas-Susquehannock offered their support in exchange for generous promises from the new governor.[84]

Neighborly Love

Risingh may have been able to satisfy the diverse European and Indian constituencies of the Delaware Valley, but Dutch and English authorities in neighboring colonies still refused to acknowledge New Sweden's right to occupy lands along the Delaware. Risingh tried to convince them otherwise. The thirty-seven-year-old economist appeared to be well suited to the task, having traveled and studied in the Netherlands and England as a younger man. His later economic writings reflect an active engagement with contemporary thought originating in both nations. Historian Eli F. Heckscher described him as "a product of the Dutch intellectual climate" who was most notable as "an exponent of the Dutch influence," while Sven Gerentz has argued that he was "clearly English-oriented."[85] In *Itt Uthogh om Kiöp-Handelen eller Commercierne* (an excerpt published in 1669 from his larger unpublished and unfinished work, *En Tractat om Kiöp-Handelen*) Risingh made the bold assertion that "freedom in religion" in Holland had made it "rich in people, goods, and money" while drawing in merchants and trade from Europe and other parts of the world.[86] His thoughts on the success of the Dutch were in line with those of Sweden's high officials, including chancellor Axel Oxenstierna, who wrote in the early 1640s that "no one can teach us better than *Hålländerne*."[87] Yet for Oxenstierna and for Risingh the ultimate goal was not simply to imitate the Dutch but to adapt their methods to conditions in Sweden (and New Sweden). Cosmopolitanism would serve the *patria*.

As governor Risingh put his theory into practice. He advocated sending "a French hat-maker" and "some Dutch farmers" to work in the colony, and he tentatively proposed allowing English planters from the Chesapeake "to buy land and to settle here." Risingh acknowledged that it might be dangerous to permit English settlers to buy land within their limits, noting that in New Netherland the English had "bought and borrowed land from the Hollanders with the result that they have later pressed them out." But he also suggested that New Sweden would benefit from having "a good man on our side in Virginia who could settle his servants here."[88] Shortly after his arrival Risingh had accepted the Dutch freemen from Fort Casimir with open arms and had renewed alliances with the Lenape and Minquas-Susquehannock. Before coming to the Delaware, he had negotiated trading agreements with the English and French governors at St. Christopher. Now he hoped to persuade New Sweden's immediate colonial neighbors of the virtues of cooperation and commerce.

Risingh sent friendly letters to officials in Maryland and New Netherland shortly after he reached New Sweden. He wanted the Marylanders to stop luring away his settlers, but he also hoped to refute their claims to the territory. In his letter to Stuyvesant, Risingh offered "all neighborly good wishes." He claimed that Fort Casimir had been transferred to Swedish control "without hostilities" and urged the Dutch governor to let their superiors settle their dispute. In the meantime, he sent vice factor Svensson to Connecticut to deliver letters to officials there and to purchase food for New Sweden's settlers, "as we were completely destitute, and all the people would either perish from hunger or run away." The colony needed friends simply to survive.[89]

A day after sending his letter to Stuyvesant, Risingh received a letter from the governor welcoming his arrival and promising cooperation against the Indians. Maryland's officials also responded quickly. About a week after Risingh had dispatched two men to Maryland to deliver his message, they returned with a representative from the colony, Thomas Ringgold, the justice of the peace at Kent, Maryland.[90] He presented a letter from the governor and council of Maryland that discussed the matter of New Sweden's runaway colonists. The letter stated that after some investigation Maryland's officials had decided that the settlers were not required by contract to stay or to serve under New Sweden's government. The settlers were free to stay in Maryland. Maryland's officials nonetheless offered good wishes and promised to trade with the Swedish colony in the future. Ringgold even encouraged New Sweden's officials to set up a trading post along the route from Fort Christina to the Chesapeake Bay so that they could trade more efficiently with one another.[91]

During his visit Ringgold also gave them advice for dealing with their Indian neighbors. He warned the Swedish officials not to allow Indians to move so freely within their colony, as they could be "murderous" when given the opportunity. Nor should the colony permit sales of guns or powder to them, as they had used such weapons to "shed much Christian blood, especially English blood." The Swedish officials denied that their colony had sold any guns to the Indians, claiming instead that the Indians' guns were "not Swedish, but rather English and Dutch." But now that the other Europeans had provided them with weapons, Risingh said, the Swedes would have to follow their example in order to maintain the Indians' friendship. If the Indians demanded guns, then the Swedes would oblige them.[92]

A week after Ringgold left Fort Christina, a larger delegation from Maryland arrived to announce its claims to the territory. Its members were probably guided there by Gotfried Harmer, New Sweden's former fur trader, whom Risingh blamed for enticing his settlers to flee to the English. The leader of the mission, Edward Lloyd, traced the English claim from first discovery to Lord Baltimore's royal charter and finally to Sir Edmund Plowden's abortive attempts to plant a colony along the river. New Sweden's officials replied to the first claim by denying that discovery could give possession. If it did, then "the English would have no part of America which the Spanish had first discovered." Likewise, King James's grant to Lord Baltimore was no more effective in granting possession than was the pope's decision to divide the world between the monarchs of Castile and Portugal. "The English, the French, and the Dutch have, in practice, by having occupied and populated large tracts of land in America, shown that this grant did not have any power." And just as the English occupied lands that had been discovered by others, so were "we Swedes . . . free to occupy those lands which we could obtain from their owners." Risingh and his officers then considered the various forms of legal title to the possession and ownership of lands and asserted that the English could not claim a title to the Delaware Valley by any of these means. The Swedes, by contrast, had purchased or received as gifts most of the territory from its original owners, the Indians.[93]

Neither side was willing to accept the other's arguments, but the English still promised "all good neighborly friendship," despite their differences. One of the representatives, Thomas Marsh, "the wealthiest man there," arranged to ship ten cows to the colony and offered to sell them as much tobacco on credit as they wished. If Maryland's men could not convince New Sweden's officers to give up their claims, they could at least make money trading with one another until the issue was settled. Meanwhile, of course, they would continue to accept New Sweden's runaways into their ranks.[94]

Marylanders were not the only Englishmen with claims to the Delaware Valley. Soon after confirming the purchase of lands from the Lenape sachems Ahopameck and Pemenatta, nine New Englanders were captured at Tinicum Island. The men lacked passports from their governments, which raised suspicions. They claimed that "at home they had heard that the Swedes here were mostly dead or so sick that they were neither able to raise anchor on the ship nor to depart" and that they had come to aid the ailing colonists. Risingh and his officers suspected that the men were spies and placed them under guard. The only commission the nine could provide was signed by themselves and George Baxter, an English settler who lived at Gravesend, near Manhattan.[95]

The document stated clearly that "because they had heard that all the Swedes in New Sweden were dead, they wished to come and take possession of the territory in the service of the English protector." Despite the affront, Risingh and his officers did not want to become enemies of the "English nation," so they simply chose to send the men away under escort.[96]

Just five days after the interrogation of the nine Englishmen, a ship arrived from New Haven bearing a letter from that colony's governor, Theophilus Eaton. In his letter Eaton outlined his colony's claims to lands along the Delaware River and complained about Printz's collusion with the Dutch. At the same time he proposed establishing free trade between their two colonies. "We shal as freely ingage not to disturbe eyther your selves or other Nations in any of their just right but to live . . . in all Neighbourly love and Correspondency," he wrote.[97] In the response he drafted, Risingh argued that most of the lands along the river were under the jurisdiction of the Queen of Sweden. Included was a statement signed by the colony's oldest inhabitants that denied the legitimacy of New Haven's claims. Risingh's rebuff did little to temper the enthusiasm for expansion in New Haven. Instead, in September Eaton went before the commissioners of the United Colonies of New England at Hartford and petitioned for their support. They in turn wrote another letter to Risingh reasserting New Haven's rights to territory along the Delaware River.[98]

New Haven's men began making plans to assert their claim through direct action. On January 30, 1655 (Old Style) John Cooper and Thomas Munson petitioned the General Court of the Town of New Haven to provide his company of fifty or sixty men with public funds for their venture to the Delaware. They asked to receive the "protection of this jurisdiction, and that in case of any affront the jurisdiction will ingage to assist, till by the blessing of God they may be able of themselues to set up a Common wealth according to the fundamentalls for gouerm[t] laid at Newhauen." It is unclear whether the petitioners hoped to receive military assistance, but they did request "two great gunns and powder" for their company's use. The General Court approved of their plan, even going so far as to speculate how New Haven's government might be divided between the two settlements, north and south. Finally, in April 1655 the General Court agreed to provide two cannon to the group along with shot, musket balls, and gunpowder. They never had a chance to test their plan. When the time arrived, Stuyvesant and his troops had already overrun New Sweden.[99]

The Collapse

In the few months since his arrival on the Delaware River, Risingh had confirmed the loyalty of his settlers, established friendly relations with neighboring Indian communities, and parried the claims of colonial competitors while cultivating their merchants. New Sweden's territorial claims now stretched from the mouth of the bay to the falls, and the rivals who contested those claims seemed ill equipped or disinclined to resist any further. Risingh seemed to have turned the colony around. Yet for all the governor's diplomatic successes he had proved incapable of meeting the colony's needs for food and supplies, even with the aid offered by its neighbors. As settlers lost faith in their officers' ability to protect and to provide for them, the colony began to fall apart at the seams. Rumors of a Dutch invasion hastened the unraveling. Risingh soon discovered that he could rely on the loyalty of few of his own officers or colonists, despite their fervent promises to serve their monarch and their nation.

The first sign of trouble appeared on August 12, 1654, when Swedish officer Hans Månsson returned with news from Manhattan. "They said that we Swedes would starve, that the Indians were going to kill us, and that we would not receive relief from the mother country," Risingh reported. The officer also had learned that Stuyvesant intended to attack New Sweden but was awaiting further orders before he proceeded. Stuyvesant could entertain such malevolent thoughts because the governments of England and the Netherlands had just concluded a peace treaty. The announcement arrived just in time for New Netherland. According to Månsson's exaggerated estimate, New England's colonies had been planning to attack New Amsterdam with ten thousand men.[100]

Soon after Månsson's return, a number of New Sweden's senior officers asked to be released from their service. Their request seems to have been unrelated to the arrival of the bad news from Manhattan, but outside events soon linked them. At the end of September Risingh received a letter from Henrich von Elswich, a merchant in the employ of the New Sweden company, that contained more bad tidings. The company's ship, the *Gyllenhaij*, had mistakenly sailed to New Amsterdam, where Stuyvesant seized the vessel and its cargo and detained its passengers and crew. New Sweden's survival depended on the ship, for it carried a year's worth of provisions. "With the utmost effort we could not provide enough food for our people, who all must be supplied with monthly rations of food," Risingh wrote. Moreover, the colony's soldiers and officers also needed clothes and wages "so that they will not mutiny or run away." The inhabitants were turning to the tactics they had used in Printz's day.[101]

The rumors at Manhattan had come true. Relief for the colony had not arrived, and starvation was now a real possibility. The colony's weakness only encouraged further indignities and threats. Shortly after news arrived of the *Gyllenhaij*'s capture, two merchants from Maryland visited the colony. One was Thomas Bradnox, a leading planter at Kent Island, who "began to speak in a scoffing manner about us and our colony."[102] Captain Skute scolded the visitor, while Simon Lane, one of New Sweden's few Englishmen, "abused him even more angrily," so much so that Lane was placed under arrest until the morning. Bradnox's companion, Thomas Ringgold, interceded, and the matter was forgiven, but the colony was so obviously in trouble that even a visiting merchant felt no need to disguise his disdain.[103]

Stuyvesant piled on the humiliations. The director general wrote to Risingh to tell him that the English at Gravesend were planning to attack New Sweden and that Risingh could seek refuge in New Netherland if he wished to save himself, if not the rest of the colony. The threat may have been credible, as the nine Englishmen who had had been found at Tinicum Island had carried a pseudo-commission from George Baxter of Gravesend. But Risingh correctly viewed Stuyvesant's offer as "a great insult to us here, as he saw that we sat here so forsaken." The merchant von Elswich relayed Stuyvesant's offer to Risingh via two Swedes from the *Gyllenhaij* and a German officer whom he had hired at New Amsterdam. The officer "let it be known that he wanted to serve with us," although according to Risingh, he was really a spy. When the soldier returned to New Amsterdam, he provided Stuyvesant details of the colony's weakened condition.[104]

New Sweden's officials sought to reassure the colony's inhabitants that these setbacks could be overcome. At the next meeting of the court at Fort Christina on October 3, the colony's officers read the latest instructions from Sweden, including the appointment of Risingh as governor and Skute as commander of the colony's soldiers. "All were encouraged to have good hope of relief and to diligently plow and cultivate their land," wrote Risingh. He did not record how the freemen responded to these pleas. Their later actions suggest that they were not convinced.[105]

New Sweden's officers soon became concerned about traitors in their midst. Andries Hudde, a "cunning Dutchman," left on October 18 without the permission of the colony's officials. Fearing that "he had treachery in mind,"

Risingh dispatched some men to capture him. They caught him and brought him back to Fort Christina, where he was placed under arrest and questioned "as to why he wanted to run away contrary to his oath and duty." Hudde was a "bad example for the Dutch [in the colony]," Risingh wrote, "as most of them looked up to him." Although the Swedish commander wanted to punish Hudde as an example to others, the former WIC officer confessed and requested a pardon. Fort Casimir's former commander, Gerrit Bicker, also intervened on Hudde's behalf, and ultimately he was released with the warning not to attempt to leave the colony again.[106]

Hudde was not the only prominent settler with divided loyalties. A search of his possessions had revealed that Hudde, Gotfried Harmer, Hendrick Huygen, and Simon Lane were engaged in a conspiracy to draw away the colony's settlers to Maryland. Harmer, who once had served as New Sweden's main trader with the Indians, had "expressed the hope that the Swedes would be driven out of the [river]." Risingh claimed that this "ill-will in Virginia [i.e., Maryland] had been conjured up by the above-mentioned Simon Lane, who together with Gotfried Harmer, lured our people there." Huygen was another conspirator. In a letter he wrote to Harmer at the end of April 1654—six months after Printz had left the colony and nearly a month before Risingh's ship finally arrived—Huygen had advised his cousin to "go to the English," as Huygen himself planned to do once he returned to the colony. The letter purportedly showed that "through Gotfried Harmer the English in Virginia were ruining us, because all the trade that the Minquas had promised us was [now] in their hands." According to Risingh, "everything came to naught because of Huygen and Harmer," the cousins who had managed the colony's trade since it was founded by their uncle, Peter Minuit.[107]

Soon the Dutch freemen at Sandhook (near Fort Casimir / Trefaldighet) and the colony's own soldiers began to grow "rebellious." The freeman Peter Ebel and his wife reported that "the Dutch now claimed that they had been forced to swear the oath of loyalty to Her Royal Majesty," despite the fact that they had originally done so "gladly and willingly." The Swedish governor chose not to address this problem directly, instead banking on assistance arriving from Sweden and a future improvement of morale. New Sweden's soldiers next came under scrutiny. In early November Alexander Torsson, "keeper of the arms" at Fort Christina, was accused of urging the colony's inhabitants to run away at a time when "unrest was found everywhere, and people were agitated and uneasy." One man testified that Torsson had told him to go to the "Dutch in Manhattan." Torsson eventually confessed and identified others who were also involved. When Lars Olofsson was accused of encouraging colonists to leave for Manhattan, he refused to implicate anyone else, and the colony's officials hung him up in handcuffs. He admitted later that "most of the Finnish soldiers had let it be known that they wanted to escape to Virginia," that is, to Maryland. They had heard rumors that life was better there, and they feared that "here we Swedes would starve during the winter and would be attacked by the Indians."[108]

When Risingh and the colony's officials finally realized the true scale of the problem, they ordered all the soldiers to assemble at the fort. The officers reminded them of the oaths they had sworn to the queen under the Swedish flag, which was displayed before them. Bearing the banner as a sign of their sovereign and their nation, the officials told the soldiers that "now was the time to reveal if someone had encouraged them to run away or to mutiny." The soldiers assured their superiors that they intended to stay. The officials learned, however, that fugitive soldier Pål Larsson had said that "one of our 'old' men wished to lead all of them from New Sweden to Virginia." When they pressed further, another soldier, Mats Bengtsson, came under suspicion. Although he had fled during Printz's tenure as governor, he had since returned and was still in the colony's service. When officials called Bengtsson forward to interrogate him, he denied urging anyone to run away and insisted that he wished to remain in loyal service to the queen. Risingh suspected otherwise, but reliable men testified on Bengtsson's behalf and obtained his release. Ultimately, Risingh concluded that the person responsible for the whole affair was Gotfried Harmer, who had been using his connections in Maryland to encourage New Sweden's colonists and soldiers to abandon their struggling colony. The efforts to bolster the loyalties of the soldiers seemed to have worked. When Captain Skute visited Fort Christina to inspect the soldiers there, "they turned out to be good people." Skute urged them to act with "obedience, loyalty, and diligence" while promising them that additional support would arrive soon. "With time, everyone could find well-being here in our territory as well as in Virginia or other places they could imagine going."[109]

Unlike the soldiers at Fort Christina, New Netherland's former agents and settlers were not bound to stay. First, two Dutch soldiers requested permission to leave for Manhattan, and then Andries Hudde asked to go. New Sweden's officials required him to stay until they had received better news from New Amsterdam. They demanded further that Hudde, "a malicious man . . . who wished to go to the place where evil conspirations were nurtured against us," provide a written statement under oath that he would not conspire against the colony or otherwise abjure the oath of loyalty he had sworn. Meanwhile, the Dutch freemen were "suspected of planning a mutiny." After confirming their oaths of loyalty at a meeting at Fort Trefaldighet, Swedish officials sought to discipline their critics. One was the freeman and former soldier Peter Ebel, who had spoken "disparaging words about the Swedes." But he, too, received a pardon. Risingh and his officers must have realized that they any punishments they meted out would only turn against them.[110]

The crisis of authority continued into the new year. Hudde fled to New Amsterdam, despite his promises to stay. Before leaving, he had revealed to Gerrit Bicker that "he planned to harm us in New Sweden, contrary to his sworn duty and oath." Many of the Dutch freemen wanted to go to Manhattan as well. Even "some of our Swedes were also pessimistic and were biding their time to leave, because we were so threatened by the Dutch, had so few supplies, and no relief was in sight." Some had already run away, even as the colony's officers pleaded with them to wait for assistance to arrive.[111]

Meanwhile, New Sweden's Indian neighbors began to exert pressure on the colony. Risingh sent von Elswich to Manhattan so he could buy goods to appease the Indians, "who maintain the friendship of the Christians for no other reason than trade."[112] The Lenape along the river were threatening "to kill and ruin" the settlers and were undermining the colony's ability to trade with the Minquas and visiting merchants. "We must daily buy their friendship here with presents, for they are and continue to be hostile," Risingh wrote. They insisted on making their purchases half on credit and rarely paid their debts. "They run to the Minques, and there they buy beavers and elkskins, etc., for our goods, and then they proceed before our eyes to Manathas [Manhattan], where the traders can pay more for them than we do, because more ships and more goods arrive there." At the same time, Risingh claimed that the Indians on the river were "fond of us, because we do not do them any harm or act hostile towards them."[113] New Sweden's governor seemed unable to decide if the Lenape were his allies or his enemies. Given that the Lenape were divided into many distinct and loosely bound communities, his confusion may have reflected the different attitudes of the diverse native population along the river. But it also reflected the fundamental ambivalence of European attitudes toward Indians—friendships were always conditional and subject to a rapid dissolution into violence.

The summer of 1655 seemed to offer a prospect for renewal. In June four sachems from different Minquas nations had visited Fort Christina with the news that the "whole Minquas council and their united nations" had decided to give the "Swedes" a gift. They offered a piece of land along the eastern side of the Elk River, which, if successfully occupied, would have extended New Sweden's territory westward from the shores of the Delaware River to the northeastern tip of the Chesapeake Bay. With control of the major overland route to Maryland, New Sweden would be able to draw "the trade with the Minques, likewise the tobacco trade from Virginia," and thereby make Fort Christina a viable trading depot. "Many thousand families could settle there and support themselves," Risingh wrote.[114]

The grant was meant to be "perpetual" and included the land and everything on it. The Minquas also promised to provide "all the Swedish people" with free venison and maize for a year to help them get started. The Minquas required in return that the Swedes sell them cloth, guns, and all other goods they now had to purchase from the English and the Dutch. Hoping that the Swedes would serve as their dedicated arms dealers, the Minquas also asked the Swedes to set up blacksmiths and shot makers on the designated land. The Minquas' remarkable offer shocked the Connecticut merchant Richard Lord, who was present at the meeting. He noted that these were lands that "the English had long desired." Indeed, the Minquas aimed to put Swedes in this territory exactly because the English wanted it too. When the negotiations and ceremonies finished, the spokesman of the Minquas, Svanahändär (of the "true Minquas"), took Risingh by the hand. He led the Swede across the floor, telling him, "As I now lead you by the hand, so will we lead your people into the country, and maintain you there and defend you against Indians and against Christian enemies."[115]

The opportunity to extend New Sweden's territory to the Chesapeake presented the prospect of a brighter future, but that optimism soon collapsed as rumors began to circulate of an impending Dutch attack. The rumors came from multiple sources. The merchants from Maryland who had accompanied Gotfried Harmer reported that the "Hollanders" were planning to attack the colony with support from the Netherlands. They promised that the English would assist the Swedes, especially in returning deserters who had run away. Risingh thought that there was "little hope of relief if we had to seek it from them."[116]

The colony's declining fortunes led more freemen to flee to Maryland. "There was great apprehension in the whole territory and great longing for ships and relief from the mother country," but none was coming. The colony's Dutch freemen requested permission to leave for Manhattan. Swedish officials reluctantly let them go, and by June 1655 Risingh could report (almost optimistically) that the "land is now practically clear of the Hollanders." Before they left, New Sweden's officials made the Dutch freemen promise not to "conspire against us Swedes or do anything harmful to us there, in accordance with their oath." Yet they "did not keep that promise as honorable men." Instead, "they all returned with General Stuyvesant and showed him all our paths in order to attack us," Risingh later wrote.[117]

In the meantime New Sweden's officials ordered improvements to Fort Christina and Fort Trefaldighet, Stuyvesant's presumed objective. Risingh boasted that if Stuyvesant came up the river, "we will see to it that he is received in the manner of S. Martens (where he lost one of his legs), and we are in no wise afraid about this." The settlers were not so cocksure, as their Indian neighbors had informed them about the coming attack. Risingh, Skute, and von Elswich hurried to Tinicum, where the bulk of the colony's freemen lived. The officers asked them "if they would do their duty against the Hollanders, in accordance with the promise they had earlier made to Her Royal Majesty and the Swedish nation." The freemen all replied, "We will all stake our property, our lives, and our blood against the attack by Stuyvesant and the Hollanders." "As honorable men," they then joined the soldiers at the two Swedish forts and awaited the assault from New Netherland. They "willingly rose to [the forts'] defense," wrote Risingh, "although some were reluctant, as it was later to be seen."[118]

The Surrender

The Dutch governor and his forces finally arrived at the Delaware River on August 30 (Old Style). Seven vessels carried five companies of soldiers, over three hundred men in all—a number that equaled or exceeded the entire population of New Sweden at that time. The ships sailed first to the Varkens Kill, the former site of Fort Elfsborg, then to a site just south of Fort Trefaldighet. The next day the flotilla amassed once more and began to sail upriver. Although the parade of ships represented a powerful show of force, Stuyvesant's motives were not clear to the Swedish officers who were watching. When Stuyvesant had staged a similar visit to the river in 1651, he had brought eleven vessels and more than a hundred soldiers, yet they had not attempted to attack. Four years later New Sweden's officers guessed that Stuyvesant would again content himself with symbolic protests. This assumption seemed to be borne out when the first ship appeared to strike sail, an action that would have signaled the fleet had come in peace. The fort's commander, Sven Skute, consequently refused to give orders to fire as the ships passed, even as his own officers repeatedly requested permission to shoot. Skute's impromptu decision disregarded his own written orders, which directed him to fire upon any ships that tried to pass the fort.[119]

New Netherland's forces sailed unmolested past Fort Trefaldighet and landed upriver, cutting it off from Fort Christina, a distant six miles away.[120] Stuyvesant set up his command nearby at Alexander Boyer's house. Although New Sweden's officials had wanted to expel Boyer from the colony in 1654, calling him a "malicious and hateful man," his marriage to a Swedish woman in the colony had prevented them. Now despite Boyer's promises of loyalty to the Swedish regime, he was aiding his former master take over New Sweden. Peter Ebel, another New Netherlander who had sworn allegiance to the Swedish regime, had also rejoined Stuyvesant's service.

Stuyvesant next dispatched an officer to demand the fort's surrender. Skute sent Lieutenant Elias Gyllengren to meet with the emissary. Gyllengren declared that the fort belonged to the Swedish Crown and that "they would defend it to the last man." According to Lindeström, the Dutch officer retorted that they intended not only to drive the Swedes out of the fort but to expel "your whole nation that is found here in the country."[121] Later Skute met directly with Stuyvesant, and the two sets of officers agreed to convene again the next morning.[122]

The magnitude of Skute's earlier error was immediately evident to the fort's defenders. While Skute was outside the fort speaking with Stuyvesant, the freemen and soldiers inside began to mutiny. Sergeant Anders Kämpe inflamed their fears when he returned to the fort after delivering a message to Stuyvesant. Kämpe told those inside, "Men, we can never resist them." When Skute finally returned, one of his officers cried out, "The people are rebellious." Skute approached the soldiers and asked, "Will you now become rebellious, . . . now that the enemy is outside the fort?" The men answered that they could not resist the superior Dutch force assembled outside their gates. Skute then declared, "Whoever wants to be a honest man, and serve his King as an honest man, let him go from this rebellious crowd and come to me."[123] A majority of the soldiers decided to support Skute, but fifteen or sixteen refused. They were disarmed and put under arrest by their fellows. A few tried to escape. Olof Isgrå (Ice-gray), a soldier who had come with Risingh in 1654, jumped from the wall of the fort and ran to Stuyvesant's forces. Another newcomer, freeman Hindrich Johanson, snuck through the gate during the night.[124] The third soldier who attempted to run away, Gabriel Forsman, managed to get over the wall, but Lieutenant Gyllengren immediately "shot the leg off this one, and pulled him into the Fort, where he subsequently died."[125]

Skute was able to send word of the fort's dire situation to Fort Christina, but the smaller garrison upriver could offer little help. Several freemen, however, came down from Kingsessing. The officer von Elswich had visited their settlements to tell them that "the time had now come in which they could show their fidelity to Her Royal Majesty of Sweden by helping to defend Her Majesty's fortresses." Four of the "mutineers" of 1653, Sven Gunnarsson, Matts Hansson, Hans Månsson, and Per Rambo, immediately joined von Elswich, as did Mats Bengtsson, whom Risingh had once accused of trying to lure settlers to Maryland.[126] Although the governor sent about "nine or ten of the best freemen" from the upriver settlements to reinforce Fort Trefaldighet, they arrived too late, and Dutch forces captured all but two, who escaped under fire.[127] Skute eventually gave up the fort to Stuyvesant, who further outwitted the Swedish officer by not specifying where the soldiers were to go when they surrendered. The captain assumed that the agreement allowed the soldiers to leave the fort and reinforce Fort Christina, but Stuyvesant instead imprisoned the men aboard his ships. Within a week Stuyvesant's forces had surrounded Fort Christina on all sides. According to Risingh, they "killed our cattle, goats, pigs, and poultry, demolished our houses, and pillaged the people of their possessions outside of the fort." Upriver Stuyvesant's forces "plundered many and stripped them down to their naked bodies." They seemed to take special pleasure in raiding Tinicum Island, where Governor Printz had once held court. They robbed Armegot Printz, the governor's daughter and Johan Papegoja's wife, of "all that she owned there and also the possessions of many others who had stored their property in that place." Unable to resist a siege, Risingh finally agreed to hand over Fort Christina to Stuyvesant.[128]

After securing his victory, Stuyvesant made a remarkable offer to New Sweden's officials. Provided "no evil or harm" followed, he would permit them to retake possession of Fort Christina, and he proposed forming an "offensive and defensive league" between the two colonies. News had reached the river that Indian fighters had attacked New Netherland's settlements around Manhattan while Stuyvesant and his three hundred men were staging their invasion of New Sweden. The timing was certainly not coincidental, and some Dutch officials at New Amsterdam accused the Swedes of fomenting the assault. One settler reported to the colony's council that "the supreme chief of the Minquasas had been here conferring upon some topics with all the Indian chiefs and he believes that the Swedes have bribed these savages and that through Swedish influences these troubles have fallen upon us in your Honor's absence."[129]

The Dutch governor now needed to return posthaste to New Amsterdam with his soldiers. Risingh and his officers considered the proposal but ultimately refused. One reason was that returning to the fort would be "dishonorable to us and to our nation." Risingh also lacked authority to make such an agreement, and he could not promise that his superiors would not seek damages or act in reprisal against the Dutch. More important, Stuyvesant's soldiers had destroyed the colony's means to support itself. Freeman Per Rambo later testified that Stuyvesant's men had not only "besieged, attacked, and ruined" the possessions of the Crown and the company; they had also ravaged the settlers' "plantations and what was on them as well as [the] cattle, hogs, chickens, and other things that served us for livelihood and food." "We would then have had to sit and starve in misery as a spectacle for the Christians as well as the Indians," Risingh later wrote.[130]

One of the conditions for the surrender was that Stuyvesant would bring Risingh and "all his people" to Manhattan, where Stuyvesant would provide them with free transportation to Sweden.[131] Risingh included this demand "for we held it better that the people should be restored to their Fatherland's service than to leave them there in misery, without the necessaries of life, in which case they would have entered the service of the Dutch or English, and never again advantaged their country." Risingh fully expected New Sweden's officers and freemen to return with him to Sweden.[132]

Captain Sven Skute was one of the colony's officers who decided to stay behind. During an investigation of Skute after the invasion, Risingh questioned his subordinate's decision not to return to Sweden. The governor asked Skute directly whether his failure to fire and the botched surrender had been intentional because "he now had taken service with the Dutch." Skute answered, "So help me God, that I have not done." Risingh continued to press him. "Why then have you sought to detach the people of the Crown [who wanted to return to] the Fatherland . . . to remain with you here in this country?"[133] One witness, Nils Utter, claimed that Skute had urged him to stay in the colony. Others testified that Skute sought to persuade the colony's soldiers to stay and that he hoped to serve the Dutch regime as

an official over them. The defeated governor was disdainful. "We have . . .
surrendered the fort to the Dutch, . . . and [one] who remains living here
cannot be regarded as [His] Royal Majesty's faithful man but as something
else." Yet many did stay, and not only Skute.[134]

Good Swedish Men

Anders Jönsson's executioners would have known him well. New Sweden's entire population in 1653 numbered only a few hundred, and a much
smaller number were in active service as soldiers. As they raised their
harquebuses to their shoulders, the soldiers took aim at themselves. They,
too, wished to leave the forsaken colony. They, too, wondered whether they
would survive another year without support from their fatherland. Would
Dutch or English rivals stage an invasion, or would the discontented Lenape
overrun them first? The soldiers killed Jönsson for a treachery they carried
in their own hearts.

Jönsson and the petitioners of 1653 had built the colony and protected
it for over a decade. Yet for all their service to the colony's masters, they
lacked security in their properties and their persons. Without those protections they wanted the freedom to find other masters who could ensure their
rights and liberties.[135] The colonists' protest, then, was designed as much to
call Governor Printz to account for his abuse of power as it was to signal
their own intent to seek succor from the colony's neighbors and rivals. Had
Risingh and the *Örn* arrived a year later, New Sweden might no longer have
existed. Stuyvesant's superiors had urged him to accept the Swedes' offer
to become their subjects, and communities along Maryland's Eastern Shore
had already welcomed many fugitives as settlers. In fact, New Sweden's head
merchant, Hendrick Huygen, and its main trader, Gotfried Harmer, seemed
engaged in a conspiracy to lead the remaining settlers across the peninsula
to Maryland. Farther afield some at New Haven were still eager to take up
Lamberton's claims, and other groups of Englishmen motivated by Cromwell's imperial ambitions appeared to be right behind them.

Yet Risingh and his two hundred settlers, soldiers, and sailors sailed into
Delaware Bay in the spring of 1654, and the colony survived. The newcomers had the good fortune that the Dutch and English republics were at war
and that their American proxies were too busy preparing to kill one another
to dispossess the Swedes. Whether the *Örn*'s arrival benefited New Swe-

den's old settlers, however, is less certain. Although Risingh brought with him new colonists and new supplies, he also brought illness and people unprepared for the conditions they faced. He captured a weak Dutch fort and expanded New Sweden's territorial claims, but in doing so he triggered a retaliatory invasion that his officers were unable, or unwilling, to repulse. Risingh's once promising career would struggle under the weight of this failure, but the settlers whose properties were razed and looted by Stuyvesant's soldiers had to face a more immediate and a more fearful prospect. Risingh would not be left to starve because of his mistakes.[136]

New Netherland's colonists at Fort Casimir had a different calculation to make. Their freemen seemed content to accept Swedish rule when Risingh first appeared on the river, but their actions in the months that followed revealed something else. Perhaps they would have remained in the colony, as they swore they would, if Risingh had kept his own promises to keep them free and secure. But it soon became apparent that New Sweden's officers had propped up the dying colony only so that it could face its deathblow standing. The end of the war between the United Provinces and England meant that Stuyvesant no longer had to fear an invasion from New England. Next the *Gyllenhaij* stumbled into the harbor at Manhattan, where Stuyvesant ordered it to be seized, thereby depriving New Sweden of the supplies it needed to sustain its newly enlarged population. Then the West India Company sent a warship full of soldiers. That was enough for Stuyvesant to make his move. It was also enough for New Netherland's former subjects to realize that their freedom and security depended on guiding Stuyvesant to his conquest.

The Lenape and the Minquas-Susquehannock nations staked their own bets on the future of the Swedish colony. The Lenape communities on the river seemed to be of various minds. Some sachems seemed eager to accommodate the new Swedish presence, if only to ensure access to the (temporary) bounty of their stores. Others apparently offered threats, open or hidden, that spooked settlers and officials alike. The Minquas-Susquehannock, by contrast, recognized that the Swedish regime offered them a lifeline. They, too, lived in a contested space. To the south was a growing and aggressive English settlement in Maryland, and to the north and west were the Haudenosaunee, the Five Nations of the Iroquois, whose alliance with the Netherlanders gave them the guns, powder, and shot that they used to fight the Minquas. The Minquas-Susquehannock recognized that their own autonomy depended on the survival of the little Swedish colony situated on "Minquas Creek." To secure New Sweden's success, they were willing to guide the Swedes to the head of the Chesapeake and to make their clients their exclusive trading partners. They promised to protect the colony from its enemies, Christian and Indian.

The Minquas-Susquehannock could not protect New Sweden from itself. Merely the rumor of Stuyvesant's intentions led settlers and soldiers to flee. People and information moved too freely for officials to wield effective powers of control. Colonists could make their own judgments concerning their best interests. Officials who wanted settlers' labor and loyalty had to entice them, to cajole them, to win their affections.[137] New Sweden's neighbors understood this dynamic. Demanding their obedience, as Printz did, merely increased their disaffection and propelled their dispersal. Risingh and his officers obtained assurances of loyalty from the colony's soldiers and freemen but seemed to doubt the strength of those promises. Yet the colony ultimately might have survived had Captain Skute followed his orders and fired on Stuyvesant's armada. Instead, drawing on years of experience on the river in which violence was only feinted, Skute did not shoot. He seemed unable to comprehend that Stuyvesant actually intended to invade; he may also have feared the consequences that would have followed from a decision to fire. Skute's efforts to rally the soldiers at Fort Trefaldighet suggest that he simply made a terrible mistake of judgment, not that he was collaborating with the invaders. Yet the disgraced captain's decision to stay in the colony—and to avoid the reckoning that awaited him in Sweden—seemed to confirm the suspicions that his loyalties were compromised.

In the end the people who distinguished themselves most for their patriotism were the very men whom Printz had branded as rebels in 1653. Shortly after Stuyvesant's arrival, several freemen faced hostile fire in order to reinforce Fort Trefaldighet. All but two were captured by Stuyvesant's soldiers. When von Elswich beseeched the freemen at the settlements upriver to "do their duty against the Hollanders," four of Printz's "mutineers" immediately joined him to aid in the defense of Fort Christina. New Sweden was *their* colony, not their officials'. These "good Swedish men" were willing to fight to protect it even as their officers failed under pressure. Drawing on a "strong feeling for *liberty* and *property*" that was widespread among peasants in early modern Sweden, these settlers had developed a powerful sense of communal identity that enabled them to survive abandonment by their sponsors, resist their governor's abuses, incorporate new arrivals, and even withstand a destructive invasion.[138]

Unlike the officers, who could return to Sweden to file their protests and seek new postings, most of the settlers chose to stay and to face an uncertain future on their own, now despoiled, ground. They had lost New Sweden, but they would keep their rights and liberties. They would gain a new form of power that came with ethnic solidarity. They would become subjects of New Netherland, but collectively, as Finns and Swedes, they would negotiate the terms of their own subjection.

5

The Swedish Nation on the South River

Jean Paul Jacquet arrived in New Netherland in early 1655. He was new to the colony but not to the West India Company, which he had served "in Brazil for many years." Now, since becoming a freeman, the former soldier hoped to "devote himself . . . to farming." WIC officials in Amsterdam urged New Netherland's governor to assist Jacquet "as much as possible" and to assign "as much land to him as he may be able to cultivate." The loyal company man was looking forward to a life in New Netherland more peaceful and settled than the one he had left behind in "Nieuw Holland," or Dutch Brazil.[1]

During the 1630s the West India Company had conquered much of the northeastern coast of Brazil. Portuguese settlers and Indian workers had produced sugar there for a century, and the region had become one of the most valuable plantation districts in the Americas. By seizing the region, the WIC's promoters hoped at once to profit from the sugar trade while also dealing a blow to the Crown of Spain, which from 1580 to 1640 was united with the Crown of Portugal. Although the WIC succeeded in wresting the territory free from the Iberian empire, the colony's plantations and mills remained largely in the hands of the Portuguese settlers who had chosen to stay in the conquered territory.[2] This arrangement was by design—the company aimed to profit by shipping and processing sugar, not by making it, so it needed the old inhabitants.[3] The local population in Brazil did not accept the change passively. In 1645, several years after the fighting had stopped, a loose coalition of planters, Indians, and Africans began an armed rebellion against their Dutch rulers.[4] They were joined by forces dispatched from Portuguese Bahia and later from Portugal itself. In short order they liberated most of the province, save for Recife, the capital of Nieuw Holland. Having been under siege for nearly a decade, on January 26, 1654, the WIC's officers finally surrendered the city and the scattered remnants of the company's possessions in Brazil.[5]

Jacquet had witnessed the first stages of the uprising in Pernambuco during the summer of 1645. At the time he was a junior officer stationed at Serinhaem, about forty miles south of Recife. Situated on a ridge above the Serinhaem River, the village had a church at one end, a monastery at the other, and twelve sugar mills arrayed around it in the countryside. A Dutch writer described it as a "delightful" place. At the center of the village stood the governor's house and some outbuildings, which were surrounded by a sixteen-sided palisade. Although it was fortified, it was hardly capable of resisting a large besieging force, which is what confronted the WIC garrison shortly after the rebellion began.[6]

By the end of July 1645 the rebels had taken command of the Serinhaem River, the source of the town's water supply and its only exit to the sea. They had plundered the Dutch plantations that circled the town, seizing slaves and slaughtering livestock. Worse was to come. Several thousand soldiers under the command of Martin Soares Moreno and Andre Vidal de Negreiros had arrived from Portuguese Bahia to help pacify the "rebellious Portuguese" who had taken up arms against the Dutch regime. Although Moreno and Vidal claimed that they had come at the request of Nieuw Holland's high council, in reality they had come to support the rebels. The post at Serinhaem was no match for them. The garrison held only eighty Dutch soldiers and about sixty Indian men. Many of the townspeople had fled to the enemy, and the town's officers had received no communication from Recife for two months. Moreno and Vidal twice summoned the fort's defenders to surrender, and on August 6 the leading officers in the fort, including Jacquet, agreed to capitulate. "We did not want to throw ourselves into a blood bath," they wrote afterward.[7]

The officers arranged protections for themselves and their soldiers, although many of the latter chose to stay in Serinhaem. Jacquet and the remaining men from the garrison were eventually transported safely to Recife. The articles of surrender, however, did not protect their Tupi allies. Instead, the "Brazilians" were declared to be subjects of the King of Portugal and handed over to the Portuguese commanders. They suffered dearly for it. After the surrender thirty-three of the Tupi men were bound to the palisades and strangled. The remaining thirty prisoners were spared death but were given to the Portuguese officers as porters. Their wives, in turn, were distributed among the Portuguese inhabitants of the town.[8]

After the fall of Serinhaem, Jacquet seems to have remained in Brazil until the colony's final collapse in January 1654. He probably departed soon afterward, along with most of the remaining Dutch population.[9] Many left for the WIC's possessions in the Caribbean, especially Curaçao, while some went to New Netherland. Others, like Jacquet, returned to Amsterdam. By the end of 1654, however, he had decided to go to New Netherland. His twenty-six-year-old wife, Maria de Carpentier, was pregnant, and Jacquet seemed to hope that his record of service in the WIC would help advance his fortunes in North America.[10] Although he may have imagined himself becoming a farmer, after less than a year's residence at New Amsterdam Jacquet accepted a commission to become the new "Vice-Director and Chief-Magistrate on the Southriver of New-Netherland."[11] His office made him New Netherland's highest-ranking official on the Delaware River, second in authority only to Stuyvesant himself.

The lower Delaware Valley was not Pernambuco, but it, too, was contested and conquered territory. New Sweden's officers had surrendered the colony to Stuyvesant less than three months earlier, and now Jacquet was in command of the captured settlements and their Finnish and Swedish population. Jacquet's memories of Serinhaem must have colored his view of his new post. Would the defeated Finns and Swedes behave as the conquered Portuguese had?

The role of Portuguese settlers in the loss of Dutch Brazil seemed to call for strict oversight of the Delaware Valley's conquered population. According to one Dutch pamphleteer, the Portuguese population of Brazil began planning its *verraderye*, or treachery, from the first hour of the conquest: "When they passed by our people by day, they presented us the best appearance in the world, and by night they assembled here to cut our people's throats." Their disloyalty came despite the generous privileges that they had received from Dutch authorities, including free exercise of religion, worship in their own churches, and participation in the courts, where "they as well as our Nation have been admitted and chosen as *Schepens* [aldermen] in the same numbers and authority."[12] Indeed, the author of another pamphlet argued that the WIC's officials showed greater favoritism to the *Portugesche Natien* than to their own *Nederlanders*.[13]

National and religious differences were at the heart of Portuguese disaffection, according to WIC officer Johannes Nieuhof, who wrote a detailed account of the uprising. He noted that the "difference of religion, language, and manners" was one cause of the inhabitants' displeasure, especially because the Dutch regime sought to impose its own alien ways on the Portuguese population. But Nieuhof also attributed the WIC's failure to its unwillingness to pursue the measures necessary to secure the territory and to populate it with Netherlanders. He argued that the West India Company should have garrisoned more soldiers in its fortresses and that it should have encouraged settlement by "our own Netherlanders and free people."[14] Such a "strong population" would have been able to keep the country secure against the enemy while also sparing the state, and the settlers, from the expenses of maintaining forts and garrisons needed to protect it. This was a matter of common sense, according to Nieuhof—conquered countries could be held in subjection by "castles and garrisons or military occupations, or through colonies and peopling." Instead, the WIC gave excessive privileges to the Portuguese inhabitants of its colony, who were allowed to keep their sugar mills and the rights to their properties. The Portuguese thus retained most of the economic power in the colony and discouraged outsiders from taking up business there. Instead of protecting the privileges of the conquered population, Nieuhof argued, the WIC should have given its own people special privileges to promote settlement.[15]

The situation of the Finns and Swedes in the Delaware Valley strongly resembled that of the Portuguese population in Dutch Brazil. In Nieuhof's terms they were different in religion, language, and manners (or culture). Lutherans were not permitted to practice their faith openly in New Netherland, and it was unlikely that New Sweden's former settlers would accept such limitations with good humor.[16] Moreover, the WIC was as unable to attract settlers and to provide adequate military support for New Netherland as it had been for Nieuw Holland. The Finnish and Swedish population far outnumbered the Dutch settlers and soldiers along the river and would continue to do so unless some remarkable migration from the Netherlands took place. Most of the colony's officers had departed, but the community's leading freemen remained behind. They, too, had reason to expect a restoration. Experience had shown that even a single well-armed ship could intimidate the river's shorthanded defenders. If the Portuguese example was any guide, the Finns and Swedes would prove themselves capable of *verraderye* as well.

A Conquered People

The embarrassing loss of Brazil shaped plans for the invasion of New Sweden as well as its aftermath. Stuyvesant's instructions made the connection explicit: "If Almighty God should deliver Fort Cr[istina] into your hands, then level it; strengthen and [ ] Casamier; and [ ] all the Swedes from the South River, especially all those who are in [ ] or from whom one might [ ] trouble in the future [if they were allowed to remain]; because a conquered or [vanquished] people are not to be trusted when the opportunity arises, as has been demonstrated in Brazil."[17] The surviving document is defective, but its meaning is clear enough: the river's new governors were to expel those among New Sweden's population who might offer trouble and to monitor those who stayed. Although New Netherland's officials wanted settlers along the river to occupy the territory, they did not want traitors in their midst. They had used force to compel New Sweden's surrender, and they would use force to impose their authority on those who remained behind.

The conventions of European warfare, however, generally recognized the rights and laws of the conquered population, and the case was no different here in the Delaware Valley. In the capitulation agreement Risingh and Stuyvesant had forged, the director of the Swedish colony (who was still the nominal commander of its colonists) retained the right to encourage "any Swedish or Finnish people who [did] not wish to depart" to do so. But "those who then intend[ed] to remain of their own free will, and earn a livelihood," would retain "the freedom of the Augsburg Confession" and the privilege to choose their own minister.[18] They would, however, only be allowed one minister. The other two were forced to return with Risingh to Sweden.[19]

Among those who chose to remain in the colony, nineteen men were recorded as swearing an oath to their new masters. In taking the oath, they swore to "be loyal and faithful to the honorable High and Mighty Lords, the States-General of the United Netherlands, together with the honorable lords, directors of the Chartered West India Company, and likewise the lords and patroons of this province of New Netherland, their director-general and councillors, already appointed or to be appointed hereafter." In addition to acknowledging this long list of superiors, they also promised to "remain without engaging or assisting in any act of hostility, sedition or conspiracy in word or deed against the same" and to conduct themselves as "obedient and faithful subject[s]" as long as they remained "at the South River of New Netherland."[20] The oath was an important part of the process of incorporation, as it represented a promise before God, and it signified that these settlers had made the decision of their own free will. By performing this meaningful demonstration of allegiance, the former subjects of the Crown of Sweden legally and publicly transferred their allegiance to their new superiors. They likewise obliged themselves to acknowledge the authority of the regime's magistrates along the Delaware.

Although these Swedish subjects had sworn to obey their new Dutch governors, those officials did not necessarily trust their former rivals. The early commands for the river's new administrators displayed a clear concern for preventing treachery among the old settlers. Jacquet's commission, for example, explicitly ordered him to treat the Swedish population as potential enemies. In fact, he was to treat them much like the Indians who lived, traded, farmed, and hunted nearby. He was instructed not to permit unauthorized free people, "especially the Swedes," to remain inside the fort or even to visit it too often, a command that applied also to the Indians. He was to be especially careful when "strange ships, yachts and vessels" arrived at the fort.[21] In order to secure the colony against outside attack, he was to make all servants and freemen promise to "help defend, if necessary, the Fort against all and every one, who may at a future time desire to attack the same." Anyone who refused to swear the oath was to be dispatched to New Amsterdam for questioning. Another section of Jacquet's commission commanded him to "look well after the Swedes" who still lived there. If Jacquet discovered settlers who were "not well affected towards the Hon[ble] Company and our native country," he was advised to force them to leave ("with all possible politeness") and, if possible, to send them to New Amsterdam "to prevent any more dissatisfaction." The Indians of the river were to receive the same "politeness," but Jacquet's instructions also directed him to guard against them and "other foreign nations."[22]

Very soon after Jacquet's arrival at Fort Christina, the river's new administrators took action against a former officer of New Sweden who had not been conducting himself in an "obedient and faithful" manner. Several witnesses stated that former Swedish captain Sven Skute had claimed to have knowledge of things "concealed and hidden" in the now abandoned fort and that he would reveal them to the new commandant if he liked him. When brought before Jacquet and the river's administrative council, Skute testified that he had made the statements "merely in jest and to ridicule Otte Grym without otherwise knowing anything about this case or that anything may have been buried." The council condemned Skute for his "frequent and improper utterances . . . against this river's government which [have caused nothing] but unrest and [tumult in the] community." Then they ordered him to be placed in confinement until the next available vessel could take him to Manhattan. There Skute would have to defend himself before the governor and high council of New Netherland, just as Jacquet's instructions had prescribed. Punishing Skute would show the Finns and Swedes that their new governors would not tolerate troublemakers.[23]

The Curious Case of the *Mercurius*

One of Jacquet's instructions as commander was to take care when un-known vessels sailed into the river. Just such a ship, the *Mercurius,* arrived in mid-March 1656, bearing 130 settlers, sailors, and officers from Sweden. More important, it carried ten cannon, five hundred pounds of gunpowder, and five hundred cannonballs. The ship had left Sweden in late November 1655, before news of New Sweden's conquest had reached the fatherland, but it possessed more than enough firepower and manpower to restore Swedish rule along the river.[24]

At New Amsterdam the Anglo-Dutch merchant and mediator Isaac Allerton informed Stuyvesant and the council of the vessel's arrival shortly after it reached the Delaware River. (Allerton, who had been at the river to trade, was also the first to inform the Swedish officers aboard the *Mercurius* that all of New Sweden's forts were now occupied by the Dutch.)[25] Considering the situation, New Netherland's officials resolved not to permit the "Swedes" to land. They issued commands to send the ship and all aboard back to Europe. The *Mercurius* could return directly to Sweden or stop first at Manhattan before making its journey home. In either case the ship and its passengers would not be allowed to stay.[26]

Stuyvesant and his councillors rightly feared that the *Mercurius* threatened New Netherland's tenuous hold on the Delaware River. The ship was well armed and well manned, and if allowed to land, its passengers would increase the ranks of the Swedish and Finnish settlers who already predominated along the river. A letter from Jacquet to Stuyvesant and the council amplified these concerns. Drawing from his experience in Brazil, Jacquet warned that "some of the Swedes, left there, were either troublesome or very dangerous." He identified in particular Sven Skute and Jakob Svensson, who had once served as New Sweden's vice factor and its emissary to the Minquas-Susquehannock. Jacquet claimed that Svensson had "held secret intelligence with the *Wilden*" in order to harm New Netherland.[27] Such accusations would have resonated loudly at Manhattan, whose neighboring settlements had suffered a series of attacks while Stuyvesant was invading the Swedish colony in 1655. Indeed, some New Netherlanders claimed the Swedes had instigated the attack through their Indian allies, the Minquas-Susquehannock, as revenge for their colony's conquest.[28]

Faced with the possibility of subversion, Stuyvesant and the council commanded Jacquet to apprehend the two men and to send them to New Amsterdam for questioning. They also dispatched twelve soldiers "in case of opposition." As a final measure, Stuyvesant and the council commanded Jacquet and his council to obtain "the usual oath of all the Swedes who have heretofore not taken the oath of allegiance and send away by every opportunity those, who refuse or contravene against it." This public performance of allegiance was meant to shore up the loyalty of the Finnish and Swedish settlers or at least to reveal those who might prove disloyal.[29]

The officials' worries initially appeared to be unfounded. Stuyvesant and the council soon received a message from the leader of the voyage, Johan Papegoja, suggesting that he would cooperate fully with their commands. Papegoja was a figure familiar to New Netherland's officials. He had served in New Sweden under governors Risingh and Printz, and he was married to Printz's daughter Armegot. Accepting Papegoja's word, New Netherland's officials gave permission for the ship to come to New Amsterdam to obtain supplies for its return to Sweden. Although they provided this gesture of hospitality, Stuyvesant and the council noted that the *Mercurius* carried "some Swedish families, who for grave reasons must not be allowed to land" along the Delaware. They added, however, that their commands had "no other intentions, but to maintain the old union and friendship of the two nations" and that they planned to leave the "dispute regarding the claims on the aforesaid Southriver to the decision of our mutual Honorable Principals."[30]

Less than two weeks later the supercargo of the *Mercurius,* New Sweden's longtime factor Hendrick Huygen, came before Stuyvesant and the Council of New Netherland. Huygen explained that his instructions required him to deliver the settlers and cargo either near or at Fort Christina in New Sweden.[31] Learning of the change of regime, he had decided instead to land at Fort Casimir to speak with Jacquet. When Huygen had asked for permission to deposit the people and their goods near Fort Christina, Jacquet had responded that he could not allow the ship to proceed without Stuyvesant's permission. Spooked by the arrival of this great Swedish ship, Jacquet had also arrested Huygen "as a traitor [*verrader*] and enemy of their state." Jacquet feared treachery from this Netherlander in Swedish service.[32]

Eventually, Jacquet allowed Huygen to travel overland to Manhattan in order to petition Stuyvesant and the council directly. Huygen tried to elicit their sympathy by describing the hardships of the innocent passengers, who had been on the ship for four months. He noted the journey's great expense to the passengers, and he claimed that by preventing their landing, New Netherland's officials were separating "parents from their children, yea, even the husband from his wife." Stuyvesant and his council may have suggested that the passengers could remain at Manhattan, but Huygen did not think that was an acceptable compromise. He argued that if the settlers could not live among their own people along the Delaware River, they would be unable to practice their religion, and they would have to "live under a foreign nation whose language and manners were unknown to them." The settlers had come to people "*N. Swecia* and no other jurisdiction or Nation." Their national attachments were not negotiable. Huygen asked New Netherland's officials to allow the *Mercurius*'s passengers to settle on abandoned lands along the Delaware River or at some other location until their respective principals could settle the matter. He pledged further that he would "keep up all proper friendship and correspondence and assist in preventing all disturbances either from Indians or Christians for the security of the subjects on both sides." Huygen anticipated that the communities of settlers and Indians in the Delaware Valley might involve themselves in the affair too.[33]

Huygen's appeals did not work. Stuyvesant and the council told him that he and his passengers could leave of their own free will, or New Netherland's officials would force them to go. The next day Huygen responded that he would order the ship and its passengers to come to New Amsterdam, where he would remain until it arrived. There would be no need to send a Dutch warship to fetch the *Mercurius*.[34]

After receiving Huygen's response, Stuyvesant and the council dispatched a message to Jacquet. They had not received any response to their commands, however, even two weeks later, after they had begun to receive reports of "some disturbances between our people and the said Swedes or Indians" on the South River. Fearing that violence had erupted, they sent an officer and a dozen or more soldiers overland to the Delaware in order to discover what had happened.[35]

A few days later Stuyvesant and the council at Manhattan finally got an answer. The *Mercurius* had run past Fort Casimir, sailed some twenty miles upriver, and landed its passengers and goods near "Matinnekonk" (Tinicum Island), at the heart of the Finnish and Swedish settlements. Stuyvesant and the members of the council responded by sending a man-of-war, the *Waagh*, to the river. The *Waagh*, which had been Stuyvesant's flagship during the siege of New Sweden, was now to be put into service to subdue the Swedish settlement a second time.[36]

Stuyvesant advised his officers to address the situation "to the greatest advantage and honor of the Company and the Dutch Nation." The other councillors agreed with his advice, although one warned that they should not attack the Swedish ship, as it had already landed its goods and people. Another councillor recommended that they judge the intentions of the Swedes and the Indians on the river and seek to settle the dispute between "the natives and our nation." The councillors feared, rightly, that the Swedes and Indians had joined together to frustrate their commands.[37]

Officials at Manhattan learned more two days later, when several reports arrived from the Delaware River. The witnesses all stated that the *Mercurius*'s commanders had not intentionally disobeyed the commands of New Netherland's government. Instead, the informants blamed local settlers and Indians. They testified that "some Swedes and Finns, joined by some savages," had boarded the *Mercurius* with Papegoja and forced it to travel past Fort Casimir. The deponents also testified that "some of the principal men of the Swedes were at the bottom of it and that also most of the other Swedes, who had taken the oath of loyalty, had in their opinion been stirred up or misled."[38]

Declaring the ship's officers to be free from blame, Stuyvesant and the council permitted Huygen to return to the Delaware on the *Waagh* so long as he promised to behave himself as a loyal subject and to promote "peace and unity between the *wilden* and Christian nations." Huygen would even be allowed to trade along the river according to the rules that applied to all other "subjects or strangers." They also offered to aid him in disciplining those who contravened his commands.[39] Huygen in turn promised to act "faithfully and obediently" and to submit to the laws of New Netherland. He agreed not to become involved in any "dissension between the Christians and the *wilden*" but, rather, to seek to settle the "differences and disturbances between Swedes, Dutch, and *wilden*" along the river. Finally, he promised to comport himself as if he were "a sworn subject of this state." As security for his claims, he placed his person and property in the disposition of New Netherland's courts of justice. The Dutch regime needed Huygen to help in restoring order on the river, and he was willing to oblige.[40]

Meanwhile, two councillors set off to investigate the incident. Their instructions directed them to settle the "differences, jealousies and dissensions" that had arisen, "whether they had arisen in the Dutch, Swedish or the Indian nation[s]." Likewise, they were to find and apprehend the instigators of the trouble and send them, along with the *Mercurius,* to New Amsterdam. If they faced any opposition or attack, they had permission to do whatever was necessary to secure the "greater safety of the said River," the fort, and the "good inhabitants." New Netherland's records do not seem to offer any further details about what happened after this point.[41]

Several months later, at the end of July 1656, Papegoja wrote to officials in Sweden about the incident. His account resembles some of the Dutch reports but offers a different point of view. He said that the *Mercurius*'s officers had intended to obey the Dutch regime's order to take the ship to Manhattan, but a large crowd of "*wilde* or Indians" had swarmed the ship when it was about to depart. In their protests to the Swedish officers, the Indians recalled the "love and friendship" that they bore for the "Swedes, above all other nations," even as they threatened to "destroy all the Christians in the country by murder and fire to the smallest child, and to exterminate Hollanders as well as Swedes" unless the ship stayed and the new arrivals traded with them as they had in the past. New Sweden's old settlers also objected in a strongly worded written protest. They said the officers would be the "cause of their ruin" and would stand guilty before God and their sovereign if the *Mercurius* left the river.[42]

These protests, by settlers and natives alike, compelled the officers to change their plans. They turned the ship back upriver and sailed past Fort Casimir, firing the Swedish salute as they passed to signal their peaceful intentions. The fort allowed the ship to proceed, despite the apparent danger. The *Mercurius* sailed all the way to Tinicum Island, where the settlers and their goods were unloaded. The ship's officers then sent word to Manhattan instructing Hendrick Huygen to return immediately. They wanted his help in settling the passengers along the river and in pacifying the river's upset Indian population.[43]

Huygen was in Stuyvesant's hands, however, and news of the trouble on the river had already reached New Amsterdam. Stuyvesant dispatched the

Waagh to the Delaware in order "to quiet the Indians and also to attack us," Papegoja wrote. But when the warship finally arrived bearing Huygen, the crisis had passed. New Netherland's officials found "no hostility" and gave the Swedish ship a friendly greeting. Indeed, they had to ask the *Mercurius*'s officers for help to free the *Waagh,* which had run aground on its way up- river. They also consulted with the Swedish officers about how to "satisfy the rebellious Indians." Together the two ships sailed back to Fort Casimir, where New Netherland's officials called for a meeting of all the peoples on the river. "There they summoned all our people together with the Indians down there to them," wrote Papegoja, "and ours as well as the new people [aboard the *Mercurius*] put themselves under their protection as in the past, until further notice. Then we made the savages understand that there now were no longer two but one nation and one people, namely Dutchmen. Then Hendrick Huygen took some cargo off the ship and carried it aboard the Dutch ship, and a gift was made to the savages under the Dutch name and flag, with which they were satisfied."[44]

Huygen had lived up to his promises in a very literal way. He had af- firmed the Dutch claims to the river and had acted, as he had said he would, as though he were a "sworn subject of this state." He had even gone so far as to provide gifts in the name of the Dutch regime from the goods the ship had brought from Sweden. The Lenape, who appeared to have interpreted the *Mercurius*'s arrival as a renewal of the Swedish-Dutch contest for the river, were no doubt disappointed to find that the defunct Swedish regime would no longer be providing them with gifts. Huygen's inspired diplomacy nonetheless seemed to reconcile the Lenape to the new status quo. Two na- tions had become one.

Overall, the different accounts of the *Mercurius*'s arrival and its aftermath provide distinct but overlapping perspectives on the event. Dutch accounts blamed the old settlers, "the principal men of the Swedes." These trouble- makers had manipulated the Lenape and the loyal body of settlers and made them accomplices to their action. Papegoja, by contrast, claimed that he and his officers had sailed the *Mercurius* past Fort Casimir because of the danger posed by the large number of Lenape who had somehow made their way aboard the ship. Their threats to massacre the European population on the river supposedly had raised the fears of New Sweden's old settlers, who also had appealed to Papegoja to land the ship. Unlike the Dutch ac- counts, Papegoja's version minimized the influence of the settlers who had boarded the ship—just as he minimized his and his officers' role in giving in to their demands. The notion that the Indians were responsible for taking over the *Mercurius* was preserved in the historical memory of the Finnish and Swedish inhabitants of the river, whose stories about the Indians often mixed the themes of love and hate that appeared in Papegoja's account. Anders Bengtsson, one of the passengers aboard the *Mercurius,* recalled in an interview nearly fifty years later "how the Dutch forbade the vessel to pass up the River, and how they ingloriously would have sent it back, had it not been for the heathens who liked the Swedes and who collected, boarded the ship, and in defiance brought it past the fort."[45] For Bengtsson the story of the *Mercurius* revealed the callousness of Dutch rule as well as the intimate connection between New Sweden's old settlers and their native neighbors.

What all the accounts make clear, however, is the weakness of official power along the river. Jacquet, a novice in this space, at first overreacted to the ship's arrival then seemed unable or unwilling to take action until he received orders from New Amsterdam. Stuyvesant and the council were just as ineffective—they could not decide whether the ship was a major threat, and their orders were either disobeyed or ignored. At this critical moment settlers and Indians, not officials, had the most agency in what was still a contested space. Huygen and Papegoja tried to talk their way out of the situation, only to give up when Stuyvesant rejected their appeals. The old settlers and the Lenape better understood the range of possibilities at hand and the limited value of deference. The official Dutch and Swedish accounts of the event do not give proper credit to these groups. The passengers, the old settlers, and their Indian allies wanted the ship to land upriver, so they took actions that they knew would force the ship's officers to cooperate. The Lenape may have hoped to destabilize Dutch control of the river, and indeed they did. Settlers were able to rejoin their families, colonists and Indians alike gained access to the ship's valuable cargo, and the local elite were able to bring new settlers into their orbit. For the old settlers and the new, the decision to seize the ship was a simple one. New Sweden had collapsed, but the "Swedish nation" and its Indian allies would continue to hold their own in the Delaware Valley.

Locating "the Swedish and Finnish Nation" on the South River

One source of the Finnish and Swedish community's strength was the concentration of their settlement upriver. Their distance from the river's forts

and officials gave them a degree of autonomy that discomfited New Netherland's administrators in New Amsterdam and in the Netherlands. As these
officials recognized—and the *Mercurius* episode confirmed—the Finnish
and Swedish settlers could mobilize considerable power along the river.
Some had their homes near Fort Christina (renamed Altena by the Dutch),
but the bulk of settlers lived farther north, in what would become Pennsylvania's Chester and Philadelphia Counties. After the conquest of 1655 New
Netherland's officers often expressed concerns that New Sweden's former
settlers might conspire to overthrow the Dutch regime on the river if they
were allowed to live so clustered together. Yet allowing them to spread out
also raised problems of governance, trade, and relations with Indians along
the river. The questionable loyalty of these settlers underlay these concerns.
Although seasoned administrators on the river eventually developed confidence in the fidelity of Finnish and Swedish settlers, newer officials and
more distant observers at Manhattan and in Amsterdam were less trusting.
They feared most of all that these settlers might act as a fifth column in the
event of a Swedish, or even an English, attempt to recapture the river.

Stuyvesant remained wary of the Finns and Swedes, but he also recognized that the best way to maintain order among them was to govern them
through their own officials. They would be able to retain their communal
identity while remaining subject to the Dutch regime, a pattern already established in the English communities that dotted the eastern edge of New
Netherland. Following the invasion Stuyvesant assigned New Sweden's settlers their own set of magistrates, mainly men who had once performed
similar roles in the Swedish colony.[46] The magistrates were of Finnish or
Swedish origin, but the deputy *schout* was Gregorius van Dyck, a Netherlander who had long served in a very similar capacity under the adminis-
trations of Peter Ridder, Johan Printz, and Johan Risingh. As deputy *schout*,
he would be the head officer of the local court, serving at once as a kind of
sheriff, prosecutor, and justice.[47] The continuities were spatial as well—the
magistrates of the Finnish and Swedish settlement held court at Tinicum Island, where Printz had once presided as governor of New Sweden. Remark-
ably, the freemen had gained more direct say in their government under
New Netherland's administration than they had as subjects in New Sweden.
Stuyvesant also issued land grants and confirmed ownership of their properties, which even New Sweden's freemen had not been able to obtain from the
New Sweden Company. Despite these notable improvements in their status,
the conquered settlers remained under the authority of Dutch officials on the

river, in New Amsterdam, and ultimately in Amsterdam itself—all of whom, to varying degrees, still viewed the Finns and Swedes as potential threats.

The "Swedish nation," however, was hardly a unified body. To start, many of the "Swedes" were not Swedish. At the time of New Sweden's conquest, as many as half of the colony's settlers may have been ethnic Finns and native speakers of Finnish, although most had been recruited within Sweden itself. Nearly all of the passengers on the *Mercurius* in 1656 were Finns, not Swedes.[48] The old guard among the settlers had lived along the river for more than a decade, but many others had been there for less than a year. If some were "principal men" capable of organizing tumults, others were younger men, women, and children, who did not possess the same authority, wealth, or position.

The fractures within the Finnish and Swedish settlements became most visible when its agents sought to make decisions for it. In April 1658, while Stuyvesant was visiting the river to examine the collection of customs duties, van Dyck and the other officials of the Swedish nation presented him with a series of requests. The first was that Stuyvesant provide them with instructions that would clearly establish their authority relative to the government of New Netherland and to the people they governed. Other requests were for a court messenger and free access to the Dutch commander at Fort Altena, in case they needed soldiers in an emergency. Their final request suggests how they aimed to strengthen their own authority through the agency of the Dutch administration. They asked that "an order be made, that nobody shall leave these boundaries without knowledge of the magistrates, much less, that the servant-man or woman of one, when they leave or run away without their master's or mistress's permission, shall be concealed by the other." In short, the officials for the Finns and Swedes were seeking outside authority so they could control members of their own "nation." The freedom of movement that bedeviled every colonial regime dependent upon bound labor also undermined the authority of the officials for the Finns and Swedes of the Delaware River. The magistrates needed support from Dutch officials to preserve and maintain existing hierarchies within their community.[49]

Stuyvesant gave his assent to each proposal in their petition. The magistrates now had even more expansive authority, complete with the power to conduct their own courts. They could issue summons, make arrests, and carry out sentences. They had access to military support. They could prevent people from leaving the community without their consent. Anyone belonging to the Swedish nation who wished to leave or had already left could be commanded by the *schout,* van Dyck, to return. Those who disobeyed could be arrested or detained. The "Swedish nation, our good and faithful subjects," would pay for the costs associated with their local government. The concessions were impressively broad. So long as the members of the Swedish nation swore an oath of allegiance to Dutch authorities, they would be treated "as if they were our own nation."[50]

The Finns and Swedes had acquired political privileges as great as those possessed by the "Dutch nation." Yet they asked for one additional privilege once they had sworn the oath of allegiance. They asked "not to be obliged to take sides, if any troubles should arise between the Crown of Sweden and our State [the United Provinces] at home." Perhaps recognizing that he might prevent trouble by recognizing the obvious, Stuyvesant agreed to this extraordinary request. At the same time, he acknowledged the appointment of three military "officers of the Swedish nation on the Southriver": Anders Dalbo, the once-troublesome Sven Skute, and Jakob Svensson, all longtime residents and former officers of New Sweden.[51] Again, Stuyvesant was trying to turn a position of weakness into one of strength. Unable to extend his own limited military resources to the Delaware River, Stuyvesant authorized the Swedish nation to defend itself. In return he permitted its members to remain neutral if their natural sovereign sought to reclaim his lost colony.

The directors of the West India Company learned of this meeting some eight months later. They were astonished by Stuyvesant's decisions. They wrote that "no reliance whatever [could] be placed" upon the "Swedish officers for that nation." Their infidelity was "inferable not only from their previous actions, but also now from their request . . . that upon arrival of any Swedish succor they might remain neutral, indeed an unheard of and bold proposition by subjects bound to this State and the Company by their oaths, who thereby clearly show the sentiments nursed in their hearts." From the perspective of the directors, the Finns and Swedes were bound to uphold their oaths even if they did not have warm feelings for their current masters. No one was foolish enough to believe that they would rally to the Dutch flag in case of a Swedish invasion, but to grant them official license to stand aside *was* truly foolish. Even if Stuyvesant no longer feared an uprising among the Swedish nation, his superiors remained doubtful.[52]

A better policy, they argued, would have been "to disarm the whole nation there, than to provide them in such manner with officers and hand them the weapons, which they will know well how to use against us not only upon the arrival of the slightest Swedish succor, but also on other occasions." In fact,

Stuyvesant would have been wiser to discharge the Swedish officers altogether and replace them with Netherlanders. The directors recommended
allowing the *schout* van Dyck and the magistrates to serve out their terms,
but once they had done so, Stuyvesant should replace them with "men of our
nation, [so] that they may be deprived so much more effectively of the means
of conspiration and confederation and so much sooner be found out." In order to prevent such cabals, the directors advocated "separat[ing] them from
each other and prevent[ing] their concentrated settlements." If the Finns
and Swedes were "scattered among our people . . . they will be less to fear."[53]

The directors' panic reflected the times. While Swedish authorities were
still protesting the seizure of their colony, English colonizers continued to
threaten New Netherland. Stuyvesant explained his approach toward the
English and the Swedes in a letter he wrote to the directors in July 1659. He
agreed that "neither the Swedes nor the English, who live under our jurisdiction or outside of it, have a great affection for this State," but he also acknowledged that "the same might be likewise supposed and sustained from
us, in case we should be conquered, from which the good God may save
us." If conquered subjects had little natural affection for their conquerors,
then their magistrates had to encourage them to develop it. The key was to
employ "a lenient method of governing them and proceeding with them,
to win their hearts and divert their thoughts from a hard and tyrannical
form of government." In order to gain the confidence of their conquered
subjects, Stuyvesant and the council had granted "the Swedish nation, at
their request, some [military] officers, that in time of necessity, against the
savages and other enemies, in case of defense, they might keep order." But
New Netherland's officials had not granted them commissions, nor had they
supplied them with weapons.[54]

Probably so that he could delay changing this policy, Stuyvesant asked
the directors for further instructions. If they still disapproved, then the government of New Netherland would discharge the Swedes' military officers.
Yet Stuyvesant added a proviso—he and his officials would act "as far as
possible agreeable to circumstances and occasion." Stuyvesant was not willing to let the directors completely override his decisions. He was acutely
aware of the limits to his power, and he realized that governing through
local authorities was more effective than imposing his own authority from
above. Disarming the settlers might even provoke the uprising that the directors so feared.[55]

"Malefactors" and Marylanders

The Finnish and Swedish settlers who lived at New Netherland's southern frontier were a threat in theory, but Stuyvesant realized that the English of Maryland were the real danger. Maryland's officials had long claimed the lower Delaware Valley as their territory. They confidently cited the colony's royal charter of 1632, which declared that Maryland's territory extended to "that Part of the Bay of Delaware on the North, which lieth under the Fortieth Degree of North Latitude . . . where New-England ends."[56] The exact location of the line was disputed, but Cecil Calvert, the second Lord Baltimore and proprietor of Maryland, was certain that his province encompassed much, if not all, of the land settled by the Dutch and the Swedes. Maryland's small population, its tumultuous politics, and its hostile relations with the Minquas-Susquehannock and Eastern Shore nations had so far prevented the proprietor from realizing his claims.

Conditions had changed by the mid-1650s. Maryland's population now numbered in the thousands, its government had made peace with the Minquas-Susquehannock, and its leading men had begun making plans to expand into the Delaware Valley.[57] The first sign of their intentions appeared in 1654, when a group of planters and officials from Maryland met with Johan Risingh, the new governor of New Sweden. In their meeting Risingh argued that actual occupation trumped the discoveries and charters that the Marylanders cited to bolster their case. The English delegation rejected Risingh's reasoning, but they promised "all good neighborly friendship" when they departed. Five years later, with the river in Dutch hands, Maryland's ambassadors would not be so complaisant.[58]

By conquering New Sweden, the West India Company had eliminated its chief rival in the Delaware Valley, but it still needed to secure its claim with settlement. As a quick solution, the WIC turned to one of its partners in the invasion of New Sweden. Because the lords of the city of Amsterdam had contributed a warship (the *Waagh*) for the conquest, the WIC repaid the debt by granting the city, as a corporation, the right to establish its own settlement along the Delaware. This colony, "Nieuwer Amstel," or New Amstel, grew up around Fort Casimir, a location already inhabited by a small number of Dutch, Finnish, and Swedish settlers. New Amstel's officers and about 167 colonists arrived from Amsterdam in April 1657. The next round of English claims to the Delaware Valley began soon afterward.[59]

Within six months of the founding of New Amstel, Indians friendly to the Dutch regime captured fourteen English fugitives near Cape Henlopen, at the mouth of the Delaware Bay. Jacob Alrichs, the new colony's director, ransomed the prisoners from their captors (presumably the Siconese) and held them until they could be sent back to Virginia. Instead of patiently awaiting their return to servitude, however, most of the men escaped, thereby dodging the debts they had accumulated in the Dutch colony as well.[60] News of the Englishmen's lingering stay prompted a stern response from the directors in the WIC's Amsterdam chamber. Under the impression that Alrichs had granted the runaways permission to become colonists at New Amstel, the directors stated that it was "a cause for concern if the same Englishmen come to settle there or increase in numbers." If officials did not effectively block this "nation" and its sweeping claims to the river, its members would attempt to "intrude there and by one opportunity or another [try] to usurp the aforesaid place as has happened on the border of New England."[61] If the men were fugitives, then Alrichs was to send them back to their colony, and if they were free, he was "to get rid of them in the most proper and decent manner (without, however, being offensive to them)." Whatever Alrichs chose to do, the directors wrote, the officers on the South River were "under no circumstances ever to admit anyone of the English nation there again, much less encourage them to come there."[62] Based on their experiences with New England's settlers and officials, the directors of the WIC knew that once English immigration began, it would be nearly impossible to stop. From the perspective of the company's officials (and many others involved in Dutch colonial ventures), the English were an aggressive, grasping people who belonged to aggressive, grasping governments.

The English of Maryland left the little colony alone for another two years. In the meantime New Amstel's settlers had struggled to keep themselves alive. The newcomers had battled disease and weather, often without success. Alrichs noted in August 1659 that during their first year "a general sickness, attended by burning fevers . . . sorely fatigued and oppressed the people, and made them groan." Agriculture and construction faltered. The second year was even worse. It was "so wet and unseasonable," he wrote, "that hardly grain enough for the people and the cattle could be saved." The shortage of food was compounded by "a multitude of new cases of sickness, [which] again broke out with such severity, that nearly the tenth part of the people lingered and lived in misery, under continual sickness, fevers, and languors." More than a hundred people died, many of them children, along with much of their livestock. "By this means, most of the labor was at a stand-still; this gave rise to scarcity and dearth; most of what the people had saved was spent in their poverty, whereupon a severe, hard and long winter followed."[63] It was an especially difficult time for Alrichs, whose "dear and beloved" wife, Maria Struys, died just after the new year in 1658. As he noted then, and would have occasion to note again, "misfortune, as it is said, seldom comes alone."[64]

Soon afterward Maryland's agents renewed their efforts to claim the western shore of the Delaware Valley. At the end of May 1659 Alrichs reported to Stuyvesant that he had begun "hearing strange rumors that the English are claiming ownership of this river or territory, and that they are definitely sending two persons here to demand and take possession of this place." Alrichs was particularly troubled because "some malefactors here"—namely, New Sweden's old settlers—seemed ready "to help bring it about." Rumors suggested that the Marylanders would grant the Swedes a special status if the territory came under English rule.[65] Although the Dutch population along the Delaware River was now larger than ever before, the Finnish and Swedish population upriver still outnumbered them. Alrichs, another alumnus of Dutch Brazil, was all too familiar with the direction that events were taking.[66]

In July Alrichs learned that Colonel Nathaniel Utie had received a commission to visit the river and to present Lord Baltimore's claims to it.[67] Utie was a young, well-connected planter who had recently received several large grants of land at the northern end of the Chesapeake Bay. He had an interest in seeing the Delaware become part of Maryland's territory—the value of his property depended on having overland access to the Delaware Bay.[68] News of the proprietor's plans spread quickly. "This has now become public knowledge here," Alrichs wrote, "producing such consternation and unrest among most of the settlers that all work has stopped and everyone is trying to flee, move away and look for the best way to escape."[69] Fearing yet another invasion of the Delaware, the colonists and their director had begun to panic.

Utie and his party finally arrived at New Amstel in early September. The coming of the English had been "dragging on in such a way and for so long that it sometimes has appeared as a dark cloud repeatedly wishing to disappear; nevertheless, its time has now come," Alrichs wrote.[70] Having waited so long for the Marylanders, Alrichs seemed unwilling to face his fear. According to the director's own chronology of events, the Marylanders had been allowed three full days (in the words of Utie's instructions) to "insinuate vnto the People there seated" that they should become subjects of Lord Baltimore.[71]

While Dutch officials dithered, Utie pressed forward. At his meeting with Alrichs and the main WIC official on the river, Willem Beeckman, Utie offered New Amstel's inhabitants a stark choice: either abandon the territory or declare their allegiance to the English proprietor. Those who accepted Maryland's government would receive "protection in theyr liues, libertys, & estates wch they shall bring with them."[72] Those who chose to stay without acknowledging their subjection to Lord Baltimore would find that "innocent blood . . . might be shed as a result." Alrichs and Beeckman tried to defend the United Provinces' and the WIC's long-standing claims to the territory, but Utie rejected their arguments. Nor was the Marylander interested in leaving the question to their principals in England and the United Provinces—they had "nothing to do with it." Ultimately, Utie did accept the Dutch officials' request for a three-week delay so they could consult with New Netherland's highest official, Director General Stuyvesant.[73]

Even before Stuyvesant had learned of Utie's embassy, he had written to the WIC's directors to describe the "deplorable and bad state of affairs" in New Amstel. Colonists were deserting to Maryland and Virginia so rapidly that "hardly 30 families remain[ed]." Of the soldiers who remained in service, most were based near the mouth of the Delaware Bay "and not without fear and danger of sooner or later being massacred by the cruel savages." New Amstel itself was left with only "8 or 10 soldiers and very few free people." Stuyvesant warned the directors that they and the colony's patrons in the city of Amsterdam needed to act soon before "greater calamities occur either by an invasion of the Swedes or English or by an attack of the savages."[74]

A day after writing this letter Stuyvesant received news of Utie's visit to New Amstel. The director general was "astonished" by Alrichs's response to the Marylanders, particularly that he had allowed them to "inquire into and spy out during 4 or 5 days the condition of the Fort, the sentiments of the Colonists, the weakness of the garrison, and then on the fifth day gave them an audience on such a frivolous demand and pretended instructions." Although his own supply of soldiers was already stretched thin, Stuyvesant sent some sixty men to the Delaware River to discourage an attack from

the Marylanders.[75] He also dispatched two ambassadors, Augustine Herrman and Resolved Waldron, to the government of Maryland. Stuyvesant
had achieved some success negotiating directly with New England's officials,
and he must have hoped that diplomacy would pacify their countrymen in
Maryland as well.

The possibility of a combined threat from the English and the Swedes
remained a concern for officials in New Netherland and in Amsterdam. A
month after Stuyvesant sent out his plea for help, the directors provided
further orders regarding governance of the Delaware. Unaware of Utie's embassy, they were still fixated on "the suspicions and doubts arisen in regard to
the Swedish nation, settled on the South River." Moreover, they had learned
that "the English may very likely intend to undertake something against us
there under the Swedish flag and name." The directors had even less reason
to trust the Swedish nation, they said, because New Netherland's officials
had formed them into a militia company "under the command of officers
of their own natio[n], whereas they rather ought to have been separated and
scattered among our people," as they had urged in their letter of eight months
prior. The directors again recommended carrying out this command "without delay, before they can get any advantage over us with the assistance of
our neighbors," that is, the English of Maryland and New England.[76]

By the time the directors' letter reached New Netherland, the danger
from Maryland had receded, and fears of cabals among the English and
the Swedes had faded. Stuyvesant appears to have ignored the directors'
commands to disarm the Finns and Swedes, and this theme does not appear again in his correspondence with the West India Company. Maryland's
officials nevertheless continued to press their claims. The intensity of the
threat was rarely so great as it was in the summer of 1659, and a year later
it seemed to fade almost altogether. This was in part because of political
instability within Maryland itself, which saw its governor and assembly declare the colony a commonwealth, only to have proprietary rule restored
eight months later. Stuyvesant attributed the calm to diversions in England.
News of the Restoration of Charles II had caused the immediate collapse of
the revolution in Maryland. It may also have derailed the imperial ambitions of Colonel Utie, who had been one of the leading supporters of "Fen-
dall's Rebellion."[77] Stuyvesant urged the WIC's directors to take advantage
of this "change and apparently fresh alliance" to resolve the English claims
to their territory.[78]

Willem Beeckman and the "Finnish and Swedish Nation"

The new calm helped to ease relations between the Swedish nation and Dutch officials along the Delaware. Managing the Finns and Swedes was the duty of New Netherland's main agent on the river, Willem Beeckman, who served as the head officer for the settlements at Fort Altena (formerly Fort Christina) and to the north. Formerly an official at New Amsterdam, Beeckman began his service on the Delaware in the fall of 1658. In a short time he seems to have established a good working relationship with the *schout* and magistrates of the Swedish nation. In December 1659 he passed along to Stuyvesant their request for a yearly tax on "each household of the Swedish or Finnish nation."[79] In February 1660, after three Indians were murdered near New Amstel, Beeckman asked van Dyck and the Swedish magistrates to mediate with their Indian neighbors, who were threatening the residents of New Amstel. According to Beeckman, the old settlers were "better acquainted with the nature and customs of the Indians than we new-comers."[80] He needed the magistrates, and they needed him.

At first, however, van Dyck and the Swedish officers declined to help Beeckman. They pointed out that the request did not come directly from the director and councillors of New Amstel, whom they viewed as having jurisdiction in the case. New Amstel's new director, Alexander d'Hinoyossa, was a notorious figure, and the "Swedish" officials undoubtedly wanted to avoid irritating him. More important, the Lenape who lived upriver had "told them that they should not concern themselves in this affair since the people of Sand Hoeck or New Amstel were not of their people."[81] The Lenape recognized the national differences among their European neighbors, and they warned the Finns and Swedes to stay out of the matter.

Stuyvesant later wrote that "two so-called Christians, one a Hollander[,] the other a Swede or Finn," had murdered the three Indians, "a man, a woman, and a boy." Their motivation disgusted Stuyvesant—they had killed the natives "only from a damnable desire of wampum." Stuyvesant was out-raged even further when d'Hinoyossa released the killers.[82] The director-general, however, tried to turn this worrying incident into something use-ful. The natives of Esopus (a region between Manhattan and contemporary Albany) were attacking settlers in New Netherland, and Stuyvesant needed soldiers and settlers who could stave off further assaults. First he demanded a trial of the murderers in order to appease the aggrieved Lenape. But he also instructed the councillor Nicasius de Sille, who was to conduct the trial, to recruit Finnish and Swedish settlers who would relocate to the Esopus area. There they might form a buffer between Indian enemies and the heart of the Dutch settlements of New Netherland.

Dutch and Swedish officials on the Delaware had already reached a settlement regarding the murders by the time that Stuyvesant had made the decision. Beeckman, van Dyck, and the magistrates of the "Swedish nation" had met with native representatives at New Amstel in early February, and after two days of negotiations, "they came to a satisfactory agreement." Although these particular sachems may have accepted the agreement, other native men continued to seek vengeance for the murders. During the meeting the officials received news that Indians had robbed and killed former WIC official Andries Hudde, who lived among the Finns and Swedes upriver. Hudde turned out to be alive after all, but Lenape raiders had plundered his farm and his possessions. When the officials reported this incident to the sachems at the conference, the Lenape leaders promised they would try to recover all that had been lost.[83]

The increased threat of violence led Stuyvesant to order the colony's "isolated farmers" to seek refuge in defensible villages. Although the safety of outlying settlers was the main concern, the request also reflected the directors' instructions to incorporate the Finns and Swedes into the Dutch settlements that predominated downriver. Stuyvesant's command coincided, in fact, with news that "about 20 families of the Finnish and Swedish nation" living on WIC lands above Fort Altena wanted to move south to New Amstel. These settlers' wishes may have aligned with the plans of the Dutch regime, but their own *schout* and magistrates sought Beeckman's aid in preventing the move. Those twenty families formed a significant bloc within the population of the Finns and Swedes, perhaps one sixth or more of the total. According to van Dyck, there were only 130 men within their community who could bear arms.[84] If these families left for New Amstel, they would no longer be part of the "Finnish and Swedish nation" that had established itself upriver.

Two years earlier the *schout* and magistrates of the Finnish and Swedish settlements had sought additional powers to police the movements of the settlers under their jurisdiction. Now they wanted to prevent members of their community from leaving their jurisdiction or acting against their wishes. In this case a group living along the western shore of the Schuylkill River near Kingsessing intended to move to an adjacent area known as "Aroenemeck," where two or three families were already settled. Others at

Kingsessing wanted them to choose a location nearer to their own farms. The *schout* and magistrates stood behind the Kingsessing settlers, although the would-be migrants insisted (rightly so, according to Beeckman) that the Kingsessing area was "entirely indefensible" and offered no means of escape from an Indian attack. Some of the Swedish magistrates, who lived on "good islands," even claimed that "they ought to be favored by having the outlying people move to them." Their preferences did not seem to carry much weight among the affected settlers, however, as none wished "to move or come to an accommodation; each one asserting the intention to keep his whole lot and cultivated land."[85]

Realizing that the settlers would not be able to come to an agreement on their own, Beeckman ordered the parties to provide him with a list stating where each intended to resettle. If the locations were consistent with Stuyvesant's ordinance, then Beeckman would permit them to move. If not, then he would decide for them. Beeckman originally gave them slightly more than a week to decide the matter, but the Finns and Swedes protested that they could not move so soon because "it would be to their great loss and the ruin of their crops for this spring, if they should have to break up by district." Beeckman granted them an extension of five or six weeks. Finally, in early April 1660 the Swedish magistrates came to Fort Altena to appeal to Beeckman "on behalf of all the separate communities." They offered a compromise. If Stuyvesant permitted them to keep their lands until they had harvested their grain, they would purchase land from the Indians at Passayunk, on the east side of the Schuylkill River, and establish a village there. Beeckman informed them that only Stuyvesant could approve such a plan.[86]

The simultaneous effort to recruit Finns and Swedes to "enter the service or to relocate at the Esopus" was proving to be a complete failure. The settlers had "no inclination whatsoever" to move to the Esopus or to become soldiers for New Netherland. Here, too, the *schout* and magistrates were involved. According to Beeckman, "The leaders of their nation admonish and urge them not to disperse themselves, but to remain hereabouts," a practice he likened to the efforts of the *schout* and magistrates to obstruct the settlers who wished to move to New Amstel. Beeckman's subsequent attempts to relocate the settlers also failed. They continued to resist moving to the Esopus, despite an apparent order to do so by Stuyvesant. "They said they would be somewhat inclined to go if there was peace with the Indians," Beeckman reported. Two weeks later he informed the *schout* and magistrates that Stuyvesant was unhappy with them because they had "discouraged and hindered the people who were inclined to go to Esopus, and had frustrated the sergeant in this matter." They "vigorously denied it."[87]

Yet some of the settlers still wished to move to New Amstel. They complained that they did not have enough contiguous land: "the small parcels scattered here and there are too difficult to fence in." Beeckman's attempts to shift these settlers to Passayunk were just as fruitless as his earlier efforts. Some settlers even claimed they were "more inclined to go to Maryland than to move and crowd in with the others" at Passayunk. A week later the *schout*, van Dyck, reported that "the community had selected some representatives" to ask Beeckman to petition Stuyvesant on their behalf so they could stay in their current settlements. Beeckman informed them again of Stuyvesant's order to move. They replied that Passayunk lacked sufficient land for pasture and thus "they could not move." Furthermore, "if they were forced to move, they would go away to where they might remain settled in peace"—a none-too-veiled threat to leave for Maryland, as some already had done. Without Stuyvesant's side of the correspondence we cannot determine how they finally resolved the matter. At the end of June 1660 Beeckman wrote to Stuyvesant to say that he would obey his order concerning the Swedes, but there is no further discussion of what that entailed. It seems unlikely, however, that the settlers paid any more mind to Beeckman's demands than they had in previous years.[88]

For two years there was no further discussion among WIC officials regarding the location of the Finnish and Swedish settlers along the Delaware. In the spring of 1661 conflict between Indians and Marylanders seemed ready to spread to the Delaware Valley, but over time that threat dissipated. Squabbles over jurisdiction within the Dutch settlements seemed to form the main part of public life during this period, or at least the part that showed up in administrative correspondence. When officials next raised the question of moving the settlers, in June 1662, the director of New Amstel sought to bring "16 or 18 families living in our district, mostly Finns," into his jurisdiction. D'Hinoyossa offered them good incentives to move. They would be free from taxes for eighteen years, they would have their own magistrates for disputes concerning less than one hundred guilders, and they would be free to practice their own religion. The affected families intended to stay on their current landholdings, however, until they could clear their new lands near New Amstel. Beeckman suggested that if the settlers did leave his own jurisdiction, the WIC could repossess their former lands and "settle Dutch farmers on it." Although the desirability of retaining the Finnish and Swedish settlers had changed over the years, New Netherland's officials were still trying to insert Dutch settlers among them whenever they could.[89]

Warring Indian neighbors and negotiations with Maryland's officials occupied the river's officiary over the next few years. Local disputes set Dutch officials and colonists against one another, but fears of invasion were less powerful than they once had been. Yet the Dutch regime on the river was not so secure that it could discount potential threats. In October 1663 the directors of the West India Company informed Stuyvesant that they had heard a rumor that Vice Admiral Hendrick Gerritsen Zeehelm, a native Netherlander in Swedish service, was preparing two ships to recover the Delaware for the Crown of Sweden.[90] Although the directors first thought this conjecture was unlikely, they had since learned it might be true. The directors intended to warn Stuyvesant and the City of Amsterdam's officers on the Delaware "so that the City may not be deprived of so fine and fertile a district and the Company not get thereby so much more dangerous and threatening neighbors." Later correspondence provided additional details about the movement of the Swedish fleet, which now appeared to be a real threat to New Netherland's possessions on the Delaware.[91]

In the meantime the WIC's directors had transferred the entire Delaware territory to the burgomasters of Amsterdam, who had overseen the New Amstel colony since plans for it began in 1656. The Finns and Swedes who had frustrated the commands of so many officials could not wield their own power to prevent the change, but their willfulness and intractability was as evident as ever. On January 5, 1664, Beeckman summoned "all the Swedes and Finns" to Fort Altena to witness his resignation. None came. On January 9 "the Swedish magistrates with many of their [nation] and the Finnish nation" finally arrived at Altena. There, at d'Hinoyossa's request, Beeckman released the settlers from their former oath, in which the directors of the West India Company and the director general of New Netherland had figured so prominently. The next day the settlers proceeded downriver to New Amstel. There they declared that "if we have been sold, then we are handing ourselves over." Although they were supposed to swear a new oath administered by the city colony's director and council, "they unanimously refused to take [it] until they had in writing those privileges of trade and other things which they had enjoyed under the Company's administration; without this [they said] that they would be forced to leave." New Amstel's administrators countered by giving the settlers eight days "to confer with the rest of their people about whether to take the oath or to leave." Rather than lose these privileges, the settlers seemed willing to split up and live under Stuyvesant's government at "Nevesins," a location across the Delaware River in what is today New Jersey. Others may have intended to go to Maryland. Again, existing records do not state exactly how officials and settlers resolved this latest impasse.[92]

An invasion from Sweden was not the solution. Writing in August 1664, seven months after the transfer of command, Stuyvesant declared: "It has been . . . a wonderful work of the Lord, worth noting and to be grateful for, that the Swedish expedition under Admiral Hendrick Gerritsen Zeehelm, prepared for and intended beyond doubt against the Southriver, has been frustrated so wonderfully by His hand and providence, at least that it has been delayed and prevented." If this expedition had succeeded, then "without doubt they of Herford [Hartford, Connecticut] and other malevolent and threatening neighbors would have on their side attacked us with all their forces."[93] Certainly, the aggressive Marylanders were included in that group. Yet neither New Englanders nor Marylanders nor Swedes were the agents of New Netherland's collapse. Instead, the conquerors of New Netherland would come directly from England itself. Within a month of acknowledging the "wonderful work of the Lord," Stuyvesant had consented to a treaty surrendering New Amsterdam to officers loyal to the Duke of York and his brother, Charles II. English forces seized the Delaware River a month later. Again, the Dutch, Finns, Swedes, and members of every other European nation along the Delaware were required to swear allegiance to the agents of a new regime. As always, their consent was conditional, and the "subjected" proved to be powerful even after their conquest.

"To Win Their Hearts and Divert Their Thoughts"

Between 1655 and 1664 the Dutch administrators of the Delaware River often voiced their suspicion or distrust of the Finnish and Swedish population they governed. With the bruising loss of Brazil fresh in every WIC administrator's mind—and the plundering of their homes and farms recalled all too clearly by the Finns and Swedes—the prospect of subversion and revolt was very real. Yet if the threats to New Netherland's survival seemed to call for a strong hand, the desire to retain these settlers and to secure the products of their labor called for a lighter touch. The Finns and Swedes may have been conquered subjects, but they had shown no special affection for their own authorities,

who had abandoned them more than once before. Further violence and up-
heaval were unlikely to improve the lives or properties of those who had
decided to stay.

These peasant farmers had good reason to seek an accommodation with
their new authorities, if only to ensure that they would retain their basic
rights and liberties and preserve the most valued aspects of their communal
life. But to keep them from rebelling, the colony's officials had to cultivate
their affections, not simply demand their obedience. Authority was secured
through consent and co-optation, not by command and coercion. Settlers
had acquired power of their own by embracing their subjection and asserting collective, "national" privileges. As imperious as he could be, Stuyvesant
understood the dynamics of this relationship. Jacquet did not. Complaints
from a wide spectrum of colonists led to his recall after less than sixteen
months in office. The lessons of Serinhaem did not apply along the Delaware River.[94]

New Netherland's officials worked closely with the representatives chosen by the Finnish and Swedish settlers, and together they developed a
practical system of governance. It was only effective because Dutch officials knew the limits of their authority and power. Saddled with the task of
convincing settlers to relocate, Beeckman found himself thwarted at every
turn. The settlers who spoke for the Finns and Swedes were savvy enough
to realize that open disobedience could lead to catastrophe, so they—like
Stuyvesant in his dealings with the WIC's directors—commonly employed
strategies of delay, requests for special allowances, and other techniques of
indirect resistance or accommodation. But even when "some of the principal men of the Swedes" actively disregarded Dutch commands, as in the
Mercurius episode, they went unpunished, and shadowy unnamed malefactors and tetchy Indians were given the blame.

These techniques seemed to work well enough when the territory was
not under direct threat, but such occasions were few and far between. The
specter of a Swedish invasion kept Dutch officials from trusting their Finnish and Swedish subjects too much, and Marylanders continued to assert
their claim to the territory. In fact, the Marylanders' equal measures of appeals and threats seemed to have had a dissolving effect on all kinds of
authority along the Delaware. The English colony to the south seemed to
promise equal if not greater opportunities than anything the Dutch could
offer or that the Finns and Swedes could obtain as a group.

Although such fickle settlers would seem to make an unstable basis for a colonial regime, New Netherland's administrators on the Delaware could not help but rely on them to keep their own colonial project alive. The Finns and Swedes were productive farmers, and they served the regime as messengers, interpreters, officials, workers, and even soldiers. They brokered peace and traded with Indians when neophyte Dutch administrators could not. They also acted as an anchoring population, however undependable, that was not allied to the English, who threatened New Netherland from the southwest and the northeast.

The Finns and Swedes also benefited from their association with New Netherland. The regime provided soldiers and forts dedicated to their defense, although they were located downriver from most of their settlements. More important, the Dutch regime served as a bulwark for local officials' authority. The backing of New Netherland's officials allowed the local magistrates to maintain a specific kind of order within their own communities, one in which they could control people's movements and wield power in social relationships that depended on fixing people in space. They could pressure the new Finnish settlers to stay under their jurisdiction, and they could ensure close regulation of their own community. And when it suited their purposes, they could turn their authority against the Dutch regime, too.

The contested nature of this colonial space eventually began to undermine even these local forms of power and authority. Settlers continued to pursue opportunities in competing jurisdictions. Some went to Maryland, while others sought to improve their lot by moving within New Netherland and aligning different sets of Dutch officials against one another. The bases of ethnic authority would erode even further once the Delaware Valley became part of New York. English settlers soon began to flood into the region, bringing with them a very different kind of social and political order. Within two decades they had transformed this contested territory into a diverse but secure corner of Anglo-America.

6

From Conquest to Consent

The father has the look of a man who was a "*Master of his Art,* both as a Seaman, and as a General."[1] At his hip he wears a sword; in his right hand he cradles a baton. His left hand gestures toward a ship edging its way out of the frame. For twenty-five years he has served in the English navy. His service has brought him plaudits and punishment; the careworn expression reveals the sacrifices that have accompanied a remarkable career. In 1655, in pursuit of Oliver Cromwell's "Western Design," he captured Spanish-held Jamaica and brought it into the English empire. In the next century the island became "the vital hub of British America, far and away Britain's most significant American colony."[2] Yet the admiral's failure to take Hispaniola, the lord protector's first objective, earned him five weeks in the Tower of London upon his return to England.[3] Ten years later, his fortune restored, he was the highest officer on the Duke of York's flagship, the *Royal Charles,* engaged in the first sea battle of the Second Anglo-Dutch War. There at Lowestoft, his son later wrote, the victory was nearly complete: "About Twenty Four Ships were Taken, Burnt, and Sunck; Two Thousand Five Hundred Prisoners (said to be) brought home, besides what were slain, and wounded of the *Hollanders;* at the expence of but one old *Duch Prize* (that for want of sail fell into their Body) and about Three Hundred English Men slain."[4] The success was worthy of commemoration, and in the spring of 1666 royal favorite Sir Peter Lely painted the likeness of the now-retired forty-five-year-old.[5]

Health waning, joints aching with gout, Sir William Penn turned his weary
eyes to his "owne affaires in Ireland" and to the prospects of his eldest son
and namesake.[6]

The son had his portrait painted too, some six months after his father's,
to mark his twenty-second birthday. He wears a suit of black armor, which
stands in contrast to his pale, delicate face. The armor reminds us of the
father's martial exploits but also of the son's, who had sailed with his father
before the Battle of Lowestoft and had carried dispatches between the fleet
and the king. A year later, while the father was having his portrait painted,
the son was in Ireland attending to his family's estates, properties that the
government had seized from rebels his father had helped to defeat. During his time in Ireland the son played his own part in suppressing a rebellion, this one among soldiers garrisoned at Carrickfergus, near Belfast.[7] The
mutineers, mainly Scottish Presbyterians, had seen neither food nor pay
for several months, relying "wholly on such fish as they could find on the
shore, and even sea plants, which they boiled."[8] The admiral's son eagerly
joined the government's forces as a volunteer. "Observing his forwardnesse
on the occasion of repressing the late Mutiny," the Duke of Ormonde, the
lord lieutenant of Ireland, offered the young man command of a company
of soldiers at Kinsale, near Cork.[9] Had the father not already held the post
as a sinecure for himself, the son might have embarked on a successful
military career of his own. Instead, the elder Penn warned his restless son,
"I wish your youthful desires mayn't outrun your discretion."[10]

Discretion was not the younger Penn's strong suit. Just a few years earlier, in his second year of studies at the University of Oxford, he had been
"banisht [from] the College" for his dissenting beliefs. He later wrote that he
had experienced "persecution" as a student but that the Lord had sustained
him "in the midst of that hellish darknes & debauchery." His father was
furious with him for leaving Oxford and upon his return home responded
with "bitter usage, . . . whipping, beating, & turning out of Dores."[11] The
younger Penn's sojourn in Ireland seemed to offer the chance for a return
to respectability, yet within a year of his adventure at Carrickfergus, he had
begun attending Quaker meetings at Cork. He seems to have officially joined
the fellowship sometime before November 1667, when he and eighteen other
Quakers were arrested "for being present att a Riotous and Tumultuary assembly."[12] In 1668 he was back in London debating theology with Presbyterians, and by the end of the year he had been sentenced to prison for some
of his printed remarks. He spent eight months in "close confinement" in the

Tower of London, receiving "only a few approved visitors, and no exercise or fresh air," according to the modern editors of his papers.[13] After Penn published an apology, the king finally ordered him to be released to his father, the exasperated admiral. Within a year the son was back in prison, arrested first for participating in a Quaker meeting in August 1670 then held after his remarkable acquittal because he had refused to remove his hat before the court. Rather than pay the fine, he declared that he intended to stay in Newgate prison until "some clearer way will suddenly be found out to obtain my liberty." Eventually the willful son relented and accepted his father's assistance. He came home just days before his father's death on September 16, 1670.[14]

By this time the younger Penn had become a leading spokesman for Quaker causes and religious toleration in England. The admiral's wealth and influence made the dissenter's advocacy possible. On his father's death Penn inherited some twelve thousand acres in County Cork, Ireland. Rents from these confiscated lands would make up about half of the son's income in the years that followed.[15] More important, the father's expenditures on behalf of the English Royal Navy during the Second Anglo-Dutch War—"at least £11,000," the son claimed—had never been reimbursed by the Crown.[16] Instead of pushing for the full settlement of the debt, in 1680 Penn convinced the Crown to grant him a charter to lands along the Delaware River.

Penn's desired grant was across the river from West New Jersey, a newly established proprietary colony governed by a number of Quaker trustees, including Penn himself. The western shore, on the other hand, belonged to the admiral's longtime patron, James, the Duke of York, as part of his own proprietary colony of New York. This territory, which once belonged to New Netherland and New Sweden, was already occupied by as many as two thousand Dutch, English, Finnish, and Swedish settlers, along with the river's Lenape population.[17] Soldiers under the duke's command had taken possession of the river from the Dutch West India Company twice before—by force in 1664 and by treaty ten years later. Penn's province, named in honor of the admiral, not the Quaker, was carved out of this contested territory, which had been won "by the point of the Sword."[18] In later years Penn countered Lord Baltimore's claims to lands along the Delaware by citing the rights that came with conquest. He argued that even if Maryland's proprietor once "had a just Pretence to this River and former Possession too[,] which he never had[,] yet being by the Dutch taken and by the King taken from the Dutch it becomes the Conqueror's."[19] And the conquerors, royal brothers James and Charles Stuart, had given it to Penn.

Penn as proprietor sought to gain the consent of the Indians and Europeans who already inhabited his province, but they assented to his rule only after others had taken over the territory by force. The occupants of this space would have understood very well what Penn meant when he wrote in *An Essay towards the Present and Future Peace of Europe* (1693) that "what cannot be controuled or resisted, must be submitted to." Yet their submission was never complete or unconditional, and settlers and rival governments both proved capable of renewing the contest for this territory. As Penn noted in his appeal for a cosmopolitan government in Europe, articles of peace might give sanction to conquest, but "that doth not alwayes extinguish the Fire, . . . [and] it lies, like Embers under Ashes, ready to kindle so soon as there is a fit matter prepared for it." The national and ethnic attachments that appeared to be severed by conquest were more resilient than the conquerors realized. Only after English sovereignty in the Delaware Valley became a settled fact could Penn's vision of a peaceable and pluralistic society become a reality. Only then, "when Conquest [had] been confirmed by a *Treaty* and conclusion of Peace," could a morally superior title be established, through "that which is the security of better Titles, *Consent*." But first the gun smoke had to clear, and the embers in the ashes had to die out.[20]

From New Netherland to New York

The last phase of the contest for the Delaware Valley began in the early 1660s. For decades English colonists and colonizers had urged their officials to take action—or better yet, to allow *them* to take action—against the so-called interlopers on the Hudson and the Delaware Rivers. Lord Baltimore was still goading his officials and settlers to invade New Amstel, and colonial agents in England were urging their restored monarch to seize all of New Netherland. Meanwhile, English merchants' attempts to force their way into the Atlantic slave trade—led by none other than the Duke of York himself—created a whole new set of claims against the Dutch West India Company and the United Provinces' officials. The cacophony of protests seemed to achieve their desired effect. By the summer of 1663 Charles II's Council for Foreign Plantations had drawn up plans to make the inhabitants of New Netherland "acknowledge and submitt to His Ma[jesty's] governm[ent] or by force to compell them thereunto or expulse them."[21] The next spring the king gave his brother James, the Duke of York, a patent for lands extending

from Maine to the Delaware River. Shortly thereafter, "the King's Commissioners to Massachusetts" received instructions to reduce "the Dutch in or
neare Long Island or any where within [the] limitts of our owne dominions
to an entire obedience to our government."[22] Attacks on WIC ships and outposts along the coast of West Africa had already begun, and an invasion of
New Netherland was soon to follow.

By October 1664 English forces had obtained the surrender of all of
New Netherland's major forts along the Hudson and Delaware Rivers. Pieter Stuyvesant wisely gave up New Amsterdam without a shot on September 6, 1664. On the Delaware River, however, New Amstel's Alexander
d'Hinoyossa—who had profited tremendously from his private commerce
with Marylanders—refused to submit to English commander Sir Robert
Carr and his two warships bearing 130 men. The capture of the fort did
not take long. Two broadsides from Carr's frigates were followed by the
storming of the fort. "The losse on our part was none; the Dutch had tenn
wounded and 3 killed," Carr wrote afterward.[23]

Once the shooting had stopped, the seamen and soldiers turned "consequently to plundering," with Carr's consent.[24] He and his officers profited mightily from the looting. Twenty years later Dutch officer Gerrit van
Sweeringen gave a report of the raid to officials in Maryland, who were
collecting evidence to counter William Penn's claims to the lower Delaware
Valley. According to van Sweeringen, the invaders took from "the Citty of
Amsterdam and the Inhabitants thereabout one hundred Sheep and thirty
or forty horses[,] fifty or sixty cowes and Oxon[,] The Number of betweene
Sixty and Seventy Negroes[;] Brewhouse[,] Still house[,] and all materialls
thereunto belonging the produce of the Land for that Yeare [such] as Corne
[and] hay . . . being all to the value so neere as I now can remember of Foure
Thousand pounds sterling." The English also made off with guns, powder,
and ammunition; twenty-four cannon; plows and farming equipment;
a saw mill; and even "nine sea bu[o]yes with their Iron chaines." The human
spoils were not limited to the Africans whom Carr and his men confiscated.
"The Dutch Soldiers were taken prisoners & given to the Merchantman that
was there in recompense of his Service and into Virg[inia] they were transported to be sold," van Sweeringen said. All that the unfortunate officer
managed to save for himself was "some household stuffe and a Negroe I gott
away and some other moveables S[r] Robert Carr did permitt me to sell."[25]

The conquerors just as thoroughly ransacked the small community of
forty-one Mennonites who had recently settled at the old site of Swanen-

dael, near the mouth of the bay. Led by Pieter Corneliszoon Plockhoy, the utopian project was meant to be a kind of democratic commune where property and decisions would be shared by all.[26] Poet and former New Netherlander Jacob Steendam offered words of encouragement in a poem accompanying Plockhoy's *Kort en Klaer Ontwerp* (1662), a pamphlet promoting the endeavor:

> New Netherland's South River,—second Amazon,
> For you a pleasure garden on its banks concedes.
> Choose you the Swanendael, where Osset had his throne,
> Or any other spot your avocation needs.
> You have the choice of all; and you're left free to choose;
> Keep the conditions well, and you have naught to lose.[27]

In fact, at the gateway to a contested territory Plockhoy's peace builders had much to lose. Carr's men seized everything belonging to "the Quakin[g] Society of Plockhoy to a very naile."[28]

At New Amstel the invaders limited most of their depredations to the property belonging to the Dutch regime and its officers. Before the fighting began, Carr had negotiated the consent of the "Sweede" as well as the Dutch "Burgurs & townesmen" to the English takeover.[29] Much as Pieter Stuyvesant and Johan Risingh had done nine and ten years earlier, Carr sought to turn settlers' mutable allegiances to his advantage. For three days before attacking the fort at New Amstel, he negotiated with representatives of the freemen who lived along the river. His instructions explicitly directed him to pursue this policy. As he approached the fort "possessed by the Dutch," Carr was to summon the colony's governor and its inhabitants "to yield obedience to his Majestie as the rightfull Sovereign of that Tract of Land." He was to inform them that the king had "graciously" allowed them to possess their land and property "with the same privileges And upon the Same Terms, which they do now possess them Only that they Change their Masters, whether they be the West India Company or the City of Amsterdam." Carr's instructions included special consideration for the Swedish population along the river, who were represented as members of a nation that might welcome the English takeover. "To the Swedes you Shall remonstrate their happy return, under a Monarchicall Government and his Majesties good Inclination to that Nation, and to all men who shall Comply with his Majesties Rights and Title in Delaware without Force of Arms," his instructions read. But if Carr found that he could not subdue the territory by force, he was to seek the aid of the governor of Maryland "and of all other English who live near the dutch plantations" to "reduce the place." Carr was to deflect Marylanders' claims to the river by noting that the king would settle any such claims in the future.[30]

The agreement that Carr forged with the colony's "burgomasters" on October 1, 1664, confirmed the existing liberties of the settler population in exchange for their promise of allegiance. Carr represented "his Majesty of Great Britain," while the burgomasters acted "on the Behalf of themselves, and all the Dutch and Swedes Inhabiting in Delaware Bay and Delaware River." According to the agreement, "whoever of what Nation soever" peacefully submitted to the king's authority would have their properties protected "by his Majesties Laws and Justice." Anyone who took the oath of allegiance would become "a free Denizen" and would "enjoy all the privileges of trading into any of his Majesties Dominions, As freely as any Englishman." Settlers were to retain their religious liberties, and the conquered colony's magistrates were to keep their official powers for at least six months. The agreement was designed to preserve the settlers' most important rights and liberties, including the right to leave. If "any Dutchman, or other person" wanted to leave the colony, he would be free to depart with his goods for up to six months after the agreement had been signed.[31]

The conquest of New Netherland set off a string of protests in several European capitals. Diplomats from the United Provinces protested to Charles II for years afterward without effect. The Swedish government also became involved, as it had been seeking redress for the loss of New Sweden for nearly a decade. A year after New Netherland's conquest of the colony, the Swedish ambassador to the United Provinces, Harald Appelbom, presented a memorial to the States General demanding restitution and payment for damages but gained no headway with the uncooperative West India Company. The government of Charles X of Sweden made plans in the late 1650s to recapture New Sweden, but hostilities closer to home prevented their execution. Again in 1663 and 1664, Appelbom petitioned the States General to restore New Sweden. On each of these occasions the States General referred the Swedish agent to the WIC, whose representatives denied all of the claims against it. After the English takeover of New Netherland, the Swedish government continued to demand restitution from the States General, but it also turned its attention to the English government. These efforts gained greater impetus in early 1669, when authorities in Sweden received a report that five hundred families of their former subjects remained in the territory of New Sweden.

Over a period of several months the Swedish ambassadors to England and the Netherlands pressed for restoration of the lost colony, without success. These negotiations continued into the early 1670s, but they, too, proved futile.[32]

The Rebellion of the Long Finn

The 1669 report of New Sweden's five hundred abandoned families sparked a revival of Swedish diplomatic action in Europe. It also coincided with a remarkable "rebellion" that implicated a large proportion of the Swedish and Finnish population of the Delaware Valley.[33] The most detailed account of the event was recorded some eighty years after the fact by the Finnish-Swedish naturalist Pehr Kalm during his time in Pennsylvania. Kalm interviewed many of the descendants of New Sweden's original settlers and in the summer of 1750 recorded a story about the uprising.[34] His informant was Jacob Bengtson, a descendant of several prominent settlers of New Sweden. Bengtson's parents (Anders Bengtsson and Gertrude Rambo), his maternal grandfather (Peter Rambo), and his wife's grandfather (Peter Kock) either witnessed the events or participated in them. Yet they, like most of New Sweden's old guard, did not support the "impostor by the name of Königsmark."[35]

According to Bengtson, the leader of the revolt was Swedish by birth, but he shared no relation to his supposed namesake, the late Swedish military hero Count Otto Wilhelm Königsmark. In fact, this false Königsmark had been sent to Maryland "to serve a number of years as a servant or slave." He escaped bondage and fled to "his fellow-countrymen in New Sweden," now under English rule. Pretending to belong to the Königsmark family, he claimed that "the Swedish fleet lay outside in the Bay and would at the first opportunity capture the land from the English." He tried to convince his listeners "to cast off the foreign yoke . . . [and] to join in slaying the English" once they had received news of the fleet's arrival.[36]

The impostor was quite credible, persuading a "large proportion of the Swedish colonists," who hid him and protected him. They supplied him with "the best food and drink they had, so that he lived exceedingly well," despite his concealment. But they did more than just feed their guest. Although the city of Philadelphia did not yet exist in 1669, Bengtson claimed that the man's protectors "went to Philadelphia and bought powder, bullets, lead, etc., to be ready at the first signal." Finally, after the false Königsmark summoned the "Swedes" to a meeting, he "exhorted them to throw off the yoke, reminded them of what they had suffered, and finally asked them whether they held with the King of Sweden or the King of England."[37] With this rousing call to arms, one part of the meeting immediately declared its support for the King of Sweden. They still thought of themselves as Swedish subjects and maintained an affection for their country and king.

Yet before these reborn patriots could take any action, "Peter Kock pointed out that since the land was English and the settlement had been duly ceded to the English crown he ought to support the English sovereign." Peter Kock had come to New Sweden in 1641 as a punishment for misdeeds committed while he was a soldier in Sweden, but twenty-eight years later he was a justice in the Upland Court, whose jurisdiction included the upriver settlements where most of the Finnish and Swedish population lived. Now he was "Kaptain Kock."[38] After calling for allegiance to the English sovereign he now served, he "ran out, slammed the door, and braced himself in front of it," crying out for assistance. Eventually, the "impostor" was able to break free, although Kock managed to wound him on the hand with his knife. Once the rebel had escaped, "Kock reported the matter to the English, who set out and made the alleged Königsmarck a prisoner."[39]

In Bengtson's account Kock confronted the impostor once he had been captured. "You rogue, tell me now what is your name, for we can see enough that you are no noble."[40] The prisoner answered that his real name was Marcus Jacobson. Further questioning revealed that he was "so ignorant that he could neither read nor write." After receiving his judgment, the rebel was branded and sent to Barbados, where he was sold "as a slave." According to Bengtson, English officials subsequently confiscated half of all the Swedish collaborators' property, including their land, livestock, goods, and clothes.[41]

New York's records confirm that authorities ordered Jacobson to be "publickly & severely whipt & stigmatiz'd or Branded in the fface with the Letter (R) with an Inscription written in great Letters & putt uppon his Breast . . . for Attempting Rebellion," and then sent him to Barbados to be sold as an indentured servant "for ye space of Fower years or ye usuall tyme Servants are there sould at."[42] The records also reveal that officials fined seventy-three men and one widow for their participation in the rebellion. Their fines totaled more than twelve thousand guilders, with four men receiving fines of fifteen hundred guilders and a fifth a fine of two thousand guilders. Others, by contrast, received fines as low as fifty guilders, with the most common fine being one hundred guilders.[43]

All in all Jacobson and his supporters escaped with a relatively light punishment. Although servitude in Barbados was a virtual death sentence, Jacobson avoided immediate execution, despite the court's judgment that "yᵉ said Long ffinne deserves to dye." Even though the laws of New York mandated that "any man . . . [who] shall Traitorously deny his Majestyes right and titles to his Crownes and Dominions, or shall raise Armes to resist his Authority, . . . shall be put to Death," authorities chose instead to impose great fines on the organizers and smaller ones on their collaborators.[44] The lenience of English officials reflected not so much the self-described "Clemency & favour of the Governoʳ & Councell" as it did their profound weakness.[45] Before Jacobson's sentencing had taken place (and before his failed attempt to escape from jail), New York governor Francis Lovelace instructed the English officers at New Castle not to inflict any punishment on the conspirators. His officers should try to stop "yᵉ spreading of yᵉ contagion [so] that it grow not furthʳ" rather than "amputating or cutting of[f] any member to make yᵉ cure more perfect." As for the "poore deluded sort" who supported Jacobson, Lovelace believed the "Advice of theire owne Countrymen" was best, as "knowing their temper well, [they] pʳᵉscribe a method for keeping them in ordʳ, wᶜʰ is seuerity & laying such Taxes on them as may not giue them liberty to Entertaine any other thoughts but how to discharge them."[46] In other words, the punishment meted out to the conspirators had been devised by the Swedes' and the Finns' own headmen.

The fines on the leaders of the conspiracy were indeed very high. But for most others they seem not to have caused untold hardship, even though some six years later the New York government was still collecting fines from those who still owed.[47] In a 1671 census of European settlers along the Delaware, many if not most of the fined men's names appeared as landowners.[48] If officials had attempted to impose anything stricter, the colony might have lost many productive members of the community and alienated those who were not involved. Yet if the number of settlers who were fined indicates the actual scale of the Swedish and Finnish population's involvement, then "Königsmark's" uprising might very well have succeeded.

English-Hating Indians and Marauding Marylanders

New York's officials may have doubted the loyalties of the Swedes and Finns, but like so many insecure regimes in the Delaware Valley, they had more reason to fear their Lenape neighbors. An undated letter (ca. 1670) from five men to Captain John Carr, the commander at New Castle, indicates that Indians in the Delaware Valley still sought to exploit national differences among European settlers. The first part of the letter, signed by "Thomas S[. . .]," recounted an incident in which a group of about twenty-five Lenape tried to force their way into the settlers' houses, although they were ultimately able to keep out the intruders.[49] One of the Lenape fighters told the letter's author that they "would do us no hurt but for the English and all new Castll thay would kill man woman and Child and burne the howll plase." The second part of the letter, signed by three Finnish settlers and a former Dutch soldier, described another encounter between these Indians and one of the signers, "Andris Fines [Finn]," in which they told him "thay would do them no hurt but for y[ou] and Mr. Tom, thay would tappoose them and burne all man woman and Child." The writer added that the Indian men were "wel Loded . . . and thay say thay will kill all." Finally, at the close of the damaged letter the writer noted, "Thay say wee must still s[tay] for they will do us no hurt."[50]

Three of the five men who signed the letter lived along the Christina River at an inland area called Deer Point, located a short distance northwest of New Castle. The letter was addressed from the farm of one of the signers, "Andris Andrisones," also known as "Anders the Finn." The Indians' remarks indicated that they sought to distinguish between the older Dutch, Finnish, and Swedish settlers and New Castle's English inhabitants. Although the cause for the natives' violent displeasure with "the English and all New Castll" is not clear, other sources offer some hints. In a letter to New York's governor, dated March 9, 1670, officials William Tom and Peter Alrichs wrote that "wee are in a sad condicon . . . under the power of the Heathen." The Indians' unhappiness seemed tied to the English origins of the officials who now governed along the river. Tom and Alrichs wrote that the "sachems of the Indians give for reason of there warre that they threaten to make upon the Christians is they say where the English come they drive from there lands and bring for instance the North Virginia and Maryland and feare if not timely prevent shall doe so here." The Indians were menacing the English on the Delaware because they belonged to the same nation as the English on the Chesapeake. In the past the Lenape had supported certain European nations while blocking others. Now they were mobilizing to frighten the new English settlers while urging the older inhabitants to stay.[51]

The Marylanders created other problems for the Delaware's residents, much as they had in the decades before the territory came under English rule. In 1669 Lord Baltimore ordered the creation of two new counties along the Delaware from the mouth of the bay to the fortieth parallel, which he considered the upper boundary of his patent. Later that year the surveyor-general of Maryland wrote to Governor Lovelace, informing him that New Castle and all south of it belonged to Lord Baltimore's province. The surveying continued in the years that followed, despite the protests of New York's officials. Maryland's officials directed most of their attention to the "Whore-Kill" (from the Dutch *Hoornkil*) an isolated settlement near the mouth of the bay. Home to about fifty settlers in 1672, it had been the site of Swanendael in the early 1630s and Plockhoy's colony in the early 1660s. Most of the settlers were Dutch in origin, but several English planters from Maryland now also lived there.[52]

Maryland's government sent another surveyor to the mouth of the Delaware Bay in the summer of 1672, just after news had arrived of the start of the Third Anglo-Dutch War. To enforce Lord Baltimore's claims and to terrorize those inhabitants who did not acknowledge his authority, Maryland's government also sent an armed force under the command of a captain named Thomas Jones. There, according to Governor Lovelace, Jones and "a Party as dissolute as himselfe . . . bound yᵉ Magistrates, and Inhabitants, despitefully treated them, rifled, and plunder'd them of their Goods." When one of the settlers "demanded by what Authority, hee acted, [Jones] answer'd in noe other Language but a Cockt Pistol to his Breast, wᶜʰ if it had spoke, had forever silenc'd him." Lovelace was all the more outraged at "those violent Proceedings" because they occurred while England was at war with the Dutch Republic and "all true hearted Englishmen [were] . . . buckling on their Armorˢ to vindicate their Honoʳ & to assert yᵉ imperiall Interests of his Sacred Ma[jesty's] Rights and Dominions."[53] Lovelace's protests seem to have had little effect. In the fall of 1672 New York's governor sent orders to Captain Carr to prepare New Castle for an invasion from Maryland.[54] Lord Baltimore's men ultimately did not attack, but they would continue to set their sights on the Whorekill.

When Dutch authority was briefly restored along the Delaware River during the war, Maryland's officials seized their chance. In early December 1673 forty horsemen stormed into the town of Whorekill and demanded the submission of the inhabitants. After occupying the town for several weeks, their commander, Thomas Howell, rode back to Maryland to report to Governor Calvert. Upon his return to Whorekill, he summoned all the men in town, seized their weapons, and ordered his soldiers to torch their houses. The soldiers took the settlers' boats and left only a single building standing, a barn that by chance had not burned down. The Marylanders left the stranded settlers with no supplies, no weapons, and no means to travel, knowing full well that the closest settlement was more than sixty miles away.[55] The Whorekill's isolated inhabitants had become the latest victims of distant imperial rivalries. But they suffered so intensely because local settlers in Maryland, not royal officers in London, had declared them to be enemies of the English nation.

Inglorious Revolutions

Unlike the transitions in 1654, 1655, and 1664, the reassertion of Dutch authority over the Delaware Valley in 1673 took place without military action. When news arrived that a Dutch fleet had attacked and seized Manhattan, New York's officials at New Castle apparently ceded their authority immediately to the representatives of the new regime. In September 1673, a month after the capture of Manhattan, a group of "deputies from the Southriver" visited the commanders at "Fort Willem Hendrick" (formerly New York's Fort James) and "declared their submission to the authority of Their High: Might[inesses] the Lord[s] States-General of the United Netherlands and His Illustrious Highness, the Prince of Orange." English authority was so weak, and these revolutions had become so routine, that New Netherland's officers did not even have to visit the Delaware River to take possession of the territory.[56]

In the resulting, well-rehearsed agreement the inhabitants received privileges to free trade, freedom of conscience, and continued possession of the properties they held. The river's English, Finnish, and Swedish settlers were to have the same privileges as "all other subjects of this government," provided that they swore the required oath of allegiance. The only central point of difference from previous agreements was that the river's inhabitants had to agree to contribute their labor to the construction of a new fort. In return, however, they would be free from any taxes on their lands and excises on alcohol for three years. The river settlements retained the three court jurisdictions the English had established at New Castle, Upland, and

Whorekill. The leading Dutch official in the previous English regime, Peter Alrichs, became the new "Commander and Schout" of the Delaware settlements. He was following closely in the footsteps of his father, Jacob Alrichs, who had served as director of New Amstel from 1657 until his death in 1660. Although Alrichs was instructed to protect the inhabitants' "freedom of conscience," he was also ordered to restore the Dutch Reformed Church to its place of prominence in the colony. In New York, by contrast, there had been no official or established church of any sort.[57]

The restoration of English authority on the Delaware took place as smoothly as the handover to Dutch officials a year earlier. Although the governments of England and United Provinces signed the Treaty of Westminster in February 1674, the formal return of English rule over New Netherland / New York did not start until eight months later. As before, many of the officers in the previous regime retained their posts, Alrichs excepted, because he had "proffer'd himselfe to yᵉ Dutch at their first coming, of his own Motion and acted very violently (as their cheife Officer) ever since." The new governor, Edmund Andros, restored to the Delaware's inhabitants the "Lawes and Customes" in effect under the previous English regime. Still divided into their three court jurisdictions, the settlers of the Delaware Valley continued to manage most of their own affairs through local institutions.[58]

These institutions were usually capable of managing the disputes and differences that were a part of everyday life. Yet sometimes controversies erupted that raised old doubts about the loyalties of a settler population composed of so many different nations. One such episode occurred in 1675, when New Castle's magistrates announced at the Lutheran Church at Crane Hook that "each and every male, who belongs to the district of New Castle" would be required to help build a dike on public land and to repair another that adjoined the land of local Dutch magistrate Hans Block.[59] Because most of the church's parishioners were Finns and Swedes, officials nearly started a riot when they tried to arrest those who protested the decision.

An account written afterward by Block and signed by two other magistrates (one Dutch, one English) described the scene. First English settler John Ogle "belligerently stepped forward (in church) and said: 'We neither intend to build Hans Block's dike nor the other dike.'" New Castle's sheriff, Edmund Cantwell, answered, "You John Ogle are an Englishman and it does not become you to make such commotion among so many people," then grabbed Ogle by the arm and pushed him out of the church. When Cantwell seized Ogle, a Swede named Matthias Mathiasson de Vos ("Mathys Smith" in

Block's account), defended him, saying, "The man speaks the truth and what he says we all say." After Cantwell struck Matthiasson with his cane, the Lutheran minister Jacobus Fabritius shouted out, "The man is right, he speaks the truth, if he has to go into the stocks, then I want to go too." At first Cantwell and the magistrates tried to escort Ogle and Fabritius to a nearby yacht that would take them as prisoners to New York, but a gathering crowd began shouting "Seize it, seize it," while others "milled around with swords and clubs." Realizing that they were losing control of the situation, the magistrates set Ogle and Fabritius free. Tempers were still hot when Ogle and Block encountered each other several days later. Block accused Ogle of instigating the "recent mutiny," while Ogle warned that if "the Finns had been drunk, not much good would have come of it." When Block retorted that the order to work on the dikes was now posted at the church, Ogle replied that he thought "as much of your order as this dirt on the street" and kicked the ground with his foot.[60] Because of Block's testimony against him, Ogle was later arrested as one of the "Ringleaders" in the "late disturbance."[61]

Ogle's connection to the Finns probably came in the person of his wife, Elisabeth Petersdotter, the daughter of a soldier who had once served in New Sweden. Ogle had been a soldier too, arriving with the English force that captured New Amstel in 1664. A later petition from several inhabitants of New Castle reveals other Finnish or Swedish ties among the protesters. Of the nine men who signed the petition, seven have identifiable origins. These seven all had connections to Finns or Swedes along the river. Four were either native Finns or Swedes or their descendants; one was Dutch with a Swedish wife; Ogle was English with a Swedish wife; and another man was Dutch, but his daughter had married a Finnish man.[62] A subsequent report by William Tom, one of the chief English officials at New Castle, identified two other men, both Dutch, as having been involved in the disturbance.[63]

The minister Jacob Fabritius, on the other hand, was a more recent arrival from New York. Like his counterpart Lars Lock, who had been one of the leaders in the protest against Governor Printz in 1653 and a strong supporter of the "Long Finn" in 1669, Fabritius was eager to take his congregants' side in a conflict with their authorities. He already had a short but intense history of challenging officers of the law. He began his service as a Lutheran minister in New York in 1669, having been assigned to the colony by the Lutheran consistory in Amsterdam.[64] Within a year, however, his congregation petitioned for his removal, complaining that Fabritius was "very fond of wine and brandy, and knows how to curse and swear, too."[65] Soon afterward he left for New Castle, where a mixed group of Dutch, Finnish, and Swedish congregants had invited him to preach at the Crane Hook church. Now established along the Delaware River, the minister returned to New York for long enough to stir up further trouble there. During the short period in 1674 when New York was in Dutch hands, Fabritius improperly married a couple on his own authority, and the local court stripped him of his functions as a minister for a year. Later that year the *schout* at New Orange (the new Dutch name for New York City / New Amsterdam) brought Fabritius to court after the minister had forced his way into his wife Anna's house, pushed another woman into the road, resisted the arresting soldiers, and struck the *schout* himself.[66] Later, after the dispute about the dike at New Castle, governor Edmund Andros identified the minister as "a principall Ring Leader in causing a tumultuous disturbance" and ordered him to come to New York to explain himself. The authorities there once again stripped him of his authority to preach, citing his role in "causing a disturbance & uproare against yᵉ Magistrate" and "his former irregular life and conversation."[67] Nonetheless, two years later Fabritius would begin preaching at the new church established by the Finnish and Swedish community upriver at Wicaco.[68]

William Tom's account of the "mutiny," addressed to Governor Andros, was similar to Block's, although Tom's rhetoric reached much greater heights. He claimed that the crowd's freeing of Ogle and Fabritius foretold future anarchy. If "a plebeian faccion" could control the execution of justice "upon every occasion there frenzicall braynses pleases," the country would fall into disorder. He warned that "the Sweeds and Fynnes . . . [were] a sort of people that must be Kept under else they will rebell[,] and of that nation these here are the worse sort as by instance the Long Fynne." If these troublemakers were permitted to escape punishment, "noe man Knowes his owne[,] and trade must dye when noe man is sure of his owne estate." Tom followed this dire prediction with a list of infamous rebels in European history: "witnes former examples as Mazinello[,] John of Leyden[,] Jack Cade and Wat Tyler[,] the de Witts and in these parts since our comming the insurreccion at New yorke in the time of Generall Niccolls."[69] Andros granted Tom's request to punish the protesters. The court at New Castle levied heavy fines against those who were involved, just as it had punished the participants in the "Long Finn Rebellion" five years earlier.[70]

Memories of these incidents and the resulting bad feelings lasted a long time. In February 1680 Augustine Herrman's son Ephraim, who had become an official in the Delaware River's government, reported to fellow official "John Moll" (Jan Moll, a Netherlander) that some of the Finns and Swedes were spreading rumors about him along the river. According to Herrman, Jonas Nielsen's wife claimed that some officials who had visited New York had said "all the sweads in the river were rebellers etc. and that it was done as they supposed to make the Sweads odious in the Governors Sight and the Lyke." When Herrman asked her for the source of this information, she and others told him that "Jacob vander Veers wyfe togeather with Evert Fin at their Comming bake from New Yorke had Informed and for a Certaine truth related to them at Taokanink in a full Company of a great many people that Mr. Moll had informed the Governor that all the Sweads were rebellers against the Government and a great deal more." Herrman tried to convince the company that the rumors were false, yet he said that many others had told him the same story. Even if the rumor had been untrue, the substance of it traveled quickly among the river's Finnish and Swedish settlements.[71]

Vander Veer's wife, Christina, was probably Swedish. She may still have carried a grudge from the dike "mutiny" of five years earlier. Her Dutch husband, Jacob, formerly a soldier in New Netherland, had played a leading role in the opposition to building the dike, and officials at the river had fined him and two of his sons 460 guilders as a result. In 1679 the Dutch magistrates at the New Castle court said he had "always ben a Troublesome mutinous person and one of a turbulent spiritt from the beginning always Contending with and opposing the authority." They reported that he and his wife had been banished from New York before they came to the Delaware, and that "his lyfe and Living resembl[ed] more that of Indian then a Christian." Since coming to the river, he had been involved "in Continuall stryfe with his neighbours" and had been one of the "Cheef Ringleaders" of the "mutiny" in 1675.[72]

The other source of the rumors, "Evert Fin" (Evert Hendricksson Ek), had also protested against the dikes. He, too, had a history of confrontations with authority. He came to New Sweden in 1641 and served as a hired laborer there for seven years before becoming a freeman. He was one of the men who had protested against Governor Printz's autocratic governance in 1653. The annals of New Netherland and New York record subsequent accusations of bigamy, spousal abuse, and violent attacks against his neighbors. Based on the testimony of local Finnish and Swedish officials, Stuyvesant banished him from the Delaware River in 1663. Ever tenacious, Evert made his way back and became the captain of the local militia at Crane Hook, one of the communities along the river that strongly supported the "Long Finn Rebellion" of 1669. The river's officials fined him 300 guilders for his role in that event and 460 guilders for his participation in the dike mutiny.

This long-lived controversy demonstrates at once the persistence of national distinctions and the effects of nearly forty years of Dutch, English, Finnish, and Swedish intermingling. Many of the settlers outside New Castle who resisted the order to construct the dikes were Finns who had broken away in 1662 from the older "New Swedish" elite who lived upriver.[73] Although these settlers had separated themselves from the old settler leadership—the same people who had advocated fining the Long Finn's supporters with such "seuerity" that they would not be able to think about anything else—they retained their connections to one another and to the larger Finnish-Swedish community as a whole.[74] They also formed friendships with their new neighbors. Intermarriage, especially, fostered and reinforced cross-ethnic ties.

These rowdy representatives of a "plebeian faccion" were cosmopolitans of a very different sort from the gentleman-merchants, land speculators, and diplomats who moved so easily between colonies. They were people whose shared nonelite status encouraged connections across national or ethnic boundaries. They had the remarkable ability to alienate officials and to cause uproars under multiple regimes. Their antagonists were cosmopolitans as well. These men, such as Peter Alrichs, Ephraim Herrman, and Peter Kock, were wealthier and better established, although not necessarily from better origins. They cooperated with authorities so long as those authorities did not ask anything too onerous of them, and they served as willing mediators between communities of foreign subjects and larger systems of authority. For these men stable systems of political authority created a common institutional space in which they could occupy influential positions. By contrast, the vander Veers and Everts sought a very different kind of order. Theirs was an even more decentralized space in which diverse local settlers, not their polyglot superiors, had the ultimate say in their communities. Both groups relied on ethnic attachments to forge their identities, but the mingling of peoples over time had shaken up these categories and created new combinations. The result was a creole cosmopolitanism rooted in old national attachments yet reoriented toward a pluralistic present and future.

"Like People of One Country"

The new colony of Pennsylvania seemed to offer space both for orderly and disorderly cosmopolitanisms. A pluralistic discourse about national difference appeared at the colony's very founding. It meshed easily with the old model of political subjection, in which individuals could transfer their loyalties to a new lord in exchange for his protection. For the promoters of Pennsylvania, the Dutch, Finns, and Swedes who preceded the English did not represent sources of subversion or disorder. Their national affiliations no longer signified allegiances to empires—they were all English subjects now. The old settlers seemed incapable of threatening their more populous neighbors. In fact, they seemed to represent an earlier age that was rapidly disappearing.

William Penn's writings about the "*first Planters* in these parts" are representative in this respect. At the same time as he extolled the virtues of the old settlers, he depicted them as legacies of a less "improved" order. Penn described "the *Sweeds*" as "a *plain, strong, industrious People*, yet have made no great progress in *Culture* or *propagation* of *fruit-Trees*, as if they desired rather to have enough, than *Plenty* or *Traffick*." He attributed the lack of development to their close relationship to the Indians, who "made [the Swedes] the more careless, by furnishing them with the means of *Profit*, to wit, *Skins* and *Furs*, for *Rum*, and such *strong Liquors*."[75] Other writers marveled at the frontier skills and ways such a life produced. Thomas Paschall was amazed that "the *Swedes*" could build houses with little iron and no tool other than an ax. He noted that they are "generaly very ingenous people, . . . and have lived much at ease, having great plenty of all sorts of provisions," although they planted "but little *Indian* corne, nor Tobacco." The Swedes were well provisioned but only "ordinarily Cloathd" before the English came. Now "they have gotten fine Cloaths, and are going proud," Paschall wrote. Their cosmopolitan skill in languages was another product of life on this contested frontier: "Most of the *Sweads*, and *Finns* . . . speak *English, Swead, Finn, Dutch*, and the *Indian*."[76]

According to English accounts, the old settlers welcomed the newcomers with open arms. In his "Letter to the Society of Traders" Penn wrote that he found "*Love* and *Respect*" when he reached the river. The inhabitants offered "an universal kind *Welcome*, every sort in their way," even though they were "of several *Nations*, as well as divers *Judgments*." The Swedes in particular "kindly received me, as well as the *English*, who were few, before the People concerned with me came among them," Penn wrote. He also commended "their *Respect* to *Authority,* and *kind Behaviour* to the *English;* they do not degenerate from the *Old friendship* between *both Kingdoms.*"[77]

Penn articulated a more explicit vision of national pluralism in "A Further Account of the Province of Pennsylvania and Its Improvements." There he wrote that "the People are a *Collection* of divers Nations in *Europe:* As, *French, Dutch, Germans, Sweeds, Danes, Finns, Scotch*[,] *Irish* and *English;* and of the last equal to the rest." For all the appearance of diversity this collection of nations was essentially one people, Penn wrote. "As they are of one kind, and in one Place and under One Allegiance, so they live like People of *One Count[r]y,* [whose] Civil Union has had a considerable influence towards the prosperity of that place."[78]

Because these diverse subjects were united through their allegiance and their adherence to the new province, the new regime did not question their loyalty. Newcomers seemed more interested in the religious diversity they represented. Penn noted that the "*Dutch* have a *Meeting-place* for Religious Worship at *New-Castle,* and the *Sweedes three,* one at *Christina,* one at *Tenecum,* and one at *Wicoco,* within half a Mile of this Town."[79] Gabriel Thomas wrote that the "way of Worship the *Sweeds* use in this Countrey, is the *Lutheran,*" then went on to describe the four different English denominations in Pennsylvania.[80] The German Pietist minister Francis Daniel Pastorius divided "the Religions in this Province" into similar categories. There were the Calvinists, who were mainly English and Dutch; the Quakers, who were of no specific nation; and the Evangelicals, who were Swedes and "High-Germans."[81]

For the old European inhabitants of the Delaware Valley Penn's pluralistic ideal complemented the diverse local order they had already established, but it also subjected it to new pressures that were hard to resist. For the Dutch inhabitants at New Castle the disintegrating pressures of religious toleration, schism, and an English majority were too much to bear. Institutional neglect struck the first blow—the Dutch Reformed Church had no minister along the river between 1659 and 1679. When by chance church members finally received one, he caused a split between the Dutch and English factions within the church. The membership soon chased out the new minister, Pieter Tesschenmaeker, and requested another with less orthodox views. Their chosen replacement did not come, and in time many of the congregants moved elsewhere or joined the English Presbyterian church that had grown up in their midst.[82]

For the more numerous Finns and Swedes of the Delaware Valley, the plural order offered opportunities as well as challenges. Signs of both appeared in correspondence to officials in Sweden in 1693, when the members of the Swedish Lutheran churches along the Delaware wrote to request new ministers to fill their empty pulpits. One letter, signed by thirty church members, described the virtues of their new home. "This land is a mighty fruitful good and plentiful country, and here doth grow all sorts of grains in great plenty; and all that we sow and plant doth thrive mightily," they wrote. The letter mentioned the flourishing grain trade with the islands of the West Indies and "the great plenty of all sorts—beasts, fowls and fishes." The men worked as farmers, the women as spinners and weavers, "so that we have great occasion to thank the Almighty God for his manifold mercies and benefits, which we at his hand receive."[83]

Their community was stable and strong. "We live also in peace, friendship and amity with one another, and the Indians have not molested us for many years," they wrote. Even when they lived under foreign regimes, they prospered. "In general, we all confess and proclaim and in truth say that we have been exceedingly and mighty well treated, both in the Dutch government as well as his Majesty the King of England's time." The key to their happiness was their ability to participate in their own government. "We have always been well dealt with, seated in the court with his Majesty's justices and also in Councils, and yet do to this day. We have always had good and gracious government and we live with one another in peace and quietness," the letter explained.[84] Their avowals of peaceful settlement and good relations papered over not only the divisions among themselves but also the "mutinies" their congregations had participated in over the past half-century. This identity as loyal, obedient subjects would become central to the Finns' and Swedes' representation of themselves in the years to come.

Accompanying the request for ministers was a letter from eighty-one-year-old Peter Gunnarsson Rambo, who first came to New Sweden in 1640. In the letter to his sister Rambo discussed his marriage to Britta Mattsdotter, who "also came from Sweden, from Vasa," a largely Swedish settlement in Finland, and proudly noted the success of his seven children and thirty-seven grandchildren. Rambo wrote that he had "served faithfully . . . the Swedish regime, the Holland Dutch, and now the English." He had been a member of the local court for twenty-nine years "both in the Swedes' and the Hollanders' time." He noted with approval the Dutch government's "rule that no case [involving Swedes] should be decided at court unless the Swedes had their voice in it." Looking back on more than fifty years of life in the Delaware Valley, Rambo wrote that "our nations also live faithfully with one another, both in harmony and affection." They inhabited "a very splendid fruitful land" that offered all that they needed. Although "the surrounding lands and neighbors have had great duress from the Indians," the Swedes lived in "harmony, affection, and faithfulness" with them.[85]

New Sweden's second generation had a similarly benign view of past and present. Lars Persson Cock, the son of influential settler (and nemesis of the Long Finn) Captain Peter Kock, addressed a letter to his father's brother, Mouns Larsson. Lars wrote that his late father had come "out here to the country of New Sweden, sent by his Royal Majesty to settle the land with the others, his countrymen." His father had served as a justice in New Sweden "with the greatest loyalty," but he also had been an official "during the Holland Dutch regime . . . and in the English regime's time likewise." His father was "always in advice and counsel with them." Lars, the son, was just as active in local affairs. He was the warden of the Swedish Lutheran church at Wicaco, south of Philadelphia, and he had been a justice in the local court since 1680. He currently served the provincial government as an interpreter in its negotiations with neighboring Indians. He had married an Englishwoman, and like his father, he seemed adept at mediating between his countrymen and their new neighbors. Yet he was still conscious of his ties to old Sweden. He asked his uncle to pass along the letter to his family and relatives so that he "might receive a gladdening reply." In order for a letter to reach him, Lars noted that it should include his surname, "Cock." "Since we were living here among foreign nations," he wrote, "my late father took that surname so that we and others could be distinguished from one another." Even as he lived comfortably amid diversity, Lars nevertheless described his neighbors as belonging to "foreign nations."[86]

As pleased as Rambo and his compatriots were to renew their contact with officials in Sweden, they had not been the ones who initiated this round of correspondence. In May 1693 they had received a letter from the Swedish postmaster at Göteborg, Johan Thelin, requesting information and news about the Swedish community in Pennsylvania. The church members responded by describing their situation and their desire for support from their national church. Two earlier attempts at correspondence had received no response. They were nonetheless very happy to hear that "his Majesty of Sweden . . . does yet bear a tender and a Christian heart and care unto us, as his former old and true subjects, for our souls' good and happiness, and a lover of the Lutheran faith." They expressed thanks for the king's offer to send ministers and "godly books" to them. They wrote that they needed "two Swedish ministers that are well learned in the Holy Scriptures, and that may be able to defend them and us against all false opposers who can or may oppose any of us, and also one that may defend the true Lutheran faith which we do confess, that if tribulation should come amongst us, and we should suffer our faith, that we are ready to seal it with our blood." The Swedes may have lived contentedly among strangers, but they were less certain of their ability to fend off foreign religious sects. They needed protection from the Swedish Church in order to preserve their faith.[87]

In this new competitive religious space these "former old and true subjects" did not need twenty-seven ships or twelve hundred soldiers. Instead, they asked for two ministers, "three Sermon Books, 12 Bibles, 42 Psalmbooks, 100 of the lesser, with 200 Catechisms [and] 200 ABC books."[88] The greatest threats to their community were toleration and anglicization. They needed tools to help them protect their faith and language, not their allegiance. Although these Lutherans still thought of themselves as Finns and Swedes, their sense of national belonging had lost its direct connection to the Swedish state. Instead, they maintained their connection to Sweden and their coherence as a Swedish community through their church. Like so many of the immigrants who later joined them in Pennsylvania, they would either gain or lose their coherence as an ethnic and religious group through religious institutions and local networks.

As the imperial contest for the Delaware Valley came to a close, competition in other spaces began. Indians once again played central roles in these spaces. Many of the Lenape sold their claims along the river and headed west into lands that had once belonged to the Minquas-Susquehannock, now much reduced after their war with the Iroquois. Penn did not need to conquer the Indians in his province—surveyors and settlers were more effective than soldiers. Disease also played its part in clearing the way for the thousands of colonists who followed Penn to the Delaware Valley. Gabriel Thomas wrote that the "Dutch and Sweeds" informed him that the Indians were "greatly decreased in number to what they were when they came first into this Country." He added that the "Indians themselves [said] that two of them die to every one Christian that comes here."[89] Yet not all the Indians of the Delaware Valley died out or disappeared. Even as they moved away, they formed new combinations, new nations, out of the old. Their lands became the arena for the next round of contest, this time between the traders, settlers, and soldiers of Great Britain and France.[90]

From Logan to Franklin

Pehr Kalm had traveled the road to Germantown once before. His guide then, in September 1748, had been Peter Cock, a Swedish-born merchant who lived in Philadelphia. During their autumn ride, Kalm had marveled at the farms that lined the wooded road, each boasting an orchard thick with fruit and cornstalks "six to ten feet high . . . covered with fine green leaves."[1] On this journey in February 1750 the forest was cold and barren, and beyond the trees broad, muddy fields sprouted weeds. A few months earlier Kalm had learned that his merchant friend was dead, and it had affected him "deeply."[2] Now his riding companion was Benjamin Franklin and their destination was Stenton, the country manor of James Logan. The elderly Quaker gentleman had made his name as a politician, scholar, and scientist, but Kalm had come to know him as something else—an inveterate adversary of Pennsylvania's "ancient settlers," Kalm's fellow Swedes.[3]

Now retired from a long and controversial career in politics and trade, Logan had conducted studies in astronomy, optics, and botany. During the 1730s fellow Quaker Peter Collinson, a merchant and scientist based in London, helped to build Logan's reputation abroad by publishing his research in the Royal Society's *Philosophical Transactions*.[4] Another admirer was Kalm's mentor, the Swedish botanist Carl Linnaeus, who wrote to Collinson to praise "the ingenious Mr. Logan's experiments made in North America upon the sex of plants." In 1738 Linnaeus sent his compliments directly to

201

Logan, who was then serving as Pennsylvania's chief justice and its acting governor. These offices were merely his latest—Logan had begun his long career in 1699 as William Penn's personal secretary.[5]

Long ago Franklin had written to Logan about Kalm's arrival in Philadelphia, and since then Logan had wondered why the naturalist had not come to see him. He had doubts about the Swede's true intentions, confiding to Collinson, "I know not what to make of him." The young professor had already traveled to Canada, where over five months he had "dined many times at the Governors at Quebec," but during his time in Pennsylvania the only notable men whom Kalm had sought out were Franklin and John Bartram, the famed botanist.[6]

These men formed a friendly yet competitive circle, and Logan felt left out. Franklin and John Bartram had corresponded with Collinson since the early 1730s, Logan had introduced Bartram to Linnaeus's classification system in 1736, and two years later he recommended Bartram's botanical investigations to Linnaeus.[7] A decade afterward Collinson provided Kalm with a letter of recommendation addressed to "Friend Franklin" in which he described Kalm as "a Sweed per Nation" who had come to "Improve himself in all Natural Inquiries" and to "make Observations on your Parts of the World."[8] Since his arrival Kalm had sought out Franklin's assistance but not Logan's. Instead, he had spent "the whole last winter . . . at a Swedish Woman's House near Newcastle." Now Kalm was talking of "returning to Canada again," Logan wrote, "but on what business I cannot learn."[9] The naturalist seemed to prefer the company of Quebecois and common Swedes to Logan's own learned conversation.

Following Kalm's belated visit, Logan was inspired to give Collinson a brief imperial history of the seventeenth-century Delaware Valley. "The Swedes had a Colony Sent in this River under Christina their Queen, but because they were neglected by their own People at home, they were obliged to Surrender to the Low Dutch," he wrote. Yet the Dutch were not long secure in their possession, "being attack'd by an English Fleet and army," and forced to surrender to them in 1664. The "Same Lowlanders" were able to recover "the Countrey" but then had to "resign all their pretensions to it to the English" a year later. "This Delaware was called the South River, and the Dutch in it built the town of Newcastle," he concluded. For Logan there seemed to be little else to relate.

By this time the Swedish community along the Delaware River was more than a century old, yet Logan saw little in its history that was worth commemorating. "The Swedes are not much encreased and in my time here (now above 50 years) are much Anglified as our Term is." Doubts about their allegiances persisted: Sweden was France's ally, France was Britain's enemy, and Kalm was making mysterious visits to New France. Logan nonetheless assured Collinson that if another war were to start, there would be no reason to fear Swedish subversion. During the last war their mutual friend Franklin had managed to raise "above 120 Companies of Militia" in the province, 10 in Philadelphia alone. Franklin's militiamen would make quick work of any incipient Swedish-French cabals.[10] Ninety-five years had elapsed since the fall of New Sweden, and nearly seventy years had passed since the founding of Pennsylvania, yet the old provincial politician was still uncertain about where the Swedish settlers' loyalties lay. The Swedes were "much Anglified," but they were still not English.[11]

A Promise of Privileges

Too often historians of Pennsylvania have written about the province as though it emerged fully formed, Athena-like, from William Penn's head. Logan knew better; he understood that this "holy experiment" was built upon the ruins of older imperial ambitions.[12] Once Lenape, Swedish, and Dutch ground, the Delaware Valley now belonged to the English but only because "an English Fleet and army" had seized it and diplomacy had restored it after a Dutch fleet had retaken it. Charles II had issued Penn his charter just seven years after this latest revolution, in part to secure the river from enemies who might reclaim it again.

Logan was uniquely able to see the continuities between the old Delaware Valley and the new. He had arrived in Pennsylvania when the province was eighteen years old and he was a novice official only in his midtwenties. Two generations of Swedish and Finnish settlers had been born along the river, and a few aged members of the founding generation still survived. Although they had been English subjects already for several decades, to newcomers like Logan they appeared to be no less Swedish for it. They identified themselves as Swedes, they continued to speak Swedish (and Finnish), and they went to services led by a Swedish-born, Swedish-appointed ministry. In their few forays into provincial politics, notably in confrontations with Logan over their land rights, they openly identified as Swedes. In return Logan and the Provincial Council of Pennsylvania accused them of conspiring together as a "nation . . . to make themselves a faction" and "caball[ing]" with the government's enemies. For provincial leaders the Swedes' attempts to participate in provincial politics as a "nation" were provocative and dangerous.[13]

By 1750, when Kalm visited Logan, the Delaware Valley's "Swedes" were a living, breathing reminder that the English were not the first colonizers to occupy this river and they might not be the last. French soldiers were building fortifications in the backcountry. One war had just ended, and another war appeared likely to follow. The small number of settlers of Swedish and Finnish descent along the Delaware River may not have seemed very dangerous, but what of the Scots-Irish and Germans who now populated the backcountry? Would they prove to be loyal to the province and the British Crown? Could they become "Anglified" too? Most of the Quakers in the Delaware Valley were of British origin, but conscience-stricken pacifists were unlikely to be reliable defenders against French and Indian invasions, as Logan recognized. The popular support for forming a militia in 1747–48 suggests that even city dwellers realized that they occupied contested ground. As Franklin noted in *Plain Truth,* published in Philadelphia in 1747, "*Sacking* the City will be the first, and *Burning* it, in all Probability, the last Act of the Enemy."[14]

Logan could still see the past in the present, but looking back from the midpoint of the eighteenth century, less than two years from his death, he could also observe how much had changed. The colony's "ancient settlers" no longer seemed so foreign, and the imperial rivalry between the Dutch, the Swedes, and the English belonged to history. His neighbors in the woods were gentlemen, not "savages"; they cultivated their gardens for pleasure, not to feed their families. Men such as Franklin, Kalm, and Logan simply had not existed in North America a hundred years earlier.

The Delaware Valley had been much "improved" since the days of New Sweden, as Logan's guest discovered during his wanderings. Soon after Kalm arrived in Philadelphia, he visited the oldest house in the city. He found "a wretched old building on a hill near the river, located a little north of Wicaco[,] preserved on purpose as a memorial to the poor condition of the place before the town was built on it." This Swedish cabin was no relic of a golden age; it was a reminder of a primitive past now thankfully gone. As Kalm wrote: "Its antiquity gives it a kind of superiority over all the other buildings in town, though in itself it is the worst of all. This hut was inhabited whilst yet stags, deer, elks and beavers at broad daylight lived in the future streets, church yards and marketplaces of Philadelphia. The noise of a spinning wheel was heard in this house before the manufactures now established were thought of or Philadelphia was built. But with all these advantages the house is ready to fall down, and after a few years it will be as difficult to find the place where it stood as it was unlikely at the time of its erection that one of the greatest towns in America should in a short time stand close to it."[15]

Where ax-hewn cabins once stood in Wicaco's woods, now rose houses made of brick and stone. Kalm counted seven Protestant churches, two Quaker meetinghouses, and various places where Anabaptists, Moravians, and Roman Catholics held their services. There was a town hall, a library, a courthouse, and an academy. The city carried on a "great trade both with the inhabitants of the country and with other parts of the world, especially the West Indies, South America and the Antilles, England, Ireland, Portugal, and the various English colonies in North America." For all of its connections abroad Philadelphia remained firmly established within the British Empire—"none but English ships" were permitted to enter the port.[16]

The people of the Delaware Valley had been "improved" too. "At the arrival of the English," Kalm wrote, "the Swedes to a large extent were not much better than savages."[17] Once Indians had left the area, their influence on the old settlers dwindled. The new city's residents were as diverse and complex as its commercial connections. "The town is now well filled with inhabitants of many nations, who in regard to their country, religion and trade are very different from each other," Kalm observed. Religious and temporal liberties were perfectly secure in this cosmopolitan settlement, where one could hardly "wish for and obtain greater freedom." Freedom, in fact, was what had motivated all of these foreigners to come. "It has not been necessary to force people to come and settle here; on the contrary foreigners of different languages have left their country, houses, property and relations and ventured over wide and stormy seas in order to come hither." The result was that "Pennsylvania[,] which was no better than a wilderness in the year 1681, and contained hardly fifteen hundred people, now vies with several kingdoms in Europe in the number of inhabitants." Its inhabitants were made up of "hosts of people which other countries, to their infinite loss, have either neglected, belittled or expelled." Among these people, of course, had been the farmers and traders of New Sweden and New Netherland. They had laid the foundations for the prosperous British settlements that now surrounded their descendants.[18]

The eighteenth-century British-American empire was larger, more orderly, and more effectively monitored from the metropolis. It was also
more diverse. Distinctive populations of Netherlanders, Finns, and Swedes
remained in the conquered Delaware and Hudson Valleys, but European
immigration had created culturally plural settler societies throughout
eighteenth-century British America.[19] In North America as in Great Britain,
Britishness was not Englishness, or not always. This paradox of non-British
British Americans was a puzzle that curious men such as Collinson, Franklin, Kalm, and Logan struggled to solve. Their interest in empires and their
subjects was a practical extension of their scientific studies; they believed
that government and society were as susceptible to observation and reason
as physics and botany.

As worldly as these men were, they approached questions about national
affiliation and allegiance in the Delaware Valley from a familiar empire-
centered perspective. Logan's theme of cultural transformation was the focus of intense discussion; his comment that the term *Anglified* had become
common jargon in Pennsylvania is especially revealing. Franklin fretted
in print about "Anglifying" the Germans, while Collinson offered Franklin
"Hints Humbly proposed to Incorporate the Germans more with the English
and Check the Increase of their Power."[20] Their younger colleague Kalm had
more sympathy for non-English settlers, but he, too, observed that many of
them had adopted "English" ways in place of their own. He noted that many
Swedes in America were "ashamed to talk in their own tongue" for fear of
not being considered "real English." And while he was able to uncover some
speakers of Finnish in New Jersey, he found that "now most of them are
dead, and their descendants changed into Englishmen."[21]

Despite their differences, these early modern social scientists came to
similar conclusions. They articulated a vision of British America in which
policy and time would make non-English settlers fully "British"—Anglo-
phone in language, Protestant in religion, loyal and liberal in politics, and
integrated into a larger Anglo-American society.[22] The multitude of European "nations" within British America would become one people under one
allegiance. The change would be neither sudden nor coerced, but it would
be necessary. If authorities did not manage it properly, the empire and its
liberty might be put in jeopardy. Foreign subjects had to be incorporated
with care. As Franklin wrote to Collinson: "With regard to the Germans, I
think Methods of great tenderness should be used, and nothing that looks
like a hardship be imposed. Their fondness for their own Language and

Manners is natural: It is not a Crime. When People are induced to settle a new Country by a promise of Privileges, that Promise should be bonâ fide performed, and the Privileges never infringed: If they are, how shall we be believed another time, when we want to People another Colony?"[23] Reason, justice, and empire required tolerance of difference but only so much and only for so long. To the great frustration of men such as Franklin and Logan, the process of national transformation proved to be slow, contested, and never complete. If enlightened imperialists believed they could create subjects in their own image, they were mistaken.

Britonization

In the eighteenth-century Delaware Valley, Germans, Irish, Scots, and Swedes alike employed the languages of loyalty and liberty to assert their place in the British Empire in America. Cultural change went hand in hand with political incorporation; over time these groups became "Anglified" culturally as well as politically. While Kalm regretted the loss of the Swedes' national language and culture, Logan welcomed it, and, with the Germans in mind, Franklin and Collinson imagined ways to accelerate the process.

At a remove of two and a half centuries historians today are less likely to applaud or to criticize such change, but when they examine the cultural character of non-English settlers in eighteenth-century British America, they sometimes sound like Franklin and Logan. Echoing their terminology, historians of colonial America have described this process of cultural change as "anglicization." The term refers more generally to the tendency of colonies in British North America to follow metropolitan models identified with England, but historians have also used it to describe non-English colonists adopting the culture of their Anglo-American peers. Both senses of the term acknowledge that the power of the metropolis shaped cultural change—anglicization began in the Delaware Valley only when English royal forces conquered it—but power alone did not determine the pace and character of the change. In fact, much of the impulse behind anglicization originated in the colonists themselves, particularly among elites who were seeking to improve their societies and their own status.[24]

Historians have observed countervailing tendencies in colonial societies too. The force of anglicization sometimes met with the opposite, if not equal, force of "ethnicization."[25] Even as non-English settlers felt the pressure to adapt themselves culturally to their status as English subjects, many responded by asserting and reaffirming their national origins and attachments through forms of ethnic mobilization. While Kalm found, for example, that in New York City many residents of Dutch descent "preferred to pass for English,"[26] upriver at Albany he observed that the inhabitants spoke Dutch, had Dutch preachers, attended Dutch religious services, and possessed Dutch manners, even if their outer dress was English in style.[27] More surprisingly, the Dutch there expressed "a hatred toward the English, whom they ridicule and slander at every opportunity." Worse yet, they brazenly purchased goods that Indians had looted during attacks on New England, even though the victims were "in a manner their brothers, and . . . subjects of the same crown."[28] Meanwhile, along the Delaware River Kalm observed settlers of Finnish and Swedish descent freely absorbing the "English" culture around them, but he also found that many continued to identify themselves and to be identified by others as "Swedes." The anchor bolt for this identity was the Swedish Lutheran Church, which continued to send priests from Sweden, to provide services in the Swedish language, and to form an institution around which Finns and Swedes in the Delaware Valley could organize their communities.[29]

The Germans in the British colonies forged a similar unity on a much larger scale. "Supported by self-conscious leaders and support networks," A. G. Roeber writes, "they established a press in their own language and cultivated an extensive trade and religious communication via London and Holland to the Reich and across North America." Indeed, this "mélange of German-speakers eventually enjoyed a more unified experience in North America than they had known in Europe."[30] Elsewhere in the mid-Atlantic region, Scots of various origins and religious affiliations forged yet another type of "common community, sharing trade networks and, increasingly, participation in a unified Scottish Presbyterian church."[31] Irish settlers, by contrast, were less keen to emphasize their national origin. Instead, what cohesion they gained as a group came through their adherence to the Presbyterian Church. Over time, however, religion separated the Irish settlers as often as it united them. According to Patrick Griffin, "They overcame division by rallying around a familiar concept, Britishness."[32]

The Irish in British America did not have to shed their political allegiances to become subjects, which might help to explain why their self-identification as "Irish" was often weak. Settlers from Ulster knew long before they reached America that they were better off identifying themselves as Britons than as Irishmen. For the non-British Germans, Netherlanders, and Swedes, however, their national identities often persisted more clearly. Having lost most or all of their formal connections to European states by the eighteenth century, Germanness, Dutchness, and Swedishness in British America became forms of ethnicity, cultural affiliations that formed the basis for collective identification and action. These ethnic identities were often fluid—the products of social relationships, not simply ancestry. As Kalm discovered, some settlers could be more "Swedish" than others. Some people who identified as Swedes were not actually of Swedish origin but had married into the community or had become devoted congregants in the Swedish church. Many, of course, had Finnish origins as well. Others moved in the other direction, leaving the Swedish Lutheran Church and joining alternate religious communities or none at all.[33] Dutch and German communities in North America were even more diversely constituted. They, too, experienced a similar coalescence around their nations once they had become subjects of the British Crown.[34]

This process of ethnic formation, or ethnogenesis, was related to the broader process of creolization, in which settlers of all stripes adapted to local conditions and became rooted in local societies.[35] Creolization, like ethnicization, has often been viewed as a counterforce to anglicization.[36] But if we look at the place of non-English communities in British America, it is clear that the local and the metropolitan were not mutually exclusive; indeed, they constituted one another. The provincial Delaware Valley was dynamically attached to an expanding global empire. To adapt to the local was also to become British.

The interrelated processes of anglicization and creolization might be better understood if we consider them in a broader Atlantic frame. From the late seventeenth century forward, the different pieces of the British Empire were simultaneously developing along similar social, economic, cultural, and political trajectories. The British colonies in North America and the Caribbean notably experienced a "slow but powerful cultural and social convergence," as Jack P. Greene has convincingly argued, but it was also true that the other dominions of the British Empire were converging toward a common cultural center during the same era.[37] This cultural core was "Anglo-British," not simply English.[38] Likewise, it is more accurate to say that non-English settlers in British America were becoming British, not

"English," contrary to what Kalm and Logan claimed. They learned the common language of the British Empire, produced commodities for its commerce, participated in its state institutions, and adopted its basic political ideals and norms. Englishmen and English ways often dominated in these domains, but as the British Empire grew and developed, that cultural heritage became a more "inclusive and expansive" Britishness that others besides English people could claim.[39] "Men and women began to sense that they belonged to a larger and more diverse political community," historian Geoffrey Plank notes, "one tied together primarily by a common allegiance to the British crown and a shared commitment to the cause of Protestantism, broadly defined."[40] Rather than focusing on the cultural and political power of the metropolis and the extent of settlers' anglicization, we should be speaking of the opportunities that they pursued and the strategies they followed in a process, or practice, that might better be called "Britonization."

Settlers acquired this Britishness slowly, but when they learned how to use it, they employed it vigorously. Britishness became a way to assert and to defend rights in political discourse. As Peter Onuf notes, "It was only by imagining a transcendent, inclusive, imperial community, a greater Britain that reached across the Atlantic, that colonists could plausibly claim—to their own satisfaction, at least—the 'rights of Englishmen.'"[41] Expressions of allegiance and national identity helped to legitimate collective activities even as the individualistic character of Britishness seemed to undermine them. We see the same strategic employment of loyalties during the previous century, when Dutch and Swedish subjects asserted their allegiances in demands on their officials. Just as eighteenth-century settlers chose to become British because of what it could do for them, so did seventeenth-century settlers choose to identify themselves and others as Dutch, English, and Swedish for what it could do for them too. *Choice* might be too strong a word to use here, of course, because the alternatives were limited and often unpromising. Settlers could choose to leave their nation by escaping their colony, but in practice that meant departing the service of one master to enter the service of another. For a cosmopolitan merchant such as Augustine Herrman that might be a very lucrative move. For Swedish laborers in debt to their own officials, becoming servants in Maryland's tobacco fields was not much of a step up: Valerius Loo and Anders Hansson fled New Sweden only to die in Maryland shortly thereafter. National and imperial loyalties could be traded and exchanged but often only at a price.

From the British Nation to the Empire of Liberty

By the time a British identity had been forged in the Delaware Valley, the contest of empires had moved west, and the discourse of nations had changed.[42] In the backcountry imperial competition remained vigorous as British, French, and Indian peoples converged on disputed ground. In the Delaware Valley national differences continued to flourish but now under different terms. The character of ethnicity in this space had changed radically by the end of the seventeenth century. The world that followed shared in the world that preceded it, but it was established and it operated under conditions that were fundamentally different.

Foremost among these differences was that the Delaware Valley had now become a European space. By the early 1700s the multitude of Lenape nations that once greeted Dutch and Swedish traders had moved inland and established several related but distinct settlements along the Schuylkill, the Brandywine, the Susquehanna, and at the Forks of the Delaware. Others had begun to head west to the Ohio Country. Elsewhere in the Pennsylvania backcountry were the remnants of the Minquas-Susquehannock, who, along with some Iroquoian additions, became known as the Conestoga. They were joined by Shawnee who had come from the Ohio country; Conoy and Nanticoke who had been pressed out of Maryland; and others who had arrived from farther south, including Tutelo and Saponi from Virginia and Tuscarora from the Carolinas. Asserting authority over them all were the Haudenosaunee, the Iroquois, who claimed the region by virtue of their conquest of the Minquas-Susquehannock in the 1670s.[43]

As some nations broke apart, other communities began to form. Various Lenape bands became "Delaware" just as they began to depart the Delaware Valley. Along the Susquehanna River, the town of Shamokin became "the veritable Indian capital of Pennsylvania, albeit often a rather dismal place," writes archaeologist Barry Kent.[44] Like Philadelphia, Shamokin rarely met the expectations of moralists. In 1745 Presbyterian minister David Brainerd wrote that the town contained "upwards of fifty houses, and near three hundred persons: but of three different tribes of Indians, speaking three languages wholly *unintelligible* to each other. About one half of its inhabitants are Delawares, the others called Senekas, and Tutelas. The Indians of this place are counted the most drunken, mischievous, and ruffianly *fellows* of any in these parts; and *satan* seems to have his seat in this town in an eminent manner."[45] Similar hybrid communities had formed upriver at Wyoming (present-day Wilkes-Barre) and downriver at Paxtang. These were refugee towns inhabited by citizens of worlds dispossessed.[46]

In time these diverse peoples would find other ways to unite. Some found common cause through violence, uniting to strike against their dispossessors in raids during the Seven Years' War. Others promoted unity through renewal. Drawing from earlier nativist movements in the Susquehanna Valley, the Delaware prophet Neolin inspired a spiritual revival first among the Delaware and then among their many neighbors. "In addition to the Potawatomis, Wyandots, Shawnees, and Delawares, the prophet's message raised spirits among the Miamis, Senecas, Ottawas, Chippewas, and beyond," historian Gregory Evans Dowd writes.[47] Alfred Cave notes that "Neolin's preaching helped provide the spiritual foundation not only of Delaware unity but also of a nascent pan-Indian resistance movement." The Ottawa war leader Pontiac drew on that unity to rally opposition to the rapidly growing British military presence around the Great Lakes during the early 1760s. Ultimately, neither the prophet nor the warrior was able to establish a lasting and unified resistance to British and British American power in the aftermath of the Seven Years' War. Nonetheless, they did foster concrete forms of "intertribal cooperation" and created "coalitions . . . [that] were fairly formidable."[48]

Back east in the Delaware people's homeland, diverse populations of Europeans were forging new unities too. Their experience was very different from that of earlier generations of settlers. In the seventeenth-century Delaware Valley settler nations had been attached to imperial states in Europe seeking exclusive control of the river, its commodities, and access to its Indian neighbors. It was never clear that any one of those powers could effectively preserve its hold on this territory—or its settlers—in the struggle against the other claimants. By contrast, for all the confusion over charters and boundaries, there was no question by the mid-eighteenth century that the Delaware Valley had become British territory and that it would be ruled under laws and institutions that had their origins in Great Britain. Those who chose to live there had to accept these conditions from the start. Although the Anglo-British rulers of the eighteenth-century Delaware Valley occasionally had their doubts, they generally accepted that the non-English among them would remain loyal subjects during times of crisis. Britain's greatest rival in North America for the next century was French and Catholic, while the "foreigners" who populated the frontiers most exposed to

French depredations were either "British" or German in origin, and most were Protestants. Franklin may have doubted the Germans' loyalties, and Logan may have had questions about the Swedes, but they had little real evidence to suggest that they would act in a disloyal fashion. Indeed, the loyalty of "foreign Protestants" often seemed more noteworthy. In 1747 British officials in Nova Scotia cited the history of Pennsylvania to argue that "Swiss and German settlers could serve effectively as promoters of British imperial culture," Geoffrey Plank notes.[49]

The place of loyal settler populations on Pennsylvania's frontier contrasts sharply with the treatment given to subject populations that showed affinities with the French. Consider that one of the ways that Swedish settlers demonstrated their English allegiance was by calling for military protection against the French during the 1690s. Swedish fur traders also publically accused their newly arrived French Protestant counterparts of being disloyal and having secret attachments to New France.[50] The starkest example of anti-French sentiment in British America remains the story of the Acadians of Nova Scotia, whose refusal to swear unconditional oaths of allegiance to the British Crown led royal officials to dispossess them of their properties and to disperse them across British America during the Seven Years' War. British officials deported about seven thousand Acadians to other North American colonies, including Pennsylvania, where about five hundred deportees received a cold welcome.[51] Indeed, historian Carl A. Brasseaux writes that "the banishment to Pennsylvania constitutes one of the bleakest chapters of Acadian history."[52] John Mack Faragher estimates that overall "some 10,000 Acadians—the majority of them probably infants and children—lost their lives as a direct result of the campaign of removal from 1755 to 1763."[53]

The case of the Acadians offers a view of what might have occurred in the Delaware Valley if the conditions of colonial competition there had been different. This book might have told a much more violent story if the Lenape and the Minquas-Susquehannock had not chosen to accommodate European traders and colonizers; had these European powers not been sporadic allies as well as rivals; had religious loyalties been antagonistic, instead of merely being competitive; had the conquered settler populations not acquiesced to demands for public submission; and perhaps most important, had the victorious powers not made concerted efforts to win the cooperation of their conquered subjects.[54] Yet even in tragic Acadia, French Catholic settlers had been able to maintain cooperative relationships with their British rulers for decades on end. Only at midcentury did that re-lationship collapse, when British administrators decided to expand their efforts to anglicize the colony.[55] Among their various schemes for turning the Acadians into "English Protestants" were the importation of German and Irish Protestants, the expulsion of resident French Catholic priests, the establishment of English schools, and the promotion of intermarriage be-tween Acadian women and New England men.[56] Dispersal became their pre-ferred strategy, however, and through trickery and military coercion British officials rooted out the Acadians from Nova Scotia. Meanwhile, a supply of settlers from New England stood by, ready to take the place of the dispos-sessed, while officials and entrepreneurs such as Benjamin Franklin bought up land and sought to become colonizers in their own right.[57] By contrast, in the Delaware Valley before the 1680s no state had such power or resources, none had a new settler population that could take the old settlers' place, and none were willing to treat so callously fellow Protestants who were attached to powerful states in Europe. Indeed, the Acadians may have suffered as much as they did exactly because they had been nominal British subjects for several decades by the time of their expulsion. They had no state to protect them except the one whose agents were assaulting them.

The same might be said of the Indians, who were a vital part of this British American world but were typically denied the rights and privileges that accompanied the status of the subject. Although some British settlers were willing to accord Indians such rights, most were not.[58] The Africans transported to the Delaware Valley in increasing numbers during the eigh-teenth century were also excluded from this liberal inheritance. Consider a court case from 1737, when a Pennsylvania jury sentenced a "*Negroe* Fellow" named Sampson to death for "setting Fire to a House near the President's Country Seat"—that is, James Logan's Stenton.[59] Logan, the president of the Provincial Council, argued against the jury's appeal for clemency. Sampson had "threatened Resentments" against Logan and the occupant of the house, and he had a "wicked Disposition" and a "bad Character." More important, "so henious a Crime" could not pass unpunished, Logan claimed, because the "insolent Behaviour of the Negroes in and about the city . . . require[d] a strict hand to be kept over them." Although the Provincial Council decided to spare Sampson's life, they may have done so only to allow Sampson's owner to sell the man as a slave "beyond Seas to any Colony, Dominion, or State not subject to or depending on the Crown of Great Britain, so as that he do not return into this Province."[60] And who was Sampson's privileged

owner? Historians say it was Logan himself.[61] Sampson could be banished
and sold because he was not a true subject of the Crown. The "rights of Englishmen" belonged only to British subjects, and in the eighteenth-century
Delaware Valley only white European settlers and their descendants could
become British.

Discourses about nations and allegiances also shaped the next imperial
struggle these British Americans faced. As Franklin wrote in an English
newspaper in 1768, "The allegiance of the distant provinces to the crown
will remain for ever unshaken, while they enjoy the rights of Englishmen."
But if they were to lose the "right of legislation" under the consent of the
Crown, then they would be "no longer fellow subjects, but the subjects of
subjects."[62] Eight years later, a half-mile from the Delaware River, Franklin and his fellow representatives of the self-described "British Nation" in
North America declared themselves "absolved from all Allegiance to the
British Crown."[63] Among the subjects reborn as citizens was Franklin, the
old Anglifier. He came to regret his diatribes against Africans, Germans,
and Indians and deleted them from later editions of his works. Franklin became the model of the cosmopolitan American, elected an honorary fellow
of the Royal Society of Edinburgh, member of the Royal Academy of History
of Madrid, and member of the Russian Imperial Academy of Sciences. He
was also a patriot who, at eighty-one years of age, served simultaneously as
president of Pennsylvania, delegate to the Constitutional Convention, and
president of the Pennsylvania Society for Promoting the Abolition of Slavery and the Relief of Free Negroes Unlawfully Held in Bondage.

Despite Franklin's profound change of heart, Africans and Indians, those
"savage nations," remained either ambiguously inside or decidedly outside
the bounds of the new nation's expansive citizenship—becoming a republic
had not changed that.[64] By contrast, according to the 1790 Naturalization
Act, "any alien," the subject of a foreign sovereign, could become a citizen
so long as he was "a free white person . . . of good character" who had lived
within the United States for two years and was willing to swear an oath to
support the Constitution. Just as the British Empire had encouraged the
settlement of foreign Europeans within its extended dominions and certi-
fied their allegiance with loyalty oaths, so did its American successor. Yet
foreigners' loyalties came under close scrutiny when invasion threatened
from abroad.[65]

In the new republic Americans continued to draw on old discourses
about subjects, nations, and empires and the allegiances that bound them

all together. All too successfully, they modeled their growing republic after the expansive British Empire from which it was born. The citizens of the United States created a new "empire of liberty" and a new imperial nation.[66] At its worst the new nation authorized the subjugation and destruction of the nonwhite noncitizens within its borders. At its best it offered a commitment to universal liberty even as it failed to extend that liberty to all.

During the American Revolution provincial British colonists became American citizens, and Americans became citizens of the world. The legacy was lasting. "Settled by the people of all nations, all nations may claim her for their own," Herman Melville wrote in *Redburn: His First Voyage* (1849). "We are not a nation, so much as a world." During World War I Randolph Bourne declared that "colonialism has grown into cosmopolitanism"; the American, he claimed, is "a colonial of the world." The American nation became ever more global, if not worldly, as its commerce, culture, and power spread in the century that followed. In our own doubtful century of wars and revolutions we imagine a cosmopolitan future where liberty is universal and nations follow Hobbes's "Fundamental Law of Nature; which is, *to seek Peace, and follow it.*"[67] Until then we might do well to build communities such as the one that Peter Gunnarsson Rambo described in 1693, in which "our nations . . . live faithfully with one another, both in harmony and affection."[68]

NOTES

INTRODUCTION

1. Thomas Holland to the Earl of Salisbury, October 30, 1609, in *Calendar of the Manuscripts of the Most Honourable the Marquess of Salisbury . . . Part XXI (1609–1612)*, ed. G. Dyfnallt Owen (London: Her Majesty's Stationery Office, 1970), 152.

2. Henry Hudson's journal of his second voyage, in Samuel Purchas, ed., *Haklvytvs Posthumus, or, Pvrchas His Pilgrimes* (London: H. Fetherston, 1625), 3:570, 578.

3. John Meredith Read, *A Historical Inquiry Concerning Henry Hudson, His Friends, Relatives and Early Life, His Connection with the Muscovy Company and Discovery of Delaware Bay* (Albany: Joel Munsell, 1866), 29.

4. Robert Juet's journal, in Purchas, *Haklvytvs Posthumus*, 3:581.

5. Juet's journal, in Purchas, *Haklvytvs Posthumus*, 3:590.

6. Holland to the Earl of Salisbury, October 30, 1609, in Owen, *Calendar of the Manuscripts of the Most Honourable the Marquess of Salisbury*, 152.

7. See Emanuel van Meteren, *Emanuels van Meteren historie der Neder-landscher ende haerder na-buren oorlogen ende geschiedenissen, tot den iare M.VI.c XII* (In s'Graven-Haghe: Hillebrant Iacobssz, 1614), 628d.

8. For Hudson's final voyage, see Peter C. Mancall, *Fatal Journey: The Final Expedition of Henry Hudson—A Tale of Mutiny and Murder in the Arctic* (New York: Basic Books, 2009).

9. Thomas A. Janvier, *Henry Hudson: A Brief Statement of His Aims and Achievements* (New York: Harper & Brothers, 1909), 140.

10. Henry Hudson's journal of his second voyage, in Purchas, *Haklvytvs Posthumus*, 3:575.

11. The phrase in the quote comes from the oath made by the mutineers before seizing Hudson, as reported in Abacuk Pricket's account of the fourth voyage, in Purchas, *Haklvytvs Posthumus*, 3:603.

12. Sir Edward Coke, "Postnati. Calvins case," in *The Reports of Sir Edward Coke Knight* (London, 1658), 587.

13. Philip Ford, *A Vindication of William Penn, Proprietary of Pennsilvania, from the late Aspersions spread abroad on purpose to Defame him* (London: Printed for Benjamin Clark, 1683), 2.

14. Israel Acrelius, *Beskrifning om de Swenska Församlingars Forna och Närwarande Tilstånd, uti det så kallade Nya Swerige, Sedan Nya Nederland . . .* (Stockholm: Harberg & Hesselberg, 1759), 118. See also Acrelius, *A History of New Sweden; or, The Settlements on the River Delaware,* trans. William M. Reynolds (Philadelphia: Historical Society of Pennsylvania, 1874), 111.

15. Ford, *Vindication of William Penn* (1683), 2.

16. Richard S. Dunn and Mary Maples Dunn, eds., *The Papers of William Penn* (Philadelphia: University of Pennsylvania Press, 1982), 2:337–38.

17. See the short biographies of the signers, in Dunn and Dunn, *Papers of William Penn,* 2:338.

18. Roughly in order of their first attempted claim, they included New Netherland, Virginia, New Sweden, New Haven, New Albion, Maryland, New Amstel, New York, New Jersey, and Pennsylvania.

19. For an analysis of national identity in Britain's American colonies, see Jack P. Greene, "Empire and Identity from the Glorious Revolution to the American Revolution," in *The Oxford History of the British Empire,* vol. 2: *The Eighteenth Century,* ed. P. J. Marshall (Oxford: Oxford University Press, 1998), 208–30. For studies of English or British identity in the early modern era, see esp. Richard Helgerson, *Forms of Nationhood: The Elizabethan Writing of England* (Chicago: University of Chicago Press, 1992); Colin Kidd, *British Identities before Nationalism: Ethnicity and Nationhood in the Atlantic World, 1600–1800* (New York: Cambridge University Press, 1999); and Linda Colley, *Britons: Forging the Nation, 1707–1837,* 2d ed. (New Haven: Yale University Press, 2009). For Dutch and Scandinavian examples, see Willem Frijhoff and Marijke Spies, *1650: Bevochten Eendracht* (The Hague: Sdu Uitgevers, 1999); and Harald Gustafsson, "The Eighth Argument: Identity, Ethnicity, and Political Culture in Sixteenth-Century Scandinavia," *Scandinavian Journal of History* 27.2 (2002): 91–113.

20. On medieval understandings of kingdoms and nations, see esp. Susan Reynolds, *Kingdoms and Communities in Western Europe, 900–1300,* 2d ed. (New York: Oxford University Press, 1997), 250–54.

21. John Minsheu, *Hegemon eis tas glossas. id est, Ductor in Linguas, The Guide into Tongues* (London: William Stansby and Melchisidec Bradwood, 1617), 324, 102, 356.

22. Eric Hobsbawm comes to different conclusions in his wider-ranging analysis of the term *nation* in *Nations and Nationalism since 1780: Programme, Myth, Reality* (Cambridge: Cambridge University Press, 1992), 14–18.

23. See Elizabeth Mancke, "Empire and State," in *The British Atlantic World, 1500–1800,* ed. David Armitage and Michael J. Braddick (New York: Palgrave Macmillan, 2002), 175–95. On the application of Calvin's Case and Sir Edward Coke's opinion outside England, see Daniel Hulsebosch, "The Ancient Constitution and the Expanding Empire: Sir Edward Coke's British Jurisprudence," *Law and History Review* 21.3 (Fall 2003): 439–82.

24. For the proliferation of legal spaces in the colonial world, see esp. Lauren A. Benton, *Law and Colonial Cultures: Legal Regimes in World History, 1400–1900* (New York: Cambridge University Press, 2002); and *A Search for Sovereignty: Law and Geography in European Empires, 1400–1900* (New York: Cambridge University Press, 2010).

25. See, for example, Ignacio J. Gallup-Diaz, *The Door of the Seas and Key to the Universe: Indian Politics and Imperial Rivalry in the Darién, 1640-1750,* rev. ed. (New York: Columbia University Press, 2005).

26. For the use of the term *nation* by Indians and Europeans, see Nancy Shoemaker, *A Strange Likeness: Becoming Red and White in Eighteenth-Century North America* (New York: Oxford University Press, 2004), esp. 6–8.

27. Benedict Anderson coined the term *nation-ness* in order to provide a more evocative and encompassing term for *nationality,* the quality of being national. Extending Anderson's concept, literary scholar Thomas J. Scanlan notes that in early English colonial narratives "'nation-ness' need[ed] . . . 'colonial-ness.'" Anderson, *Imagined Communities: Reflections on the Origin and Spread of Nationalism,* rev. ed. (London: Verso, 2006), 4; Scanlan, *Colonial Writing and the New World, 1583-1671: Allegories of Desire* (New York: Cambridge University Press, 1999), 37.

28. On the links between lived national and ethnic identities, see esp. Richard Jenkins, *Rethinking Ethnicity: Arguments and Explorations* (London: Sage, 1997); Rogers Brubaker, Margit Feischmidt, Jon Fox, and Liana Grancea, *Nationalist Politics and Everyday Ethnicity in a Transylvanian Town* (Princeton: Princeton University Press, 2006); Thomas Hylland Eriksen, *Ethnicity and Nationalism: Anthropological Perspectives,* 3d ed. (London: Pluto Press, 2010).

29. Francis Bacon, "The Argument of Sir Francis Bacon . . . In the Case of the Post-Nati of Scotland," *The Works of Francis Bacon* (London, 1753), 2:164.

30. Charles T. Gehring, ed., *Delaware Papers (English Period): A Collection of Documents Pertaining to the Regulation of Affairs on the Delaware, 1664-1682* (Baltimore: Genealogical Publishing Co., 1977), 19 (hereafter cited as *DE*).

31. Frederick Cooper, *Colonialism in Question: Theory, Knowledge, History* (Berkeley: University of California Press, 2005), 30.

32. Peter Sahlins, *Boundaries: The Making of France and Spain in the Pyrenees* (Berkeley: University of California Press, 1989), 9.

33. Hugo Grotius, *The Most Excellent Hugo Grotius, His Three Books Treating of the Rights of War and Peace,* trans. William Evats (London: Printed by M.W. for Thomas Basset . . . and Ralph Smith . . . , 1682), 527.

34. For a comparative analysis of the links between local and national conceptions of citizenship in early modern Europe, see Tamar Herzog, *Defining Nations: Immigrants and Citizens in Early Modern Spain and Spanish America* (New Haven: Yale University Press, 2003), chap. 8.

35. John G. Reid et al., *The "Conquest" of Acadia, 1710: Imperial, Colonial, and Aboriginal Constructions* (Toronto: University of Toronto Press, 2004), 20–21.

36. For a useful study that explores the connection between modern allegiances and identities, see Arthur Aughey, "National Identity, Allegiance and Constitutional Change in the United Kingdom," *Nations and Nationalism* 16.2 (2010): 335–53.

37. William Penn, *A Further Account of the Province of Pennsylvania and Its Improvements . . .* (London, 1685), 2–3. For the intensification of racial differences in Pennsylvania, see esp. James Merrell, *Into the American Woods: Negotiators on the Pennsylvania Frontier* (New York: Norton, 1999); and Peter Silver, *Our Savage Neighbors: How Indian War Transformed Early America* (New York: Norton, 2008).

38. For contemporary examples, see Scott L. Malcomson, "The Varieties of Cosmopolitan Experience," in *Cosmopolitics: Thinking and Feeling beyond the Nation,* ed. Pheng Cheah and Bruce Robbins (Minneapolis: University of Minnesota Press, 1998), 238–40; and, more generally, James Clifford, "Mixed Feelings," in *Cosmopolitics,* 362–70.

39. Margaret C. Jacob, *Strangers Nowhere in the World: The Rise of Cosmopolitanism in Early Modern Europe* (Philadelphia: University of Pennsylvania Press, 2006), 3–5, 11.

40. See Karen O. Kupperman, *Indians and English: Facing Off in Early America* (Ithaca: Cornell University Press, 2000); Alison Games, *Migration and the Origins of the English Atlantic World* (Cambridge, Mass.: Harvard University Press, 1999); Games, *The Web of Empire: English Cosmopolitans in an Age of Expansion, 1560–1660* (New York: Oxford University Press, 2008); April Lee Hatfield, *Atlantic Virginia* (Philadelphia: University of Pennsylvania Press, 2003); Claudia Schnurmann, *Atlantische Welten: Engländer und Niederländer im Amerikanisch-Atlantischen Raum, 1648–1713* (Köln: Böhlau, 1998); Cynthia J. Van Zandt, *Brothers among Nations: The Pursuit of Intercultural Alliances in Early America, 1580–1660* (New York: Oxford University Press, 2008); Christian Koot, *Empire at the Periphery: British Colonists, Anglo-Dutch Trade, and the Development of the British Atlantic, 1621–1713* (New York: New York University Press, 2011). In a different context Ira Berlin has argued for the existence of a class of "Atlantic creoles" who mixed African, European, and American attributes and were "cosmopolitan in the fullest sense." Berlin, *Many Thousands Gone: The First Two Centuries of Slavery in North America* (Cambridge, Mass.: Harvard University Press, 1998), 17.

41. Hans Kohn, *The Idea of Nationalism: A Study in Its Origins and Background* (New York: Macmillan, 1944), 202–3; Hobsbawm, *Nations and Nationalism Since 1780,* 14.

42. See Nicholas Canny and Anthony Pagden, *Colonial Identity in the Atlantic World, 1500–1800* (Princeton: Princeton University Press, 1987), 271–76; Nicholas Canny, "Writing Atlantic History; or, Reconfiguring the History of Colonial British America," *Journal of American History* (December 1999): 1093–1114; James Sidbury and Jorge Cañizares-Esguerra, "Mapping Ethnogenesis in the Early Modern Atlantic," *William and Mary Quarterly,* 3d ser., 68.2 (April 2011): 207.

43. Schnurmann, *Atlantische Welten,* 375–76.

44. Charles T. Gehring, trans. and ed., *Delaware Papers (Dutch Period): A Collection of Documents Pertaining to the Regulation of Affairs on the South River of New Netherland, 1648–1664* (Baltimore: Genealogical Publishing Co., 1981), 276 (hereafter cited as *DD*).

45. *SENTENTIE By den Kryghs-Rade gewesen Over Alexander D'Hinyossa* (1672).

46. On the early history of the Lenape, see esp. C. A. Weslager, *The Delaware Indians: A History* (New Brunswick: Rutgers University Press, 1972); Ives Goddard, "Delaware," in *Handbook of North American Indians,* vol. 15: *Northeast,* ed. William C. Sturtevant and Bruce G. Trigger (Washington, D.C.: Smithsonian Institution, 1978), 213–39; Amy C. Schutt, *Peoples of the River Valleys: The Odyssey of the Delaware Indians* (Philadelphia: University of Pennsylvania Press, 2007); Gunlög Fur, *Colonialism in the Margins: Cultural Encounters in New Sweden and Lapland* (Leiden: Brill, 2006); and Dawn Marsh Riggs, "Pax Lenape: The Peaceable Kingdom of the Pennsylvania Indians," *Indigenous Policy* 17.2 (2006), *www.indigenouspolicy.org.* On the Minquas-Susquehannock, see esp. Francis Jennings, "Glory, Death, and Transfiguration: The Susquehannock Indians in the Seventeenth Century," *Proceedings of the American Philosophical Society* 112.1 (1968): 15–53; Barry Kent, *Susquehanna's Indians* (Harrisburg: Pennsylvania Historical and Museum Commission, 2001); Sharon D. White, "To Secure a Lasting Peace: A

Diachronic Analysis of Seventeenth-Century Susquehannock Political and Economic Strategies" (Ph.D. diss., Pennsylvania State University, 2001). In general this work will employ the term *Minquas-Susquehannock* to refer to the group that historians and anthropologists usually call the "Susquehannock," except when referring to quotations that identify the group by another name. The combined name is meant to emphasize that the Dutch and English accounts cited in this work may or may not have been referring to a single "nation."

47. Bruce Robbins, "Actually Existing Cosmopolitanisms," in Robbins and Cheah, *Cosmopolitics*, 2.

1. CLAIMING HUDSON AND HIS DISCOVERIES

1. Hessel Gerritsz, *Descriptio ac delineatio Geographica Detectionis Freti* (Amsterdam: Ex officina Hesselij Gerardi., 1612). See the English translation in *Henry Hudson the Navigator: The Original Documents in Which His Career Is Recorded, Collected, Partly Translated, and Annotated with an Introduction*, ed. G. M. Asher (London: Hakluyt Society, 1860), 187.

2. For Hudson's background, see Asher, *Henry Hudson the Navigator;* Henry Cruse Murphy, *Henry Hudson in Holland: An Inquiry into the Origin and Objects of the Voyage Which Led to the Discovery of the Hudson River, with Bibliographic Notes* (The Hague: M. Nijhoff, 1909); Thomas A. Janvier, *Henry Hudson: A Brief Statement of His Aims and Achievements* (New York: Harper & Brothers, 1909); Llewellyn Powys, *Henry Hudson* (New York: Harper & Brothers, 1928); and I.N.P. Stokes, *The Iconography of Manhattan Island, 1498–1909* (1915–28; repr., New York: Arno Press, 1967).

3. See Edmund Morgan, *American Slavery, American Freedom: The Ordeal of Colonial Virginia* (New York: Norton, 1975), chaps. 1–2; and Kenneth R. Andrews, *Trade, Plunder and Settlement: Maritime Enterprise and the Genesis of the British Empire, 1480–1630* (New York: Cambridge University Press, 1984).

4. Asher, *Henry Hudson the Navigator,* 248.

5. On Le Maire, see Simon Schama, *The Embarrassment of Riches: An Interpretation of Dutch Culture in the Golden Age* (New York: Knopf, 1987), 336–39.

6. Asher, *Henry Hudson the Navigator,* 248–51.

7. Asher, *Henry Hudson the Navigator,* 245–52.

8. Hudson's contract appears in Murphy, *Henry Hudson in Holland,* 32–34 (English), 110–11 (Dutch).

9. See Claudia Schnurmann, *Atlantische Welten: Engländer und Niederländer im Amerikanisch-Atlantischen Raum, 1648–1713* (Köln: Böhlau, 1998), 25–30.

10. John Romeyn Brodhead and E. B. O'Callaghan, eds., *Documents Relative to the Colonial History of the State of New-York* (Albany: Weed Parsons, 1853–87) (hereafter cited as *DRCHNY*), 1:2–3, 9, 16–20.

11. See Randolph Vigne and Charles Littleton, eds., *From Strangers to Citizens: The Integration of Immigrant Communities in Britain, Ireland, and Colonial America, 1550–1750* (Portland, Ore.: Sussex Academic Press, 2001).

12. Leo Bagrow, *History of Cartography,* 2d ed., rev. and enlarged by R. A. Skelton (Cambridge, Mass.: Harvard University Press, 1966), 251.

13. J. Franklin Jameson, ed., *Narratives of New Netherland, 1609–1664* (New York: Scribner, 1909), 4.

14. Stokes, *Iconography*, 2:41.

15. Van Meteren, *Emanuels van Meteren historie*, 628d. See also van Meteren, *Belgische ofte Nederlantsche Oorlogen ende Geschiedenissen* (Utrecht, 1611), reprinted in Murphy, *Henry Hudson in Holland*, 119–21.

16. Hudson's contract with the VOC referred to Jodocus Hondius's assistance during the negotiations. See Murphy, *Henry Hudson in Holland*, 110.

17. Murphy, *Henry Hudson in Holland*, 119.

18. Murphy, *Henry Hudson in Holland*, 66 (English), 120 (Dutch).

19. Robert Juet's journal, in Purchas, *Haklvytvs Posthumus*, 3:589.

20. Jameson, *Narratives of New Netherland*, 38. Compare Juet's account in Purchas, *Haklvytvs Posthumus*, 3:590.

21. Murphy, *Henry Hudson in Holland*, 67 (English), 120 (Dutch).

22. My translation from the Dutch in Murphy, *Henry Hudson in Holland*, 121.

23. Thomas Holland to the Earl of Salisbury, October 30, 1609, in Owen, *Calendar of the Manuscripts of the Most Honourable the Marquess of Salisbury*, 152.

24. My translation from Murphy, *Henry Hudson in Holland*, 121.

25. My translation from Murphy, *Henry Hudson in Holland*, 121.

26. Murphy, *Henry Hudson in Holland*, 68.

27. My translation from Murphy, *Henry Hudson in Holland*, 111.

28. My translation from Murphy, *Henry Hudson in Holland*, 111.

29. David Pietersz. de Vries, *Korte Historiael ende Journaels Aenteykeninge van verscheyden voyagiens in de vier deelen des wereldts-ronde, als Europa, Africa, Asia, ende Amerika gedaen* (Hoorn: Voor David Pietersz. de Vries, 1655), 114. See also the translation in Jameson, *Narratives of New Netherland*, 188.

30. Peter Heylyn, *Cosmographie: in four bookes: containing the chorographie and historie of the whole world, and all the principall kingdomes, provinces, seas and isles thereof* (London: Printed for Henry Seile, 1652), bk. 4, 110. "Beauchamp Plantagenet" claimed that Hudson "sold his Discovery, plots and cards to the Dutch," in *A Description of the Province of New Albion* (London: Printed by James Moxon, 1650), 8.

31. Heylyn, *Cosmographie*, 111. See also John Ogilby, *America* (London: Printed by the author, 1671), 169.

32. William Smith, *The History of the Province of New-York*, ed. Michael Kammen (Cambridge, Mass.: Belknap Press of Harvard University Press, 1972), 10.

33. Johannes de Laet, *Nieuvve Wereldt Ofte Beschrijvinghe van West-Indien . . .* (Leiden: Isaack Elzevier, 1625), 83–84. See also Jameson, *Narratives of New Netherland*, 36–37.

34. Adriaen van der Donck, *Beschryvinge van Nieuvv-Nederlant* (Amsterdam: By Evert Nieywenhof, 1655), 1–4.

35. My translation of Hessel Gerritsz, *Verhael van d' ontdeckinghe van de nieu-ghesochte Strate in 't Noordwesten . . . ghedaen door Mr. Hendrik Hudson Enghels-man* (1612), in Murphy, *Henry Hudson in Holland*, 128.

36. Jameson, *Narratives of New Netherland*, 78. Cleves, or Kleve, was a German city and duchy in the lower Rhineland with strong links to the Dutch Republic.

37. Nicolaas Cornelis Lambrechtsen (van Ritthem), *Korte beschrijving van de ontdekking en der verdere lotgevallen van Nieuw-Nederland . . .* (Middelburg: S. van Benthem, 1818). See also the translation in Asher, *Henry Hudson the Navigator,* 165–66.

38. *DRCHNY,* 1:5.

39. *DRCHNY,* 1:10–12. On the New Netherland Company, see Simon Hart, *The Prehistory of the New Netherland Company: Amsterdam Notarial Records of the First Dutch Voyages to the Hudson* (Amsterdam: City of Amsterdam Press, 1959); Oliver A. Rink, *Holland on the Hudson: An Economic and Social History of Dutch New York* (Ithaca: Cornell University Press, 1986), chap. 2; and Jaap Jacobs, *New Netherland: A Dutch Colony in Seventeenth-Century America* (Leiden: Brill, 2005), 34–37.

40. Rink, *Holland on the Hudson,* 74; and Hart, *Prehistory of the New Netherland Company,* 36.

41. *DRCHNY,* 1:2–3.

42. *DRCHNY,* 1:2–3.

43. For a discussion of varying responses to national difference among the founders of New Plymouth, see Cynthia Van Zandt, "The Dutch Connection: Isaac Allerton and the Dynamics of English Cultural Anxiety in the *Gouden Eeuw,*" in *Connecting Cultures: The Netherlands in Five Centuries of Transatlantic Exchange,* ed. Rosemarijn Hoefte and Johanna C. Kardux (Amsterdam: VU University Press, 1994), 51–76.

44. According to William Bradford, "Our honourable nation of England [was] the first of nations whom the Lord adorned therewith after the gross darkness of popery which had covered and overspread the Christian world." Bradford, *Of Plymouth Plantation, 1620–1647,* ed. Samuel Eliot Morison (New York: Knopf, 1952), 3.

45. Bradford, *Of Plymouth Plantation,* 16–17, 25.

46. G. Mourt, *Relation Or Iournall of the beginning and proceedings of the English Plantation settled at Plimoth in New England* (London: Printed for John Bellamie, 1622).

47. Mourt, *Relation Or Iournall,* 3.

48. Edward Winslow, *Hypocrisie Unmasked* (London: Printed for John Bellamy, 1646), 89.

49. Nathaniel Morton, *New-Englands Memoriall* (Cambridge, Mass.: Printed by S. G. and M. J. for John Usher of Boston, 1669), 3–4.

50. *DRCHNY,* 3:6.

51. *DRCHNY,* 3:10. See *DRCHNY,* 3:9–10, for the proposal that a group of Walloon settlers provided to Carleton.

52. Henri A. and Barbara Van der Zee, *Sweet and Alien Land: The Story of Dutch New York* (New York: Viking, 1978), 35.

53. *DRCHNY,* 3:7.

54. *DRCHNY,* 3:7. The records of the States General confirm that this warning was heard at the highest level of the state. See *DRCHNY,* 1:8.

55. Andrews, *Trade, Plunder and Settlement,* 260–61.

56. M. C. Ricklefs, *History of Modern Indonesia since c. 1300,* 2d ed. (Stanford: Stanford University Press, 1993), 29.

57. Bernard H. M. Vlekke, *Nusantara: A History of the East Indian Archipelago* (Cambridge, Mass.: Harvard University Press 1944), 124.

58. See Benjamin Schmidt, *Innocence Abroad: The Dutch Imagination and the New World, 1570–1670* (New York: Cambridge University Press, 2001), 291–301.

59. Heylyn, *Cosmographie*, 6, 20.

60. Nicolaes van Wassenaer, *Historisch Verhael alder ghedenck-weerdichste Geschiedenissen die hier en daer in Europa . . .*, trans. in *Narratives of New Netherland, 1609–1664*, ed. J. Franklin Jameson (New York: Scribner, 1909), 73.

61. A.J.F. van Laer, ed. and trans., *Documents Relating to New Netherland, 1624–1626, in the Henry E. Huntington Library* (San Marino, Calif.: Huntington Library, 1924), 5.

62. Van Laer, *Documents Relating to New Netherland*, 55.

63. Van Wassenaer, *Historisch Verhael*, 75.

64. See Carole Shammas, "English Commercial Development and American Colonization, 1560–1620," in *The Westward Enterprise: English Activities in Ireland, the Atlantic, and America, 1480–1650*, ed. Kenneth R. Andrews, Nicholas P. Canny, and P.E.H. Hair (Detroit: Wayne State University Press, 1979), 172; R. A. Houston, "Colonies, Enterprises, and Wealth: the Economies of Europe and the Wider World," in *Early Modern Europe*, ed. Euan Cameron (Oxford: Oxford University Press, 1999), 158; and Mancke, "Empire and State," 175–95.

65. Mancke, "Empire and State," 177.

66. Heylyn, *Cosmographie*, preface, 3.

2. COSMOPOLITAN PATRIOTISM AND THE FOUNDING OF NEW SWEDEN

1. A bibliography of Usselincx's writings between 1608 and 1622 appears in J. Franklin Jameson, *Willem Usselinx: Founder of the Dutch and Swedish West India Companies*, in *Papers of the American Historical Association*, 2.3 (New York: Putnam, 1887), 349–52, 361–62.

2. Milja van Tielhof, *The "Mother of All Trades": The Baltic Grain Trade in Amsterdam from the Late 16th to the Early 19th Century* (Leiden: Brill, 2002), 177.

3. Van Tielhof, *"Mother of All Trades,"* 172.

4. On Usselincx's interest in Danzig, see Catharina Ligtenberg, *Willem Usselinx* (Utrecht: A. Oosthoek, 1914), 93.

5. For a discussion of cosmopolitan patriotism in a contemporary context, see Kwame Anthony Appiah, "Cosmopolitan Patriots," *Critical Inquiry* 23.3 (Spring 1997): 617–39.

6. Jameson, *Willem Usselinx*, 14–21.

7. Drafts of Usselincx's commission and charter written in Dutch (probably by Usselincx himself) can be found in the National Archives of Sweden (Riksarkivet). See also Jameson, *Willem Usselinx*, 215.

8. For a summary of its contents and its similarity to his previous proposals, see Jameson, *Willem Usselinx*, 98–100.

9. Jameson, *Willem Usselinx*, 100–114.

10. See *Sweriges Rijkes General Handels Compagnies Contract* (Stockholm, 1625); and *DRCHNY* 12:2–7.

11. *Sweriges Rijkes General Handels Compagnies Contract;* and *DRCHNY* 12:2–7.

12. Jameson, *Willem Usselinx*, 103.

13. This is drawn from the language of the Swedish *Octroy Eller Privilegium* (Stockholm: Hoos Ignatium Meurer, 1626). The German version in *Argonautica Gustaviana* (Frankfurt am Main: Caspar Rödteln, 1633) has slightly different phrasing.

14. *Octroy und Privilegium,* in *Argonautica Gustaviana; DRCHNY,* 12:9–10.

15. *Aen alle vroome Nederlanders,* in *Argonautica Gustaviana.*

16. *Außführlicher Bericht uber den ContractBrieff,* 32, in *Argonautica Gustaviana.*

17. *Außführlicher Bericht uber den ContractBrieff,* 32–33, in *Argonautica Gustaviana.*

18. Jameson, *Willem Usselinx,* 123–32.

19. Jameson, *Willem Usselinx,* 138–45, 152–62.

20. *Patent* (1633), in *Argonautica Gustaviana.*

21. *Mercurius Germaniae,* 1–3, 11, 23–25, in *Argonautica Gustaviana.* See Jameson's summary of the contents of *Mercurius Germaniae,* in *Willem Usselinx,* 164–67.

22. Jameson, *Willem Usselinx,* 171–82.

23. Usselincx to Jan Beyer, March 16, 1639, quoted in G. W. Kernkamp, "Zweedsche archivalia. Brieven van Samuel Blommaert aan den Zweedschen rijkskanselier Axel Oxenstierna, 1635–1641," in *Bijdragen en Mededeelingen van het Historisch Genootschap (Gevestigd de Utrecht)* (hereafter cited as *ZA*) (1908), 29:147–48 n. 1.

24. Jacques Mévisse, "Ohain a Perdu New York," *Revue du Cercle d'Histoire et de Généalogie de Grez-Doiceau et Beauvechain* 11.3 (2004), www.orlans-amo.be/cghl/articles/OHAIN_NY.html; Tobias Arand, "Peter Minuit aus Wesel: Ein rheinischer Überseekaufmann im 17. Jahrhundert," in *Schöne Neue Welt: Rheinländer Erobern Amerika* (Wiehl: Martina Galunder, 2001), 20.

25. David Fors Freeman, "Wesel and the Dutch Revolt: The Influence of Religious Refugees on a German City, 1544–1612" (Ph.D. diss., Emory University, 2002), 134.

26. Andrew Pettegree, *Emden and the Dutch Revolt: Exile and the Development of Reformed Protestantism* (Oxford: Oxford University Press, 1992), 20, 231; Freeman, "Wesel and the Dutch Revolt," 75–77, 307.

27. Freeman, "Wesel and the Dutch Revolt," 258, 266–67.

28. Jonathan I. Israel, *The Dutch Republic: Its Rise, Greatness and Fall, 1477–1806* (New York: Oxford University Press, 1995), 407.

29. John Thomas McNeill, *The History and Character of Calvinism* (New York: Oxford University Press, 1954), 277.

30. Freeman, "Wesel and the Dutch Revolt," 309 n. 1.

31. Freeman, "Wesel and the Dutch Revolt," 347.

32. Israel, *Dutch Republic,* 407.

33. Jesse A. Spohnholz, "Strangers and Neighbors: The Tactics of Toleration in the Dutch Exile Community of Wesel, 1550–1590" (Ph.D. diss., University of Iowa, 2004), 400, 403.

34. Quoted in Spohnholz, "Strangers and Neighbors," 401.

35. Spohnholz, "Strangers and Neighbors," 412.

36. Israel, *Dutch Republic,* 498.

37. Usselincx, *Mercurius Germaniae,* 1, in *Argonautica Gustaviana.*

38. Arand, "Peter Minuit aus Wesel," 20–21.

39. For evidence and analysis of Minuit's church affiliations, see *Ecclesiastical Records, State of New York* (Albany: James B. Lyon, 1901), 1:52–53; Arand, "Peter Minuit aus Wesel," 20–22; and J. G. Sardemann, "Peter Minuit, First Governor of New Netherlands," *The Historical Magazine and Notes and Queries Concerning the Antiquities, History and Biography of America* (1868), 2d ser., 3:208.

40. Arand, "Peter Minuit aus Wesel," 23. Minuit's experience as a diamond cutter may have factored into his employment in seeking valuable stones and minerals.

41. Isaack de Rasière to the Amsterdam Chamber of the WIC, September 23, 1626, in A.J.F. van Laer, ed. and trans., *Documents Relating to New Netherland, 1624–1626, in the Henry E. Huntington Library* (San Marino, Calif.: Henry E. Huntington Library and Art Gallery, 1924), 175–76, 192.

42. C. A. Weslager and A. R. Dunlap, *Dutch Explorers, Traders and Settlers in the Delaware Valley, 1609–1664* (Philadelphia: University of Pennsylvania Press, 1961), 258. The document appears to be a seventeenth-century English translation of a now missing Dutch document.

43. Weslager and Dunlap, *Dutch Explorers,* 266–69.

44. See the end matter in Joannes de Laet, *Historie ofte Iaerlijck Verhael* (Leiden: Bonaventuer & Abraham Elsevier, 1644); see also C. A. Weslager, *A Man and His Ship: Peter Minuit and the "Kalmar Nyckel"* (Wilmington, Del.: Kalmar Nyckel Foundation, 1989), 65.

45. De Rasière to the Amsterdam Chamber, September 23, 1626, in van Laer, *Documents Relating to New Netherland,* 228.

46. Kiliaen van Rensselaer to Johannes de Laet, June 27, 1632, in A.J.F. van Laer, ed. and trans., *Van Rensselaer Bowier Manuscripts, Being the Letters of Kiliaen Van Rensselaer, 1630– 1643, and Other Documents Relating to the Colony of Rensselaerswyck* (Albany: University of the State of New York, 1908) (hereafter cited as *VRBM*), 197.

47. *VRBM,* 219, 233.

48. De Rasière to the Amsterdam Chamber, September 23, 1626, in van Laer, *Documents Relating to New Netherland,* 240 (my trans.).

49. Albert Eekhof, *Jonas Michaëlius: Founder of the Church in New Netherland* (Leyden: Sythoff's, 1926), 63–64, 68–69. The quotes are modified from Eekhof's English translation of the Latin text.

50. See van Wassenaer, *Historisch Verhael,* 12:37, for a reference to "Ian Huych" as one of the "Krank-besoekers." See also *Narratives of New Netherland,* 83 (trans. of van Wassenaer, November 1626) and 124 (Michaëlius to Smoutius, August 11, 1628).

51. *Ecclesiastical Records, State of New York,* 55.

52. *Ecclesiastical Records, State of New York,* 53–54.

53. Arand, "Peter Minuit aus Wesel," 28.

54. *ZA,* 5–15. Although Blommaert later claimed he was leaving Borneo because he feared being massacred by the natives of Sukadana, he had also been recalled by the VOC, which had received reports that the company had been "greatly defrauded there by unfaithful clerks" (15).

55. *ZA,* 16. On Reynst, see Jonathan Israel, *Dutch Primacy in World Trade* (New York: Oxford University Press, 1990), 60, 68, 71.

56. *ZA,* 21.

57. Quotes from *VRBM,* 157, 166, 175. For "Blomaerts kil," see the early map of Delaware Bay that appears as fig. 1 in Weslager and Dunlap, *Dutch Explorers.*

58. On the European copper trade with Africa in this period, see Eugenia W. Herbert, *Red Gold of Africa: Copper in Precolonial History and Culture* (Madison: University of Wisconsin Press, 2003), chap. 6. On the European trade in copper with Africa and America, see Laurier Turgeon, "The Tale of the Kettle: Odyssey of an Intercultural Object," *Ethnohistory* 44.1 (Winter 1997): 1–29.

59. See Byron J. Nordstrom, *The History of Sweden* (Westport, Conn.: Greenwood Press, 2002), 54; and Amandus Johnson, *The Swedish Settlements on the Delaware*, 2 vols. (Philadelphia: Swedish Colonial Society, 1911), 91.

60. On the copper monopoly, see Maarten Roy Prak, *The Dutch Republic in the Seventeenth Century*, 123. See also Leos Müller, "The Dutch Entrepreneurial Networks and Sweden in the Age of Greatness," in *Trade, Diplomacy and Cultural Exchange: Continuity and Change in the North Sea Area and the Baltic, c. 1350–1750*, ed. Hanno Brand (Hilversum, Netherlands: Uitgeverij Verloren, 2005), 58–74.

61. For examples of Blommaert's high status within the WIC, see *ZA*, 39–40.

62. *ZA*, 41.

63. Jonathan I. Israel, *Conflicts of Empires: Spain, the Low Countries and the Struggle for World Supremacy, 1585–1713* (Rio Grande, Ohio: Hambledon Press, 1997), 69.

64. Arand, "Peter Minuit aus Wesel," 28.

65. Israel, *Conflicts of Empires*, 70–71.

66. Friedrich Prinzing, *Epidemics Resulting from Wars* (New York: Clarendon Press, 1916), 28, 49–50, 67–73.

67. *ZA*, 44.

68. *ZA*, 45–46.

69. My translation from the Swedish in Johnson, *Swedish Settlements*, 98 n. 25.

70. Like Usselincx, Blommaert, and Minuit, Spiring's family originally came from the southern Netherlands. Spiring's origins and his connection to Sweden are discussed in Badeloch Noldus, "An 'Unvergleichbarer Liebhaber': Peter Spierinck, the Art-Dealing Diplomat," *Scandinavian Journal of History* 31.2 (2006): 174–75. For Spiring's relationship with Oxenstierna, see, among others, Stellan Dahlgren, "Pieter Silfvercrona," *Svenskt Biografiskt Lexicon* (Stockholm: Svenskt Biografiskt Lexikon, 2004), 157:190–93; Johnson, *Swedish Settlements*, 695–96; Noldus, "'Unvergleichbarer Liebhaber,'" 173–85; Noldus, "Loyalty and Betrayal: Artist-Agents Michel le Blon and Pieter Isaacsz, and Chancellor Axel Oxenstierna," in *Your Humble Servant: Agents in Early Modern Europe*, ed. Hans Cools, Marika Keblusek, and Badeloch Noldus (Hilversum, Netherlands: Uitgeverij Verloren, 2006), 54–55.

71. *ZA*, 104.

72. *ZA*, 106–10, 115; Johnson, *Swedish Settlements*, 102, 104–5.

73. Johnson, *Swedish Settlements*, 105–15.

74. *ZA*, 146–47.

75. Quotes are drawn from the original affidavit (in German), which is reproduced in Johnson, *Swedish Settlements*, after p. 184; and from the translation in Albert Cook Myers, ed., *Narratives of Early Pennsylvania, West New Jersey, and Delaware, 1630–1707* (New York: Scribner, 1912), 86–89. On "ceremonies of possession," see Patricia Seed, *Ceremonies of Possession in Europe's Conquest of the New World, 1492–1640* (New York: Cambridge University Press, 1995).

76. *DRCHNY*, 1:592.

77. A.J.F. van Laer, trans., and Kenneth Scott and Kenn Stryker-Rodda, eds., *Council Minutes, 1638–1649* (Baltimore: Genealogical Pub. Co., 1974), 7. See also Johnson, *Swedish Settlements*, 186; and *DRCHNY*, 12:19.

78. Letter from Jerome Hawley to Secretary Windebanke, May 8, 1638, in *DRCHNY*, 3:20.

79. *DRCHNY*, 3:20.

80. *ZA,* 163.

81. *ZA,* 138–39.

82. John Taylor, *Newes and Strange Newes from St. Christophers of a tempestuous Spirit, which is called by the Indians a Hurry-Cano or whirlewind* (London, 1638), 4–6; *ZA,* 177.

83. Taylor, *Newes and Strange Newes,* 6.

84. *ZA,* 177–78.

85. *ZA,* 162.

86. Amandus Johnson Papers (hereafter cited as AJP), 55:1; see Johnson, *Swedish Settlements,* 124 n. 19, for the Swedish.

87. AJP, 54:2 (in German), 55:1 (English trans.).

88. Blommaert to Axel Oxenstierna, June 6, 1637, in *ZA,* 117–19.

89. For the names and shares, see AJP, 57:3; and Johnson, *Swedish Settlements,* 106. For a discussion of the influence of family networks in early modern Amsterdam and New Netherland, see Willem Frijhoff, "Neglected Networks: Director Willem Kieft (1602–1647) and His Dutch Relatives," in *Revisiting New Netherland: Perspectives on Dutch America,* ed. Joyce Goodfriend (Leiden: Brill, 2005), 156.

90. Blommaert trained as a merchant in Vienna under his uncle, Daniel Hoefnagel (*ZA,* 5). Note that Usselincx met with a merchant named Hoeffnagel when he was in Göteborg in 1623 (Jameson, *Willem Usselinx,* 91).

91. *ZA,* 4.

92. Bessels was married to Margaretha Reynst, the sister of Blommaert's wife, Catharina. See *ZA,* 19; and Matthijs Antonius van Rhede van der Kloot, *De Gouverneurs-Generaal en Commissarissen-Generaal van Nederlandsch-Indië* ('s-Gravenhage: W. P. Van Stockum, 1891), 27. Both families were also important collectors of tulips. See Anne Goldgar, *Tulipmania: Money, Honor, and Knowledge in the Dutch Golden Age* (Chicago: University of Chicago Press, 2007), 125.

93. Jaap Jacobs, *New Netherland: A Dutch Colony in Seventeenth-Century America* (Leiden: Brill, 2005), 70. For the Verbrugge family's activities, see Oliver A. Rink, *Holland on the Hudson: An Economic and Social History of Dutch New York* (Ithaca: Cornell University Press, 1986), chap. 7; and Janny Venema, *Beverwijck: A Dutch Village on the American Frontier, 1652–1664* (Albany: State University of New York Press, 2003), 197–98, 239–42.

94. Carl Boyer, *Ship Passenger Lists: New York and New Jersey, 1600–1825* (Westminster, Md.: Heritage Books, 2007), 100.

95. C. A. Weslager, "The City of Amsterdam's Colony on the Delaware 1656–1664; With Unpublished Dutch Notarial Abstracts," *Delaware History* 20 (1982): 80. The relationship between van de Water and Minuit may have continued through Hendrick Huygen, the son of another of Minuit's sisters: "Sieur Isacq van de Water, merchant at Amsterdam, Holland," is mentioned in a case connected to "Hendrick Huygens," in Berthold Fernow, trans. and ed., *Minutes of the Orphanmasters Court of New Amsterdam, 1655–1663* (New York: Francis P. Harper, 1907), vol. 2 ("Minutes of the executive boards of the Burgomasters of New Amsterdam"), 57.

96. Blommaert to Axel Oxenstierna, January 28, 1640, in *ZA,* 178–79, 187.

97. Jameson, *Willem Usselinx,* 138.

98. Blommaert to Axel Oxenstierna, January 28, 1640, in *ZA,* 188.

99. Johnson, *Swedish Settlements,* 131–32.

3. GOOD FRIENDS AND DOUBTFUL NEIGHBORS

1. Van Wassenaer, *Historisch verhael*, 5:40–41.

2. Jameson, *Willem Usselinx*, 85.

3. Willem van Brederode, *Op jacht naar Spaans zilver: Het scheepsjournaal van Willem van Brederode, kapitein der mariniers in de Nassause vloot (1623–1626)*, ed. Anne Doedens and Henk Looijesteijn (Hilversum: Uitgeverij Verloren, 2008), 52–53.

4. Van Brederode, *Op jacht naar Spaans zilver*, 2.

5. Robert Kerr, *A General History and Collection of Voyages and Travels* (Edinburgh: William Blackwood, 1824), 10:193.

6. Benjamin Schmidt, *Innocence Abroad: The Dutch Imagination and the New World, 1570–1670* (New York: Cambridge University Press, 2001), 198.

7. Kris E. Lane, *Pillaging the Empire: Piracy in the Americas, 1500–1750* (Armonk, N.Y.: M. E. Sharpe, 1998), 85.

8. Schmidt, *Innocence Abroad*, 176.

9. "FORMULAR Deß Manifest und Vergleich-oder Contract-brieffes," in *Argonautica Gustaviana*.

10. Schmidt, *Innocence Abroad*, 181–83; Donna Merwick, *The Shame and the Sorrow: Dutch-Amerindian Encounters in New Netherland* (Philadelphia: University of Pennsylvania Press, 2006), 49–52. On the origins, context, and application of *Mare Liberum*, see Richard Tuck, *The Rights of War and Peace: Political Thought and the International Order from Grotius to Kant* (New York: Oxford University Press, 1999), chap. 3; and Martine Julia van Ittersum, *Profit and Principle: Hugo Grotius, Natural Rights Theories and the Rise of Dutch Power in the East Indies, 1595–1615* (Leiden: Brill, 2006).

11. Among them was one new arrival, an Angolan named Anthony, who had been purchased as a slave in the Caribbean.

12. Johnson, *Swedish Settlements*, 207.

13. Jacobs, *New Netherland*, 53–54.

14. Carol E. Hoffecker et al., eds., *New Sweden in America* (Newark: University of Delaware Press, 1995), 292, 348.

15. He arrived either on the first voyage in 1638 or on the second in 1640. Johnson, *Swedish Settlements*, 699.

16. For backgrounds of some other participants in the first voyage, see Weslager, *Man and His Ship*, 113–15.

17. Selections from Kieft's correspondence with the directors of the Amsterdam chamber of the WIC, from app. 1 of "Deduction or Clear Account," January 28, 1656, *DRCHNY* 1:592.

18. Ridder may have been the son of Dutch merchant Hans Hollander Ridder and a Finnish mother, Anna Robertsdotter, and thus may have spoken Finnish as well as Dutch. See Weslager, *Man and His Ship*, 165; Johnson, *Swedish Settlements*, 691–92; Hoffecker, *New Sweden in America*, 173, 348.

19. Johnson, *Swedish Settlements*, 200.

20. Ridder to Axel Oxenstierna, May 13, 1640, in AJP, 55:2 (English trans.).

21. Ridder to Oxenstierna, May 13, 1640, in AJP, 55:2.

22. Fleming to Axel Oxenstierna, July 1, 1639, in AJP, 55:1.

23. Blommaert to Oxenstierna, January 28, 1640, in *ZA*, 188.

24. Blommaert to Oxenstierna, January 28, 1640, in *ZA*, 185. Andries Hudde called van Dyck "een hagenaer." "Dutch Delaware River settlement administrative records, 1646–1664" (A1878), New York State Archives, vol. 18.

25. See Johnson, *Swedish Settlements,* 128–30.

26. Ridder to Axel Oxenstierna, December 1640, in AJP, 55:2.

27. Blommaert to Oxenstierna, January 28, 1640, in *ZA*, 188.

28. Plantagenet, *Description of the Province of New Albion,* 17.

29. *DRCHNY,* 1:593.

30. See van Laer, *Documents Relating to New Netherland, 1624–1626,* 262 n. 12.

31. *ZA*, 190.

32. *ZA*, 173.

33. Oxenstierna to Fleming, in AJP, 54:2; my translation modified from the one given in AJP, 55:1.

34. Fleming to Oxenstierna, June 8, 1639, trans. in AJP, 55:1.

35. See Johnson, *Swedish Settlements,* 139–40.

36. For the charter in German, see AJP, 54:2; see also AJP, 55:2.

37. Johnson, *Swedish Settlements,* 142.

38. Johnson, *Swedish Settlements,* 143.

39. See Hans Norman, "The New Sweden Colony and the Continued Existence of Swedish and Finnish Ethnicity," in Hoffecker, *New Sweden in America,* 189, table 1, which states that there were sixty-eight men in the colony in 1640.

40. Johnson, *Swedish Settlements,* 143.

41. *The Journal of John Winthrop, 1630–1649,* ed. Richard S. Dunn et al. (Cambridge, Mass.: Harvard University Press, 1996), 403.

42. Charles J. Hoadly, ed., *Records of the Colony and Plantation of New-Haven, from 1638 to 1649* (Hartford, Conn.: Case, Tiffany, & Co., 1857), 91. Five of the ten were nonresidents, so Lamberton was actually among the top five resident planters. New Haven's population numbered 419 at the time. Edward Elias Atwater, *History of the Colony of New Haven to Its Absorption into Connecticut* (Meriden, Conn.: Journal Publishing Co., 1902), 131.

43. L. H. Roper, "The Ties That Bound: The Conception of Anglo-America, 1617–1667," *Journal of Early American History* 1 (2011): 143.

44. Hoadly, *Records,* 91. On Turner's background in Massachusetts and New Haven, see Atwater, *History of the Colony of New Haven,* 121–22; and Edward R. Lambert, *History of the Colony of New Haven, before and after the Union with Connecticut* (New Haven: Hitchcock & Stafford, 1838), 51.

45. Hoadly, *Records,* 40. His previous experience in warfare included participating in the party that invaded Block Island and staged the first assault against the Pequots in 1636. See John Underhill, *Newes from America* (London: J.D. for Peter Cole, 1638), 3; Lion Gardener, *Relation of the Pequot Warres* (Hartford, Conn.: Hartford Press, 1901), 9.

46. Cotton Mather, *Magnalia Christi Americana: Or, the Ecclesiastical History of New-England, from Its First Planting in the year 1620. unto the Year of our LORD, 1698* (London: Printed for Thomas Parkhurst, 1702), bk. 1, 27.

47. See the map of New Haven in Myron Andrews Munson, *The Munson Record: A Genealogical and Biographical Account of Captain Thomas Munson* (New Haven: Munson Association, 1895), 1:8. Eaton's name and what seems to be Davenport's name appear in protests issued by Lamberton in 1643. See Amandus Johnson, ed., *The Instruction for Johan Printz, Governor of New Sweden* (Philadelphia: Swedish Colonial Society, 1930) (hereafter cited as *Instruction*), 231–32.

48. See *Instruction*, 231–32.

49. Mather, *Magnalia Christi Americana*, bk. 1, 25.

50. William Hubbard, *A General History of New England: From the Discovery to MDCLXXX*, 2d. ed. (Boston: Charles C. Little & James Brown, 1848), 321.

51. Hubbard, *General History of New England*, 14.

52. Amandus Johnson suggested that this expedition might have actually taken place a year later. Johnson, *Swedish Settlements*, 213–14.

53. John Winthrop, *Winthrop's Journal: "History of New England," 1630–1649*, in *Original Narratives of American History*, ed. James Kendall Hosmer, 2 vols. (New York: Scribner, 1908), 2:35.

54. *DRCHNY*, 2:144. See also Johnson, *Swedish Settlements*, 214–15; and Isabel M. Calder, *The New Haven Colony* (New Haven: Yale University Press, 1934), 77.

55. Calder, *New Haven Colony*, 64; Dunn, *Journal of John Winthrop*, 387.

56. Hendrick Huygen to Peter Spiring, November 28, 1641, in AJP, 56:1.

57. Lamberton may also have visited the river the year before, as he was recorded as having purchased cattle on Virginia's Eastern Shore on March 29, 1641. Hatfield, *Atlantic Virginia*, 45, 243. His interest in the Delaware Valley's fur trade supposedly stemmed from a voyage to Virginia during the winter of 1638–39. See Charles H. Levermore, *The Republic of New Haven: A History of Municipal Evolution* (Baltimore: Johns Hopkins University, 1886), 90.

58. George Lamberton's protest, April 19, 1642, in *Instruction*, 231 n. 14a.

59. Johnson, *Swedish Settlements*, 211.

60. See *DRCHNY*, 2:141–43, for New Netherland's protests against the English settlers in Connecticut in 1640–41.

61. Van Laer, *Council Minutes*, 144–46.

62. David Pulsifer, ed., *Records of the Colony of New Plymouth in New England . . . Acts of the Commissioners of the United Colonies of New England* (Boston: William White, 1859), 1:181.

63. Weslager and Dunlap, *Dutch Explorers*, 138.

64. Johnson, *Swedish Settlements*, 215; Pulsifer, *Records of the Colony of New Plymouth*, 1:189.

65. Dunn, *Journal of John Winthrop*, 402; Weslager and Dunlap, *Dutch Explorers*, app. B, 300–301; Calder, *New Haven Colony*, 77; Johnson, *Instruction*, 68.

66. See Amandus Johnson's biography of Printz, in *Instruction*, 4–15.

67. *Instruction*, 92–94.

68. Brahe to Printz, November 9, 1643, in *Instruction*, 156–57.

69. *Instruction*, 4–5.

70. *Instruction*, 94–96.

71. Brahe to Printz, November 9, 1643, in *Instruction*, 156.

72. *Instruction,* 163.

73. *Instruction,* 94–96.

74. *Instruction,* 78.

75. *Instruction,* 70.

76. *Instruction,* 72.

77. *Instruction,* 72–76.

78. My translation from *Instruction,* 67–69, 78–80.

79. *Instruction,* 25.

80. The fort is described in David Pietersz. de Vries, *Korte Historiael ende Journaels Aenteykeninge van verscheyden voyagiens in de vier deelen des wereldts-ronde, als Europa, Africa, Asia, ende Amerika gedaen* (Hoorn: Voor David Pietersz. de Vries, 1655), 184–85; and Andries Hudde's report (1645–48), in *DD,* 1.

81. *Instruction,* 107–8.

82. *Instruction,* 112. The other major new fort, built in April 1643 on Tinicum Island near the mouth of the Schuylkill River, was called "New Göteborg." By early 1644 the location became the colony's new capital and by 1646 the home of Printz's blockhouse, or "mansion," Printzhof, and a new church. See *Instruction,* 25–28; and Marshall Becker, "Ethnohistory and Archaeology in Search of the Printzhof: The 17th Century Residence of Swedish Colonial Governor Johan Printz," *Ethnohistory* 26.1 (Winter 1979): 15–44.

83. See table 1 in Hans Norman, "The New Sweden Colony and the Continued Existence of Swedish and Finnish Ethnicity," in Hoffecker, *New Sweden in America,* 189.

84. *Instruction,* 107–8.

85. "Henrik Huygens Schuldbok," Handel och Sjöfart, Nya Sverige series, vol. 196, Riksarkivet, Stockholm.

86. See Hudde's report, in *DD,* 1.

87. *Instruction,* 124.

88. Printz's Report of 1644, in *Instruction,* 112–13.

89. *Instruction,* 114–15. For additional details regarding Plowden's venture, see C. A. Weslager, *The English on the Delaware: 1610–1682* (New Brunswick, N.J.: Rutgers University Press, 1967), 76–88; L. H. Roper, "New Albion: Anatomy of an English Colonisation Failure, 1632–1659," *Itinerario* 32.1 (2008): 39–57; and Clifford Lewis, "Some Recently Discovered Extracts from the List Minutes of the Virginia Council and General Court, 1642–1645," *William and Mary College Quarterly Historical Magazine,* 2d ser., 20.1 (January 1940): 62–78.

90. See *Instruction,* 254.

91. Printz's Report of 1644, in *Instruction,* 115.

92. Dunn, *Journal of John Winthrop,* 710.

93. Printz's Report of 1644, in *Instruction,* 113.

94. Lamberton's protest, in *Instruction,* 232.

95. *Instruction,* 238–39.

96. Proceedings at Court in New Sweden, July 10, 1643, in *Instruction,* 242.

97. Translations of John Winthrop's and Johan Printz's Latin correspondence are available in AJP, 55:3.

98. Winthrop, quoted in *A Volume Relating to the Early History of Boston, Containing the Aspinwall Notarial Records from 1644 to 1651* (Boston: Municipal Printing Office, 1903), v.

99. Dunn, *Journal of John Winthrop*, 504. For a discussion of Aspinwall's venture, see Weslager, *English on the Delaware*, 123–32; and Louise A. Breen, *Transgressing the Bounds: Subversive Enterprises among the Puritan Elite in Massachusetts, 1630–1692* (Oxford: Oxford University Press, 2001), 129–30.

100. Dunn, *Journal of John Winthrop*, 521–22.

101. *Instruction*, 222.

102. See Johnson, *Swedish Settlements*, 707–8; and Joseph J. Mickley Manuscripts, Historical Society of Pennsylvania, "Musterrals 1641–49."

103. *Instruction*, 117.

104. On the attack, see Frank E. Grizzard and D. Boyd Smith, eds., *The Jamestown Colony: A Political, Social, and Cultural History* (Santa Barbara, Calif.: ABC-Clio, 2007), 134–36.

105. *Instruction*, 119.

106. For an early reference to the large scale of the maize trade, see Huygen to Spiring, November 28, 1641, in AJP, 56:1. Marshall Joseph Becker argues that the Swedish colony was dependent on the maize trade with the Lenape throughout its existence. See Becker, "Lenape Maize Sales to the Swedish Colonists: Cultural Stability during the Early Colonial Period," in Hoffecker, *New Sweden in America*, 121–36.

107. *Instruction*, 117–18.

108. *Instruction*, 124.

109. For New Netherland's wars with the Munsee, see Paul A. Otto, *The Dutch-Munsee Encounter in America: The Struggle for Sovereignty in the Hudson Valley* (New York: Bergahn Books, 2006).

110. On the Hartford Treaty, see Sabine Klein, "'They Have Invaded the Whole River': Boundary Negotiations in Anglo-Dutch Colonial Discourse," *Early American Studies: An Interdisciplinary Journal* 9.2 (2011): 324–47.

111. Hudde report, in *DD*, 2.

112. *DD*, 2–4.

113. *DD*, 5. On Lindeström's manuscript map of the Delaware River and Bay, "Mirekats Kijl" appears a short distance upriver from "Kiki-menskijl," present-day Neshaminy Creek. See Johnson, *Swedish Settlements*, 2:514ff.

114. *DD*, 16.

115. *DD*, 5.

116. "Dutch Delaware River settlement administrative records, 1646–1664"; *DD*, 5–6.

117. "Dutch Delaware River settlement administrative records, 1646–1664."

118. *DD*, 7.

119. *DD*, 7.

120. *Instruction*, 133–34.

121. *Instruction*, 132–33.

122. *Instruction*, 136.

123. *DRCHNY*, 12:40. The sachems' visit to New Amsterdam was probably part of a greater mission to conduct diplomacy with the Iroquois and perhaps the Mohawks in particular. For the Hurons' role in prompting the mission, see Reuben G. Thwaites, ed., *The Jesuit Relations and Allied Documents* (Cleveland: Burrows Brothers, 1898), 33:129–33.

124. On Loockermans's origins, see Jameson, *Narratives of New Netherland*, 376.

125. Stuyvesant to Hudde, in *DD*, 22–23.

126. On the national origins of the men, see *DD*, 24; *DRCHNY*, 12:603; *Register of New Netherland*, 132; and Teunis G. Bergen, *Register in Alphabetical Order, of the Early Settlers of Kings County, Long Island* (New York: S. W. Green's Son, 1881), 246, 346.

127. *DRCHNY*, 12:57.

128. Van Tienhoven to Stuyvesant, November 9, 1648, in *DD*, 19.

129. Loockermans to Verbrugge, May 27, 1648, quoted in Jaap Jacobs, *New Netherland: A Dutch Colony in Seventeenth-Century America* (Leiden: Brill, 2005), 71.

130. Hudde's report, in *DD*, 9.

131. *DD*, 9–10.

132. *DD*, 10.

133. Undated memorandum, in *DD*, 18.

134. *DD*, 10–11.

135. Boyer to Stuyvesant, September 25, 1648, in *DD*, 12–13.

136. *DD*, 18.

137. *DD*, 12–13.

138. Hudde's report, in *DD*, 11.

139. Testimony by Adriaen van Tienhoven, Alexander Boyer, Davidt Davitsz, Symon Root, Johannes Markus, and Harmen Jansz., November 6, 1648, in *DD*, 15–16.

140. Van Tienhoven to Stuyvesant, November 9, 1648, in *DD*, 18.

141. Hudde to Stuyvesant, May 16, 1662, 19:29, in *DD*, 271–72.

142. Stuyvesant to Hudde, May 13, 1649, 19:31, in *DD*, 273–74.

143. See also the freemen's purchase of lands on the east side of the river in April 1649, in *DRCHNY*, 12:48–49.

144. Stuyvesant to Printz, July 24, 1650, app. B, in *DD*, 362.

145. For more on the disastrous voyage of the *Katt*, see Johnson, *Swedish Settlements*, 266–80; and Sprinchorn in Keen, *PMHB* (1884), 8:28–32.

146. Sten Carlsson, "The New Sweden Colonists, 1628–1656: Their Geographical and Social Background," in *New Sweden in America*, ed. Carol E. Hoffecker et al. (Newark: University of Delaware Press, 1995), 176. The number of workingmen in the colony actually fell, however, from ninety-three to eighty-three between 1643 and 1648.

147. Printz to Brahe, August 1, 1650, in *Instruction*, 177.

148. Printz to Brahe, August 1, 1650, in *Instruction*, 177–78.

149. *DD*, 25.

150. *DD*, 29; and "Dutch Delaware River settlement administrative records, 1646–1664."

151. See Klein, "'They Have Invaded the Whole River.'"

152. *DD*, 34.

153. Printz to Oxenstierna, August 1, 1651, in *Instruction*, 180–81.

154. Johnson, *Swedish Settlements*, 436.

155. *DRCHNY*, 1:597.

156. *DRCHNY*, 1:598. WIC officials later claimed that Arent Corssen had purchased land along the Schuylkill River in 1633 (*DRCHNY*, 1:588), which matches the date the sachems offered here. Hudde orchestrated a second purchase in 1648 that confirmed and completed Corssen's purchase of 1633, for which he had apparently not fully paid the sachems. *DRCHNY*, 1:593.

157. *DRCHNY,* 1:598.

158. *DRCHNY,* 1:599.

159. Johnson, *Swedish Settlements,* 438–39. A photostat of the manuscript appears between pp. 438 and 439. Mitatsimint appeared as "Mitot Schemingh" in the 1638 affidavit of the New Sweden purchase. Myers, *Narratives of Early Pennsylvania,* 87.

160. *DRCHNY,* 1:599–600.

161. *DRCHNY,* 1:596–97.

162. *Instruction,* 181.

163. For Stuyvesant's response, see *DRCHNY,* 12:69–70; more generally, see Calder, *New Haven Colony,* 191–92; and Weslager, *English on the Delaware,* 144–46. *Instruction,* 183.

164. See Printz to Oxenstierna, August 30, 1652, in *Instruction* 184; and Printz to Brahe, July 14, 1653, in *Instruction,* 190.

165. See Oxenstierna to Printz, September 1647, in *Instruction,* 169, 174.

166. *Instruction,* 185–86.

167. Printz to Brahe, December 1, 1653, in *Instruction,* 193; Printz to Oxenstierna, April 26, 1653, in *Instruction,* 187.

168. Both groups apparently were "Minquas," but their relationship to one another is unclear.

169. *Instruction,* 187–88.

170. Ondaaiondiont may have been mistaken or misled. A new Swedish church had been built on Tinicum Island in 1646, and Printz's instructions (1643) suggest that there was a small church at Fort Christina before he arrived. Johnson, *Swedish Settlements,* 366–67. See also Thomas Campanius Holm, *Kort Beskrifning om Provincien Nya Swerige aff America* (Stockholm, 1702), 73.

171. Thwaites, *Jesuit Relations,* 33:133–35.

172. For Printz's increasingly bleak view of the prospects for conversion, see *Instruction,* 151–53, 164–55.

173. Dunn, *Journal of John Winthrop,* 503.

174. "Motives & Reasons for the Petition of the Governor & Company of New Albion" (1635), quoted in Roper, "New Albion: Anatomy of an English Colonisation Failure, 1632–1659," *Itinerario* 32.1 (2008): 42. See also Plantagenet, *Description of the Province of New Albion,* 6.

175. For Indians' interest in the catechism, see Erick Björk to Israel Kolmodin, October 29, 1697, in Thomas Campanius Holm, *A Short Description of the Province of New Sweden,* ed. and trans. Peter Du Ponceau, in *Memoirs of the Historical Society of Pennsylvania* (1834), 3:100.

176. Campanius Holm, *Kort Beskrifning,* 160–61.

177. Campanius Holm, *Kort Beskrifning,* 183.

178. For accounts of Swedish sales of guns to Indians, see Plantagenet, *Description of the Province of New Albion* (1648), 18; Lindeström, *Resa till Nya Sverige,* ed. Alf Åberg (Stockholm: Natur och Kultur, 1962), 132; and Lindeström, *Geographia Americae: With an Account of the Delaware Indians; Based on Surveys and Notes Made in 1654–1656,* ed. Amandus Johnson (Philadelphia: Swedish Colonial Society, 1925), 227.

179. Quote from Brant Aertsz van Slichtenhorst's testimony in Janny Venema, *Beverwijck: A Dutch Village on the American Frontier, 1652–1664* (Albany: State University of New York Press, 2003), 43. For other contemporary comments about gun sales to Indians in New Netherland,

see "Journal of New Netherland" (1647), in *Narratives of New Netherland, 1609–1664,* ed. J. Franklin Jameson (New York: Scribner, 1909), 274; Plantagenet, *Description of the Province of New Albion;* "Answer to the Representation of New Netherland" (1650), by Cornelis van Tienhoven, in Jameson, *Narratives of New Netherland,* 368; and Magistrates of Heemstede (Hempstead) to the (WIC) Directors at Amsterdam, September 35, 1651, in *DRCHNY,* 2:157.

180. From an extended and slightly different version of this quote in Janny Venema, "The Court Case of Brant Aertsz van Slichtenhorst against Jan van Rensselaer," *De Halve Maen* (Spring 2001): 6.

181. *Instruction,* 74.

182. The only apparent exception was Edmund Plowden, whose efforts to colonize the Delaware Valley were especially unsuccessful. For examples of colonizers' recognizing indigenous land ownership, see Van Twiller to the "Governoʳ of the Englishe Collonye att the Massachusetts Baye," October 4, 1633 (New Style), in *DRCHNY,* 3:19; Winthrop to Printz, September 18, 1643, in *Instruction,* 210–11; Printz to Winthrop, January 12, 1644, in *Instruction,* 213; Lamberton's testimony in *Instruction,* 231–32 n. 14a; and Stuyvesant's dialogue with the sachems at Fort Casimir in 1651, *DRCHNY,* 1:597. For an account of English arguments about possession, see Stuart Banner, *How the Indians Lost Their Land: Law and Power on the Frontier* (Cambridge, Mass.: Harvard University Press, 2005), chap. 1, "Native Proprietors."

183. *DRCHNY,* 1:597.

184. Hudde report, in *DD,* 9–10.

185. *Instruction,* 238.

186. Printz to Oxenstierna, August 30, 1652, in *Instruction,* 185.

187. Natives killed four men on a fur-trading voyage from Boston in the spring of 1645. See Johnson, *Swedish Settlements,* 398.

188. Campanius Holm, *Kort Beskrifning,* 173–79.

189. Winthrop to Printz, in *Instruction,* 212.

190. Printz to Winthrop, January 1644, in AJP, 55:3.

191. Printz to Winthrop, January 1644, in AJP, 55:3.

192. *Instruction,* 219.

193. *Instruction,* 220.

194. Dunn, *Journal of John Winthrop,* 521–22.

195. Dunn, *Journal of John Winthrop,* 480.

196. Thomas Hobbes, *Leviathan, Or the Matter, Forme, and Power of a Commonwealth Ecclesiasticall and Civil* (London: Andrew Crooke, 1651), 185, 62.

4. REBELS AND GOOD SWEDISH MEN

1. Johnson, *Swedish Settlements,* 316–17.

2. Alf Åberg, *The People of New Sweden: Our Colony on the Delaware River, 1638–1655* (Stockholm: Natur och Kultur, 1988), 58.

3. Johnson, *Swedish Settlements,* 243, 304–5, 452.

4. Lindeström, *Geographia Americae,* 86–87.

5. Lindeström, *Geographia Americae,* 86.

6. Johnson, *Swedish Settlements,* 339; Johnson, *Instruction,* 183.

7. Stellan Dahlgren and Hans Norman, eds., *The Rise and Fall of New Sweden: Governor Johan Risingh's Journal 1654–1655 in Its Historical Context* (Stockholm: Almqvist & Wiksell, 1988) (hereafter cited as *Risingh's Journal*), 149.

8. AJP 54:3 (Swedish), 55:4 (English trans.).

9. See Peter S. Craig, *The 1693 Census of the Swedes on the Delaware: Family Histories of the Swedish Lutheran Church Members Residing in Pennsylvania, Delaware, West New Jersey & Cecil County, Md., 1638–1693* (Winter Park, Fla.: SAG Publications, 1993).

10. *Risingh's Journal,* 185.

11. Johnson, *Instruction,* 165–66, 173, 175, 179.

12. Johnson, *Instruction,* 177.

13. Johnson, *Instruction,* 183–85.

14. Johnson, *Instruction,* 185–88.

15. Johnson, *Instruction,* 190–94.

16. Johnson, *Instruction,* 193–96.

17. Johnson, *Swedish Settlements,* 702; Craig, *1693 Census,* 26–27, 33, 41, 56.

18. AJP, 55:2: "List of Persons," May 3, 1641. See also Johnson, *Swedish Settlements,* 151–53.

19. AJP, 55:2, April 13, 1641; Craig, *1693 Census,* 60; Johnson, *Swedish Settlements,* 705, 712.

20. Johnson, *Swedish Settlements,* 152, 704.

21. For background on Olof Stille, see Fritz Nordström, "Olof Stille of New Sweden," *Swedish American Genealogist* 6.3 (1986): 97–106; Peter S. Craig, "The Stille Family in America," *Swedish American Genealogist* 6.4 (1986): 141–76; Hans Ling, "Olov Stille," at www.colonials-wedes.se/Olof_Stille.htm; and Peter S. Craig, "Olof Persson Stille and His Family," at www.co-lonialswedes.org/forefathers/Stille.html. The last was originally published in *Swedish Colonial News* 1.16 (Fall 1997). See also AJP, 55:2: "List of Persons"; Craig, *1693 Census,* 46; Johnson, *Swedish Settlements,* 711.

22. Johnson, *Swedish Settlements,* 702, 711–12, 722.

23. For further background on the forest Finns, see Terry G. Jordan and Matti E. Kaups, *The American Backwoods Frontier: An Ethnic and Ecological Interpretation* (Baltimore: Johns Hopkins University Press, 1989). See also Per Martin Tvengsberg, "Finns in Seventeenth-Century Sweden and Their Contributions to the New Sweden Colony," 279–90; Juha Pentikäinen, "The Forest Finns and Transmitters of Finnish Culture from Savo via Central Scandinavia to Delaware," 291–301; and Terry G. Jordan, "The Material Cultural Legacy of New Sweden on the American Frontier," 302–18, all in *New Sweden in America,* ed. Carol E. Hoffecker, et al. (Newark: University of Delaware Press, 1995).

24. Andersson had previously served as a soldier at Fort Älvsborg at Göteborg but had been sent to the colony as punishment for a crime. Jochim later married Ella Stille, Olof's daughter. See Craig's biography of Andersson at www.colonialswedes.org/Forefathers/AnderssonFinn. html, originally published in *Swedish Colonial News* 3.2 (Spring 2005).

25. Catharine's mother was probably a sibling of the Stille brothers. See Craig's account of the Lom family at www.colonialswedes.org/Forefathers/Lom.html, originally published in *Swedish Colonial News* 1.12 (Fall 1995).

26. In 1654 the settlers put together an expanded version of the petition. In it they accused Printz of selling the colony's provisions to New Netherland, trading furs with New Englanders,

and shipping silver and pelts to Holland on his own account. AJP, 54:3 (Swedish), 55:4 (English trans.).

27. The 1654 document added further details about Printz's abuse of the widow "Karin the Finn." They claimed that he had beat her, imprisoned her in chains at Fort Elfsborg for an entire year, and prevented her from feeding her own young children. "From that she lost her mind [and] could not remain among other people, but [she] stayed in the woods . . . and snow and other horrors, and she died insane from the world," they wrote. The petitioners claimed that Printz did all this to Karin so that he could take possession of her family's house and land for his own use. AJP, 54:3 (Swedish), 55:4 (English trans.).

28. AJP, 54:3 (Swedish), 55:4 (English trans.).

29. AJP, 54:3 (Swedish), 55:4 (English trans.).

30. Stuyvesant to the Directors of the WIC, Amsterdam Chamber, October 6, 1653, in *DRCHNY,* 1:600.

31. Craig, *1693 Census,* 3.

32. Johnson, *Swedish Settlements,* 705, 711.

33. He is recorded as having purchased a plantation from William Leeds on September 10, 1655, and another piece of land on October 22, 1655. He sold a piece of the first purchase in March 1656. By February 1657 he was being sued for debt. See *Archives of Maryland,* 54:37, 54, 59, 84.

34. Another possibility is Anders Andersson (Homman), who served as soldier in the 1640s and later lived at Kingsessing and in Gloucester County, New Jersey. See Johnson, *Swedish Settlements,* 706, 713; Craig, *1693 Census,* 71–72. He may have been neither man, as in October 1657 an Andrew Anderson is mentioned as a witness for an indenture for "Margrett Anderson," daughter of Anders and Anna Hansson. *Archives of Maryland,* 54:124–25. Anders died in 1655, and Anna was remarried a year later to Andrew Elena, a Spaniard. See Craig, *1693 Census,* 66; and George Adolphus Hanson, *Old Kent: The Eastern Shore of Maryland* (Baltimore: John P. Des Forges, 1876), 60.

35. See *Archives of Maryland,* 54:31. Both Loo and Hanson were dead by the end of 1655 (35).

36. Svensson later returned to the Delaware River and served on the Upland Court in 1681–82 and the Pennsylvania Assembly in 1683. See Craig, *1693 Census,* 33–34.

37. *Risingh's Journal,* 163.

38. Papegoja to Per Brahe, July 15, 1644, in *Instruction,* 160–62.

39. The two men may have been Hendrick Mattsson the Swede and Matts Hansson, the gunner whose brother Anders had fled with his family to Kent Island. Craig, *1693 Census,* 3.

40. *Risingh's Journal,* 156–57.

41. *Risingh's Journal,* 163.

42. Johnson, *Swedish Settlements,* 479–82; *Risingh's Journal,* 133; Lindeström, *Geographia Americae,* 27–28; Per Lindeström, *Resa till Nya Sverige,* ed. Alf Åberg (Stockholm: Natur och Kultur, 1962), 28.

43. Lindeström, *Geographia Americae,* 33; *Risingh's Journal,* 137–39. The negotiations between Whitelocke and Queen Christina led to an agreement that "the colonies of New Sweden and the English . . . [should] embrace a sincere friendship . . . [and] abstain from all troubles and injuries to the other" and ensure their "mutual preservation" until their respective limits were determined by their commissioners. See Whitelocke, *A Journal of the Swedish Embassy in the Years 1653 and 1654* (London: Longman, 1855), 2:242.

44. Lindeström, *Resa till Nya Sverige*, 34, 37.

45. Lindeström, who had a talent for exaggeration, wrote that the *spanske* "shot at us the whole night." Lindeström, *Resa till Nya Sverige*, 37; Lindeström, *Geographia Americae*, 41.

46. *Risingh's Journal*, 141; Lindeström, *Geographia Americae*, 46; Lindeström, *Resa till Nya Sverige*, 40–41.

47. Lindeström, *Geographia Americae*, 44–45; Lindeström, *Resa till Nya Sverige*, 39–40; *Risingh's Journal*, 1, 39–41.

48. Lindeström, *Geographia Americae*, 66–67; Lindeström, *Resa till Nya Sverige*, 52–53; *Risingh's Journal*, 143.

49. Lindeström, *Geographia Americae*, 73; Lindeström, *Resa till Nya Sverige*, 57.

50. *Risingh's Journal*, 145; Lindeström, *Geographia Americae*, 82.

51. Lindeström, *Resa till Nya Sverige*, 64.

52. *Risingh's Journal*, 151.

53. *DRCHNY*, 1:603.

54. *DRCHNY*, 12:46–47.

55. *DRCHNY*, 1:602.

56. Lindeström, *Geographia Americae*, 87.

57. *DRCHNY*, 12:75.

58. *Risingh's Journal*, 150–51.

59. *DRCHNY*, 1:601. See also *Risingh's Journal*, 155.

60. Lindeström, *Geographia Americae*, 88.

61. Risingh's 1654 Report, in *Narratives of Early Pennsylvania, West New Jersey, and Delaware, 1630–1707*, ed. Albert Cook Myers (New York: Scribner, 1912), 147.

62. For a reference to Aaltje as Gerrit Bicker's wife, see *The Minutes of the Orphanmasters of New Amsterdam, 1655 to 1663*, ed. Berthold Fernow (New York: Francis P. Harper, 1902), 1:94.

63. *DRCHNY*, 1:605.

64. *Risingh's Journal*, 155–57.

65. *Risingh's Journal*, 159.

66. In December 1655 Boyer recorded the baptisms of two sons at New Amsterdam. See Thomas G. Evans, ed., "Baptisms from 1639 to 1730 in the Reformed Dutch Church, New York," in *Collections of the New York Genealogical and Biographical Society*, vol. 2 (1901; repr., Upper Saddle River, N.J.: Gregg Press, 1968). Originally from Leiden, Boyer had formerly served as an assistant officer at Fort Nassau and had since become a freeman. See A.J.F. van Laer, ed., *New York Historical Manuscripts: Dutch*, vol. 3: *Register of the Provincial Secretary, 1648–1660* (Baltimore: Genealogical Pub. Co., 1974), 122.

67. *Risingh's Journal*, 161.

68. *Risingh's Journal*, 167, 183.

69. *Risingh's Journal*, 167; Lindeström, *Geographia Americae*, 125.

70. Lindeström identified one of the freemen's spokesmen as "Matts Hansson Nylänning," which suggests that he was the Matts Hansson from Borgå/Porvoo, which is located in the Finnish province of Nyland/Uusimaa. Hansson had been a soldier in the service of Klas Fleming but had been sent to the colony as punishment. Lindeström, *Geographia Americae*, 125.

71. *Risingh's Journal*, 173–75. For the text of the oath, see AJP, 55:4.

72. *Risingh's Journal*, 170–71.

73. See Johnson, *Swedish Settlements,* 507–8; and Myers, *Narratives of Early Pennsylvania,* 148–49. On tenants of the nobility in Sweden, see Michael Roberts, *Gustavus Adolphus: A History of Sweden, 1611–1632,* 2 vols. (New York: Longman, 1951–58), 2:50–56; Eli F. Heckscher, *An Economic History of Sweden* (Cambridge, Mass.: Harvard University Press, 1954), 127; and Maria Ågren, "Asserting One's Rights: Swedish Property Law in the Transition from Community Law to State Law," *Law and History Review* 19.2 (2001): 252–53.

74. *Risingh's Journal,* 175.

75. Lock came to New Sweden in 1648; Stille had been a freeman in the colony since 1641. See Peter Stebbins Craig, *1671 Census of the Delaware* (Philadelphia: Genealogical Society of Pennsylvania, 1999), 32 and 15, respectively.

76. See the 1654 petition in AJP, 55:5.

77. *Risingh's Journal,* 184. The text of this expanded petition is in AJP, 55:4.

78. Lindeström, *Geographia Americae,* 126; *Risingh's Journal,* 167. This seems to have been a common practice when Europeans abandoned their forts in the Delaware Valley.

79. For the names and origins of the sachems, see Lindeström, *Resa till Nya Sverige,* 75.

80. Lindeström, *Geographia Americae,* 128.

81. Lindeström, *Resa till Nya Sverige,* 75.

82. For the deed, see AJP, 55:5. Pemenatta claimed that Mitatsimint had given him the land before his death.

83. *Risingh's Journal,* 187–89. For negotiations with the Mantes Indians from the east side of the river, see *Risingh's Journal,* 199, 235–37.

84. *Risingh's Journal,* 179, 197, 199.

85. Eli F. Heckscher, *An Economic History of Sweden* (Cambridge, Mass.: Harvard University Press, 1954), 114–15; Sven Gerentz, "Johan Risingh och hans Tractact," *Ekonomisk Debatt* 15.8 (1987): 663. Gerentz was responding to Johan Lönnroth, "Johan Risingh," *Ekonomisk Debatt* 15.5 (1987): 407–12.

86. Johan Claesson Risingh, *Itt Uthogh om Kiöp-Handelen eller Commercierne* (Stockholm: Nicolaum Wankijff, 1699), 98.

87. My translation from the Swedish in Erik Thomson, "Swedish Variations on Dutch Commercial Institutions, 1605–1655," *Scandinavian Studies* 31.2 (2005): 333.

88. Risingh's 1654 Report, in *Narratives of Early Pennsylvania, West New Jersey, and Delaware, 1630–1707,* ed. Albert Cook Myers (New York: Scribner, 1912), 142, 149.

89. *Risingh's Journal,* 161–65. For details of his mission, see Johnson, *Swedish Settlements,* 573.

90. For a brief biography of Ringgold, see *Archives of Maryland,* 54:xvi–xvii. He was a Puritan from Virginia who had settled on Kent Island in 1650. Two years earlier Ringgold was one of the men at Kent Island who, along with Anders Andersson, Johan Ericksson, and Anders Hansson, had sworn the oath of loyalty to the English Commonwealth. *Archives of Maryland,* 54:4–5.

91. *Risingh's Journal,* 171.

92. *Risingh's Journal,* 173.

93. *Risingh's Journal,* 179–81.

94. *Risingh's Journal,* 181.

95. Baxter lived at the southwestern end of Long Island, under New Netherland's jurisdiction. He served as an arbitrator for New Netherland in the Hartford Treaty negotiations of

1650 but later became a prominent defender of English claims to New Netherland. Calder, *New Haven Colony,* 190.

96. *Risingh's Journal,* 193.

97. AJP, 55:5.

98. Calder, *New Haven Colony,* 204–5. For Eaton's letter and the affidavit challenging New Haven's purchase, see AJP, 55:5.

99. Hoadly, *Records,* 2:129–32. See also Johnson, *Swedish Settlements,* 575–79.

100. *Risingh's Journal,* 197–99.

101. *Risingh's Journal,* 201–7.

102. A brief summary of Bradnox's long, villainous career (culminating in the death of his servant, Thomas Watson) appears in *Archives of Maryland,* 54:xvii–xviii.

103. *Risingh's Journal,* 207.

104. *Risingh's Journal,* 209.

105. *Risingh's Journal,* 211.

106. *Risingh's Journal,* 215–17.

107. *Risingh's Journal,* 217.

108. *Risingh's Journal,* 219–21.

109. *Risingh's Journal,* 219–21, 225.

110. *Risingh's Journal,* 223, 227.

111. *Risingh's Journal,* 229–31.

112. *Risingh's Journal,* 231.

113. "Report of Governor Johan Rising, 1655," in *Narratives of Early Pennsylvania, West New Jersey, and Delaware, 1630–1707,* ed. Albert Cook Myers (New York: Scribner, 1912), 157.

114. *Risingh's Journal,* 236–37.

115. *Risingh's Journal,* 239; "Report of Governor Johan Rising, 1655," 160.

116. *Risingh's Journal,* 241.

117. *Risingh's Journal,* 241; Myers, *Narratives of Early Pennsylvania,* 164.

118. *Risingh's Journal,* 243.

119. *Risingh's Journal,* 245; and AJP, 55:6

120. C. A. Weslager, "A Ruse de Guerre—and the Fall of New Sweden," *Delaware History* 23.1 (Spring–Summer 1988): 2–6. See "Examination of the Commandant Swen Skute," in AJP, 55:6.

121. Lindeström, *Geographia Americae,* 260; Lindeström, *Resa till Nya Sverige,* 154.

122. Weslager, "Ruse de Guerre," 10; AJP, 55:6, 64:8.

123. AJP, 55:6.

124. For Isgrå's later career in Maryland, see Peter S. Craig, "Oluf Matthiasson, alias Olof Isgrå, alias Oliver Caulk and his Caulk/Calk Descendants," *Swedish Colonial News* 2.8 (Spring 2003), www.colonialswedes.org/Forefathers/Matthiasson.html.

125. Weslager, "Ruse de Guerre," 11.

126. Johnson, *Swedish Settlements,* 602. For von Elswich's full report, dated February 12, 1656, at Stockholm, see the transcription in AJP, 54:4.

127. *Risingh's Journal,* 249.

128. *Risingh's Journal,* 253. See also von Elswich's report in AJP, 54:4.

129. DRCHNY, 12:99. For the strongest case for a Swedish-Susquehannock origin for the war, see Van Zandt, *Brothers among Nations,* chap. 7, "Nations Intertwined."

130. *Risingh's Journal,* 261–63; see also the report of the discussions by Risingh, his officers, and some freemen, in AJP, 55:6.

131. *DRCHNY,* 12:104.

132. "Relation of the Surrender of New Sweden, by Governor Johan Clason Rising, 1655," in *Narratives of Early Pennsylvania, West New Jersey, and Delaware, 1630–1707,* ed. Albert Cook Myers (New York: Scribner, 1912), 176.

133. AJP, 55:6.

134. Weslager, "Ruse de Guerre," 15–16.

135. For a discussion of the rights-based mentality of Swedish peasants, see Eva Österberg, "Folkets mentalitet och statens makt," in *Folk Förr: Historiska Essäer* (Stockholm: Atlantis, 1995), 171–97.

136. Rather, it was the "obsession" to complete his *magnum opus, En Tractat om Kiöp-Handelen,* that was "mainly responsible for his death in misery in 1672." Heckscher, *Economic History of Sweden,* 114.

137. For the Swedish government's efforts to keep "the people in a good mood" in order to rally support for its midcentury wars, see Anna Maria Forssberg, *Att hålla folket på gott humör: Informationsspridning, krigspropaganda och mobilisering i Sverige 1655–1680* (Stockholm: Stockholms Universitet, 2005), 310.

138. Österberg, "Folkets mentalitet och statens makt," 195–96.

5. THE SWEDISH NATION ON THE SOUTH RIVER

1. Letter from the Directors of the WIC to Pieter Stuyvesant, November 23, 1654, in *DRCHNY,* 12:87.

2. Robin Blackburn, *The Making of New World Slavery: From the Baroque to the Modern, 1492–1800* (New York: Verso, 1997), 197.

3. The WIC also reserved to itself the privilege of providing the colony with the slaves who produced the sugar. See P. C. Emmer, *The Dutch Slave Trade, 1500–1850* (New York: Berghahn Books, 2006), 18; Blackburn, *Making of New World Slavery,* 195, 212.

4. On the failure of the Dutch regime to win the allegiances of the colony's diverse population, see Ernst Pijning, "Idealism and Power: The Dutch West India Company in the Brazil Trade (1630–1654)," in *Shaping the Stuart World, 1603–1714: The Atlantic Connection,* ed. Allan I. Macinnes and Arthur H. Williamson (Leiden: Brill, 2006), 207–32.

5. On the revolt and the Portuguese reconquest of Brazil, see C. R. Boxer, *The Dutch in Brazil, 1624–1654* (Oxford: Clarendon Press, 1957), chaps. 5 and 6.

6. See the images of Serinhaem in Caspar Barlaeus, *Rerum per octennium in Brasilia* (Amsterdam: Blaeu, 1647), following p. 40f: "Serinhaim" (pl. 12) and "Civitas Formosa Serinhaemensis" (pl. 13); and "Serinhaim," in Arnoldus Montanus, *De Nieuwe en onbekende Weereld: of Beschryving van America* (Amsterdam: Jacob Meurs, 1671), following p. 454. The quote and the number of sugar mills come from Johannes Nieuhof, *Johan Nieuhofs Gedenkweerdige Brasiliaense Zee-en Lant-Reize* (Amsterdam: Voor de weduwe van Jacob van Meurs, op de Keizersgracht., 1682), 13.

7. Nieuhof, *Johan Nieuhofs Gedenkweerdige Brasiliaense Zee-en Lant-Reize,* 118–19; and "Liefhebber," *Claar Vertooch van de Verradersche en Vyantlijcke Acten en Proceduren van Poortugaal* (Amsterdam: Gedruckt by de Weduwe van Ioost Broersz. . . . , 1647).

8. Nieuhof, *Johan Nieuhofs Gedenkweerdige Brasiliaense Zee-en Lant-Reize,* 120–21. Cosmo de Moucheron's account of the surrender and the causes of the uprising is printed in "Missieven Betreffende de West-Ind. Compagnie, 1641 en 1645," *Bijdragen en Mededelingen van het Historisch Genootschap,* 3:378–84. Nieuhof's account of the surrender appears to be based on Moucheron's statement. See also Mark Meuwese, *Brothers in Arms, Partners in Trade: Dutch-Indigenous Alliances in the Atlantic World, 1595–1674* (Leiden: Brill, 2012), 174. For a native perspective on the massacre, see Lodewijk Hulsman, "Brazilian Indians in the Dutch Republic: The Remonstrances of Antonio Paraupaba to the States General in 1654 and 1656," *Itinerario* 1 (2005): 51–78.

9. On the diverse composition of the population in "Dutch" Brazil, see Pijning, "Idealism and Power," 215–24.

10. On Jacquet's Swiss ancestry and his origins in the German city of Nuremberg, see Edwin Jacquett Sellers, *Genealogy of the Jacquett Family,* rev. ed. (Philadelphia: Allen, Lane, & Scott, 1907), 70–75. On Maria de Carpentier, see Edwin Jacquett Sellers, *Allied Ancestry of the Van Culemborg Family of Culemborg, Holland* (Philadelphia: Allen, Lane, & Scott, 1915), 63.

11. *DRCHNY,* 12:113–14.

12. "Liefhebber," *Iournael ofte Kort Discours / nopende de Rebellye ende verradelijcke Desseynen der Portugesen / alhier in Brasil voorgenomen / 't welck in Junio 1645. is ontdeckt* (Arnhem: Jan Jacobsz., 1647).

13. *Brasilsche Gelt Sack* ([Amsterdam?]: Gedruct in Brasilien op't Reciff in de Bree-Bijl, 1647). For a contemporary Portuguese perspective that was circulated in the Netherlands, see *Manifest door d'inwoonders van Parnambuco uytghegeven tot hun verantwoordinghe op 't aennemen der wapenen teghens de West-Indische Compagnie* ([Netherlands], 1646).

14. Nieuhof, *Johan Nieuhofs Gedenkweerdige Brasiliaense Zee-en Lant-Reize,* 234.

15. Nieuhof, *Johan Nieuhofs Gedenkweerdige Brasiliaense Zee-en Lant-Reize,* 229, 234, 237.

16. Frederick James Zwierlein, *Religion in New Netherland: A History of the Development of the Religious Conditions in the Province of New Netherland, 1623–1664* (Rochester: John P. Smith, 1910), 122–23, 188–93.

17. *DD,* 37 (ca. September 1655). See also *DRCHNY,* 12:100.

18. *DD,* 43.

19. This limited concession was a product of necessity, not generosity. See the letter by Megapolensis and Drisius to the Classis of Amsterdam, August 5, 1657, in Jameson, *Narratives of New Netherland,* 395–96; and Zwierlein, *Religion in New Netherland,* 123–24.

20. *DD,* 47.

21. For Jacquet's commission, see *DRCHNY,* 12:113–16.

22. *DRCHNY,* 12:115–16.

23. *DD,* 48–49. "Otte Grym"—Otto Grimm, but elsewhere "Greyn" (*DD,* 77)—arrived in New Sweden with Risingh in 1654. See Johnson, *Swedish Settlements,* 718.

24. Johnson, *Swedish Settlements,* 632–35.

25. Johan Papegoja to Erik Oxenstierna, July 30, 1656, in *AJP,* 55:6.

26. *DRCHNY,* 12:120.

27. *DRCHNY,* 12:121; Council Minutes, 6:348, New York State Archives.

28. See Van Zandt, *Brothers among Nations,* chap. 7, "Nations Intertwined."

29. *DRCHNY,* 12:121; Council Minutes, 6:348, New York State Archives.

30. *DRCHNY,* 12:121; Council Minutes, 6:349, New York State Archives.

31. Huygen was one of three merchants with interests in the newly reorganized New Sweden Company (renamed the American Company). See *Risingh's Journal,* 8. He left New Sweden with Governor Printz in 1653.

32. *DRCHNY,* 12:122; Council Minutes, 6:358, New York State Archives.

33. *DRCHNY,* 12:122–23; Council Minutes, 6:358, New York State Archives.

34. *DRCHNY,* 12:123–24; Council Minutes, 6:360, New York State Archives.

35. *DRCHNY,* 12:124; Council Minutes, 6:378, New York State Archives.

36. *DRCHNY,* 12:125.

37. *DRCHNY,* 12:125; transcription of Council Minutes, vol. 8, New York State Archives, by Janny Venema of the New Netherland Project.

38. *DRCHNY,* 12:126.

39. *DRCHNY,* 12:126; my translation is from the transcription of Council Minutes, vol. 8, 8:4, New York State Archives, by Venema of the New Netherland Project.

40. *DRCHNY,* 12:126–27; my translation is from the transcription of Council Minutes, vol. 8, 8:4, New York State Archives, by Venema of the New Netherland Project.

41. *DRCHNY,* 12:127–28.

42. Papegoja to Erik Oxenstierna, July 30, 1656, my translation from AJP, 54:3 (Swedish transcript) and 55:6 (English trans.).

43. Papegoja to Erik Oxenstierna, July 30, 1656, in AJP, 54:3, 55:6.

44. Papegoja to Erik Oxenstierna, July 30, 1656, in AJP, 54:3 (Swedish) and 55:6 (English trans.).

45. Pehr Kalm, *The America of 1750: Peter Kalm's Travels in North America,* ed. Adolph B. Benson (New York: Dover Publications, 1964), 723.

46. *DD,* 69.

47. Weslager, *New Sweden on the Delaware,* 189–90.

48. Carlsson, "The New Sweden Colonists," in *New Sweden in America,* 179–80. Carlsson estimates that before 1654 the Finnish element may have composed about 30 percent of the population. The arrival of the *Örn* and the *Mercurius,* however, brought many more Finns to the River.

49. *DRCHNY,* 12:211–12.

50. *DRCHNY,* 12:211–12.

51. *DRCHNY,* 12:212.

52. *DRCHNY,* 12:232–33.

53. *DRCHNY,* 12:232–33.

54. *DRCHNY,* 12:246–47.

55. *DRCHNY,* 12:246–47.

56. Quote from the English translation of Maryland's charter in *A Relation of Maryland* (1635), reprinted in *Narratives of Early Maryland, 1633–1684,* ed. Clayton Colman Hall (New York: Scribner, 1910), 102.

57. Lois Green Carr, Russell R. Menard, and Lorena S. Walsh, *Robert Cole's World: Agriculture and Society in Early Maryland* (Chapel Hill: University of North Carolina Press, 1991), 15. For the Susquehannock's treaty with Maryland, see the *Archives of Maryland*, 3:277–78; and Francis Jennings, *The Ambiguous Iroquois Empire: The Covenant Chain Confederation of Indian Tribes with English Colonies from Its Beginnings to the Lancaster Treaty of 1744* (New York: Norton, 1987), 121–22. For the new interest in the upper Chesapeake in the late 1650s, see William G. Duvall, "Smuggling Sotweed: Augustine Herrman and the Dutch Connection," *Maryland Historical Magazine* 98 (Winter 2003): 394–95.

58. *Risingh's Journal*, 175–81. According to an account recorded by William Penn's agents in 1684, Printz sent a delegation from New Sweden to Maryland in 1651 to discuss the English colony's potential claims to the Delaware Valley. See A. R. Dunlap and C. A. Weslager, "More Missing Evidence: Two Depositions by Early Swedish Settlers," *Pennsylvania Magazine of History and Biography* 91:1 (1967): 39.

59. C. A. Weslager, *Swedes and Dutch at New Castle* (Wilmington, Del.: Middle Atlantic Press, 1987), 98.

60. *DD*, 117.

61. *DD*, 122–23.

62. *DD*, 123; *DRCHNY*, 2:54.

63. *DRCHNY*, 2:69.

64. *DD*, 134.

65. *DD*, 143.

66. For references to Alrichs in Brazil from 1637 to 1651, see the registers of births in Dutch Brazil, "Doopregister der Hollanders in Brazilië," in *Algemeen Nederlandsch Familieblad*, vols. 5–6 (1888–89). He seems to have been appointed a bookkeeper in Brazil in 1636. See A.J.F. van Laer, "Minutes of the Amsterdam Chamber of the Dutch West India Company, 1635–1636," *New York Genealogical and Biographical Record* 49 (1918): 219, 226–27.

67. *DD*, 147. For details regarding Utie's instructions, see *Archives of Maryland*, 3:365.

68. On Utie's family and land grants in the upper Chesapeake, see "Captain John Utie, of Utimaria, Esq.," *William and Mary Quarterly* 4.1 (1895): 52–58. See also Hatfield, *Atlantic Virginia*, 106.

69. *DD*, 148.

70. *DD*, 149.

71. Utie's instructions appear in *Archives of Maryland*, 3:365. For the Dutch commanders' accounts of the meeting, see *DD*, 149, 152, 163.

72. *Archives of Maryland*, 3:365.

73. *DD*, 153.

74. *DRCHNY*, 12:254.

75. *DD*, 162.

76. *DRCHNY*, 12:271.

77. For an account of this period, see Aubrey C. Land, *Colonial Maryland: A History* (Millwood, N.Y.: KTO Press, 1981), 54–56.

78. *DRCHNY*, 12:332.

79. *DD*, 183.

80. *DD*, 188.

81. *DD*, 188.

82. *DRCHNY,* 12:305.

83. *DD*, 199; *DRCHNY,* 12:314.

84. *DD*, 189, 353. Given that a large proportion of the Finns and Swedes were male, twenty families might have formed a sizable part of the total community.

85. *DD,*191.

86. *DD*, 192–93.

87. *DD*, 192–93, 195, 199.

88. *DD*, 199, 201, 206.

89. *DD*, 283.

90. In Swedish sources he is known as Henrik Gertson / Gerdtsson Sjöhjelm.

91. *DRCHNY,* 12:445–46.

92. *DD*, 341–42.

93. *DRCHNY,* 12:455.

94. *DRCHNY,* 12:167–73.

6. FROM CONQUEST TO CONSENT

1. William Penn, *Truth rescued from imposture . . .* (London[?], 1670), 27.

2. Vincent Brown, *The Reaper's Garden: Death and Power in the World of Atlantic Slavery* (Cambridge, Mass.: Harvard University Press, 2008), 13. On the conquest of Jamaica, see esp. Stephen Saunders Webb, *The Governors-General: The English Army and the Definition of the Empire, 1569–1681* (Chapel Hill: University of North Carolina Press, 1979); and Carla Gardina Pestana, *The English Atlantic in an Age of Revolution, 1640–1661* (Cambridge, Mass.: Harvard University Press, 2004).

3. William Isaac Hull, *William Penn: A Topical Biography* (New York: Oxford University Press, 1937), 19.

4. Penn, *Truth rescued from imposture,* 26. On the Battle of Lowestoft, see Gijs Rommelse, *The Second Anglo-Dutch War (1665–1667): Raison d'état, Mercantilism, and Maritime Strife* (Hilversum: Verloren, 2006), 126–32.

5. Hull, *William Penn,* 21. The portrait is in the Greenwich Hospital Collection of the National Maritime Museum in London.

6. Sir William Penn to Sir George Lane, February 8, 1666, in Dunn and Dunn, *Papers of William Penn,* 1:39.

7. On the mutiny and its larger context, see Richard L. Greaves, *Enemies under His Feet: Radicals and Nonconformists in Britain, 1664–1677* (Stanford: Stanford University Press, 1990), 110–11.

8. George Hill, ed., *The Montgomery Manuscripts (1603–1706) . . .* (Belfast: Archer & Sons, 1869), 1:424 n. 106.

9. James Butler, first Duke of Ormonde, to Sir William Penn, May 29, 1666, quoted in Dunn and Dunn, *Papers of William Penn,* 1:42 n. 6.

10. Sir William Penn to William Penn, July 17, 1666, in Dunn and Dunn, *Papers of William Penn,* 1:42.

11. "An Account of my Journey into Holland & Germany," July 22–October 12, 1677, in Dunn and Dunn, *Papers of William Penn,* 1:496.

12. William Penn to the Early of Orrery, ca. November 4, 1667, in Dunn and Dunn, *Papers of William Penn,* 1:51.

13. Dunn and Dunn, *Papers of William Penn,* 1:81.

14. Dunn and Dunn, *Papers of William Penn,* 1:180.

15. Richard S. Dunn, "Penny Wise and Pound Foolish: Penn as a Businessman," in *The World of William Penn,* ed. Richard S. Dunn and Mary Maples Dunn (Philadelphia: University of Pennsylvania Press, 1986), 38–39.

16. Mary K. Geiter, *William Penn* (Harlow, England: Longman, 2000), 33.

17. Edwin B. Bronner, *William Penn's "Holy Experiment": The Founding of Pennsylvania, 1681–1701* (New York: Temple University Publications, 1962), 21.

18. William Penn, *An Essay towards the Present and Future Peace of Europe . . .* (London, 1693), 23.

19. Samuel Hazard, ed., *Pennsylvania Archives* (1890), 16:385–86.

20. Penn, *Essay towards the Present and Future Peace of Europe,* 23–24.

21. *DRCHNY,* 3:46.

22. *DRCHNY,* 3:51.

23. Sir Robert Carr to Colonel Nicolls, October 13, 1664, in *Pennsylvania Archives,* 2d ser., 5:577.

24. Sir Robert Carr to Colonel Nicolls, October 13, 1664, in *Pennsylvania Archives,* 2d ser., 5:577.

25. *Archives of Maryland,* 5:416.

26. On Plockhoy and his colonial project in America, see Henk Looijesteijn, "'Born to the Common Welfare': Pieter Plockhoy's Quest for a Christian Life (c. 1620–1664)" (Ph.D. diss., European University Institute, 2009), chaps. 10–11; and Evan Haefeli, *New Netherland and the Dutch Origins of American Religious Liberty* (Philadelphia: University of Pennsylvania Press, 2012), chap. 9. On the intellectual context, see also Jonathan Israel, *Radical Enlightenment: Philosophy and the Making of Modernity, 1650–1750* (New York: Oxford University Press, 2002), 175–80.

27. William Loring Andrews, *Jacob Steendam, Noch vaster: A Memoir of the First Poet in New Netherland* (New York: Dodd, Mead & Co., 1908), 60.

28. *Archives of Maryland,* 5:416–17.

29. Sir Robert Carr to Colonel Nicolls, October 13, 1664, in *Pennsylvania Archives,* 2d ser., 5:577.

30. *DE,* 1–2.

31. *DE,* 2–3.

32. See Johnson, *Swedish Settlements,* 655.

33. Evan Haefeli offers a thorough examination of the uprising, its origins, and its aftereffects in "The Revolt of the Long Swede: Transatlantic Hopes and Fears on the Delaware, 1669," *PMHB* 130.2 (April 2006): 137–80.

34. This version of the tale comes from Kalm's diary of his travels, published in Swedish in *Pehr Kalms Resa till Norra Amerika,* ed. Fredrik Elfving and Georg Schauman (Helsingfors: Mercators tryckeri aktiebolag, 1929), 4:227–28, and in English in *The America of 1750:*

Peter Kalm's Travels in North America, ed. Adolph B. Benson (New York: Dover Publications, 1964), 732–33. (Note that Benson mistakenly translated Kalm's abbreviation for Jacob, "Iac.," as "Isaac.") An anonymously authored account, similar in language to the Bengtson-Kalm account, is found in the Joseph J. Mickley Swedish Manuscripts, 1636–1811, at the Historical Society of Pennsylvania. Evan Haefeli's transcription and translation of this account can be found in "Revolt of the Long Swede," 174–78. For another translation of this account, see G. B. Keen, trans., "An Account of the Seditious False Königsmark in New Sweden," *PMHB* 7 (1883): 219–20. Comparison of the different versions suggests that the Mickley Manuscripts account is a modified copy of the Bengtson-Kalm account, perhaps drafted by Kalm after 1759, as the author of the account in the Mickley Manuscripts refers to Israel Acrelius's relation of the episode in *Beskrifning om de Swenska Församlingars Forna och Närwarande Tilstand . . .* (Stockholm: Harberg & Hesselberg, 1759), 123. Acrelius's summary, drawn from Andreas Rudman's notes during his time as a minister in Pennsylvania, is very similar to the summary that Kalm first gave in his diary (drawn from the same notes) before he interviewed Bengtson about the event. See Benson, *America of 1750,* 724; and Elfving and Schauman, *Pehr Kalms Resa till Norra Amerika,* 4:193.

35. For the genealogy of the Bengtson family, see Peter S. Craig, "Anders Bengtsson and His Bankson & Bankston Descendants," *Swedish Colonial News* 1.20 (Fall 1999).

36. Benson, *America of 1750,* 732.

37. My translation from the Swedish in Elfving and Schauman, *Pehr Kalms Resa till Norra Amerika,* 4:228.

38. Elfving and Schauman, *Pehr Kalms Resa till Norra Amerika,* 4:228.

39. Benson, *America of 1750,* 732–33.

40. My translation from Elfving and Schauman, *Pehr Kalms Resa till Norra Amerika,* 4:228.

41. Benson, *America of 1750,* 733.

42. *DRCHNY,* 12:469, 472.

43. *DE,* 7–10. See also *DRCHNY,* 3:186.

44. *Collections of the New-York Historical Society* (1811), 1:326.

45. *DRCHNY,* 12:472.

46. *DRCHNY,* 12:465.

47. *DRCHNY,* 12:471. Around the time of the uprising the New York government began collecting quitrents from settlers who had patented lands along the Delaware River, perhaps feeding resentment toward their subjected status. See *DRCHNY,* 12:490–92; *DE,* 27–29; and the discussion in Haefeli, "Revolt of the Long Swede," 171.

48. Craig, *1671 Census of the Delaware.*

49. The author may have been Thomas Snelling, a former English soldier associated with the two of the signers.

50. *DE,* 19.

51. *DE,* 11.

52. Craig, *1671 Census of the Delaware,* 74–75.

53. *DRCHNY,* 12:500.

54. *DRCHNY,* 12:503–4.

55. See Weslager, *English on the Delaware,* 212–15.

56. *DRCHNY,* 12:507–8.

57. *DRCHNY,* 12:507–12.

58. *DRCHNY*, 12:513–14.

59. *DE*, 85. Block was formerly a gunner at New Amstel.

60. *DE*, 87.

61. *DRCHNY*, 12:536.

62. See Craig, *1671 Census of the Delaware.*

63. *DE*, 92–93. One of the men's names was later crossed off the letter.

64. Fabritius was a native of Silesia in Poland and had most recently served as a minister in Hungary until the Ottoman invasion of the country. Jeannette Eckman, *Crane Hook on the Delaware, 1667–1699: An Early Swedish Lutheran Church and Community with the Historical Background of the Delaware River Valley* (Newark: University of Delaware, 1958), 55.

65. His parishioners' complaints appear in A.J.F. van Laer, trans., *The Lutheran Church in New York, 1649–1772: Records in the Lutheran Church Archives at Amsterdam, Holland* (New York: New York Public Library, 1946), 64–76.

66. For background on Fabritius and his various clashes with officials, see Thomas Holcomb, *Sketch of Early Ecclesiastical Affairs in New Castle, Delaware, and History of Immanuel Church* (Wilmington: Delaware Printing Co., 1890), 17, 19–26. Evidence of his encounters with the law appears in Berthold Fernow, ed., *The Records of New Amsterdam from 1653 to 1674 Anno Domini*, vol. 7 (New York: Knickerbocker Press, 1897). For his career as a minister in New York and along the Delaware, see Evan Haefeli, "The Pennsylvania Difference: Religious Diversity on the Delaware before 1683," *Early American Studies: An Interdisciplinary Journal* 1.1 (Spring 2003): 48–50.

67. *DRCHNY*, 12:538, 540.

68. Haefeli, "Pennsylvania Difference," 49.

69. *DE*, 92–93. See Haefeli, "Revolt of the Long Swede," 153.

70. See *Records of the Court of New Castle* (Lancaster, Pa.: Wickersham Print Co., 1904 35), 1:162–63.

71. *DE*, 299.

72. Craig, *1693 Census*, 113.

73. *DD*, 283.

74. *DRCHNY*, 12:465.

75. William Penn, *A Letter from William Penn, Proprietary and Governour of Pennsylvania in America, to the Committee of the Free Society of Traders . . .* (London: Andrew Sowle, 1683), 7–8. See also the version of Penn's letter in *Narratives of Early Pennsylvania, West New Jersey, and Delaware, 1630–1707*, ed. Albert Cook Myers (New York: Scribner, 1912), 217–44. For similar remarks about the Dutch and Swedes, see Gabriel Thomas, *An Historical and Geographical Account of the Province and Country of Pensilvania, and of the West-New-Jersey in America . . .* (London: A. Baldwin, 1698), 2–3. The moral criticism implicit in Penn's remark was made explicit by other, less circumspect authors. See Francis Daniel Pastorius's criticisms of the old settlers' influence on the Indians in *Umständige Geographische Beschreibung Der zu allerletzt erfundenen Provintz Pensylvanaiae* (Frankfurt: Andreas Otto, 1700), trans. in Myers, *Narratives of Early Pennsylvania*, 385–86.

76. Thomas Paskell [Paschall], *An Abstract of a Letter from Thomas Paskell of Pennsilvania to His Friend J. J. of Chippenham* (London: John Bringhurst, 1683). See also Myers, *Narratives of Early Pennsylvania*, 250–52.

77. Penn, *Letter from William Penn*, 1, 8.

78. William Penn, *A Further Account of the Province of Pennsylvania and Its Improvements . . .* (London, 1685), 2–3.

79. Penn, *Letter from William Penn*, 8.

80. Thomas, *Historical and Geographical Account of the Province and Country of Pensilvania*, 51. See also Myers, *Narratives of Early Pennsylvania*, 335.

81. Pastorius, *Umständige Geographische Beschreibung*, 387.

82. See Haefeli, "Pennsylvania Difference," 52–60.

83. Craig, *1693 Census*, 159–60.

84. Craig, *1693 Census*, 159–60.

85. Craig, *1693 Census*, 161.

86. Craig, *1693 Census*, 162–63.

87. Craig, *1693 Census*, 158.

88. Craig, *1693 Census*, 158.

89. Myers, *Narratives of Early Pennsylvania*, 344.

90. See esp. Schutt, *Peoples of the River Valleys;* Merrell, *Into the American Woods;* Jane T. Merritt, *At the Crossroads: Indians and Empires on a Mid-Atlantic Frontier, 1700–1763* (Chapel Hill: University of North Carolina Press, 2003); and Richard White, *The Middle Ground: Indians, Empires, and Republics in the Great Lakes Region, 1650–1815* (New York: Cambridge University Press, 1991).

EPILOGUE

1. Pehr Kalm, *The America of 1750: Peter Kalm's Travels in North America*, ed. Adolph B. Benson (New York: Dover Publications, 1964), 48–49.

2. Kalm, *America of 1750*, 625.

3. On Logan's scientific pursuits, see Frederick B. Tolles, "Philadelphia's First Scientist: James Logan," *Isis* 47.1 (March 1956): 20–30.

4. Peter Collinson, *"Forget not Mee & My Garden . . .": Selected Letters, 1725–1768, of Peter Collinson*, ed. Alan W. Armstrong (Philadelphia: American Philosophical Society, 2002), 50 n 2.

5. Tolles, "Philadelphia's First Scientist," 20–30.

6. Logan to Collinson, February 28, 1750, in Benjamin Franklin, *The Papers of Benjamin Franklin*, ed. Leonard W. Labaree (New Haven: Yale University Press, 1959–), from the digital edition at www.franklinpapers.org (hereafter cited as *Franklin Papers*).

7. Collinson, *"Forget not Mee & My Garden,"* 15; Tolles, "Philadelphia's First Scientist," 29.

8. Collinson to Franklin, June 14, 1748, in Collinson, *"Forget not Mee & My Garden,"* 146–47.

9. Logan to Collinson, February 28, 1750, in *Franklin Papers*.

10. On Franklin's militia, see Joseph A. Leo Lemay, *The Life of Benjamin Franklin*, vol. 3: *Soldier, Scientist, Politician, 1748–1757* (Philadelphia: University of Pennsylvania Press, 2009), chap. 1.

11. Logan to Collinson, February 28, 1750, in *Franklin Papers*.

12. The famous phrase *holy experiment* appears in William Penn to James Harrison, August 25, 1681, in Dunn and Dunn, *Papers of William Penn*, 2:108. For overviews of the history of the Del-

aware Valley before Pennsylvania's founding, see esp. Carl Bridenbaugh, "The Old and New Societies of the Delaware Valley in the Seventeenth Century," *Pennsylvania Magazine of History and Biography* 100.2 (1976): 145–63; and Sally Schwartz, "Society and Culture in the Seventeenth-Century Delaware Valley," *Delaware History* 20.2 (1982): 98–122.

13. See the minutes for the meeting in Philadelphia of August 17, 1709, in *Minutes of the Provincial Council of Pennsylvania* (Philadelphia: Joseph Severns and Co., 1852), 2:481. Penn's representatives responded similarly in their "Report on the Petition of the Swedes, 1721," which appears in Samuel Hazard, ed., *Pennsylvania Archives* (Philadelphia: Joseph Severns & Co., 1852), 1:172–77.

14. Benjamin Franklin, *Plain Truth: Or Serious Considerations on the Present State of the City of Philadelphia, and Province of Pennsylvania* (Philadelphia: Printed by Benjamin Franklin, 1747), 13.

15. Kalm, *America of 1750,* 34.

16. Kalm, *America of 1750,* 19, 27.

17. Kalm, *America of 1750,* 711.

18. Kalm, *America of 1750,* 33.

19. On pluralism in British America, see esp. Ned C. Landsman, "Pluralism, Protestantism, and Prosperity: Crevecoeur's American Farmer and the Foundations of American Pluralism," in *Beyond Pluralism: The Conception of Groups and Group Identities in America,* ed. Wendy F. Katkin et al. (Urbana: University of Illinois Press, 1998); and Landsman, "Roots, Routes, and Rootedness: Diversity, Migration, and Toleration in Mid-Atlantic Pluralism," *Early American Studies: An Interdisciplinary Journal* 2.2 (Fall 2004): 267–309.

20. Collinson, *"Forget not Mee & My Garden,"* 171.

21. Kalm, *America of 1750,* 683, 717.

22. On the broader imperial discourse about the meaning of British subjecthood and its relation to colonial populations, see esp. Geoffrey Plank, *An Unsettled Conquest: The British Campaign against the Peoples of Acadia* (Philadelphia: University of Pennsylvania Press, 2000); and Patrick Griffin, *American Leviathan: Empire, Nation, and Revolutionary Frontier* (New York: Hill & Wang, 2007).

23. Benjamin Franklin to Peter Collinson, [1753?], in *Franklin Papers.*

24. On anglicization, see esp. Jack P. Greene, *Pursuits of Happiness: The Social Development of Early Modern British Colonies and the Formation of American Culture* (Chapel Hill: University of North Carolina, 1988); T. H. Breen, "An Empire of Goods: The Anglicization of Colonial America, 1690–1776," *Journal of British Studies* 25 (1986): 467–99; Michael Kammen, *Colonial New York: A History* (New York: Scribner, 1975); Richard L. Bushman, *The Refinement of America: Persons, Houses, Cities* (New York: Knopf, 1992); John M. Murrin, "The Legal Transformation: Bench and Bar in Eighteenth-Century Massachusetts," in *Colonial America: Essays in Politics and Social Development,* Stanley N. Katz and John M. Murrin, 3d ed. (New York: Knopf, 1983), 540–72; and Brendan McConville, *The King's Three Faces: The Rise and Fall of Royal America* (Chapel Hill: University of North Carolina Press, 2006).

25. For studies of colonial British America and the early United States that employ the concept of ethnicization, see Joyce D. Goodfriend, *Before the Melting Pot: Society and Culture in Colonial New York City, 1664–1730* (Princeton: Princeton University Press, 1994), 219–20; Willem Frijhoff, "Dutchness in Fact and Fiction," in *Going Dutch: The Dutch Presence in America,*

1609–2009, ed. Joyce D. Goodfriend et al. (Leiden: Brill, 2008), 347; Frijhoff, "Inventing an Old Fatherland: The Management of Dutch Identity in Early Modern America," in *Managing Ethnicity: Perspectives from Folklore Studies, History and Anthropology,* ed. Regina Bendix and Herman Roodenburg (Amsterdam: Het Spinhuis, 2000), 123–24; and Steven M. Nolt, *Foreigners in Their Own Land: Pennsylvania Germans in the Early Republic* (University Park: Pennsylvania State University Press, 2002).

26. Kalm, *America of 1750,* 626.

27. Kalm, *America of 1750,* 343. On conflicts at Albany between the Dutch and the English during the seventeenth and early eighteenth centuries, see Donna Merwick, *Possessing Albany, 1630–1710: The Dutch and English Experiences* (New York: Cambridge University Press, 1990).

28. Kalm, *America of 1750,* 614–15.

29. See Daniel Lindmark, *Ecclesia Plantanda: Swedishness in Colonial America* (Umeå, Sweden: Institutionen för Litteraturvetenskap och Nordiska Språk, Umeå Universitet, 2005); and Landsman, "Pluralism, Protestantism, and Prosperity," 117–18.

30. A. G. Roeber, "'The Origin of Whatever Is Not English among Us': The Dutch-Speaking and the German-Speaking Peoples of Colonial British America," in *Strangers within the Realm: Cultural Margins of the First British Empire,* ed. Bernard Bailyn and Philip Morgan (Chapel Hill: University of North Carolina Press, 1991), 221.

31. Landsman, "Pluralism, Protestantism, and Prosperity," in Katkin et al., *Beyond Pluralism,* 119.

32. Griffin, *People with No Name,* 158.

33. Lindmark, *Ecclesia Plantanda,* chap. 7.

34. See Roeber, "'Origin of Whatever Is Not English among Us,'" 220–83.

35. James Sidbury and Jorge Cañizares-Esguerra, "Mapping Ethnogenesis in the Early Modern Atlantic," *William and Mary Quarterly* 68 (2011): 181–208.

36. Robert Olwell and Alan Tully, eds., intro., in *Cultures and Identities in Colonial British America* (Baltimore: Johns Hopkins University Press, 2006), 1–17. Recent attempts to apply the concept of creolization to colonial North America and the early United States include David Buisseret and Steven G. Reinhardt, eds., *Creolization in the Americas* (College Station, Tex., 2000); John Brooke, "Ecology," in *A Companion to Colonial America,* ed. Daniel Vickers (Malden, Mass.: Blackwell, 2003); Sean X. Goudie, *Creole America: The West Indies and the Formation of Literature and Culture in the New Republic* (Philadelphia: University of Pennsylvania Press, 2006); Ralph Bauer and José Antonio Mazzotti, eds., *Creole Subjects in the Colonial Americas: Empires, Texts, Identities* (Chapel Hill: University of North Carolina Press, 2009); John Smolenski, *Friends and Strangers: The Making of a Creole Culture in Colonial Pennsylvania* (Philadelphia: University of Pennsylvania Press, 2010).

37. See Greene, *Pursuits of Happiness,* 170–71; Colley, *Britons;* Colin Kidd, "Integration: Patriotism and Nationalism," in *A Companion to Eighteenth-Century Britain,* ed. H. T. Dickinson (Malden, Mass.: Blackwell, 2002), 377–78; Eliga H. Gould, "A Virtual Nation: Greater Britain and the Imperial Legacy of the American Revolution," *American Historical Review* 104 (1999): 476–89; Ned C. Landsman, "Nation, Migration, and the Province in the First British Empire: Scotland and the Americas, 1600–1800," *American Historical Review* 104 (1999): 463–75; David Armitage, "Making the Empire British: Scotland in the Atlantic World, 1542–1707," *Past and Present* 155 (1997): 34–63.

38. See Krishan Kumar, *The Making of English National Identity* (New York: Cambridge University Press, 2006), chap. 1.

39. Olwell and Tully, intro., *Cultures and Identities in Colonial British America*, 15.

40. Plank, *Unsettled Conquest*, 4.

41. Peter S. Onuf, *Jefferson's Empire: The Language of American Nationhood* (Charlottesville: University of Virginia Press, 2000), 6.

42. Onuf, *Jefferson's Empire*, 152.

43. Schutt, *Peoples of the River Valleys*, 63-69.

44. Kent, *Susquehanna's Indians*, 100.

45. John Styles, ed., *The Life of Brainerd: Missionary to the Indians* (Boston: Samuel T. Armstrong, 1812), 155.

46. Weslager, *Delaware Indians*, 192.

47. Gregory Evans Dowd, *A Spirited Resistance: The North American Indian Struggle for Unity, 1745-1815* (Baltimore: Johns Hopkins University Press, 1992), 34.

48. Alfred A. Cave, "The Delaware Prophet Neolin: A Reappraisal," *Ethnohistory* 46 (1999): 283.

49. Plank, *Unsettled Conquest*, 117.

50. *Minutes of the Provincial Council of Pennsylvania*, 2:334, 396-97.

51. Plank, *Unsettled Conquest*, 149.

52. Carl A. Brasseaux, *The Founding of New Acadia: The Beginnings of Acadian Life in Louisiana, 1765-1803* (Baton Rouge: Louisiana State University Press, 1987), 47. See also John Mack Faragher, *A Great and Noble Scheme: The Tragic Story of the Expulsion of the French Acadians from Their American Homeland* (New York: Norton, 2005), 376-81; Wilton Paul Ledet, "Acadian Exiles in Pennsylvania," *Pennsylvania History* 9.2 (1942): 118-28; William B. Reed, *The Acadian Exiles, or French Neutrals in Pennsylvania* (Philadelphia: Historical Society of Pennsylvania, 1858).

53. Faragher, *Great and Noble Scheme*, 425.

54. For examples of expulsions following conquest of colonial territory, including an English proposal in 1673 to "expel all the Dutch" from New Amsterdam, see Faragher, *Great and Noble Scheme*, 118-19.

55. Plank, *Unsettled Conquest*, chap. 5.

56. Plank, *Unsettled Conquest*, 118-20; Francis Parkman, *France and England in North America*, vol. 2: *A Half-Century of Conflict* (Toronto: George N. Morang, 1898), 176; William Shirley, *The Correspondence of William Shirley* (New York: Macmillan, 1912), xxvi.

57. See William Otis Sawtelle, "Acadia: The Pre-Loyalist Migration and the Philadelphia Plantation," *Pennsylvania Magazine of History and Biography* 51 (1927): 244-85.

58. Sir William Johnson was engaged in a contemporary discussion about whether Indians in British territory could become subjects. He believed that in time they could become subjects once they gave up their claims to be a "free people" and acquired civilization. See Griffin, *American Leviathan*, 34-36.

59. *Pennsylvania Gazette*, August 18-25, 1737.

60. *Minutes of the Provincial Council of Pennsylvania*, 4:243-44, 259.

61. Gary Nash, *Forging Freedom: The Formation of Philadelphia's Black Community, 1720-1840* (Cambridge, Mass.: Harvard University Press, 1988), 12.

62. *The Gentleman's Magazine, and Historical Chronicle* (London, 1768), 38:6-7; it also appears in *Franklin Papers*.

63. *Declaration of Independence* (Philadelphia: John Dunlop, 1776).

64. Robert W. Tucker and David C. Hendrickson write: "The Empire of Liberty was to be made up of one people, dedicated to liberty under republican institutions. There was to be no place here for subjects, only for citizens. This was why, in principle, Negroes could have no permanent position within the palladium of freedom and why, in practice, Indians as well had to be excluded from it." *Empire of Liberty: The Statecraft of Thomas Jefferson* (Oxford: Oxford University Press, 1992), 161.

65. See Douglas Bradburn, *The Citizenship Revolution: Politics and the Creation of the American Union, 1774–1804* (Charlottesville: University of Virginia Press, 2009). On the connections between English, colonial, and American conceptions of citizenship, see James H. Kettner, *The Development of American Citizenship, 1608–1870* (Chapel Hill: University of North Carolina Press, 1978).

66. Thomas Jefferson used the phrase once in 1780, and historians have been using it ever since. See Jefferson to George Rogers Clark, December 25, 1780, in *The Papers of Thomas Jefferson* (Princeton: Princeton University Press, 1950–), 4:237–38.

67. Hobbes, *Leviathan*, 64.

68. Craig, *1693 Census,*161.

INDEX

incursions and, 82, 94–95; English incursions and, 81, 82–84; fort construction by, 81; Indians and, 80–81, 85–86, 95–96; instructions to, as governor of New Sweden, 77–81; isolation of, 113–15; land sales dispute and, 100; "mutiny" of 1653 in New Sweden and, 117–18, 127, 128, 144, 237n26–238n27; New Netherlands under Hudde, conflict with, 87–91; Stuyvesant and, 97–98; Winthrop, correspondence with, 107–8

Quadickho, 91, 105
Quakers, 179–80

Ragueneau, Paul, 103
Rambo, Peter Gunnarsson (Per), 116, 142, 143, 185, 198–99, 216
Rasière, Isaack de, 46–47, 71
Reede, Godard, 72
Reid, John, 9
religion: churches in New Sweden, 235n170; diversity in Pennsylvania, 197–200; Dutch Reformed factions, 197; "heathens" vs. Christian fellowship, 89; Lutheranism in New Netherland, 151, 152; Lutheranism in New Sweden, importance of, 78–79; Lutheran requests for new ministers, 198, 199–200; Lutheran vs. Reformed, 70, 73; Mennonites, 182–83; missionary goals, 35; national belonging and state vs., 200; Protestant alliances and conflict, 60, 65, 66, 67, 108; Quakers, 179–80; struggle with Spain and, 45; trade vs. conversion, 103–4; Wesel and, 44
Rensselaer, Kiliaen van, 47, 50
Rensselaerswyck Colony, 97
Reynst, Gerrit (Gerard), 50
Ridder, Peter Hollander, 68–69, 74, 76, 77, 229n18
Ringgold, Thomas, 131, 240n90
Risingh, Johan Claesson: capitulation agreement with Stuyvesant, 152; colony collapse and, 134–40, 144–46; death of,

242n136; *En Tractat om Kiöp-Handelen*, 130, 242n136; on fleeing settlers, 119; on Fort Casimir capture, 124; Indians, interactions with, 128–29, 138–39, 145; invasion and surrender to Stuyvesant, 140–44; Maryland's land claims to, 131–32, 165; "mutiny" of 1653 and, 113, 127, 128; neighboring colonies, interactions with, 130–33; voyage to New Sweden, 120–22
Roeber, A. G., 208
Roper, L. H., 74

Sahlins, Peter, 8
Sampson, 214–15
Sandhook (Sand Hoeck), 100, 136, 170
Schmidt, Benjamin, 32
Schnurmann, Claudia, 11
schout, 161–64, 170–73, 191
Schuylkill River: Dutch-Swedish conflict on, 87; English settlement on, 76–77; feudal fears on, 127–28; Fort Beversreede, 92–95; land claims status, 99; Swedish forts on, 81, 90–91, 232n82
Scots in British America, 208
Separatists, 27–29
Serinhaem, Brazil, 149–50
Seven Years' War, 212, 213
Shamokin, 211–12
Siconese, 47, 166
Sigismund III Vasa of Poland, 36
Sille, Nicasius de, 170–71
Sinquees, 98, 100, 105
Skute, Sven: appointment as commander, 135; decision not to return to Sweden, 143–44; Dutch attack and, 140, 141–44; Fort Beversreede and, 95; Fort Casimir, capture of, 124; Fort Christina inspection, 137; Maryland merchants and, 135; as military officer in Finnish-Swedish community, 163; punished as troublemaker, 153–54
slave trade, Atlantic, 181, 242n3
slaves, 65, 185, 214–15
Smith, John, 2, 17, 19

131; harsh terms of, 92–93; language and, 104; in maize, 233n106; Minuit and fur trading, 47; missions vs., 103–4; New Netherland and, 25–26, 92; New Sweden and supply fluctuations, 91; Printz vs. Hudde and, 87–91; settlers forbidden, 117; "spoiled," 92, 105; in tobacco, 81–82

Trip, Elias, 51

Tupi, 149–50

Turner, Nathaniel, 74, 83, 103, 230n45

United Provinces. *See* Netherlands

Upland, 4

Upland Court, 186

Usselincx, Willem: background, 49–50; biography, 36; Blommaert compared to, 49; cosmopolitan vision of, 11; Hoeffnagel family and, 228n90; motivations of, 60–62; pay petition, 64; proposals and projects of, 35–37; Swedish South Company and, 36, 38–44

Utie, Nathaniel, 167–69

Utrecht colony, New Sweden, 71–74, 79

Varkens Kill settlement, 76, 77, 79–80, 81, 83

Vereenigde Oostindische Compagnie (VOC). *See* Dutch East India Company

Veer, Jacob vander, 194, 195

Verbrugge, Gillis, 59

Verhulst (or van der Hulst), Willem, 33, 46, 47–48

Virginia, 19, 56, 82–83, 85, 236n182. *See also* Maryland

Vliegende Hert (ship), 57

Vliet, Cornelius van, 69–70

VOC (Vereenigde Oostindische Compagnie). *See* Dutch East India Company

Vries, David de, 21

Waagh (man-of-war), 157, 159, 165

Waldron, Resolved, 169

Walloons, 17, 44, 46, 49

Wappanghzewan, 100–101

Wassenaer, Nicolaes, 24, 32, 64

Water, Isaac van de, 59

Water, Jan Hendricksz van de, 57, 59

Wesel, 44–45

Wheeler, John (Johan Hwiler), 117, 118

Whitelock, Bulstrode, 121, 238n43

Whorekill, 189–90

WIC. *See* Dutch West India Company

Wicaco, 88, 193, 199, 204–5

Windebanke, Francis, 56

Winslow, Edward, 28–29

Winthrop, John, 74, 83, 84, 107–8

Wissemmenetto, 93, 105–6

witchcraft accusations, 118

York, James, Duke of, 178, 180, 181–82

Zeehelm, Hendrick Gerritsen, 174–75